Lexeme-Morpheme Base Morphology

SUNY Series in Linguistics

Mark Aronoff, Editor

Lexeme-Morpheme Base Morphology

A General Theory of Inflection and Word Formation

Robert Beard

STATE UNIVERSITY OF NEW YORK PRESS

Published by
State University of New York Press, Albany

© 1995 State University of New York

For information address State University of New York Press,
State University Plaza, Albany, NY 12246

Production by Laura Starrett
Marketing by Fran Keneston

Library of Congress Cataloging in Publication Data

Beard, Robert, 1938–
    Lexeme-morpheme base morphology : a general theory of inflection and word formation / Robert Beard.
        p.   cm. — (SUNY series in linguistics)
    Includes bibliographical references (p.) and index.
    ISBN 0-7914-2471-5 : $89.50. — ISBN 0-7914-2472-3: $29.95
    1. Grammar, Comparative and general—Morphology.   I. Title.
II. Series.
P241.B43   1995
415—dc20   94-30216
                                                   CIP

10   9   8   7   6   5   4   3   2   1

Contents

Acknowledgments

As usual, a project such as the one that brought forth the present book was not carried out alone or in a vacuum. In addition to the intellectual forebears of the morphological theory outlined in this work, many friends and colleagues have contributed even more directly to the book itself. Leonard Babby originally suggested my stay as a research fellow at Cornell in 1983–1984, where work on this book began. Len also lent me his four-volume set of Archi grammar which contributed materially to the thinking that follows. Wolfgang Dressler long ago advised me on how to proceed against the odds with a complex theory like LMBM and has materially helped shape the theory with cogent criticism in his published works. Annette Ellis's Bucknell honors thesis yielded several important ideas including the structure of the argument against lexical prepositions in chapter 10. Joan Maling's comments on chapters 12 through 14 led to major improvements. Andrew Spencer and Andrew Carstairs-McCarthy gave the manuscript detailed readings at two different stages and provided comments which caught several oversights and led to rethinking of several parts. Norbert Corver and Henk van Riemsdijk provided crucial discussion of prepositions in Dutch and elsewhere. Steven Franks and Gerald Greenberg have supplied advice on syntax throughout the ordeal of bringing the LMBM theory together. Jorge Hankamer provided several examples from Turkish. Slava Yastremsky was kind enough to verify the Russian examples, and Peter Morris-Keitel, the German ones. Much of the material contained herein has benefitted on its way to the book in various forms from the comments, written and spoken, of Mark Aronoff, Geert Booij, Ursula Doleschal, Jaap van Marle, Bogdan Szymanek, Amanda Pounder, Richard Sproat, and Jan Don.

Preparation of the manuscript has benefitted from several of my research assistants, whose diligence and care smoothed the road on many occasions. Francine Falvo did much of the bibliographic work and Brooke Bitner contributed to work on the manuscript in too many ways to enumerate. My secretary, Florence Silverman, has supported many aspects of the project, too many in fact to remember. Christine Worden and Laura Starrett of SUNY Press played vital roles in seeing the manuscript to press. My heartfelt thanks to all of them.

Primary financial support for the project has derived from the research funds of the Ruth Everette Sierzega Chair in Linguistics and from the office of the Dean, College of Arts and Sciences, Bucknell University. I am particularly grateful to Eugenie P. Gerdes, Dean of that College, for assisting with generous travel funds and other crucial support in the preparation of the manuscript. My children, Jeffrey and Owen, have always been a great comfort to me. They were particularly kind to entertain themselves and even take over my chores when this project absorbed all my attention. My parents, Kathleen and LaVerne Beard, were kind enough to contribute the solace of their vacation home on Topsail Island, NC toward the initial draft of the book. Finally and foremost, I owe the greatest debt to my wife, Faye, not only for carrying the full load of our family through much of the project, but for supporting the project enthusiatically from beginning to end and, indeed, for funding a significant portion of it. It is to her, and to our enduring friendship, that the final product is dedicated.

Preface

The book you have chosen to open represents an ambitious project which began in 1960 with my University of Michigan M.A. thesis in Slavic linguistics. My advisor, James Ferrell, asked me to devise as many word formation rules for contemporary Russian adjectives as I could. He insisted that the rules must be "predictive" to be of any value, though he admitted his doubt that such rules were possible. By the time I had finished the thesis, I shared his doubts.

I was encouraged to continue my pursuit of the elusive predictive word formation rule in my Ph.D thesis, presumably under the assumption that it would keep me occupied while the members of my committee traveled. From 1961–1964 I managed to work wholly unsupervised in Yugoslavia and the US on adjectival word formation in Serbo-Croatian. Since linguists at Michigan at the time exhibited little curiosity about what Noam Chomsky was doing, I was surprised to find Milka Ivić assigning *Syntactic Structures* in her syntax course in Novi Sad. But I read it and R. B. Lees' classic *English Nominalizations*, too. Without proper supervision, I began thinking in the same strange ways as these two luminaries.

Lees came across a problem which led him to suspect that nominalization might comprise discrete processes of derivation and affixation, but did not pursue the idea. I found much evidence that the rules of Serbo-Croatian adjective derivation were distinct from the affixation rules. Without appropriate supervision, I was able to complete a draft of my dissertation that developed this line of thought. My committee was unimpressed; however, I received my Ph.D on the basis of a revised version containing only a short introduction and the chapter on affixation.

I took up a position at Bucknell in 1965 with the assignment to build a Russian literature and linguistics program but the idea would not go away: Leitner, Kiefer, and Matthews separated derivation from affixation in the early '70's to solve specific problems of morphology. Aronoff's first monograph carried a suggestion of the same idea the year of my first publication in *Language* (1976). Karcevskij and Bazell, I discovered later, had written about the problems that separation resolves and Bazell had even suggested the solution in the '40's. This simple but revolutionary idea opened the way to studying morphological categories and their relation to

ix

syntax free of the distraction of phonology. I could not understand why it neither swept linguistic research off its feet nor went away.

Over the ensuing years, encouraged by the work of the pioneers mentioned above, I pursued the implications of what is now THE SEPARATION HYPOTHESIS across dozens of languages and all the lexical categories. My first book, *The Indo-European Lexicon*, pointed out that if we look beyond the phonology of affixation, we see IE languages sharing a single lexicon: the same derivational categories, rules, and principles. This led to the conclusion that grammatical morphemes and lexemes cannot be the same type, stored in the same component or copied into phrases and words in the same way, for no IE languages share the same affixes. The present book combines this conclusion with the Separation Hypothesis for the first time in a complete theory of grammar which distinguishes all lexicology from allomorphy.

Morphology, its categories and marking system, is the glue that holds words and sentences together. Lexical derivation maps derived words to their lexical bases in ways that semantics can interpret. Inflectional derivation maps the relations of lexical bases in phrases. Affixation, both derivational and inflection, maps words and phrases onto phonology. Finally, derivation of both types maps onto affixation and other types of morphological marking. While this last mapping is the heart of morphology, the relation of derivation to syntax and semantics and affixation to phonology are also important aspects of morphology. Recent research by myself and others has raised a mountain of evidence against the direct mapping of syntax to semantics or syntax to phonology.

List of Figures

List of Tables

List of Symbols

1PL	1st Person Plural
1SG	1st Person Singular
1ST	1st Person
2ND	2nd Person
2PL	2nd Person Plural
3PL	3rd Person Plural
3RD	3rd Person
3SG	3rd Person Singular
ABL	Ablative Case
ABS	Absolutive Case (Subj of Intransitive, Obj of Transitive verbs)
ACC	Accusative Case
ACT	Active Voice
ADES	Addessive Case (''on'')
ADV	Adverb
AFF	Affix
ART	Article
BEN	Benefactive Case (Purposive with an animate noun)
CAUS	Causative
CLS1	Noun Class 1
CLS2	Noun Class 2
DAT	Dative Case (''to, for'')
DES	Desiderative
DUB	Dubitative
EMPH	Emphatic
EMPPRED	Emphatic predicator
ERG	Ergative Case (Subject of Transitive verbs)
FAGR	F-Agreement (Feminine)
FEM	Feminine (Natural) Gender
FUT	Future Tense
GEN	Genitive Case (''of'')
GOAL	Goal Case Function (''to'')
IMP	Imperative Mood
IND	Indicative Mood
INES	Innessive Case (''in'')

INF	Infinitive
INST	Instrumental Case (''with, by'')
LOC	Locative Case (''at'')
MAGR	M-Agreement (Masculine)
MAS	Masculine (Natural) Gender
NAGR	N-Agreement (Neuter)
NEC	Necessitative (''need to'')
NEG	Negative
NEU	Neuter Gender
NOM	Nominative Case
NULL	Null Morphology (Omitted morpheme)
OBJ	Object
OBL	Obligative
PART	Participle
PL	Plural
POSS	Possessive
POT	Potential
PPP	Past Passive Participle
PREP	Preposition
PRES	Present Tense
PROG	Progressive Imperfective Aspect
PRT	Particle
PST	Past Tense
REFL	Reflexive
REL	Relativizer (marks relational adjectives or nouns)
SG	Singular
SOC	Sociative Case (''with (someone)'')
SUB	Subject
TRAN	Transitive
VAL	Validator

Chapter One

The Agenda of Morphology

1. SETTING OUR BEARINGS

Morphology is superficially the sum of all the phonological means for expressing the relations of the constituents of words, of words in phrases, and of the phrasal constituents of sentences. The key element of morphology is the WORD, a symbol comprising mutually implied sound and meaning. The central purpose of morphology, therefore, is to map sound to meaning within the word and between words. The issues of morphology are what constitutes linguistic sound, what determines linguistic meaning, and how the two are related. Since these questions are central to the linguistic enterprise in general, morphology should be the centerpiece of language study. Yet, instead of gravitating to the center of linguistics during the recent Generativist revolution in language studies, in the past few decades morphology has all but vanished from the agenda of linguistic inquiry.

One reason for this malaise of the discipline is the unresolved flaws in the European Structuralist model of morphology inherited by Generativist theory—zero morphology, empty morphology, morphological asymmetry. Perhaps for this reason, the Generativist tradition has yet to find a firm place for morphology in its theoretical models. Indeed, some Generativists argue that morphology does not even exist outside the general principles of syntax and phonology, and the storage capacities of the lexicon. The reason for the underestimation of morphology's contribution to the sentence is the Generativists' simple view of the morpheme. From Plato to Baudouin, the word was taken to be the smallest linguistic sign. Since Baudouin, however, "the minimal meaningful unit of language", has been the MORPHEME, the sublexical constituent of words. While the status of the word as a linguistic sign is uncontroversial, the term "word" itself has defied all attempts at definition; indeed, this recalcitrance prompted the original interest in the proposition that morphemes are the primitive linguistic signs. The result is a genuine quandary: morphemes fail to behave consistently like signs and words defy definition.

The second reason for the malaise in the discipline is that while the word and morpheme have two sides: the semantic and phonological, only for a brief period in the 19th century did research treat both sides evenly in any attempt to account for the relation between the two. The initial interest of the Greeks centered exclusively on the semantic side of words, their various categories and subcategories. Over the centuries interest slowly shifted, not to a balanced scrutiny of the meaning and sound of morphemes, nor to the crucial relation between the two, but rather to the exclusive study of the phonological side of morphemes that dominated the Structuralist school.

The next section, a brief overview of this historical shift, outlines this imbalance and provides a frame of reference for the present work. The central issues and assumptions of morphology, which this book will address in subsequent chapters, will be drawn from this historical survey.

1.1 A BRIEF HISTORY OF MORPHOLOGICAL STUDIES

The Stoic philosophers (Diogenes Laertes, Apollonius) first defined the word as a bilateral association of "the signifier" (τὸ σημαῖνον) and "the signified" (τὸ σημαινόμενον). The Greeks did not analyze the word; they considered the word the smallest indivisible meaningful linguistic element. They used the formal regularities existing between words only as clues to grammatical and semantic categories. They defined the lexical classes, noun and verb (including adjectives among the former), and undertook the first investigations into Gender. Aristotle advanced these studies with his definition of words other than nouns, verbs, adjectives, and adverbs as "conjunctions" or "connectives" (σύνδεσμοι). He defined this latter class in terms of their relational functions and their lack of referential meaning in isolation. This distinction is an important one that will be restored and refurbished in the next chapter.

The Classical Greek philosophers then focused on the categories expressed in words without formally analyzing words. This fascination with semantic categories continued in Alexandria even though the Alexandrian grammarians are credited with converting language study from a subdiscipline of philosophy to an independent "technical" discipline. The Alexandrians expanded the number of recognized grammatical categories, defining them in terms of the formal characteristics of their inflectional paradigms as well as their referential properties.

Aristarchus and Dionysius Thrax categorized words into the canonical eight parts of speech, but their categories, too, were restricted to whole words, and did not include any analysis of sublexical elements. By the time of Dionysius, the Alexandrians had identified three Tenses (Present, Past, Future), two Aspects (Perfective, Imperfective), and three Voices

(Active, Passive, Middle) among verbs. Dionysius reported 22 subclasses of nouns: proper, collective, generic, specific, appellative, and so forth; three Genders: Masculine, Feminine, Neuter; three Numbers: Singular, Dual, Plural; the five Cases: Upright, Generic, Dative, Causal, Vocative; two species: primitive and derivative, which had seven subspecies: patronymic, possessive, comparative, superlative, hypocoristic, denominal, and deverbal; and three shapes: simple, compound, and double compound. The Alexandrians did not associate these categories with distinct morphemes; rather, they simply sorted out whole words with inflectional variations expressing these categories. However, the individuation of all these categories laid the foundations of our understanding of lexical behavior across the succeeding centuries.

The Latin grammarians continued the Greek tradition with greater dexterity. In *De Lingua Latina* (47–45 B.C.), Marcus Varro classified the major parts of speech according to two properties: Case or Tense. Assuming much like Chomsky (1981) that either of these properties could be absent or present in a form, he came to the very modern conclusion that Latin has four major categories, not the N, V, A, P yielded by $[\pm N, \pm V]$, but (i) nominals (Ns and As), which he might have symbolized as $[+Case, -Tense]$, (ii) verbs, $[-Case, +Tense]$, (iii) participles, $[+Case, +Tense]$, and (iv) adverbs, $[-Case, -Tense]$.[1]

Varro also distinguished attested from potential paronyms, noting that *unguentum* "perfume" has a Plural *unguenta* because of the existence of several kinds of perfume. Were similar differences in the kinds of olive oil and vinegar to arise, so would Plurals *olea* "olive oils" and *aceta* "vinegars". However, Varro is perhaps best known for his discussions of the extensive violations (*anomalia*) of derivational regularity, for instance, the indeclinable nouns, the irregular Comparatives like *bonum, melius, optimum,* and derivational irregularities like those of (1.1):

(1.1) a. vin-um "wine"   vin-aria "wine shop"
       b. unguent-um "perfume"   unguent-aria "perfume shop"
       c. car-o "meat"   *carn-aria "butcher's shop"

Instead of the expected *carnaria,* the word for "butcher shop" in Latin is *laniena.* So the discovery of lexical exceptions to morphological patterns is ancient, indeed.

Despite their interest in paradigms, the Latin grammarians, like their predecessors, explored sublexical derivational properties only minimally and focused most of their efforts on the categories and etymologies. Problems such as those listed in (1.1) were not discussed in terms of differences in affixation; rather, the major categories were seen as whole words with "flexible ends", the concept which underlies the current term, "inflection". Not until Priscian (*Institutiones grammaticæ,* Books 9–10) do we find rules predicting inflected forms. Even here the rules predict the form of a whole word from that of another whole rather than from the behavior of sublexical elements. For example, Priscian's rule for the Past Imperfective is as follows (from Kiel, 1857–1870, II, 457–58: quoted here from Matthews 1972: 10–11, my translation):

> *præteritum imperfectum . . . a præsenti fieri sic: in prima quidem et in secunda coniugatione et quarta in "eo" desinente a secunda persona ablata "s" finali et addita "bam": "amas amabam", "doces docebam", "is ibam"; in tertiæ vero omnibus verbis et quartæ in "io" desinentibus prima persona mutat "o" in "e" productam et assumit "bam": "lego legebam", "facio faciebam", "venio veniebam".*

> The Past Imperfective . . . is formed from the Present like this: for the 1st and 2nd Conjugation and the 4th Conjugation ending in *eo:,* the final *s* is deleted from the 2nd Person and *bam* is added: *amas amabam, doces docebam, is ibam;* for all verbs in 3rd Conjugation, however, and [those of] the 4th in *io, o* is changed into *e* and *bam* is added: *lego legebam, facio faciebam, venio veniebam.*

Primary interest here focuses on disambiguating the categories themselves rather than on the allmorphy of the "accidents" of ending which symbolized them.

The study of the word strayed little beyond the accomplishments of the Latin grammarians throughout the Middle Ages and Renaissance. From a contemporary perspective, one might question how much morphological study had in fact been conducted up to this point, since the means of signaling categories generally remained all but wholly beyond the pale of interest. Reuchlin (1506) finally introduced the analysis of words in terms of roots and affixes to European audiences, a practice he had observed in the works of the Hebrew grammarians. In a more influential work a century and a half later, Schottelius (1663) extended Reuchlin's division by distinguishing *Stammwörter* STEMS, *Hauptendungen* MAIN (= derivational) ENDINGS, and *zufällige Endungen* ACCIDENTAL (= inflectional) ENDINGS, thereby recognizing differences in inflection and derivation for the first time.

Schottelius' work began a shift toward a balanced study of the signified and the signifier. By and large, however, morphological research did not advance beyond the work of Reuchlin and Schottelius until the turn of the 19th century, when the discovery of the Hindi grammarians generated an interest for formal decomposition. The Indian grammars from Pāṇini's *Aṣṭādhyāyī* (ca. 500 BC) on distinguished derivation and inflection. They contained formal rules governing the behavior of sublexical elements, for example, Pāṇini's AFFIXES (*pratyaya*) and AUGMENTS. Pāṇini's affixes could be replaced before the surface level or deleted to accommodate zero morphology; empty realizations were also possible. All these wonders began to emerge in European word study on the wave of proofs that Sanskrit was related to the languages of Western Europe, which culminated in William Jones' famous report to the Royal Society in 1786.

Von Humboldt (1836) turned attention outside the IE family, introducing infixation and incorporation to European theoreticians. Since these new types of morphology are formally, not categorially, distinguished from other types of morphology, von Humboldt was led to conclude that the variation in the SOUND FORM (*Lautform*) is the primary element distinguishing languages. Thus the first language typology, von Humboldt's isolational, agglutinative, and inflectional types, is based exclusively on formal distinctions. Morphology had become a fairly clear component of grammar and its formal side, an accepted fact. Schleicher (1859) next produced the first formal theory of morphology. A forewarning of things to come, it dealt solely with the possible structural relations of affixes and stems as a basis for predicting language typology.

The influential work of von Humboldt and Schleicher, however, did not spell the end of categorial studies. Neogrammarians like Brugmann and Delbrück consistently discussed both the form and the grammatical functional categories associated with them in their monumental works at the end of the 19th century. The Neogrammarians, in fact, first distinguished lexical classes (N, V, A, Adv) from the categories of grammatical functions, for example, Number, Person, Gender. Indeed, the brief Neogrammarian period represents the apogee of morphological studies balancing concern for content with that for form. The phenomenon was short-lived, however, for the Structuralist school accelerated the shift away from the study of morphological categories to the exclusive study of the allomorphy.

The Structuralists' point of departure was the Classic assumption that the relation of all lexical and morphological sound to meaning is direct, mutual implication; Saussure even adopted the Greek terms, "signifier" and "signified." Baudouin then combined the Greek concept of the sign with the newly discovered sublexical units to reorient the definition of the sign from the word as a whole to its sublexical elements. Baudouin placed roots, affixes, and inflectional endings into a single natural class, which he called, for the first time, "morpheme". He originally defined his new concept as "the simplest psycho-linguistic elements in the guise of sound" (Baudouin de Courtenay 1889). But in Baudouin de Courtenay (1895), he refined this definition to "that part of the word which is endowed with psychological autonomy and for that reason is not further divisible" [tr. E. Stankiewicz (1972)]. Baudouin, therefore, not only distinguished sublexical units; he raised the status of affixes to that of the stems that bear them, defining both identically.

Saussure, mindful of the problems with Baudouin's definitions, carefully avoided the term ''morpheme'' in his lectures and associated his definition of the sign only with words. Bloomfield, however, carried Baudouin's definitions even further. Having shifted the classical definition of the word as a bilateral sign to the morpheme, Bloomfield then took the next logical step, to place all morphemes in the lexicon, previously the storage component of words (Bloomfield 1933, 161–63). Bloomfield's overall vision of morphology included (i) Baudouin's Single Morpheme Hypothesis, which unifies all sublexical elements under the single rubric ''morpheme''; (ii) the Sign Base Morpheme Hypothesis, which defines all such morphemes as signs, directly related associations of form and meaning; and (iii) Bloomfield's own Lexical Morphology Hypothesis, which locates all such morphemes in the lexicon, where they are subject to the same selection and copying processes, without distinguishing the behavior of stems from that of affixes. This cluster of independent assumptions will be referred to throughout this book as the LEXICAL MORPHEME HYPOTHESIS (LMH), a hypothesis that dominates the contemporary language sciences.

Simultaneous to listing grammatical morphemes in the lexicon, Bloomfield denied any relevance of semantics to the study of linguistics. This step led to an abrupt shift of interest away from morphological categories altogether to Trubetskoi's MORPHOPHONEMICS, allomorphy pure and simple. When Nida completed the first structuralist treatise on morphology (Nida 1946), it represented little more than a set of discovery procedures for isolating affixes and determining their allomorphy. It simply ignored the categories that affixes express.

Not all thinkers were unaware of the problems with the structuralist assumptions. Saussure (1916) pointed out the fundamental contradiction of ZERO MORPHS to his theory of the linguistic sign and the complications in defining the word raised by compounds and contractions (one word or two?). In 1929 Karcevskij discovered MORPHOLOGICAL ASYMMETRY in Russian inflection: the same ending may mark more than one grammatical function, while any given function may be marked by more than one ending. The inflectional ending -*a* in Russian, for example, marks NomSg-Fem, GenSgMas/Neu, and NomPlNeu. It is therefore multifunctional. On the other side, each of these Case functions, say, NomSg, is marked not by one, but by a set of endings: NomSgFem = -*a,* NomSgMas = -∅, NomSgNeu = -*o*. Karcevskij saw a major problem for sign theory in this since such patterns are not found among stem morphemes.

Bazell examined many problems with the structuralist approach to morphology: asymmetry, zero morphology, the bias in favor of form. His most enlightened criticism identified THE CORRESPONDENCE FALLACY, the presumption that an analysis at one linguistic level isomorphically corresponds to the analysis of the same object at other levels. Examining the problem of morphological asymmetry discovered by Karcevskij, Bazell (1949, 1952) argued that it follows neither that the phonological analysis of a word will isomorphically correspond to the semantic, nor that, because of this, no analysis is possible. Bazell chided attempts to conceive of such morphemes as the English Past Tense marker in *sang* as an ablaut variant of the suffix *-ed*. It does not follow from the fact that these two markers express the same grammatical function, he reasoned, that they are identical at any other level. It is quite possible that each level is defined in its own terms (in which case a set of principles mapping one level to the other will be required of linguistic theory).

Despite the catalogue of problems facing sign-based morphology compiled by Bazell, Saussure, and Karcevskij, neither Structuralism in its decline nor Generativism in its rise addressed the shortcomings of Bloomfield's assumptions. In its first two decades, the Generative Revolution ignored morphology. Aronoff's dissertation on derivational morphology (Aronoff 1976) was published 19 years after Chomsky's *Syntactic Structures*. It is true that the Natural Phonology movement of the late 1970's (Hooper 1976) was a response to the level of abstraction allowed by the allomorphy of Chomsky and Halle (1968). However, initial concern focused primarily on phonological issues of allomorphy rather than the elementary questions of morphology. Recent schools of GB morphology, such as Lexical Morphology and Autosegmental Morphology, started out as Kiparsky's Lexical Phonology and the Autosegmental Phonology of Goldsmith, respectively. Neither of these theories deals with meaning explicitly, though meaning is curiously the basis of the determination of formal units. Both theories assume Bloomfield's three principles on the nature and place of morphemes in grammatical theory (LMH).

The history of morphological studies, in conclusion, teaches us that the critical objects of morphological research are lexical and grammatical categories, sublexical phonological constituents and, crucially, the relation between the two. The course of this history has witnessed a shift from the exclusive study of categories to an exclusive study of formal elements. Only very recently, and only in the work of a handful of contemporary morphologists, has morphological research returned to a balanced study of both form and function (see Carstairs-McCarthy 1992a: chapter 6); however, the question of the relation between categories and exponents remains largely unexplored terrain.

1.2 A SURVEY OF CURRENT AGENDAS

Having surveyed the history of word studies from the Greeks to modern times, the next step is to examine current research programs in morphology to determine our bearings. To redress the current imbalance in allomorphic and semantic studies of morphology, we need first to understand that imbalance as it presently stands. This section, therefore, will review current research programs in morphology with a view toward assessing their contribution to the core concern of morphology: the relation of linguistic sound and meaning.

Recent work in morphology has, by and large, continued the Structuralist emphasis on allomorphy, though some studies have returned to the issue of grammatical categories. Carstairs-McCarthy (1989) refers to the Structuralist approach as the "bottom-up" approach, because it focuses on phonological issues at the expense of semantic ones. The "top-down" approach focuses on the semantic side of morphology or, more correctly, on the combinations of grammatical categories which grammatical morphemes, inflectional and derivational, mark. Those who approach morphology from either direction seldom deal with the whole morpheme, sound and meaning. "Bottom-up" and "top-down" frameworks usually focus on the phonological or categorial side of the morpheme, respectively, without reference to the other, the most common assumption being that the two are simply directly associated with each other.

Research in morphology associated with the GB school of grammatical studies all share in the common basic assumptions of the LMH mentioned in the discussion of Bloomfield above. Lieber (1981a: 35) claims, for example, that "affixes differ from non-affix morphemes only in that affixes have as part of their lexical entries, frames indicating the category of items to which they attach as well as the category to which they belong". She emphasizes also that "especially important for the theory to be developed below is the fact that lexical entries for affixes are identical to lexical entries for non-affix morphemes, except for the presence of subcategorization information in the entries of the former" (37).

The appeal of this hypothesis lies in its simplicity: it provides only one basic grammatical element, the morpheme, which is more or less isomorphic with referential terms and predicates. This element is stored in a single component, the lexicon, and is copied into words and phrases by the same simple selection rule that interprets the symbol of a minimal projection and copies an appropriate lexical item onto it from the lexicon. The assumption that affixes belong to the same categories as stems (N, V, A) and are inserted like stems, allows lexical derivation to be conflated with compounding. That is, the copying of a prefix into a derivation is the same process as adding an attribute to an noun to form a compound: *do* → *undo, boat* → *houseboat*.

The simplicity of this approach, in fact, is such that Pesetsky (1985), Sproat (1985), and Di Sciullo and Williams have concluded that the lexicon does not contain a rule component. Rather, the lexicon is boring: "The lexicon is like a prison—it contains only the lawless, and the only thing that its inmates have in common is lawlessness" (Di Sciullo & Williams 1987: 3).[2] The principles of derivation and inflection, the inheritance of category features, subcategorization frames, and the like, are those of syntax. The lack of research into the nature of grammatical categories in the published accounts of GB morphology is thus justified by the assumption that grammatical categories differ in no way from those of syntax.

1.2.1 Level-Ordered (Stratal) Morphology

Kiparsky (1982), Halle and Mohanan (1985), Booij and Rubach (1987), and Inkelas (1993) have sought to develop morphological and phonological systems void of diacritic features like [±Latinate], while explaining the different types of phonological changes that take place at the boundaries of Latinate and native affixes in English. English, for example, has two negative prefixes, the Latinate (*in-*) and the native (*un-*). When attached to stems, the Latinate prefix undergoes assimilation across a broad range of consonants, for example, *immovable, incorrect* ([ɪŋkərɛkt]), *irrelevant, illegal*, to which *un-* is not susceptible, as in *unmoved, uncompromising, unreal, unlikable*. Chomsky and Halle (1968) posited two types of boundary, a morpheme boundary " + " and a word boundary "#," stipulating that the lexical representation of *un-* would be /ən#/ and that for *in-* would be /ɪn + /. Since "#" was a word boundary marker, only postcyclic phonological changes which occur across word boundaries were allowed between *un-* and its stem, while morphophonemic alternations were allowed across the morpheme boundary " + ."

Although Chomsky and Halle distinguished two types of boundaries, they could not account for a major generalization: while word-boundary affixes may be attached to both word-boundary and morpheme-boundary (Latinate) affixes, it is not generally possible to attach morpheme-boundary affixes to word-boundary (Germanic) affixes. For example, the suffix *+ion* motivates morphophonemic changes in the stems to which it attaches: *submit : submission; deride : derision*, so it must be assigned a morpheme boundary. The native suffix *#ing*, on the other hand, does not, so it needs a word boundary: *ride : riding; roll : rolling*. Consequently, while it is possible for *#ing* to occur outside *+ion: positioning, (air) conditioning, requisitioning, +ion* cannot occur outside *#ing*.

Allen (1978) proposed that rather than distinct boundaries, affixes are attached at different levels of derivation, so that morpheme-boundary affixes simply attach to stems at an earlier stage of derivation than word-boundary affixes. Phonological rules apply cyclically so that all phonological rules relevant to a given affix apply immediately upon attachment, before the next affix is copied. This is accomplished by Kiparsky's BRACKET ERASURE PRINCIPLE, which erases the brackets around an affix when all P-rules relevant to it have applied. P-rules continue applying inside brackets until all brackets are erased. Level I affixes require allomorphic operations; they are inserted at a higher level than those affixes which involve only regular phonological alternations and no allomorphic ones. This ordering captures the generalization that the '' + '' boundary affixes tend to occur closer to the stem and not outside a ''#'' boundary affix without postulating different types of boundaries. This approach is called STRATAL MOR-PHOLOGY.

Stratal Morphology raises the question of whether there are different classes of operations on morphemes and whether they affect the order of affixes in lexical and inflectional derivations. Notice that this brand of morphology speaks only to the issue of the order of these CLASSES of affixes or operations, not to the order of specific affixes within those classes. For example, while Stratal Morphology predicts the order of the set of cyclic suffixes like *+ ion, + ous, + ity* vis-à-vis the set of noncyclic suffixes like *#er, #ing, #en,* it does not predict the order of the affixes within these sets, for example, why we find derivations with *+ ous + ity (generosity)* but not ** + ous + ion,* e.g. **generosion.* The predictions of Stratal Morphology are thus very general and require further specification to be useful.

1.2.2 Word-and-Paradigm Morphology

Matthews (1972, 1991) and S. Anderson (1982, 1992) argue for a separation of inflectional affixation from the ''morphological representations'' (grammatical feature inventory) of lexical items. These advocates of WORD-AND-PARADIGM (WP) morphology argue for unordered morphosyntactic features in the morphological representation and the application of unordered realization rules which attach affixes or otherwise modify a lexical stem (reduplication, metathesis, and so forth). Affixation is therefore the result of operations on stems, rather than listed items. Although Matthews and Anderson offer theories of mapping of morphological to phonological representations, they say little about the nature of the categories featured in those representations.

Matthews developed the classical WP approach to morphology by refining and elaborating the rules of Prician's *Institutiones Grammaticæ.* From this Classical point of departure, he developed a formal model particularly adept at handling the problems encumbering sign-based morphology pointed out by Karcevskij and Bazell: morphological asymmetry, and null and empty morphology. In place of an ordered arrangement of morphological functions for a Latin form like *ferri,* such as, [FER- + Infinitive + Passive], Matthews proposes a simple statement of unordered morpholexical features like ''the Passive Infinitive of FERO'' (Matthews 1972: 106). Independent phonological operations interpret these features. One such realization rule might be: ''the terminal ending (or Termination) *-i:* is selected if the word is characterized by the elements Ist, Singular, Perfect-ive and Present Indicative'' (Matthews 1972: 107–108).

An interesting claim of WP morphology is that the ordering of inflec-tional desinences is a matter of language specific morphotactics. Moreover, contra the MIRROR PRINCIPLE of Baker (1985), morphological features are not mapped one-one onto affixes in fusional languages as they sometimes seem to be in agglutinative languages. Rather, inflectional derivations are built up from stems by algorithmic operations, which may map one feature onto two or more affixes or more than one feature onto one affix. Mat-thews, however, is careful to explain that his WP framework may be valid only for fusional languages; an Item-Arrangement or Item-Process model may be better suited for agglutinative languages. Affix order can be crucial in agglutinative languages like Turkish: *Türk-ler-dir* means "they are the Turks" while *Türk-tür-ler* means "they are Turkish." Here the order of affixes seems to isomorphically follow that of the morphosyntactic fea-tures. Hence the cost for Matthews' compelling solution to the problems of fusional morphology may be the universality of his model.

Anderson's A-MORPHOUS MORPHOLOGY is an extension of what was previously called the EXTENDED WP MODEL (Anderson 1982). Anderson (1992) returns to the Aspects model of syntax (Chomsky 1965) in postulat-ing terminal syntactic nodes with complex symbols containing just those category features necessary for inflection: Number, Gender, and Case fea-tures for nouns, Person, Number, and Tense features for verbs. This pro-vides a source for the morphosyntactic feature representation that Mat-thews assumed. Anderson maintains Matthews' claim that the features of a morphosyntactic representation are unordered, but adds that they are LAYERED; that is, they accumulate in ordered layers. This accounts for languages like Turkish, where some affixes are ordered vis-à-vis each other, but others are not. Features within layers trigger those affixes whose order is irrelevant; features ordered with respect to each other trigger or-dered affixes. Anderson in particular notes that layering accounts for the ordering of Subject and Object agreement in languages which maintain both. The order of the pronominal affixes more often than not determines whether they are coindexed with the Subject or Object position.

Derivational morphology and compounding are processes altogether different from inflectional processes in the WP model. Because they see differences in productivity and rates of idiomaticity radically different among lexical and inflectional derivates, Matthews and Anderson assign lexical derivation exclusively to the lexicon. This was a major issue in the 1960's and 1970's in Europe; Fleischer, Dokulil, Kubriakova, Vinogra-dov, Zemskaia, and many others have written extensively on it, generally concluding that the two morphologies are distinct but without establishing clear and reliable criteria for distinguishing them. Perlmutter (1988) dubbed this hypothesis the SPLIT MORPHOLOGY HYPOTHESIS. Since the origin of morphosyntactic features is syntax and word formation processes operate from the lexicon, the WP model with Split Morphology accounts for the distinction of inflection and word formation. It also accounts for the LEXICALIST HYPOTHESIS (= Lexical Integrity Principle), that the operations of syntax have no access to the internal structure of lexical items.

WP morphologies raise at least three fundamental issues. First, is there a universal order of (derivational and) inflectional morphemes and, if so, what determines that order? Matthews denies a universal order of fusional morphemes but leaves the door open for a model of agglutinative morphology that might specify order. Anderson provides layered morphological representations, which can accommodate both strictly ordered and unordered markers. Second, what is the relation between morphological expression and the category it expresses? If the relation is not everywhere homomorphic, there must be more than one derivational level and a set of principles for mapping one level onto the other, principles which account for ordering and scope differences between levels. Matthews was the first to explore the indirect articulation of grammatical categories in inflection and to postulate mechanisms for mapping between the categorial and phonological levels. Finally, is inflection radically distinct from lexical derivation and compounding? Although much has been written on this subject, it remains an unsettled issue.

1.2.3 The Morphological Structure of Word Syntax

Word Syntax raises the question of whether lexical rules and morphology exist at all. Rather than special lexical rules constraining derivational and inflectional operations, Word Syntax proposes that the principles of GB syntax constrain them. Baker (1988a, 1988b), Lieber (1981a, 1983, 1992), Roeper and Siegel (1978), Roeper (1987), Scalise (1984), Selkirk (1982), Di Sciullo and Williams (1987), and Halle and Marantz (1993) argue that word formation processes are constrained by argument structure inherited from the stem plus the principles of GB syntax. Selkirk, for example, claims that internal (Object) arguments of verbs in compounds must be satisfied in a compound just as they must be satisfied in a VP. Moreover, just as an external (Subject) argument cannot be satisfied within the VP, it also cannot be satisfied within a compound. Hence *tree-eating of pasta* is ruled out because the Object, *pasta,* must be satisfied within the compound. By the same principle, *girl-swimming* is ruled out because *girl* must serve the function of Subject in the compound. *Pasta-eating in trees* is perfectly acceptable.

To account for the lexical categories of derived words, Williams posited his controversial RIGHT-HAND HEAD RULE, that the rightmost element of derivations and compounds is always the head and categorizes the neologism, for example, $[re[read_V]]_V$, $[house_N[boat]_N]_N$, and $[bak_V[er]_N]_N$. He takes advantage of the status of affixes as listed objects with its implication that affixes belong to the same lexical classes as do stems. It follows that affixes are the lexical heads of derived words. It also follows that prefixes will not change the category of the stems to which they attach, as suffixes do. By and large, this prediction is realized in English and a few other languages, but not in predominantly prefixing languages like Yoruba or left-branch compounding languages like Vietnamese.

Recent Word Syntax studies have focused on thematic relations (Agent, Patient, Recipient) of argument structures for which verbs subcategorize. They have shown that these relations must be inherited by derivations or compounds from their underlying bases and that such inheritance precludes any further use of them by syntax in the phrase. For example, the Agentive sense of *driver,* by these accounts, derives from the Agent relation in the argument structure of *drive*: [Agent ____ (Theme)]. Once an argument role is linked to an affix by derivation, as [Agent] is linked to *-er* in this case, it is unavailable for further lexical or syntactic service. *Man-driver* should not be interpretable as "a man who drives" since the Agent argument of *drive* has been assigned both to the suffix *-er* and, in the compound attribute, to *man*. The same applies to the syntactic construction *a driver of a man* where *man* and *-er* would also have to be assigned the same Agent argument. *Truck-driver* and *the driver of the truck* are acceptable since *truck* is assigned the unoccupied Theme (Patient) role in either case.[3]

Some recent Word Syntax literature has gravitated toward proof that word formation and inflection do not exist as discrete components of grammar, that is, do not possess their own rules and categories. Sproat (1985), Baker (1988a), and Lieber (1992) argue explicitly that the principles of morphology are just those of GB syntax applied to lexical structure. Word Syntax is of interest, therefore, because it focuses on the categories of morphology and what determines them. It thereby complements the theoretical work of the allomorphic research of Stratal Morphology also conducted within the GB model, and certainly frames two of the major questions on the agenda of morphology: do words have internal structure? and are the terminal elements in all that structure lexical items?

1.3 SEPARATING THE CENTRAL FROM PERIPHERAL ISSUES

Argument linking and inheritance, on the one hand, and autosegmental representations and level ordering, on the other, raise issues of constraints on the categorial and formal sides of morphology, respectively, and must be dealt with in the chapters to follow. However, these treatments of categories and allomorphy do not get at the central issue of morphology: the relation between the two. Because morphology bridges the levels of meaning and sound, this issue is paramount to morphological research. How is it that phonological expressions convey meaning when we speak? What are the constraints on the mapping of meaning to sound at the atomic level? This issue is not a trivial one because the widespread occurrence of zero and empty grammatical morphemes brings sign theory itself into question in ways which cannot simply be ignored as they have been in the recent past.

The literature up to now has revealed several types of morphological objects and operations. Lexemes, morphemes, stems, and roots are the fundamental objects of morphology, while the most salient operations are derivation, conversion, transposition, compounding, affixation, revowelling, reduplication, contraction, and metathesis. No complete list of grammatical categories has been compiled and the number seems to be quite large though closed. The list would include such expressive derivational categories as Diminution, Augmentation, Pejorativity, Affection, and functional categories such as Subjective (*baker*), Objective (*employee*), Instrumental (*mixer*), Locational (*bakery*). A workable theory of morphology in any viable model of grammar must not merely account for all these operations, categories, and objects, but also demonstrate how they interact and interrelate.

The fundamental questions of morphology which emerge from the ancient and current research on the structure of words, then, seem to be the following:

1. What are the grammatical atoms, the basic elements of language:
   a. the morpheme (lexical and grammatical)?
   b. the lexeme and the grammatical morpheme?

2. How are phonological, grammatical, and semantic representations of the basic grammatical elements related at each of their respective levels:
   a. directly (biuniquely)?
   b. indirectly (conditionally and, if so, how)?
   c. both?

3. How many morphologies are there:
   a. inflectional and derivational (Split Morphology)?
   b. only one (Integrated Morphology)?

4. What are the categories of morphology?
   a. What is the outer limit on their number and what determines it?
   b. What is the nature of these categories?
      (1) grammatical or semantic?
      (2) How are derivational and inflectional categories related?

5. What are morphological rules:
    a. special morphological operations (WP morphology)?
    b. lexical insertion + allomorphy (Lexical Morphology)?
    c. the operations of syntax (Word Syntax)?

6. Finally, what adjustments to syntactic theory are required to accommodate a theory of morphology?

This book will develop a model of lexicology and morphology focused specifically on these issues.

1.4 BASIC PRINCIPLES

In order to develop answers to the questions catalogued in the previous section, we need a base of central truths to draw upon during our investigations that will serve as anchors and a point of departure for the argumentation. Over the history of linguistics few principles have become so axiomatic as to provide such a base; however, the first two principles below seem to me to be axiomatic. They are followed by three theoretical principles of modern linguistics and cognitive science which seem firmly established even though troubled by lingering questions of detail.

I. *The uncontroversial prototypical major class lexical items (nouns, verbs, and adjectives) consist of nonnull, mutually implied (directly articulated) phonological, grammatical, and semantic representations.*

This principle is a specification of the Stoic (and subsequently Saussurian) definition of the classical linguistic sign. Throughout this book, noun, verb, and adjective stems will be referred to as "prototypical major lexical class items". "Prototype" is used in this context to distinguish these uncontroversial lexical items from other potential types of lexical items, which some morphologists argue must belong to an independent morphological component. That Principle I holds for these three classes of lexical items has been assumed for centuries and is, to my knowledge, uncontroversial. The exact status of adverbs, however, is controversial. Manner adverbs seem to derive rather freely from qualitative adjectives while spatio-temporal adverbs do not seem to do so. It is widely recognized that items referred to as adverbs in the past in fact are several marginally connected classes. This category will be examined in what follows and most of the items composing it will be included under Principle I. All types of bound and free grammatical morphemes are considered controversial and are included among the data investigated here. The central issue of chapter 2 will be whether grammatical morphemes are covered by this principle. Whether the phonological representation may be null is an issue which still emerges from time to time, so it will also be examined in chapter 2.

II. *Prototypical major class lexical items constitute synchronically open classes.*

The lexical stock of the prototypical major lexical classes may be expanded synchronically by lexical derivation and a wide variety of logical, nongrammatical means described as LEXICAL STOCK EXPANSION by Beard (1987b): borrowing, loan translation, onomatopoeia, blending, backformation, clipping, acronymization, and the like. Whether the lexicon also contains some closed classes is an issue at stake in the remainder of this book. The point of Principle II is that the closed status of classes like prepositions and auxiliaries may not be ignored, which brings into question their assignment to the lexicon. In order to mix the two types of classes, one must first prove that nothing of significance motivates the distinction, that is, the differences between grammatical relations and semantic classes.

III. *Prototypical major class items belong to one and only one lexical class (category).*

Principle III means that each uncontroversial major class item belongs to a single, discrete lexical class. A major class item may be a noun, verb, or adjective but not both a noun and verb. Items like *love*, therefore, which have both a verbal and a nominal sense, are either accidental homonyms, or one is a principled derivate of the other. The assumption here is that the lexical categories are distinct and mutually exclusive, overlapping nowhere, but that they are related to each other by rules whose nature is an empirical question. Notice that this principle does not speak to the issue of SQUISHES (Ross 1972), that is, MIXED CATEGORIES (Lefebvre and Muysken 1988). The category to which a major class item belongs may in fact be a mixed category, which derives its properties from two other, pure categories. However, if a major item belongs to a mixed or pure category, it belongs to that one category alone unless it is shifted to another by derivation. The reason that this principle is desirable, aside from the rigor it imparts to the model, is that it motivates derivation rules. Without Principle III there is no explanation of why languages have derivation rules, especially transposition (chapter 8), whose unique purpose is to convert members of one class to another.

IV. *The operations of an autonomous module have no access to operations internal to any other module.*

This is the principle of modularity as presented by Chomsky (1981) and Fodor (1983). If we assume that objects and operations of various grammatical subcomponents are distinct, we assume that they interact in only one way: the output of one set may be the input of another set. The operations of one distinct module or component cannot interact in any way with those of another. Hence, if the evidence shows the conditions on morphological rules to be compatible with those of syntax, the two grammatical components cannot be independent. However, if the conditions on their operations are incompatible, we must conclude that the two constitute discrete components, either one of which may operate only on the input or output of the other.

An important implication of Principle IV is that the outputs of various modules will reflect the nature of that module. In terms of the lexicon and syntax, this means that should the lexicon and syntax contain similar categories or operations, lexical output will nonetheless differ from syntactic output over the same categories and operations. Moreover, the differences will reflect the different natures of the modules involved: lexical output will always be words, while syntactic output will always be phrases, whatever similarities the two modules might otherwise share.

V. *The parameters of morphology are universal.*

This is the principle of Universal Grammar (UG), revised by Chomsky (1981) to make clear the claim that the components of grammars of various languages are not necessarily identical but simply share a universal set of parameters. These parameters exhibit a limited range of settings which may vary from language to language. Assuming this claim as axiomatic commits the remainder of this book to a search for a set of categories and operations available to all languages. The possibility that the grammatical categories of English represent a different set of parameters from those of, say, Mohawk, will not be entertained, even though it is an equally reasonable a priori assumption. Principle V is thus little more than a stipulation at this point, an attempt to restrict the enormous range of theoretical possibilities to an addressable set.

1.5 CONCLUSION

This book is a work of lexicology and morphology at the edge of syntax rather than at the edge of phonology. Because work on allomorphy since the Generative Revolution has been conducted at the expense of methodical examination of morphological categories, we have a much clearer picture of the interface of morphology and phonology than we have of the lexicon-morphology and syntax-morphology interfaces. For this reason, the present work will concentrate on categories and the abstract operations of derivation rather than on allomorphy. Within these areas, this book will recommend some rather bold changes in syntactic and lexical theories. The benefit of taking these radical demands seriously is a more complete, more integrated overall theory of language.

NOTES

1. This theoretical consistency demonstrates that the ancients were just as capable of becoming prisoners of their theoretical models as are we.

Apparently Varro, in his fervor to maintain mathematic symmetry, ignored the fact that participles represent an entirely derived class while the other three are fundamentally lexical.

2. Compare this definition with Bloomfield (1933: 274): "The lexicon is really an appendix of grammar, a list of basic irregularities."

3. The fact that *man-driver* may be interpreted as "a man who drives" is usually explained in terms of a second compound type, that is, [*man*] [*driver*] versus [*truck driv*]er.

Chapter Two

The Aristotelean Hypothesis

2.1 THE LEXICAL MORPHEME HYPOTHESIS

This chapter will demonstrate that the three interrelated notions named in chapter 1 "the Lexical Morpheme Hypothesis" (LMH) is untenable as a whole or in part. These notions are, in review, (i) Baudouin's Single Morpheme Hypothesis, the claim that all sublexical elements, stems and affixes alike, are "morphemes"; (ii) the Sign Base Morpheme Hypothesis, which defines all such morphemes as signs, isomorphic associations of form and meaning; and (iii) Bloomfield's Lexical Morphology Hypothesis, which locates all morphemes in the lexicon, where they are subject to the same selection processes. We will examine the most explicitly articulated models of LMH in the current literature, that of Lieber (1981a, 1992) and Scalise (1984). Since these three works do not diverge in their assumption of LMH, which is the focal concern here, Lieber's work has been chosen as a focus because it deals more pointedly with the crucial threats to LMH, that is, zero and empty morphology, and other unlexemelike behavior in affixes.[1] Other work in the Word Syntax framework conforms to Lieber's model in all basic principles and will be referred to from time to time when specifics warrant.

This chapter will demonstrate that in all definitionally crucial respects, major class lexical items differ from affixes so drastically as to preclude their being processed in the same component as the former. Even though Aristotle did not recognize affixes in his grammatical studies, I refer to this hypothesis as Aristotelean, since Aristotle was the first to separate minor from major class items. He was persuaded that the former are distinguished first by their meaninglessness outside context. While Ns, Vs, and As are commonly used as extralinguistic labels (as in *restaurant, garage, gas, slow, stop, hot, danger*), articles, auxiliaries, conjunctions, prepositions and affixes cannot be so used. For example, *the, those, can, should, to, from, of, with* simply have no labeling function.[2] Aristotle's CONNECTIVES (σύνδεσμοι), articles, conjunctions, and apparently prepositions, are also distinguished by their special function of marking grammatical relations between lexical items, hence his term "connectives."

This is precisely the conclusion of this chapter: affixes are in a class with free minor class items like articles, auxiliaries, adpositions, conjunctions, and some pronouns. These items as a class bear no semantic content but reflect grammatical functions which are managed by other components, specifically, by the lexicon and syntax. Because grammatical morphemes are interpretable only contextually, like Aristotle's minor class connectives, they are uninterpretable outside their grammatical context. Affixes and other grammatical morphemes so differ from major class lexical stems, in fact, that no basis exists for claiming that they are elements of the same component, the lexicon. The successful grammatical theory, therefore, must be based on discrete lexemes and grammatical morphemes.

The first step in proving this hypothesis is to demonstrate the faults of the simpler theories which assume a single basic linguistic element, a morpheme with insignificant lexical and grammatical variants. The next two sections discuss the limits of such theories. Section 2.2 will outline a set of assumptions central to all Word Syntax models by examining the arguments of Lieber and those who base their models on her assumptions. Section 2.3 will then systematically test four cardinal predictions of that model, showing that each fail. Along the way, we will discover the central problems of morphology, that is, empty morphemes, zero morphemes, operations like reduplication, and polyfunctionality, and investigate some commonly proposed solutions, such as homonymy, conversion, and feature percolation.

2.2 Lieber's Version of the Lexical Morpheme Hypothesis

Lieber (1981a, 1992) assumes X-bar theory with its impoverished base component and enriched lexicon. The base rules do not assign case or θ-roles to tree nodes; rather, these are assigned from the feature inventory of the governing lexical classes to NPs within their governing domains.[3] Within this framework, a word formation theory that captures the structural parallels between phrases and words must provide a means of changing the lexical class of underlying stems in those cases where the lexical class does change, as in the case of deverbal Subjective nominalizations like, $bake_V$ → $bak\text{-}er_N$, for X-bar syntax does not have the power to change lexical class. Now, if affixes are essentially identical with stems, they must bear lexical class (category) features like stems. These features may be assigned to derivational nodes by simple conventions that copy those features from the feature inventory of the affix to the maximal projection of the structure of the derived word. Lieber explains lexical derivation in three steps, illustrated in (2.1).

(2.1)

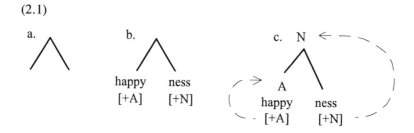

The word formation process begins with a lexical structure generated in accord with the principles of X-bar theory (2.1a). Lexical selection then fills this structure with stems and affixes, both lexical items, a process which observes subcategorization frames so that affixes are selected for the appropriate class of stems (2.1b). To account for the lexical class of the new word, Lieber (1981a) proposes four percolation conventions. The first two assign the lexical class feature of the stem to the first nonbranching node and that of the affix to the first branching node, as in (2.1c). Affixes which do not change the class of lexical derivates, for example, the prefix *counter-*, are listed in the lexicon without a lexical class. A third percolation convention specifies that in these cases the lexical class of the stem will percolate to the head. Di Sciullo and Williams (1987: 26–28) refer to this concept as RELATIVIZED HEADS, since heads are thereby relative only to specific features. Because *counter-* contains no [±N, ±V] feature, this featurization is inherited from the stem. The fourth convention specifies that the right-hand constituent of a compound will determine the lexical class of the compound.

Interest in the basic theory of LMH derives from its simplicity: there is but one lexicon, which contains but one type of item, the morpheme. McCarthy (1981) and Marantz (1982) have even demonstrated how Semitic revowelling and reduplication, processes which plagued Structuralist morphology, may be reduced to lexical selection if lexical selection and phonological operations are appropriately enriched. The morpheme under this interpretation is simply a fully specified or underspecified isomorphic sign, written into phrase structures by a single set of selection principles. Any changing of lexical class or category is illusion, the result of behavior that follows the Principles and Parameters framework. We would need strong motivation to abandon a theory of such elegance.

A potential threat to LMH is the zero morph(eme). Since zero morphology changes the lexical class and semantics of an underlying stem without affixation, it could undermine LMH, requiring another kind of rule, unrelated to lexical selection. The only candidate is the traditional operation of CONVERSION (Fleischer 1975: 74–76; Guilbert 1975: 73–80), which Lieber (1981a, 1981b)) adopts with little comment (although she redefines it in Lieber 1992). Lieber originally explained the relations in *(to) frame* : *(a) frame*, *(to) run* : *(a) run* with the nondirectional redundancy rule V ↔ N. The derivational direction we sense in these examples is a function of an autonomous semantic component irrelevant to formal descriptions and hence not requiring a description in Lieber's strictly grammatical model—also the position of Bloomfield. Since both sides of a conversional equation must be lexically listed, productive conversion is precluded.

Other unproductive lexical and inflectional relations are captured in MORPHOLEXICAL RULES, Bloomfield's name for morphological redundancy conditions holding over listed items in the lexicon (Bloomfield 1939). These rules of the lexical storage component "mimic" productive M-operations and account for subregular, morphologically determined phonological relations by simply asserting that they are related. Since reduplicative affixation was unproductive in Latin, Lieber would list *mord-* : *momord-*, *spond-* : *spopond-*, *curr-* : *cucurr-* independently. A morpholexical rule within lexical storage would then specify that the two stems are related via a rule of reduplication which applies only to stems marked for the rule:

(2.2) $C^0 C^1 V C^2$

   | | | |

   1 2 3 4 → 1 2 3 2 3 4

This arrangement captures the facts that the occurrence of reduplicative Perfective affixes is unpredictable, but given the subclass of verbs that do exhibit this form of marking, the phonology of the relation is regular.

2.3 THE CENTRAL ASSUMPTIONS OF LEXICAL MORPHOLOGY

At the beginning of this chapter we noted that LMH rests on three assumptions critical to the definition of the lexicon: (i) the morpheme is the only minimal element of grammar; (ii) the morpheme is a linguistic sign; and (iii) all morphology resides in the lexicon. The remainder of this chapter will attempt to disprove LMH by first showing that these assumptions describe only major class items, that is, lexemes, and fail to account for the facts of derivational and inflectional morphology. It will then show that the inclusion of affixation in the lexicon leads to confusion within the model, which, as a result, fails to predict major aspects of the behavior of linguistic elements.

This section is based on the assumption that the prototypical major class items (N, V, A) are lexemes as defined by Principles I–III of chapter one; specifically, they are *"mutually implied (= directly articulated) phonological, grammatical, and semantic representations"* (Principle I). If affixes are signs with the same definitional properties as prototypical lexical signs, we would predict the following. First, since all lexemes must be at least partially phonologically specified by Principle I, neither zero nor empty lexemes can exist. It follows that zero and empty affixes also cannot exist. Second, affixes should belong to open classes and hence be subject to the same sort of synchronic lexical derivation that Principle II allows of prototypical lexemes. Third, affixes should belong to one and only one lexical class as is required of uncontroversial lexical items by Principle III. Finally, affixes should be listable items like other lexemes, not operations or processes more akin to syntactic or phonological rules.

If affixes are to be coclassified with prototypical lexemes, we would expect them to share most of the attributes of prototypical lexemes. If they do not, certainly if they share none of these attributes, the argument for coclassification and a unified lexicon collapses under the weight of evidence and we should look for a radically different framework to account for grammatical phenomena.

2.3.1 Omissive and Empty Morphology

Since it departs from the assumption that affixes are lexical signs, the first challenge to the Lexical Affix Hypothesis of LMH is that of ZERO MORPHOLOGY. If affixes are lexemes, since prototypical lexemes are never null or empty by Principle I, zero and empty affixes also should not exist, yet both are ubiquitous. How might supporters of LMH circumvent this ostensible loss of generalization?

Zero Lexemes

One approach is to challenge Principle I. Mel'čuk (1979) argues that Russian possesses at least two zero lexical stems. His first example is the Russian verb *byt'* ("to be"), which is not phonologically realized in the present tense.

(2.3) a. on zdes'   b. on byl zdes'   c. on budet zdes'
        "he (is) here"   "he was here"   "he will-be here"

This argument for a zero lexeme does not go through because the Present Tense form of *byt'* "be" is at most a null variant of a lexeme which is elsewhere phonologically realized. But Mel'čuk's story is not merely caught on an argument from allomorphy. Chvany (1975: 45–93) shows that Russian has two items with the same realization: *byt'*. One is an existential predicate, the other a copula.

(2.4)   a. est' kniga   b. byla kniga
            there-is book   there-was book
            "there is a book"   "there was a book"

(2.5)   a. kniga (*est') na stole   b. kniga byla na stole
            book [is] on table   book was on table
            "the book is on the table"   "the book was on the table"

Although Chvany argues that the existential predicate is a lexical item, both these categories are purely morphological. The copula functions simply as a Tense/Aspect marker with the power to agree in Gender and Number—all grammatical functions. Existence is also a grammatical category, for it is marked by the Genitive on Subjects (2.6) and Objects (2.7).

(2.6)   a. otvet prišel   b. otvet-a ne prixodilo
            answer-NOM arrived   answer-GEN not arrive
            "the answer arrived"   "no answer arrived"

(2.7)   a. on poslal otvet   b. on ne posylal otvet-a
            he sent answer-ACC   he not sent answer-GEN
            "he sent an answer"   "he didn't send an answer"

The crucial factor in determining whether the Nominative or Accusative, on the one hand, or Genitive, on the other, is used to mark Subjects and Objects in negated phrases, is whether the phrase implies the nonexistence of the reference (Babby 1980a). If Negation and Existence may be expressed by the Case system, they must be grammatical functions as well as conceptual categories since Case is a grammatical category. Mel'čuk hence has not proven that *byt'* "be" is a lexeme.

Mel'čuk proposes another null lexeme: the Subject of Neuter and so-called "Plural" impersonal constructions like (2.8):

(2.8)   a. menja sbi-l-o   s   nog-∅
            1STACCSG knock-PST-NEU from leg-GENPL
            "Something knocked me off my feet"

         b. menja sbi-l-i   s   nog-∅
            1STACCSG knock-PST-PL from leg-GENPL
            "Someone knocked me off my feet"

Mel'čuk claims that these verbs must take their agreement from the Subject noun which is not phonologically realized. Indeed, the common assumption is that the Subject here is the empty category, *pro*. Russian is a *pro-*

drop language and hence does not require an overt Subject, even though the verb exhibits various patterns of agreement in its absence.

But Mel'čuk assumes that only lexemes can be Subjects. In a *pro*-drop construction, agreement comes from the morphological representation of a phonologically null pronoun, *pro*. The real issue then, which Mel'čuk does not address, is whether *pro* is a lexeme or grammatical morpheme. Both the Animacy marked in (2.8b) and the Plurality, which -*i* marks elsewhere in the Russian verbal paradigm, are grammatical properties. It follows that data like (2.8) may be explained easily and more profitably without recourse to the lexicon, a point which will emerge more clearly as future chapters unfold.[4]

The most dramatic claim of zero lexemes is found in Anceaux (1965). Anceux claims that Nimboran, a language spoken in New Guinea, contains a total of 12 verbs (of the 300 or so he studied) with phonologically null stems. That the verbs for "be" and "become" are among the 12 does not surprise us in light of the discussion of Mel'čuk's data; however, Anceaux's list includes the verb stems for "bring", "dream", "extend", "go", "hear", "kiss", "laugh", "make cat's cradles", "say", and "sleep". For example:

(2.9) a. $\emptyset$-rár-be-d-u   → rebedú
       BRING-Prt-6Loc-Fut-1st   I will bring from here to above

       b. $\emptyset$-tam[+A]-t-um   → temtím
       KISS-Prt-Prs-3n   She kisses (here)

Anceaux's case for null lexemes, however, is far from convincing; he provides no allomorphic rules at all, even though the verbal data he presents is rife with phonological variation, as in the three distinct verbs he posits for the single meaning "to signal": *kyéb-, iyé-, yé-*. Anceaux is so struck with the similarities in these three perfectly synonymous stems that he mentions them twice (144, 151); nonetheless, he counts them as three synonyms. He admits that one of his zero lexemes is a member of a similar triplet, all meaning "say to": *u-, i-* and null (124–25, 151). He shows no curiosity at the fact that *u-* has no Plural and that *i-* occurs only in the Plural, and simply lists the null variant without comment. In fact he allows that three more of his zero stems have phonologically realized variants: *réi-* "sleep" (124, 158), *ty-* "hear" (129), and *kiá-* "laugh" (129). The reflective reader can only wonder whether the remainder of his ten null lexical morphemes (not counting the grammatical morphemes for "be" and "become") have phonologically realized forms which are phonologically incompatible with some contexts.[5]

The critical role of a full description of allomorphy and allophony in determining the validity of null stems may be illustrated by a verb in Russian thought previously to have no stem: *vy-nu-* "take out". The preverb *vy-* means "out" and *-nu* is a Semelfactive Perfective suffix. The Imperfective form of this verb is *vy-nim-aj-*, whose stem vowel /i/ is expected to elide in the Perfective, as in the Perfective-Imperfective pairs, *so-bra-* : *so-bir-aj-* "gather, collect", *vy-zv-a-* : *vy-zyv-aj-* "call out, cause". If the vowel elides from an underlying **vy-nim-nu-*, the result is **vy-nm-nu-*, both of whose nasals would assimilate to the final one, producing the ostensible null stem. Thus we cannot claim that Russian has even a null suppletive meaning "take", given a complete description of the (morpho)phonology; Anceaux's claim of null lexemes in Nimboran, by extension, cannot be adequately assessed until a complete description of the phonology of that language is available.

Conversion

According to Principle I, lexemes must be linguistic signs and thus presuppose an obligatory phonological representation; so, Lieber was originally right in wanting to avoid affixes without forms. (Lieber 1992 embraces them because of a redefinition of conversion, to which we will turn directly.) Sign-based morphology assumes that lexical and grammatical meaning is directly conveyed by sound; this implies, a priori, the absence of sound entails the absence of lexical or grammatical meaning. As Tables

Table 2.1   Deadjectival Causative Verbalization

	Affixed		*Unaffixed*
wid-en	legal-ize	pur-ify	to thin
damp-en	normal-ize	solid-ify	to slow
deep-en	steril-ize	humid-ify	to warm

Table 2.2   Resultative Nominalization

	Affixed	*Unaffixed*
a paint-ing	a state-ment	a slice
an etch-ing	a declar-ation	a roll
a carv-ing	a confess-ion	a find

2.1 and 2.2 demonstrate, however, this is not always the case. The elegance of LMH will not be undermined by zero morphology if it may appeal to another kind of morphological relation altogether to explain it. Lieber follows the European morphologists, who account for zero morphology as a process wholly distinct from derivation, namely, CONVERSION. Conversion implies that the affixed and unaffixed forms of Tables 2.1 and 2.2 are unrelated.

The conversion relation may be expressed by a directional or nondirectional redundancy rule or by a productive directional rule. The distinction of productive lexical derivation and redundant conversion is appealing in its suggestion that the two processes are distinguished by the qualitative differences distinguishing regular derivations from stored idioms. But (2.10–2.12) demonstrate that differences in productivity do not respect the line between conversional and derivational pairs. While (2.10b) is more productive than (2.10a), (2.11a) is more productive than (2.11b); (2.12a) and (2.12b) are of equal productivity.

(2.10)   a. **Latinate Denominal Verbs:**
         (to) rubber-ize, categor-ize, container-ize, crystal-ize, winter-ize
         b. **Native Denominal Verbs:**
         (to) paint, name, package, frame, winter, fork, paddle, ship

(2.11)   a. **Particleless Deverbal Subjectives:**
         (a) writ-er, design-er, driv-er, teach-er, runn-er, lead-er
         b. **Verb-Particle Subjectives:**
         (a) run-away, stand-in, drop-out, cut-up, knock-out, walk-on

(2.12)   a. **Native Perfective Nominals:**
         (a) crack, drive, launch, rerun, remake, splash-down, cave-in
         b. **Latinate Perfective Nominalizations**
         (a) collis-ion, explos-ion, invas-ion, deriv-at-ion, investig-at-ion

If two unrelated productive processes with the same functions existed side by side, one mimicking the other, we would expect them to apply to the same stems with the same lexical results, differing only in the definitional quality of the components involved. For example, Lexical derivates such as *widen* and *deepen* are generated alongside analytical constructs with the same grammatical meaning and similar form produced by syntax: *make/get wide*, *make/get deep*. Duplicate output like this would be convincing evidence for discrete components operating over lexical derivation and conversion, but we do not find it. (2.13–2.14) exemplify the typical case: wherever we find an affixed derivation, we do not find a conversional pair and vice versa.

(2.13)   a.   (to) double : *endouble   a'.   (to) *noble : ennoble
         b.   (to) right : *righten   b'.   (to) *thick : thicken
         c.   (to) warm : *warmen   c'.   (to) *deep : deepen

(2.14)   a.   (a) cut : (a) cutting   a'.   (a) *write : (a) writing
         b.   (a) bend : (a) *bending   b'.   (an) *etch : (an) etching
         c.   (a) spit : (a) *spitting   c'.   (a) *carve : (a) carving

Although occasional overlaps like *a cut* : *a cutting*; *to winter* : *to winterize* occur, they appear to be semantically motivated exceptions, so that separate definitions for "lexical derivation" and "conversion" contribute nothing to their clarification.

The introduction of conversion into the grammar in fact necessitates an ad hoc convention, COMPLEMENTARY BLOCKING, to explain the curious distribution that excludes just those stems undergoing conversion from lexical derivation and vice versa. Such a convention is highly suspect, in that complementary distribution usually marks an underlying grammatical regularity unifying the data, and thus cannot be taken as a basis for the fundamental distinction Lieber seeks.

A more likely explanation is that omissive marking is simply another type of morphological expression in a framework different from Lieber's, a framework that provides for such expression in paradigms. Thus, we do not find omissively marked derivates with overtly marked synonyms for the same reason that we generally do not find one derivation with different overt affixes, as in *sterilify* and *sterilize,* or *breakability* and *breakableness.* The reason is that one form suffices in most instances to express one concept and blocks synonyms (Aronoff's Blocking Principle, Pinker's Unique Entry Principle, Kiparsky's Avoid Synonymy Principle). Only if a derivate may have more than one reference do two forms emerge in speech. This usually means that one or both have been idiomatized, for example, *emergence* and *emergency, reference* and *referral.* This is exactly the pattern to which pairs like *to winter* : *to winterize*; *a cut* : *a cutting* conform.

LMH might abandon redundancy rules altogether as an account of zero morphology in favor of directional conversion rules in the sense of Williams (1981: 257). Peter Cole has suggested by personal communication that it is possible that rules of affixational word formation feed such directional conversion rules. This would explain the complementary distribution of the two types of derivation; however, it does not address the question of why two theoretically unrelated components assign the identical categories in exactly the same combinations to the same classes of bases. Remember, the only difference between the two sets of rules is that the output of one receives overt phonological marking and the output of the other does not. The more obvious explanation is that both sets involve the same semantic derivation but that the output in some contexts is overtly marked while in other contexts it is not, a more straitforward explanation which receives independent support (see Chapter 3).

Lieber (1992) attempts to account for all derivational morphology in terms of the principles of extended GB theory, thereby ridding grammar entirely of morphological principles. It follows that she now cannot accept conversion as a morphological process. Instead, she embraces zero morphology in those instances where the meaning of zero-marked forms is consistent with overt analogs and restricts conversion to simple lexical relisting, such that a lexeme of class X is reinserted in the lexicon as a member of class Y. It follows that the meanings of conversional forms will not be grammatically related to those of their bases, so that they will be noticeable in speech as are other ''creative coinages'' since they are new items, and productive derivations will be blocked from this type of conversion since the output of productive rules are not listed.

Despite this change of direction, Lieber still does not address the failures of zero lexemes described in this chapter. Nor does the effort to reduce conversion to simple relisting overcome criticism. For example, Lieber (1992: 163), claims that were she to introduce a new verb, *to knob,* she could imagine the verb having any of the meanings ''to imitate a knob'', ''to assault someone with a knob'', ''to put a knob on something''. Of course, the same is true of non-zero coinages (*to lionize, vilify, liquidate*). But the three meanings selected by Lieber reflect the regular morpholexical functions Manner, Means, and Possessional, respectively. Manner is semantically interpreted as [LIKE(XY)]; Means, as [USE(XY)]; and Possessional, in a transitive verb, would correspond to [CAUSE (X, HAVE(YZ))]. The evidence for regularity lies everywhere in data on conversion adduced by Lieber.

Finally, Lieber argues that absence of such forms as **we happinessed, *we hopelessed, *we gave the car a Midasize*, supports the position that conversion is unrelated to derivation since they show that conversion does not apply to productively derived words. In these instances, however, either no affixes are available or, if so, they are also blocked, as in **happinessen, *enhopeless, *happinessify, Lenin gave Russia an *industrialize/ *industrialization*. The restriction here, whatever it is, applies equally to affixed and unaffixed forms. Even were this not the case, Lieber's new framework does not prevent **we happinessed* because the verb could be derived by the addition of zero affixes which are now included in the lexicon.

The problems with demonstrating that derivation and conversion are distinct in some meaningful sense are simply too great to make the endeavor profitable. We are left with the conclusion that zero morphology is just that, the omission of morphological spelling in the face of executed derivation. The possibility that the grammatical functions elsewhere marked by affixes may be present in the absence of any articulated expression of them then distinguishes affixes sharply from lexical stems.

Empty Morphology

Empty morphology is also a well-established property of affixation which does not characterize lexical stems. Williams (1981) and Lieber (1981a) account for the lack of categorial and subcategorization effects in prefixes like *counter-* by not assigning class or subcategorization features to their lexical representation in the lexicon. This allows such prefixes to attach to stems of all three lexical classes, for example, *counterclaim$_N$*, *countersue$_V$*, *counterintuitive$_A$*, without changing the class of the stem to which they attach. However, allowing some lexemes to belong to no lexical class whatever immediately raises the question of whether they are in fact subject to the principles determining lexemes, for by Principle III, described in chapter 1, all of the uncontroversial, prototypical lexemes belong to one and only one class.

Affixes like *counter-,* however, do not represent the real difficulty associated with empty morphemes. Although *counter-* may have no grammatical content, it certainly has semantic content. Languages brim with examples of affixes with neither grammatical nor semantic content, a striking deviation from the norm for a lexical item, given the otherwise strong semantic character of the lexicon. 2.15 illustrates obligatory and optional English affixes which are totally empty.

(2.15)   a. dram-at-ic(al)
         b. syntact-ic(al)
         c. class-ic(al)

The suffix *-at* is an imported stem extension, which Greek bases sometimes require for reasons germane only to Greek morphology. The suffix *-al* occasionally offers a means of distinguishing two meanings of an ambiguous adjective, as in *economic* versus *economical*; however, in (2.15) it is so empty as to be optional.

The other interesting aspect of emptiness is that it may be a variable rather than a constant state of a given affix. Notice that the meaningful suffix in (2.15), *-ic,* plays an empty role in the adjectives of (2.16).

(2.16)   a. Marx-ist(ic)
         b. social-ist(ic)
         c. capital-ist(ic)

We might be tempted to explain (2.16) as a denominal adjectivization from the underlying N: *a Marxist → Marxist-ic*. However, this would result in a productive violation of the blocking constraint since the output of such a rule would have a meaning identical with that of the class of synonymous adjectives, as in a *Marxist experiment*. The only alternative is that the underlying form is the adjective which is used as a noun, as so many adjectives are.[6] This means that the suffix *-ic,* which is the ostensibly meaningful suffix in (2.15), in (2.16) must be empty. To posit theoretical homonyms, say, $-ic_1$, $-ic_2$; $-al_1$, $-al_2$, to account for these semantic differences, would merely double the number of such suffixes without ruling out empty morphemes; empty *-ic* and *-al* remain.

Examples like (2.15) and (2.16) cannot simply be written off as regular signs with null semantic content because objects cannot be definitionally the equivalent of any of their parts. Bierwisch (1988: 19) refers to the ontological category of objects as a GRANULATED DOMAIN, a domain whose elements may be made up of parts which themselves are not elements of the domain. Bierwisch uses the conceptual category of SUBSTANCE for comparison. Members of the category SUBSTANCE cannot be reduced to parts which are not members of the same category, that is, which are not substances themselves. For example, there is no part of water which is not water itself (at least, not so far as water is related to primary experience rather than to physics). An OBJECT like a dog, however, does comprise parts which are not themselves dogs: ears, legs, eyes, a tail. If signs are objects defined as mutually implied associations of phonological, grammatical, and semantic representations, they comprise a granulated domain. It follows that none can be simply a phonological representation, as empty morphs are generally defined; that is what a phonological representation is. By the same reasoning, they do not comprise only a grammatical or semantic representation (zero morphemes).

Advocates of LMH must provide a convincing account of such anomalies within their theory; moreover, they must do so without redefining the term "morpheme" so that it approaches the definition to be offered in chapter 3, that is, an empty phonological modification of a stem only conditionally associated with a grammatical function. If LMH is to retain an interesting position, it must salvage the claim that affixes are simple signs like lexemes, for it is this claim that provides the hypothesis with its elegance and appeal and distinguishes it from competing hypotheses. To redefine a subset of signs in the direction of competing theories would simply concede the point.[7]

2.3.2 Derivation and Affixes

Lieber (1981a, 1981b) finds evidence that affixes are subject to conversion exactly as are lexemes; however, conversion has just been discredited. Can Lieber's examples of affix conversion then be explained as lexical derivation with omissive marking, operating over affixes? Since lexemes are subject to lexical derivation, evidence that affixes are subject as well would partially substantiate the claim that affixes are lexemes. Lieber argues that affixes do undergo derivation, referring to the German suffix *-ig* in A : V pairs like *ängst-ig* "afraid" : *ängst-ig-en* "frighten", *kräft-ig* "strong" : *kräft-ig-en* "strengthen". Lieber accounts for these examples by an unmarked operation on the suffix *-ig* alone, rather than on the stem as a whole. The same rule, A → V, would also account for lexical pairs like *grün* "green" : *grün-en* "to green", *steif* "stiff" : *steif-en* "stiffen".

This argument does not go through, however, because the position it opposes, that the entire adjective stem, *ängst-ig-*, undergoes verbalization like the entire stems *grün* and *steif*, is equally supported by the data. The point is therefore moot, given the fact that such affixal derivation would never be marked by any morphology not equally applicable to the stem as a whole. The only proof of affixal derivation or conversion we could hope for would be an example of an affixed affix like English ?*at-ic* or ?*ic-al*, perhaps produced by a compounding lexical rule. But such extended exponence is not derivational, because the morphemes involved never express lexical derivational functions. *Dram-at-ic* does not differ at all derivationally from *theatr-ic* or *dram-at-ic-al*. We must concede that affixes do not derive and rationalize this fact in our theory.

It cannot be argued that affixes do not derive because they are bound since no necessary relation holds between boundness and underivability, cf. bound lexemes like *dent-* may be quite productive : *dent-ist, dent-al, dent-ate, dent-oid, dent-icle*. It is true that affixes belong to a closed class, so let us imagine Lieber's argument for excluding prepositions from compounding and lexical derivation, extended to include affixes. Lieber (1983: 262) maintains that a special constraint is required in the lexicon to prevent the operation of lexical derivation on prepositions because prepositions form a closed class and lexemes susceptible to derivation must belong to open classes. A natural extension of this argument could preclude affixes from reflecting lexical derivational relationships for the same reason.

We would have to assume such an argument would lead to the additional complexity of several storage subcomponents in a lexicon, one containing open classes, the other, closed ones. But this move cuts affixes off from lexemes and classifies them as a separate type of morphological marking. Following this line of argumentation, LMH must still concede that affixes are different from lexemes in yet another aspect. This concession is all the argument against LMH needs on this point. The argument against LMH in this chapter is based on the accumulated evidence on four such independent points. This concession represents the second argument against LMH, which forces it to concede that lexemes and affixes cannot be treated identically. Let us now turn to the third prediction of LMH mentioned at the outset of the chapter.

2.3.3 The Principle of Unique Lexical Class

The lexical listing of affixes is supported by one fact in particular: in the structure of a lexically derived word under LMH, the affix may be said to assign the lexical class and subcategorization features to the node dominating the lexical bases to which they attach, as in [[*bak*]er]$_N$. This is a natural effect of the Projection Principle if affixes have lexical listings like prototypical lexemes. However, if affixes possess lexical class and subcategorization like prototypical lexemes, they would by Principle III be limited to the possession of only one lexical class feature. Although it is conceivable that an affix might belong to more than one lexical class and assign its lexical classes in dependence on context, such behavior would not be lexemic. Lexemes have only one lexical class and whenever a lexeme ostensibly belongs to more than one lexical class, it is either an accidental homonym (*pear* : *pare* : *pair*) or is involved in a derivational relation like *a frame* : *to frame*. Since the preceding section has eliminated the possibility of derived affixes, LMH now predicts that, with the exception of accidental homonyms, affixes must belong to one and only one lexical class.

The evidence against the prediction that affixes are restricted to a unique lexical class can be quite spectacular, as (2.17–2.20) demonstrate.

(2.17) The boy is **cutting** flowers   (Progressive Verbal Aspect)

(2.18) He ruined his knife **cutting** flowers   (Deverbal Adverb)

(2.19) a. His **cutting** the flowers dismayed us   (Gerundive)
  b. **Cutting** is for the birds   (Imperfective Nominalization)

  c. He brought his **cuttings** in   (Resultative Nominalization)

(2.20) a. The boy **cutting** the flowers is cute   (Present Participle)
  b. a very **cutting** remark   (Subjective Adjective)

Not only does -*ing* mark verbs (2.17), adverbs (2.18), nouns (2.19), and adjectives (2.20), it marks both inflectional (Aspect, participles, deverbal adverbs and gerundives) and lexical derivational categories (Subjective adjectives, Resultative nominals). Other affixes mark narrower ranges of derivational and inflectional relations, for example, -*ed*, -*s*, -*en*.

In German the most notable polyfunctional affix is -*en*. It productively marks nominals (*das Lesen*), Infinitives (*lesen*), 1st and 3rd Person Plural verbs (*wir/sie lesen*), every nominal case, Singular and Plural, except NomSg: *einen Neuen* (Acc), *einem Neuen* (DatSg), *eines Neuen* (GenSg) "a new one" and *die/die/den/der Neuen* (Nom/Acc/Dat/GenPl) "the new one," plus strong verb Past participles (*gelesen*), Material adjectives (*leinen* "linen", *wollen* "woolen"), and others. The German suffixes *-er* and *-e* manifest similar though less inclusive functional ranges.

Lieber (1983: 269, fn. 21) recognized the problem but dismissed it as minor. Lieber claimed that whether the problem of polyfunctional affixes is resolved by polysemy or homonymy is irrelevant; however, LMH is in fact theoretically compelled to posit homonymous variants, as Halle and Mohanan (1985: 63) recognize. A polysemous *-ing* in the LMH framework would result in lexical class assignments like (2.21), since the GB framework posits no derivational source of lexical classes save lexical items. But lexical entries such as that required for *-ing* in (2.21) are precluded by Principle III. There simply are no prototypical lexemes belonging simultaneously to three distinct lexical classes and hence no unproblematic way to multiply classify affixes without distinguishing affixes from lexemes in yet another way.

(2.21)

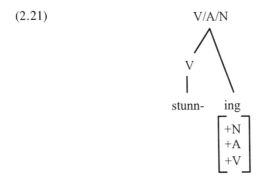

This difficulty explains why Lieber, like Halle and Mohanan, is forced to postulate several theoretically homonymous suffixes *-ing* to settle the issues of polyfunctionality. Listing affixes like *-ing* (2.17–2.20) as lexical homonyms may seem unproblematic for LMH; certainly, homonymy is a common property of prototypical lexical items. However, homonymy does not salvage the LMH enterprise; the evidence for homonymy among grammatical morphemes is weak.

There are three types of evidence of homonymy: diachronic, derivational, and allomorphic. Diachronic evidence, such as the spelling variation in *pair, pear, pare,* demonstrates a clear historical distinction among synchronic homonyms, reflected in previous phonological representations which were distinct. Such diachronic evidence does suggest that two homonymous suffixes are historically responsible for English *-er*. In Old English the Comparative suffix was written *-re* or *-ra* and the Subjective suffix, *-ere*. The historical status of these suffixes offers no proof of their synchronic status; however, in some US dialects, these historical differences parallel allomorphic variations. These dialects drop the velar before the comparative *-er*, as in [lɔŋ-er], but not before the subjective, as in [siŋg-er]. So affix homonymy can be demonstrated on diachronic and synchronic grounds but such evidence is available only for *-er,* and that is weak and not general. Moreover, the faint evidence of homonymous suffixes expressed by *-er* distinguishes only the Comparative adjective suffix from the deverbal nominal; the Subjective, Objective, and Instrumental functions of the nominal *-er* have never and do not now exhibit any evidence of homonymy, nor do most other ostensibly homonymous affixes.

SPE (Chomsky & Halle 1968: 86) provides allomorphic evidence for homonymous variants of *-ing.* SPE claims that *twinkling* in the nominal sense of ''an instant'' has two syllables and elsewhere contains an epenthetic schwa rendering the same word in three syllables. This evidence is again very weak, however, because in most English dialects the disyllabic and trisyllabic pronunciations are free variants. Moreover, even if this were a dependable test for distinguishing the Perfective nominalization from other applications of *-ing,* it would account for only two of the seven functional distinctions in (2.17–2.20) and nothing similar applies to the German data just mentioned.

Closer examination of the problem reveals that affix homonymy is not even a good hypothesis for a solution to the problem posed by (2.17–2.20). If we compare the properties of what would be affix homonymy with those of prototypical lexical homonymy, we again find no basis for comparison. Unlike prototypical lexemes, the form of affixes and the functions they express both fall into separate closed, grammatical categories, cross-referenced in paradigms like that in Table 2.3.

Table 2.3   Three English Derivations

	Qualitative Adjectiv- izations	Subjective (Agentive) Nominalization	Objective (Patientive) Nominalization
-ee	. . .	escap-ee	draft-ee
-er	dri-er	dry-er	fry-er
-ist	Marx-ist	Marx-ist	. . .
-ant	domin-ant	migr-ant	rehabilit-ant
(*-∅*)	salmon	cut-up	slice

There is a difference between lexical homonymy and any definition of homonymy based on data like that of Table 2.3. The function of the nominal *-er,* for example, does not DRIFT randomly, to use Sapir's term, or expand according to the SEMANTIC EXTENSION SCHEMAS of Booij (Beard 1990). The meanings of affixes skip cleanly from one derivational function to another: Subjective, Objective, Instrumental.[8] Even the highly idiomatic functions of *-er* generally come from this limited set of derivational functions, as in Locative: *diner,* Action nominal: *merger,* Objective nominal: *loaner.* The referential range of the set of English affixes is thus determined by the range of meaning in the closed set of grammatical categories. Lexical homonyms exhibit no such semantic consistency and no categorial parallels whatever: *bear*$_V$, *bear*$_N$, *bare; pair, pear, pare.*

In conclusion, then, the problem of polyfunctional affixes like English *-ing* cannot be solved by polysemy in an LMH framework. But neither does homonymy work; introducing it would be a purely theoretical maneuver. No consistent allomorphic or other empirical evidence supports affix homonymy, and the attributes of affix homonymy diverge widely from those of prototypical lexical homonymy. LMH cannot explain polyfunctional affixes within its theoretical architecture and thus must invoke ancillary theories of some unique type of morphological homonymy to account for evidence like that of (2.17–2.20) and Table 2.3.

2.3.4 Reduplication

The only unassailable shared trait of lexemes and affixes would seem to be their necessary phonological realization. However, even this apparent common property dissipates under scrutiny. We have already examined phonologically null and empty affixes and noted the absence of corresponding null and empty major class items. Another threat to the claim that affixes are lexical items that can be stored in the lexicon is what seem to be not morphological items, but morphological operations on stems. Affixes resemble lexemes to the extent that they may be copied onto lexeme stems by the same sort of rule that copies stems to their structural position. However, operations like reduplication resist description as listable items of any sort, despite attempts to describe them as lexemes.

McCarthy (1981, 1982, 1984), Marantz (1982), Yip (1982), Archangeli (1983), and Lieber (1987) are supporters of LMH who have recast the phonological issues of morphology to account for processing as the selection of phonologically underspecified lexical items. Their Autosegmental Phonology allows phonologically partially specified items comprising only CV templates to be listed in the lexicon along with fully specified items. By extending the domain of phonology to allow copying from the stem to these templates or from vowel clusters to stem internal positions, morphological processes become a combination of lexical selection and phonological operations.

Marantz claims that reduplicated phonological material on the surface of a derived word originates as the reduplication of the entire base. This proposal is forced by the restriction on Autosegmental Phonology, which prohibits association lines from crossing. If only the superficially reduplicated material is reproduced originally, these line inevitably cross, as

(2.22)

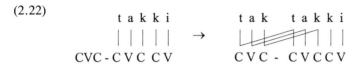

(2.22) shows. For this reason, Marantz proposes that the entire base reduplicates but only those reduplicated segments which can find a position in the affix CV template actually surface, as (2.23) illustrates.

(2.23)

Marantz's solution is attractive in that it captures the gradient from complete stem reduplication to the complete phonological specification of regular affixes which seems to characterize affixation. Complete stem reduplication is necessary for the sort of reduplication we find in Indonesian (2.24), where adverbs are generated from a variety of lexical classes by this process, for example:

(2.24) a. coba "try"   coba-coba "tentatively"
        b. fajar "dawn"   fajar-fajar "at dawn"
        c. kira "guess"   kira-kira "approximately"

Reduplication, however, represents a gradient from the phonologically fully unspecified stem and affix reduplication to fully specified affixation, with varying degrees of phonological underspecification separating these two poles. Notice that while the Indonesian and Tagalog are derived by reduplicating 100% of the stem, the Greek Perfective prefix in (2.25) is only 50% reduplicated while the Tsimshian Plural prefix (2.26) is ⅓ reduplicated:

(2.25) a. bio- "live"   be-biō-k- "have lived"
        b. game- "marry"   ge-gamē-k- "have married"
        c. lȳ- "unfasten"   le-lȳ-k- "have unfastened"

(2.26)   a. dasx "squirrel"   dik-dasx "squirrels"
        b. seyp "bone"   sik-seyp "bones"
        c. yexł "spit"   yik-yexł "spit (Plural)"

Reduplication is thus simply a variant of affixation and Marantz's approach accounts for the full spectrum of affixation.

Marantz's approach, however, invokes special copying conventions which apply exclusively to grammatical morphemes and not to other lexical phonological representations. Reduplication in this view involves three separate operations, each with its own conditions and constraints; only the first of these resembles the sort of lexical selection required by prototypical lexemes. The second operation is the reduplication of the stem to which the affix template is attached. The third operation, the drawing of association lines, may indeed result from general principles as McCarthy and Marantz claim, but the discussion over the exact nature of these principles remains quite lively. The important point to draw here, however, is that even on Marantz's hypothesis reduplication remains a process, as well as a set of items.

The ultimate point is that prototypical major class items, whose nature is not in dispute but enjoys general concensus, cannot be represented phonologically by revowelling or reduplication. All prototypical major class items, which affixes must match in all essential respects to achieve lexical status, must be phonologically prespecified in the lexicon and matched with a cognitive concept. Like fully specified affixes, revowelling and reduplication presuppose prototypical lexemes in that they are defined wholly in terms of some class of lexemes. However we notationally characterize reduplication, it remains a process that mimics some part of a lexical stem and attaches the result of that mimicry to some part of a lexical stem. The definitions of regular affixation and revowelling are similarly bound to that of the prototypical lexeme. If one set of objects presupposes another, the two sets must be distinguished and one must logically precede the other. The effect of the Autosegmental approach to reduplication and revowelling, then, is to conceal a distinction critical to the effectiveness of the model. Failure to make such a distinction should lessen the predictive accuracy of the model.

A morphology that represents all morphemes as processes rather than items will be much more internally consistent than morphology extended by an autosegmental treatment of revowelling and reduplication. If we do not begin with the assumption of lexically listed affixes, the operations proposed by McCarthy and Marantz become quite natural types of stem modification and lose their markedness vis-à-vis uncontroversial lexemes. Reduplicating a prefix or suffix is an unsurprising variation of spelling one out; revowelling is a mundane variation of infixation. However, these operations are radically different from the simple selection and copying of N, V, and A stems which are always fully prespecified phonologically. The autosegmental approach cannot capture this or the other fundamental differences between morphological relations in the lexicon and those in syntax as we will see in growing detail as this book progresses.

2.4 CONCLUSIONS

This chapter began with an examination of the three underlying assumptions of LMH: (i) Baudouin's Morpheme Base Hypothesis, which unifies all the lexical and grammatical elements under the single rubric "morpheme"; (ii) the Sign Base Morpheme Hypothesis, that all such morphemes are homomorphic signs; and (iii) Bloomfield's Lexical Morphology Hypothesis, which locates all morphemes so defined in the lexicon, where they are subject to lexical copying into word structures like stems. These three principles describe an extremely attractive theory of morphology that appears to conflate the processes of compounding, lexical derivation, and inflection, and reduce them to the process of lexical selection. The chapter then set out to see if in fact morphological operations on stems could be so reduced. The method was to compare affixal means of marking with the selection of prototypical lexical items, since affixes must share the definitional properties of lexemes if they are to be lexical items. The ideal would be Lieber's: morphological items and operations are virtually identical with those of prototypical lexemes.

It turns out that affixes in fact share none of the properties by which we identify the prototypical lexemes. Affixes often function without semantic content or grammatical function (empty morphemes), yet the meanings associated with them may be present in their absence (zero morphemes). They and the grammatical categories they express belong to tightly closed classes that cannot be expanded by any derivation rules. The same affix (for example, *-ing*) may be added to derivates of all three major lexical classes, and hence if it belongs to any one, it must belong to all. Finally, there seems no escaping the fact that at least some derivational morphemes must be described as processes distinct from the selection process that accounts for lexical items in phrases. It is important to note that all affixes share the four properties described in this chapter, while no lexemes share any of them. Lexemes share a set of properties that affixes do not share. The definitions of the two, therefore, are mutually exclusive.

The importance of the fact that grammatical morphemes of all types, items and operations, presuppose lexemes cannot be overemphasized. Bound grammatical morphemes cannot be defined other than as modifications of the phonological forms of major class lexical items. It follows from this undeniable fact that all major class lexical items must have fully specified phonological representations. Bound grammatical morphemes are by definition prefixes added to the front of a lexical stem, suffixes added to the back of a lexical stem, or infixes inserted inside a lexical stem. All other morphological processes, including revowelling and reduplication, are operations on a lexical base in the same sense. It also follows from this reasoning that lexemes and bound grammatical morphemes must be categorically distinct, for the former must logically precede the latter, and all lexemes, but not bound grammatical morphemes, must be phonologically fully specified.

NOTES

1. Lieber (1992) does not depart from LMH but attempts to build a case for the claim that morphology does not exist independent of syntax (Sproat 1985). Compare, for example, her lexical entry for the suffix *-ize*, where "LCS" signifies the lexical conceptual structure and "PAS" indicates predicate argument structure:

$$-\text{ize }]_{N,A}\text{——}]_V$$
[ayz]
LCS: [CAUSE($[_{Thing}$], [BE (LCS of base)])]
PAS: x

with her entry for *run*:

$$\text{run }[V\text{——}]$$
[rʌn]
LCS: $[_{Event}\text{GO}([_{Thing}$], $[_{Path}$])]
PAS: x

The text makes it clear that zero morphology is treated as a set of such entries, identical except in the omission of the phonological representation.

2. It is the case that pronouns are sometimes found in contexts where only lexemes should be. In the US, for example, towels are sometimes monogrammed "Hers" and "His," and in middle English the personal pronouns were used in compounds like *he-goat, she-wolf.* However, notice that the former represent humorous misusages. The towels are designated not for any male and female, but exclusively for a woman and her husband—idiosyncratic meanings far outside that of the pronouns. Also, the meaning of *he-goat* and *she-wolf* is "male goat", "female goat", not "third-person masculine goat" and "third-person feminine wolf". Third Person is completely irrelevant to the semantic interpretation of these pseu-

docompounds. Minor class items used in labelling and derivation therefore always idiomatically and ungrammatically replace deducible lexemes like WIFE and FEMALE.

3. Nominative, of course, is the exception. It is assigned by Infl to the only NP within its governing domain, its specifier, the Subject NP.

4. Bloomfield (1939) mentions another possible zero lexeme but does not describe it in enough detail to permit comment. Inkelas (1993: 610, fn. 37) attributes two zero lexemes to Bloomfield (1962: 63), one meaning "use", the other, "say." However, Bloomfield makes clear on p. 155 that the stem for "use" is *aw-*, which regularly "contracts" before vowels, and that the stem for "say" is *εN-*, which alternates with zero in a limited range of allomorphic contexts.

5. Anceaux also admits that in certain cases the positions of the null stems are filled with an Object marker, as in the Infinitives *tá-siŋ* "to hear, *tá-siŋ* "to make cat's cradles", and *rá-siŋ* "to dream". Other interpretations suggest themselves: the stems here are *tá-* and *rá-*, subject to haplology or some form of assimilation. The point is that a precise account of stem allomorphy will be particularly important in the final analysis of these suppletives.

6. In fact, this account is the only one possible. See Beard (1984) for the details.

7. Aronoff (1976: 10–16) also offers strong criticism of Saussure's biunique sign as a basis for a definition of the grammatical morpheme, criticism which may be added to that supplied here. Beard (1987b) expands on Aronoff's discussion and advances an LMBM solution for the problems he explores.

8. Chapter four discusses morphological "homonymy" in more detail.

Chapter Three

An Outline of Lexeme-Morpheme Base Morphology

INTRODUCTION. GRAMMARS WITH LEXEME-MORPHEME
BASE MORPHOLOGY

The preceding chapter demonstrated that LMH does not hold together at several points: in its most interesting form, it predicts no zero affixes, no under-specified affixes, no empty affixes, and no multiply classified affixes, or at least predicts some of these properties in lexical stems. The facts of morphological asymmetry discussed by Karcevskij and Bazell, that one affix may express zero to several grammatical functions and any one function may be expressed by zero to several affixes, evade LMH. LMH accounts for this seamless, unitary phenomenon with a patchwork of ancillary theories: conversion, zero morphology, homophony, and synonymy.

Another problem, as we have seen, is that bound grammatical morphemes presuppose lexical stems since they are operations on such stems; that is, affixation, revoweling, and mutation are all modifications of the phonological representations of N, V, and A stems, which never apply to affixes. If affixes and stems are equivalent morphemes, we might expect languages in which morphological categories are basic and lexical ones modifications of them. In these languages "affixes" would always be accented and have no allomorphy, while stems are generally unaccented and motivate allomorphy. If the lexical head of *driv-er* serves the Agentive function, why then is the marker of the Agent phonologically dependent upon the lexical modifier, the stem? Yet languages whose phonological dependencies isomorphically map the categorial ones seem not to exist.

These two problems surrender aspects of their own resolution. The problem of morphological asymmetry suggests that the rules determining the phonological representation of bound grammatical morphemes are independent of the rules determining their grammatical or morphosyntactic representation. Functional rules may provide a lexical stem with as many as three category functions while the morphology spells only one affix to mark them, as in the *-o* in Latin *amo*, which expresses 1st Person + Singular + Indicative. Conversely, the functional rules may provide no category function, yet the morphology will spell out one or more affixes, such as *-at* and *-al* in English adjectives like *dram-at-ic-al*. We are not free to assume that *-o* is a lexeme which "means" 1st Person Singular Indicative, for such a meaning would consist entirely of universal grammatical categories expressed elsewhere with three distinct markers. If we wish to represent this universality in grammar we must do so with rules and principles independent of the purely language-specific rules of affixation.

The fact that affixes presuppose prototypical lexical items implies that affixation is theoretically subsequent to inflectional derivation. That is, N, V, A selection, the structuring of the lexical and inflectional representation of words, and operations on their nonphonological grammatical (morphosyntactic) feature inventory, must occur prior to affixation. Assuming for reasons to follow that inflectional derivation in this sense, rules of government and agreement, for example, occurs in syntax, the morphological spelling component which interprets the output of these rules must be situated beyond syntax in a model of grammar. Theories of morphology that distinguish lexemes from bound grammatical morphemes in this way, situating morphological operations outside the lexicon, will be henceforth referred to as LEXEME-MORPHEME BASE MORPHOLOGY.

Lexeme-Morpheme Base Morphology (LMBM), then, characterizes a set of grammars with highly constrained morphological systems that address the problems raised in chapters 1 and 2 by assigning lexemes and grammatical morphemes to discrete components within grammar. LEXEMES in LMBM are defined unexceptionally in terms of open class signs in compliance with Principle I. They are direct associations of properly specified sequences of phonemes, grammatical features, and semantic intensions, that is, noun, verb, and adjective stems. All and only the items conforming to this definition are allowed in lexical storage.

Bound grammatical morphemes, on the other hand, are defined as morphological spelling operations in the literal sense of "morphological": modifications of the phonological form (Greek *morphé*) only of lexemes. These modifications MARK, EXPRESS, or SPELL the same closed grammatical categories, lexical and syntactic, as do free grammatical morphemes. Free grammatical morphemes are independent items requiring syntactic positions, which cannot be assigned by the lexicon. For this reason free grammatical morphemes such as articles, prepositions, pronouns never mark lexical derivational categories but only inflectional ones. Free grammatical morphemes must also be stored in an autonomous morphological component but somehow distinguished from bound morphemes.[1] The spelling operations and listed free morphemes together account for all and only the closed-class markers of languages. LMBM therefore starkly discriminates open- and closed-class linguistic objects. Figure 3.1 outlines a typical LMBM model of grammar.

Figure 3.1

A Typical LMBM Grammar with Autonomous Morphology

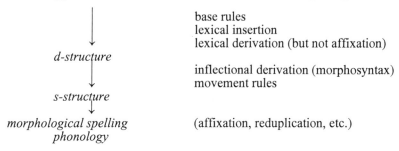

Figure 3.1 is not necessarily a real-time biological model implying that derivation takes place chronologically before affixation when it occurs during speech: processing does not necessarily follow the course shown by arrows. Performance operations may proceed horizontally, left to right, taking the components of Figure 3.1 as levels and processing token sentences in parallel across all levels (Berwick and Weinberg 1984, Rumelhart and McClelland 1987). Figure 3.1, then, reflects four autonomous cognitive modules: syntax, the lexicon, morphology, and phonology, which probably operate in that order. Base structure generation, movement, and inflectional derivation as defined above may operate in parallel within one syntactic module.

3.1 THE SEPARATION HYPOTHESIS (CONDITIONED INDIRECT ARTICULATION)

The distinction of lexemes and grammatical morphemes implies that the elementary units of language are characterized by discrete ways of conveying meaning. Lexemes unquestionably are the DIRECT ARTICULATION of meaning by sound in the Saussurian sense. Grammatical morphemes, on the other hand, are defined in terms of an indirect, context-sensitive, often paradigmatic means of reference (CONDITIONED INDIRECT ARTICULATION), for example:

(3.1) $\emptyset \rightarrow$ *-er* IFF [+ Agent] and no verb particle OR [+ Comparative] and monosyllabic base or disyllabic base ending in /i/.

This lexeme-morpheme conception of morphology goes a step farther than Matthews' WP model of morphology in distinguishing lexemes and grammatical morphemes. On the basis of the evidence adduced in chapter 2 and the chapters to follow, the lexeme-morpheme distinction explicitly prohibits any synchronic interaction between lexemes and grammatical morphemes beyond (i) the modification of the phonological formant (only) of the lexeme by the rules of bound morphology, and (ii) the copying of free morphemes in the functional projections of phrase structure.

Furthermore, and contrary to Matthews (1974), bound derivational morphemes do not differ in any significant respect from inflectional ones (THE INTEGRATED SPELLING HYPOTHESIS). Indeed, section 2.3.3 reminded us that not only do we find the same morpheme often serving both derivational and inflectional duties, but the most productive affixes in any given language consistently serve such double-level duties. The morphological component hence must be independent of either of those levels, but it must be able to express derivational paths defined on either level. Bound morphology thus comprises two independent, dissociated processes, which will be referred to here as ''derivation'' and ''morphological spelling''. The domains of derivational operations are the lexicon (lexical derivation) and syntax (inflectional derivation), and derivation applies to the grammatical representation of a lexeme only, that is, to such grammatical features as $+$ Singular, $-$ Plural, $+$ Feminine, $-$ Masculine of a lexeme's feature inventory (Matthews' ''morphological representation'').

Morphological spelling does not determine in any way the grammatical representation of lexemes, but merely marks them by modifying the phonological representation of the lexeme. (3.2–3.5) define these concepts more precisely.

(3.2)   The only minimal grammatical elements of language are lexemes, L, and free morphemes, M'.

(3.3) L is the set of indivisible nuclei, $l_1, l_2, \ldots, l_n$, each comprising a mutually implied triplet, $p \leftrightarrow g \leftrightarrow r$ (as in Figure 3.2), and
$p =$ a nonnull, lexically specified sequence of phonemes ($=$ phonological representation or matrix)
$g =$ a nonnull set of features specifying lexical and syntactic categories ($=$ the grammatical representation or feature inventory)
$r =$ a nonnull set of semantic features ($=$ semantic representation or feature inventory).

(3.4)   Free grammatical morphemes, M', are empty syntactic markers of grammatical functions to be defined later.

(3.5) *L* and *M'* allow four and only four mutually independent types of operations:

    (a) A lexical operation is any modification of any *g* proper to the lexicon;

    (b) An inflectional operation is any modification of any *g* proper to syntax;

    (c) A spelling operation, $m^\wedge$, of the set $M^\wedge$, is any modification of *p* of any fully specified lexeme, *l*, or free morpheme, *m'*, conditioned by *c*, for example, $p \rightarrow p + m^\wedge / c$, where *c* comprises *p*-, *g*-, and/or *r*-features);

    (d) A semantic operation is any modification of *r*.

The representation of lexemes will be abbreviated henceforth as $p \leftrightarrow g \leftrightarrow r$. As Figure 3.2 implies, the orientation of the double-headed arrow signifying mutual implication is moot.

Figure 3.2

The Structure of a Lexeme

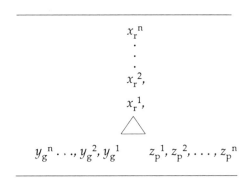

(3.6) approximates the lexical entry for the Turkish verb *gel-* "come".

(3.6)

$$g = \begin{bmatrix} +\text{Verb} \\ \text{Subj} \_\_ \end{bmatrix}$$
$$\updownarrow$$
$$p = \quad /\text{gel}/$$
$$\updownarrow$$
$$r = \begin{bmatrix} \text{GO(X)} \\ \text{TO(Y) FROM(Z)} \end{bmatrix}$$

The STEM (= root or stem), *p*, by (3.3) becomes a purely phonological phenomenon, and morphological spelling operations upon it are purely phonological. Spelling operations never modify grammatical (*g*) or semantic (*r*) representations; the rules which operate over the sets $G = \{g_1, g_2, \ldots, g_n\}$ and $R = \{r_1, r_2, \ldots r_n\}$ must be compatible with the type of categories over which they operate. *G* (morpholexical, morphosyntactic), *R* (semantic), and *P* (morphological spelling) rules, in keeping with Principle IV of chapter 1, must be discrete, thus all the categories of (3.2–3.5) are mutually exclusive. DERIVATIONAL RULES, as those rules operating on grammatical categories G will be called henceforth, have no access to phonology, thus cannot directly effect phonological changes. *G* includes the MORPHOLEXICAL categories of the lexicon and the MORPHOSYNTACTIC inflectional categories of syntax.

Spelling operations, $M^\wedge$, account for bound morphemes: affixes, prosodic variations like *survéy* : *súrvey*, revoweling schemes such as *write* : *wrote*, or any other phonological modification of the stem allowed by both morphotactics and phonotactics. The complete range of morphological means for marking grammatical categories, *M*, include all free morphemes, *M'*, and all morphological spelling operations; in effect, $M = M^\wedge + M'$.

The disambiguation of lexical and inflectional derivation from morphological spelling processes and free items that characterizes LMBM predicts all the puzzling phenomena of morphology quite naturally with the architecture of the model itself. No further constraints or ancillary theories are required, for all the possible mismatches of the three components involved are realized. Zero morphology is derivation (lexical or syntactic) without subsequent spelling operations; empty morphemes are spelling operations without concomitant derivation. Morphological asymmetry results from using several markers to express a single derivation or a single marker to express several derivational operations. No further types of mismatches are logically possible and none occur. All mismatches possible under LMBM occur widely and productively.

The description of the lexeme in (3.3) represents necessary and sufficient conditions on the linguistic sign: no meaning without fully specified sound, no sound without fully specified meaning. LMBM stores only signs defined in this, the strictest possible way in the lexicon. This predicts that only prototypical lexemes are lexemes and that zero and empty lexemes are impossible. All morphological means of marking grammatical categories—bound spelling operations and free grammatical morphemes, are handled by an autonomous morphological component. This component spells out the phonological modifications of the stem which express the various categories of *g* in any given lexical representation, *l,* or copies free grammatical morphemes into appropriate structural positions provided by

syntax. Although LMBM requires an independent morphological component, its separation of lexemes and morphology permits both the lexicon
and the morphological component to be defined in the strictest possible
terms. All open classes are lexical and the lexicon contains only open
classes; all closed classes are grammatical and the grammar comprises only
closed classes. In order to distinguish the LMBM morphological component, which cannot modify grammatical or semantic features in any way,
from more traditional morphological components, I will refer hereafter to
a MORPHOLOGICAL SPELLING or simply MS-COMPONENT.

Figure 3.3 demonstrates how derived lexemes with directly related
sound and meaning may be generated without any direct relation between
the rules of derivation and those of morphological spelling, or between the
meanings and forms over which they operate. In Figure 3.3 *P*, the set $\{p_1,$
$p_2, \ldots p_n\}$, symbolizes the phonological representation of the lexical feature inventory of major class lexical items and *G*, the set $\{g_1, g_2, \ldots g_n\}$,
the grammatical representation.

Figure 3.3

Derivational and Spelling Operations in LMBM

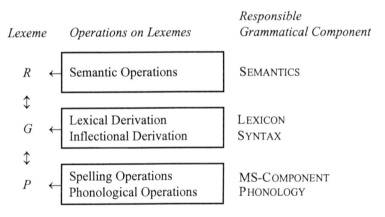

A grammatical morpheme expresses only certain grammatical categories—lexical and syntactic—in a fixed set of contexts, that is, paradigmati-
cally. One-one sound-meaning relationships among grammatical morphemes are not characteristic but accidental, a function of the number of
morphemes available in a given language. The catalogue of categories is
universal and constant. It is the lexeme that manages the mapping of morphological meaning to phonology, for only the lexeme maintains direct
articulation, that is, mutual implication, marked here by the symbol of
mutual implication, "↔" (or " ↕ "). So long as grammatical morphemes

presuppose lexemes, they need not be directly bound to the categories which they represent, not even if they are syntactically free.

The relation between the derivational and MS-operations, as Figure 3.3 demonstrates, consists in their operation on the same objects, lexemes. However, they carry out distinct operations on two different parts of lexemes, a situation which cannot be expressed by the isomorphic affix of LMH. Although MS-operations often parallel those of derivation, they need not do so in one-one fashion. This capacity has led Motsch (1987) to quite rightly suggest that LMBM affixation rules might operate "without any semantic or syntactic information". However, it does not follow from the claim that morphological spelling (MS-) rules operate independently of derivation that the two are totally unrelated; grammatical morphemes are defined in terms of their reactions to lexical and syntactic features. The lexeme, which is the focal point of both processes, provides the only constant mapping of meaning to sound. This is why Matthews found that only the word is a sign, not the individual morphemes which may constitute a word.

3.2 The Independence of Derivational and Morphological Spelling Conditions

The Separation Hypothesis implies that morphological spelling has no access to the internal workings of derivation; it operates in true modular fashion, solely on the output of derivation rules. This means that the conditions on derivations should differ from those on affix spelling. Moreover, it implies that MS-rules cannot distinguish features added by derivation from inherent lexical features irrelevant to derivation. To see that this is true, consider the set of suffixes used to mark the deadjectival nominalizations in English: *-th, -ce, -ity, -ness*. The deadjectival nominalization rule operates with only one constraint: the input must be a qualitative, not a relational adjective. This rule does no more than transpose underlying qualitative adjectives into nouns (see chapter 7 for the details of transposition). However, the wide range of productive and unproductive morphological markings that identify this nominalization demonstrates that the conditions on affixation are far more intricate than those on the derivation and are unrelated to the "no relational adjective" constraint on derivation.

(3.7) a. warm   warm-th
       b. intelligent   intelligen-ce
       c. readable   readabil-ity
       d. slow   slow-ness
       e. white   white

The suffixation rules applying to the derivatives in (3.7) must have access to (a) the current category of the stem, (b) some evidence of its previous category, (c) the phonology of the final syllable of the stem for /-Iti/ and /-s/, and (d) the semantics of the color terms for the (optional) null marking: conditions absolutely irrelevant in the determination of the derivative's meaning. Moreover, while some of these conditions are derivational, most are inherent. Though the suffix *-ce* is conditioned by the deadjectival nominal, it is also conditioned by the final /nt/ of the stem; the suffix *-ity* does not mark the deadjectival nominal in general but just those ending on /l/. Affixation truly operates on conditions that differ radically from those determining derivation (meaning).

The form-function relation of LMBM is not the most obvious or logical relation between derivational forms and functions. The logically simplest way to change the meaning of lexemes is to concatenate distinct sound sequences each paired with an isomorphically fixed meaning, as argued by the Natural Morphologists (Mayerthaler 1981; Wurzel 1984). Compounding is the most obvious way to enrich the lexicon, because the lexicon offers the largest selection of referential categories. To use a closed set of affixes, which often phonologically alter the stem to which they attach and are often altered themselves for no semantic profit, is inefficient. It is even less efficient to use the same marker to express several different functions in as many contexts while expressing any one of the same functions via several different markers. Omitting markers is positively *non sequitur*. Such a system is grossly inefficient unless the mechanism carrying out the calculus required by the system is designed to execute precisely these operations and does so as well as or better than it recognizes a simple sign. The nature of morphology discovered in chapter 2 is intriguing for its suggestion that the brain is not designed to process the simplest conceivable language. We will return to this point in the present chapter's conclusion. Now, however, let us examine the basic operations of morphology, those of derivation and stem modification.

So far we have examined (i) the tripartite lexeme sharing a set of grammatical categories with syntax, (ii) a set of L-derivation rules and a set of I-derivational rules operating on lexical grammatical categories, and (iii) a MS-component situated after all syntax, supplying two types of expressions for both types of derivation: (a) bound morphemes, modifications of the phonological representation of lexemes only, and (b) free morphemes, stems themselves, which require syntactic positions. The next section focuses on I-derivation.

3.3 INFLECTIONAL DERIVATION

Word formation operations on the categorial features of grammatical representations will be referred to as LEXICAL DERIVATION or simply L-DERIVA-

TION. L-derivation rules might be called CATEGORY FEATURE RULES since they operate on the grammatical category features (G) of lexical feature inventories and never on the phonological (P) or semantic (R) representations. However, we wish to distinguish the category feature rules of the lexicon from the inflectional derivation rules which operate on similar features relevant only to syntax, such as Person and Case. Many morphologists have argued that the latter rules are rules of the syntax; chapters 5 and 6 will review those arguments. Here, let us simply assume that derivation and inflection are distinct aspects of morphology because the grammar contains two different types of grammatical functions—$G : G_L$, inherent (morpho)lexical categories, and G_I, (morpho)syntactic inflectional categories. L-rules operate on lexical grammatical categories (G_L) interior to the word in the lexicon, while inflectional (I-) derivation operates on the functional categories (G_I) in phrase structure.

This assumption is shared by current versions of Principles and Parameters GB, where the origin of inflectional features for verbs is the Agr node of IP (Chomsky 1981; 1992; Pollock 1989; Ouhalla 1990). The exact nature of both lexical and inflectional categories will be the focus of scrutiny in the chapters to come. At this point let us simply see if it is possible for an independent MS-component to account for the basic data, departing from these common assumptions about the nature of lexical and inflectional categories. The operations of an autonomous MS-component will be limited to the lexical word and the functional categories of syntax. If inflectional categories are structurally located outside lexical positions, and lexical (sub)categories are interior to the lexeme occupying that position, we have a convenient and telling means of distinguishing L- and I-derivation.

Since categorial derivation and the spelling of morphological expressions are independent processes, the central question is whether the formal expressions may be mapped accurately onto a multiply derived grammatical category representation. An examination of the multiple inflectional derivation in (3.8) will show that, given fairly precise definitions of "lexeme" and "bound morpheme" such as (3.2–3.5), the chaos anticipated by Motsch cannot arise.

(3.8) reflects the Turkish lexical base *gel-* "come", as illustrated in (3.6), raised to Infl in accord with current GB syntactic principles. The Infl node has been provided with the inflectional category requirements for "I could come" or "I could not come", that is [+Potential, ±Negation, +Past, −Plural, +1stPerson]. In addition, (3.8) shows Infl bearing the five agreement features minimally required to explain the grammatical functions involved in the expressions "I could come" and "I could not come". Each have been set by an inflectional "switch" that toggles the syntactic values of these features in language-specific ways. If Negation is

(3.8)   **Infl**

$$g_I = \begin{bmatrix} \text{-Plural} \\ \text{+1stPerson} \\ \text{+Past} \\ \pm\text{Negation} \\ \text{+Potentiality} \end{bmatrix} \begin{array}{l} \leftarrow \text{Number Switch} \\ \leftarrow \text{Person Switch} \\ \leftarrow \text{Tense Switch} \\ \leftarrow \text{Negation Switch} \\ \leftarrow \text{Mode Switch} \end{array}$$

$$g_L = \begin{bmatrix} \text{Subj} \underline{} \\ \text{+Verb} \end{bmatrix} \quad \text{BASE GRAMMATICAL REPRESENTATION}$$

$$\updownarrow$$

$$p = \quad /\text{gel}/ \quad \text{PHONOLOGICAL REPRESENTATION}$$

$$\updownarrow$$

$$r = \quad [\text{COME}] \quad \text{SEMANTIC REPRESENTATION}$$

switched off, (3.8) would be the grammatical representation of *gel-ebil-di-m* "I could come" at the output of the categorial rules. If, however, the Potential verb is negated, instead of the suffix *-(y)Ebil,* the suffix *-(y)E* marks [+Potentiality], producing *gel-e-me-di-m,* which means "I could not come".

The lexical grammatical representation (g_L) is abbreviated here and the phonological representation is presented in phonemic shorthand rather than phonological matrices. The point of (3.8) is to capture the intuition that, despite the significant formal differences in the phonological representation of the surface forms of the Positive and Negative derivatives, the underlying grammatical difference is very minor, a difference accounted for by toggling binary values of one feature [±Negative]. The feature arrangement of (3.8), then, is fed into the MS-component, which reads these features and attaches affixes conditioned by these features, following the order of the features.[2]

The inflectional category features copied into the syntactic terminal node and the lexical features of the lexeme essentially merge into one complex feature inventory so far as the MS-component is concerned; its domain is the combined feature inventories, g_I and g_L. However, the fact that the copies of the inflectional features reside in a structure different from that of the lexical features explains why inflectional features, when syntactically relevant, appear on the outside of complex derived words. When the spelling operations begin to apply, the first operation can only modify the phonological base, in this case, /gel/, for that is the only phonological representation available. The MS-operations, therefore, have no alternative by the definition of (3.5c) but to begin at the confluence of the *g, p,* and *r* features. It then builds outward from the base, responding to each feature or set of features that serve as conditions on its operations. Operating from the base outward, the mechanism will arrive at the inflectional features of the terminal node last, after all lexical features have been expressed.

Feature and Affix Order

A crucial question for morphological models that dissociate derivation from morphological spelling is whether the features of a grammatical representation are ordered. This question is important because, as we just saw, the order of affixes depends upon that of the features in the stem and in Infl. If features are ordered, the question arises whether that order is an inherent, lexical order following from a semantic ordering principle such as Bybee's SEMANTIC RELEVANCE (Bybee 1985), or whether, as Anderson (1992) claims, affix ordering is language specific. To support his case, Anderson cites the position of the Possessive clitic in Finnish outside the Case marker: *kirjo-i-ssa-ni* (STEM-Number-Case-Possessive) "in my books" as compared to the suffix in related Vogul positioned inside the Case marker: *haap-an-um-t* (STEM-Number-Possessive-Case) "in my boats". The same ordering flexibility may be found in a single language. In Turkish, for example, *gelir-ler-se* and *gelir-se-ler* both mean "if they come".

On the other hand, affix order may reflect variations in semantic scope. For example, the scope of [+Negation] may be varied with respect to [+Potentiality] by varying the order of the respective affixes in Turkish:

(3.9)   a. Ahmet gel-me-yebil-ir-∅
         Ahmet come-NEG-POT-PRES-3RDSG
         "It is possible that Ahmet will not come"

         b. Ahmet gel-e-me-z-∅
         Ahmet come-POT-NEG-PRES-3RDSG
         "It is not possible that Ahmet will come"

In (3.9b), the Potential marker *-(y)Ebil* is replaced by *-e* before the Negative marker *-me,* so that the order of the grammatical features in (3.8) would seem to be motivated by the semantic scope of Negation. Matthews concluded from data such as these that feature order may be semantically crucial in agglutinative languages where in fusional ones it is irrelevant.

The initial assumption here will be that the possibility of ordered grammatical features is a universal parameter. However, fusional affixation ignores feature order, and the ordering of some agglutinative affixes with respect to each other is arbitrary. This suggests that the actual order of features is, as Anderson maintains, a variable of the parameter set by individual languages. The lack of a consistent relevance of ordering across and within languages casts doubt on Bybee's hypothesis that lexical and inflectional derivation features are ordered according to their relevance to lexical semantic categories.

3.4 THE MORPHOLOGICAL SPELLING MECHANISM[3]

In order to interpret the accumulated G-features as bound expressions like affixation, stem mutation, Semitic revoweling, reduplication, metathesis, and prosody shifts, the MS-component will have to contain a spelling mechanism capable of carrying out the following steps in approximately the order given:

(3.10)   a. Reading the Conditions on Operations
1. identify the class of the input lexeme
2. open the set of rules pertinent to that class
3. identify any relevant P- or R-features
4. read the first set of relevant features into memory

b. Execution
5. locate the stem (P-features) of the lexeme
6. execute the modification on the lexical stem conditioned by the grammatical features in memory
7. erase memory
8. Advance to the next feature and restart the process.

(3.10) elaborates the outline of the inflectional spelling operations described by Matthews (1972: 170–197), combining operations of inflectional and derivational morphological spelling. The spelling mechanism of the MS-component must access all three levels of lexical representations: that of the grammatical, the phonological, and the semantic representations as well as the complex symbols of syntactic projections. However, the spelling mechanism operates only at the phonological level, P. It therefore does not require access to any intermediate state of a derivation during the L- or I-derivation processes and simply requires "read-only" access to their outputs. This means that the MS-component need not violate Principle IV or the Lexical Integrity Principle in any way. Indeed, the syntactic origin of inflectional features will explain these principles.

If we assume that the rules which operate on the features of Number, Person, Tense, and Mood are independent of each other, the spelling mechanism cannot have access to these rules since Matthews has demonstrated that this set of features frequently receives only one affix, for example, Latin *venī-tis* "you (all) are coming", where the single suffix *-tis* conveys Present, Imperfect, 2nd Person, and Plural. Turkish morphology marks similar features independently: *gel-iyor-sun-uz* "come-PROG-2ND-PL."

For this reason, the options of the spelling mechanism must be kept open so that it may respond either to one, two, three, four, or five features with one operation.[4] This requires a memory to hold a feature without triggering any operation until the spelling mechanism compiles a set which corresponds to the possibly cumulative conditions of some MS-operation.

Once a feature or set of features has triggered an operation, the morphology must be able to erase those features in memory and advance to the next set of features. If it does not erase the features in memory that have triggered an operation, it will eventually overload the memory, causing it to fail as it iterates the same operation indefinitely, as in *gel-ebil-ebil-. . . .* Interestingly, certain affixes are capable of such repetition; EX-PRESSIVE markers, that is, Diminutive, Augmentative, Pejorative, and Endearment affixes, are especially prone to iteration. In Russian, for example, one may diminutivize *dožd'* "rain" at least twice: *dožd-ik* "dear/little rain", *dožd-ič-ek* "very dear/little rain." Native speakers are hesitant to accept more than one iteration, but there is reason to believe that more are grammatically possible (see section 7.3). However, this type of iteration results from a multiplicity of identical features reiterated in the base controlling affixation and is therefore easily accomplished by the model emerging here.

The MS-operation itself defines the part of the stem on which it is carried out, that is, whether it prefixes, suffixes, or infixes. The order of affixes hence will not necessarily follow the order of the grammatical features of the stem; however, the order of the operations on the stem will follow that order. The linear order of the prefix and suffixes in *ungrammaticality* is morphologically irrelevant. What is relevant is the order in which they were attached, the order in which the MS-operations were carried out on the stem, and that is (i) suffix *-al,* (ii) prefix *un-,* and (iii) suffix *-ity.* This order is determined by the prefix *un-,* which is added only to As and Vs and not to Ns. The semantic interpretation depends upon the G-features, whose order is unparadoxical and unambiguous.

It is possible for affixes to be concatenated in considerable number. Agglutinative languages like Turkish exhibit notably long concatenations of suffixes. (3.11) is due to Jorge Hankamer (personal communication, 1991).

(3.11)   Avrupalılaştırılamıyacaklardansınız
         Avrupa-lı -laş - tır - ıl - a -mı- yacak -lar- dan - sın -ız
         Europe-an-ize-CAUS-PASS-POT-NEG-FUT/PART-PL-ABL-2ND-PL
         "You (all) are among those who will not be able to be caused to become like Europeans"

The order of such morphemes in an LMBM model is determined by the order of the features in the derived base. If the categorial rules add grammatical features to the lexical features inventory of a base lexical item, those features will accumulate in a specific "direction"; features will accrue outwards from those of the underlying lexeme. This falls out of two entailments of (3.2–3.5).

First, the term MUTUALLY IMPLIED in (3.3) means that P, G, and R form an integral unit at every stage of derivation. This prohibits the insertion of derivational material between them by any derivational rule. Derived members of the lexemic classes, N, V, A, are defined by their outermost class, as in $[[[x_V]\ y_A]\ z_N] \in$ N. A derived lexeme, l, however, expanded by any number of grammatical features, g, remains l by (3.2), available for yet another derivation because these superordinate categories are defined by their core, not their ultimate category, for example, $l + g^*$ $\in L$, where $g^* = g^1, g^2, \ldots, g^n$. Since by definition category and form rules only apply in their specific domain, G and P, respectively, and since these domains are not changed by derivation on G and P, they remain available to further derivation. It follows that derivation perforce concatenates features from the lexical core, $G \leftrightarrow P$, "outward".

Suppose that a rule adds some feature, f, to l. This feature may only be added to its proper domain, for example, x_p, x_g or x_r, the subsets of P-, G- and R-features of l. Thus, if the feature is a G-feature, it joins the other features of x_g. Since the next G-rule will not be able to distinguish the previously inserted feature from the inherent features, and since it cannot insert any feature between the inner core of G, P, and R features, it can only concatenate the feature it controls to the features already present.

Let us now return to the Turkish example of (3.8–3.9). If derivational rules concatenate the features in the proper order, the MS-component easily realizes those features in the correct order. (3.5) prevents the insertion of any morpheme other than one capable of attaching to the base, *gel-*, during the first operation, for only the base has a fully defined lexical stem, *p*, initially. The first suffix in example (3.9a) may be conditioned by any of the three features read from the stem outwards; however, it cannot respond to [+ 1stSg] or [+ Past] until it has marked [+ Potentiality]. Since there are only two affixes for marking the Potential mode in Turkish, if the derivation is not marked [+ Negation], *-(y)Ebil* will be inserted on the first cycle. Since the output of this operation, *gel-ebil-*, is also a stem by entailment of (3.5), $x_P + y^*_{M^\wedge} = z_P$, a second MS-rule may operate on that output. Responding to a lexical base containing the feature [+ Past], it modifies the stem with the suffix *-DI* (Definite Past). This application results in *gel-ebil-di-*. The process needs only to be constrained from expressing the same feature twice; by definition it cannot insert an affix between a previously inserted affix and the stem.[5]

The operations of the spelling mechanism, therefore, can be executed only concatenatively, setting out from the stem. However, the spelling mechanism can read all the morphological features of the lexeme to which the stem belongs before beginning its operations. This is equivalent to saying that it has access to all the brackets (Fabb 1988), but without requiring sublexical bracketing of any kind.[6] Reading consecutive features from those of the lexical core outward, the spelling mechanism may then select a morpheme which expresses one, two, three, or none of the features present under the lexical stem, or it may select one in one context and another in another context. Finally, it may insert a complex of affixes to mark one feature, as in *dram-at-ic-al* (cf. *theatr-ic*).

A small memory in the spelling mechanism that fulfills the requirements of (3.10) would obviate any need for a one-one relation between a category feature and its expression. Up to five features (see fn. 4) will have to be stored in memory until a match between the features in memory and some MS-operation can be found by the spelling mechanism. However, we may assume that the moment the spelling mechanism recognizes a set of conditions and finds a match between it and some operation it controls, it performs the modification specified by that operation.

Since memory is a HORIZONTAL module in Fodor's terminology, that is, one which operates across all VERTICAL modules such as the spelling mechanism, we may assume that the MS-component possesses all the attributes of regular short-term memory, including the ability to erase or write over its contents. This capacity will be used in generating null morphology. For example, Turkish has no marker for [+ 3rdPerson]: *gel-ebil-di-∅* "he/she/it could come". The spelling mechanism may account for this by simply erasing this feature from its memory without performing any modification and continuing its processing. This avoids the dangers, mentioned in chapter 2, of assuming that zero morphology represents a lexical object. The LMBM architecture with a MS-processor containing a spelling mechanism defined by (3.10) accounts for all the relationships found among the form and sense of bound morphemes: one-many, many-one, null-many, null-one, many-null, many-one.

Let us now return to the Turkish derivation in (3.8) to see how a processor built on the principles of (3.10) would operate on an actual example. In Turkish, the suffix expressing the feature [+ Potentiality] before [+ Negation] is *-(y)E*. If [− Negation] occurs in that position or if [+ Potentiality] occurs after [+ Negation], the suffix expressing [+ Potentiality] is *-(y)Ebil*. (3.12–3.13) illustrate this.

(3.12) a. gel-di-m
        come-PAST-1ST/SG
        "I came"

        b. gel-ebil-di-m
        come-POT-PAST-1ST/SG
        "I could come"

(3.13) a. gel-me-di-m
        come-NEG-PAST-1ST/SG
        "I did not come"

        b. gel-e-me-di-m (*gel-ebil-me-di-m)
        come-POT-NEG-PAST-1STSG
        "I could not come"

The spelling mechanism must be able to read a feature ahead of its current position in order to know whether to insert *-(y)Ebil* or *-(y)E*. However, it cannot erase the Negation feature after reading it, for a discrete suffix, *-mE,* marks Negation itself.

The rules for adding affixes are always conditioned; their conditions may be phonological, lexical, inflectional, or any combination thereof. The rules for the expression of Potentiality and Negation in Turkish might be formulated as in (3.14).

(3.14) a. $\emptyset \rightarrow$ -(y)E   / [+ Potentiality, + Negation]
       b. $\emptyset \rightarrow$ -(y)Ebil   / [+ Potentiality, − Negation]
       c. $\emptyset \rightarrow$ -mE   / [+ Negation]

The spelling mechanism must read two features, [± Potentiality] and [± Negation], before selecting a process to carry out on a verb stem which will mark Potentiality. At the point in the process when the affixational operation is due to be executed, however, the spelling mechanism is resting on the feature [+ Negation]. If both the features have been copied into memory at this point, once the operation is executed, only [+ Potentiality] may be expunged from memory. In the case of Latin *venītis,* however, the speller must read the feature set [+ 2nd, + Plural, + Present, + Indicative], and [+ Active]), insert *-Vtis,* then erase all five features. If both features were erased in the Turkish example, the spelling mechanism would then move forward to the next feature, [+ Past], failing to insert the required feature of Negation, *-mE.*

In order to account for suffixes which are OUTWARDLY SENSITIVE in their allomorphy, to use Carstairs-McCarthy's term, the spelling mechanism must be able to selectively erase features. Carstairs (1987: 165–194) describes a particularly important constraint on morphology: an affix is generally sensitive only inwardly, that is, to the features and phonology nearer the base than itself. It is true, however, that an affix may be sensitive to the categorial features of an affix that occurs farther from the base than itself as long as it is sensitive to all the properties and functions of that category (THE PERIPHERALITY CONSTRAINT).[7] This is what the present Turkish example illustrates: it is not the phonology of the Negative marker *-mE* that conditions the selection of *-(y)Ebil* or *-(y)E;* it is the category Polarity, which contains the single property "Negative" in Turkish.

The LMH model has no explanation of affixes which are outwardly sensitive to categories; therefore, they must be represented as an exception to Carstairs-McCarthy's Peripherality Constraint. In an LMH model with only one morpheme, it a linguistic sign, no affix has access either to the phonological or grammatical information of a succeeding affix. This is because the G-features associated with a given affix are lexically bound to the form of the affix. The grammatical representation of an affix is thereby not available in a derived form until the phonological representation of the same morpheme is inserted into the derivation from the lexicon. LMBM models, however, because they postulate all grammatical derivation to occur prior to any affixation, can account for why outward sensitivity includes only the reading of categorial features and excludes reading phonological ones. Thus it predicts both the Peripherality Constraint and the major exception to that constraint with the architecture of the model itself.

The Peripherality Constraint is merely the effect of the definition of affixation based on the presupposition of the lexical base. It is the result of affixation applying after derivation, when all the derivational (category) features are present in the base, as illustrated in (3.8). This allows an affixation rule to look ahead to features beyond those which directly condition it. Indeed, the MS-component may look at all the features simultaneously and replace all with a single affix, as in the Latin example above. However, since affixation is the final morphological process, it cannot look ahead for phonological conditions on succeeding affixes, for they are not available at the relevant moment.

Instances of outward phonological sensitivity cited by Carstairs-McCarthy seem to involve only postcyclic phonology as predicted by the LMBM model illustrated in Figure 3.1. Morphophonemic examples of outward phonological sensitivity introduced by Carstairs-McCarthy seem to involve only inward truncation. For example, the Fulfulde Habitual marker *-atay* is truncated to *-at* before the 1st Person Singular Object marker *-am,* as in *wall-atay-mo* "keep on helping him" versus *wall-at-am* "keep on helping me" (Carstairs 1990). This may be explained in terms of stem allomorphy, assuming that *wallatay-* is the stem to which *-am* is attached. No alternation of *-atay* with *-at* conditioned by a more peripheral affix is required here.[8]

3.4.1 A Dynamic Model of Morphological Spelling Based on (3.10)

Since the LMBM model being designed here assumes that bound grammatical morphemes are spelling operations rather than items, it will require a computational mechanism as well as a storage area for free morphemes. This section will lay out the computational mechanism for affixation. The requirements imposed by (3.8) suggest that an LMBM spelling mechanism is a finite state transducer with a push-down stack. Figure 3.4 illustrates such a device.

Notice right away the familiar symbols of the individual lexeme $p \leftrightarrow g \leftrightarrow r$ to the left of Figure 3.4. While the spelling mechanism can read features from all three representational levels of lexemes, it can operate only on one: the phonological representation (3.5c). It follows that the

Figure 3.4

A Computational Model of an LMBM Morphological Speller

SPELLING OPERATIONS
V25: . . .
V26: 2=C|Pot| x, 1= +Ng : SUFFIX /E/
V27: 2=V|Pot| x, 1= +Ng : SUFFIX /yE/
V28: 2=C|Pot| x, 1= -Ng : SUFFIX /Ebil/
V29: 2=V|Pot| x, 1= -Ng : SUFFIX /yEbil/
V30: 2= x|+Ng| x, 1= x : SUFFIX /mE/
V31: . . .

Lexeme	*READER*	*MEMORY*				
		1	*2*	*3*	*4*	*5*
p	/gel/ → C	C → C	→NA	NA	NA	
g	[+Negation] → +Ng	+Ng →Pot	→ NA	NA	NA	
r	Nothing recognized	∅ → ∅	→ NA	NA	NA	

spelling mechanism requires two, perhaps three, distinct types of proces-
sors. First, it may require a filter to convert the gross feature inventory of
lexemes to the specific information relevant to the operation of MS-rules.
This means that it must do more than simply copy relevant P-, G-, or R-
features into memory. The reader must be able to detect stems like *gel-,*
locate the final segment, and determine if that segment contains a feature
or cluster of features relevant to spelling operations, in this instance,
whether it is a vowel or a consonant. The rules for allomorphically adjusting the suffixes listed under "Spelling Operations", *-(y)Ebil,* for example,
whose parenthesized segment is omitted if the final segment is a consonant,
do not need to know that the final segment is an /l/, but only whether it is
a consonant. Figure 3.4 assigns the task of filtering out for the reader the
information irrelevant to MS-rules. Finally, since the attributes of a lexeme
are of three mutually exclusive types, the reader and the memory that receives its output must keep them separate. Part of the reader's job is to
separate these types of features for, and write them systematically to,
memory. It is thus a reading and writing device, even though it is referred
to here only as a "reader".

Because an MS-operation is often conditioned by two or three features, for example, the alternation of *-(y)E* and *-(y)Ebil* in Turkish described above, the spelling mechanism must have a memory that accumulates such features until the appropriate combination triggers some stem modification such as suffixation.[9] The memory in Figure 3.4 is organized to contain a maximum of five columns, numbered from 1 to 5. Each is capable of containing at least one feature from each of the three sets of features possessed by lexemes according to (3.2–3.5). The number 5 reflects the five G-features Voice, Tense, Mood, Person, and Number, which are expressed by a single affix in such examples as Latin *venī-tis*: STEM + PRESACTIND1ST-SG, "we come". The assumption here is that no affix cumulatively expresses more than five grammatical features. The last three columns of Figure 3.4 contain "NA," for "not available", under the assumption that Turkish allows an affix to mark at most two features simultaneously.[10]

Finally, the spelling mechanism must have a catalogue of operations listing the modifications it carries out on the stems of lexemes, as well as a set of instructions for each operation. These are usually referred to as ALLOMORPHY rules. Those in Figure 3.4 exhibit conditions which indicate the column of memory in which a set of conditions must occur (1 = , 2 =) and vertical lines that refer to three registers of each column. This approach allows the spelling operations to respond simultaneously to the content of up to five columns. Thus, the same mechanism should accommodate the highly fusional languages like Latin as well as agglutinative types like Turkish. The operations described in Figure 3.4 also contain the name of one operation, suffixation, which refers to another complex algorithm defining the process of suffixation.

The conditions described after each catalogue number (V26, V27, and so forth) for the spelling operations of Figure 3.4 include not only insertion conditions but the allomorphic conditions on spelling operations as well. These conditions have been simplified here to include only the variation /y/~ $\emptyset$, which is determined by the final segment of the stem in Turkish. If the stem ends on a vowel (V), then /y/ is copied to the stem; if the stem ends on a consonant (C), then /y/ is not copied. Of course, these suffixes are also subject to vowel harmony; however, vowel harmony is postcyclic and not proper to the spelling mechanism. Presumably the operations are ordered disjunctively, beginning with suppletion, as in "/gʊd/|1 = Comp : SUBSTITUTE /bɛtr/". Now let us examine each of the three subprocessors of the LMBM spelling mechanism in Figure 3.4 and describe their contents and capacities more closely.

3.4.2 The Reader

The reader must contain a list of specific lexical G-features, $(g_1, g_2, \ldots, g_n)$, to search for. The list must include any relevant P- or R-features. These features must be exactly those which condition the spelling operations. This implies that the reader must be in possession of an exact set of the conditions on spelling operations to match with the complete feature inventory of each lexeme it surveys.[11] The reader then matches the conditional features with those located in the feature inventory of the current lexeme; upon finding a match, the reader sends a symbol to memory. The sets of conditional features used by the reader for its matching process are learned from the spelling operations subprocessor. Once the conditional features are learned, there is no need for direct communication between the reader and the spelling subprocessor during spelling operations.

The morphological spelling mechanism is a timed device and Figure 3.4 represents one tick of the timing. The mechanism changes state with every tick, and the content of each column of memory is written over that of the column to the right between states. Figure 3.4 illustrates the fourth state of the processing of the Turkish example in (3.8). Because the MS-component must begin with the core of the lexeme, the first two states copied the inherent features of the stem to memory, say, |V(er)b| and |Int-(ransitive)|. Both of these have advanced to column 3, which would require four changes of state.

When the operations subprocessor detects the feature |Vb| in column 1, it opens the directory of spelling operations applying to verbs. Some of the verbal operations are shown in Figure 3.4 with the prefix "V": V26, V27, V28. Those operations that apply to verbs and nouns might be listed in a segment of the catalogue prefixed with "NV", which would also be opened at the feature |Vb|. In its second state, when |Vb| was in column 1 and |Int| was in column 2, the directory of verb operations applying strictly to Transitive verbs will be closed, restricting operations to those applying to Intransitive verbs. The search may be restricted to other subdirectories, that is, to operations applying to verbs of specific conjugations or bearing specific tenses. In fact, funneling the search for the appropriate affix operations is the function of the features read into meaning: the search is narrowed by each conditioning feature until all inappropriate operations are eliminated.

In the derived form of *gelemedim* under consideration here (see 3.8), the reader must locate the phonological features [+ Consonant, − Vowel] in the matrix of the segment /l/ and send some symbol that the spelling subprocessor can recognize within memory. The entire stem /gel/ would be read from (3.8), but only the symbol crucial for the selection of an allomorphic variant, say, "C" for "consonant", needs to be transferred to memory for the operations device. At the same time, the reader takes up the grammatical representation of the lexeme and converts its first feature, [+ Verb], to its catalogue equivalent, |Vb|, then stores it in the first cell of the G-feature register of memory. Since nothing from the semantic representation, *r,* is relevant to the derivations under consideration, we assume that the cells in the semantic register of memory would either be empty or filled with information that no operation would recognize and thus would ignore. This brings the speller to its first state in processing Turkish *gelemedim*. Once the operations subprocessor reacts to the contents of column 1 in memory, the process continues on to the second state. To understand how the speller changes states, we need to know a bit more about the modest memory module in Figure 3.4.

3.4.3 Memory

The small, short-term memory of Figure 3.4 is not static but a common push-down stack. The content of each column advances one column rightward between each state, overwriting whatever is in the column to the right. Once the operation subprocessor reacts to the features in column 1, the reader copies |Vb| from column 1 to column 2, then moves to the second feature of (3.8), converting the subcategorization frame into |Int| (for "Intransitive"), which it copies over |Vb| in the first column. This brings it to its second state in processing *gelemedim*. To arrive at its third state, the speller copies |Int| over |Vb| in column 2, thereby erasing it, then converts the third feature of (3.8), [+ Potentiality] to |Pot|, and copies it over |Int| in column 1 of memory.

Figure 3.4 then illustrates the fourth state of the morphological speller in the interpretation of *gelemedim*. The operations processor did not react to the features |Pot| (column 1) and |Int| (column 2), for there are no operations marking this combination and it requires knowledge of the value of the Negation feature in order to choose the proper marking for |Pot|. Column 1 then advances to column 2 and the reader writes the output of its next reading of the stem, | + Ng|, to column 1. (The " + " before the "Ng" means simply "must be present"; " − " means "must not be present".) Since the operations subprocessor was not activated by the appearance of |Pot| and |Int|, the phonological representation of *gel* has not changed, so the reader will read "C" again into the phonological register of column 1. This cues the subprocessor to write *-E* rather than *-yE* onto the stem (*-yE* follows stems ending on vowels). Most if not all allomorphic adjustments may be executed in this manner, as a part of the affix selection process, rather than by rules situated after affix copying and insertion.[12]

When advancing information runs out of columns in memory, it is automatically erased by the information copied over it. This prevents an operation being conditioned twice by the same feature. For example, when the information of column 1 of the current example, |C| + Ng|∅|, is written over that of column 2, |C|Pot|∅|, the latter column is thereby terminally erased, because there is no available column to its right for it to be copied over. This process frees column 1 for new information, which would be

|V|Pst|Ø|, judging by Figure 3.4. The fifth state in processing *gelemedim* would therefore resemble Figure 3.5:

Figure 3.5

***Memory State 5 in the Processing of* gelemedim**

1		*2*		*3*	*4*	*5*
V	→	C	→	NA	NA	NA
Pst	→	+Ng	→	NA	NA	NA
Ø	→	Ø	→	NA	NA	NA

The "V" in column 1 derives from the vowel /e/ at the end of the suffix *-(y)E,* just inserted by the spelling operations under the conditions [+ Negative, + Potentiality] between states 4 and 5. Notice that the symbol | + Ng| is not erased but advances to column 2, triggering its own suffix, *-mE.* Since there is no suffix in Turkish triggered by the combination of [+ Past, + Negative], none will be copied onto the stem. Once the Negative suffix is inserted, its conditions will be overwritten by the Past Tense symbol in column 1 where it will trigger the suffixation of the Past Tense suffix -DI. By making the memory the WRITE-OVER memory of a pushdown stack, we avoid the necessity of a control on erasure, that is, every column is erased in each state by new information. However, the content of a column is retained for as many states as there are columns in memory. For Turkish, this means that the operations subprocessor has two and only two opportunities to respond to any given set of features in a single column.

This picture of the memory requirements of a dynamic morphological processor relies on the assumption that features are ordered for any given language, even though the order is not necessarily universally determined. Studies in morphology that examine affix order, like Cole (1985) and Inkeles (1993), confirm the fact that while the order of a few affixes vis-à-vis each other is free, the overall order of inflectional and derivational affixes is fixed. However, there is considerable variation in affix order from language to language. Each language will therefore require a morphotactic description specifying the relation of each feature to every other feature, as well as a description of any deviation from that order possible among affixes.

3.4.4 The Operations Subprocessor

The operations subprocessor of the spelling mechanism will obviously have to be in possession of a list of operations. The operations marked

V25–V31 in Figure 3.4 are assumed to apply cyclically and to be disjunctively ordered. The system of numeration begins with a prefix, as in the "V" in Figure 3.4, under the assumption that the lexical classes and subcategorization information are used to organize storage and retrieval of MS-rules. As mentioned above, the first features read by the speller will be the class specifiers and subcategorization frames of the base lexeme; these may be applied to limiting the range of operations over which the spelling subprocessor searches for matching conditions in memory. This adds to the efficiency of the process and reduces the time required to find a match.

All languages have affixes which attach to two lexical classes; Chukchee and Koryak, have suffixes that apply to all three classes of lexical stems.

(3.15)   a.   ərətku-k 'to shoot'   ərətku-lʔ(ən) 'shooting,
                                                           shooter'
         b.   jara-ŋə 'house'   jara-lʔ(ən) 'house-owing/owner'
         c.   nə-gənkojŋə-qen 'happy'   gənkojŋə-lʔ(ən) 'happy
                                                           (person)'

Suffixes like Chukchee *-lʔ(ən)* will be contained in an area of the spelling operations catalogue where the operations are prefixed, say, NAV, and which will be activated by the appearance of N, A, or V in the grammatical feature register of memory. This obviates the redundancy of multiple listings under the N, A, and V rules for the identical affix, with an appreciation of overall systematicity.

The operations performed by the spelling subprocessor begins with reading the potential conditions in column 2 and searching for a match among the conditions in the list of operations defined in the subdirectory by the initial features read into memory, in this case, |Vb| and |Int|. If no match is found for the features in column 2, column 1 is surveyed and the spelling subprocessor checks among its operations with two columns of conditions, and so on. When a match is found, the operation associated with the matching conditions is executed and the subprocessor returns to column 2.

The assumption to this point has been that Turkish allows a maximum of two categories to be expressed by a single affix, as in Potential + Negative. However, Turkish does have a single fusional ending, *-k,* which expresses both 1st Person and Plural but only in the Past Tense. "We could not come" in Turkish is *gel-e-me-di-k,* with the final suffix marking two categories in the vicinity of another, not one, as was the case with *-(y)E.* In other words, *-k* marks 1st Person and Plural only under the condition of Past Tense.[13] What happens in this case, the case of conditioned cumulative exponence of a fusional suffix, when two features are marked by a single affix only if a third is present? This situation can generally be handled with only two columns of push-down memory and the general assumptions introduced up to this point. To see how, let us examine the final three states during the processing of the morphological spelling of *gelemedik*.

The spelling *gelemedik,* "we could not go", will be identical with that of *gelemedim* "I could not go," through state 5. The reader in state five has recognized the [+ Past] feature and written its correlate "Pst" into the first column of memory. When the correlate reaches the second column, in state 6, illustrated in Figure 3.6, it triggers the insertion of the Past Tense ending, *-DI*.

Figure 3.6

Memory State 6 in the Processing of **gelemedik**

1	*2*	*3*	*4*	*5*
V $\twoheadrightarrow$ C $\twoheadrightarrow$ NA		NA	NA	
1st $\twoheadrightarrow$ Pst $\twoheadrightarrow$ NA		NA	NA	
$\emptyset$ $\twoheadrightarrow$ $\emptyset$ $\twoheadrightarrow$ NA		NA	NA	

The initial recognition of [+ Past] has another effect on the speller. Recall from the discussion above that the first features stored in memory are [+ Verb] and [NP___], which will be written into memory in that order. Upon recognition of the feature correlate |Vb| in the first column of memory, the operations subprocessor goes to the subdirectory of operations applicable to verbs. In state 2, "Vb" moves to the second column and "Int" (for "Intransitive") is written into column 1. At this point the operations subcomponent restricts its search for applicable operations to those carried out on Intransitive verbs. This procedure implies that affixes are stored paradigmatically in areas and subareas pretty much as they are presented in classical grammar books. When |Pst| appears in column 1 of memory, the operations subprocessor may restrict its search to that subarea of verb modification rules where only Past Tense endings are stored.

In the (sub)subarea of operations storage devoted to Intransitive Past Tense endings, the operations subprocessor finds no ending corresponding solely to "1st", the feature appearing in column 1 in the next state, illustrated in Figure 3.6. It thus remains in the same subarea until the next state, illustrated in Figure 3.7. In this state both "Pl" and "1st" are available to it and at that point, the subprocessor finds the suffixation of *-k* in its [Vb[Pst]] subdirectory and performs that operation on the current stem, *gelemedi-*.

Figure 3.7

Memory State 7 in the Processing of **gelemedik**

	1		2		3	4	5
V	$\twoheadrightarrow$	V	$\twoheadrightarrow$	NA	NA	NA
P1	$\twoheadrightarrow$	1st	$\twoheadrightarrow$	NA	NA	NA
Ø	$\twoheadrightarrow$	Ø	$\twoheadrightarrow$	NA	NA	NA

Let us now imagine the selection of a suffix which is phonologically or even morphologically motivated. That is, imagine that the selection of the suffix *-k* is conditioned by either the final vowel of the stem, which is *gelemedi-* at the point of the copying of *-k,* or by the preceding suffix, *-di.* Both situations are certainly prevalent. If the suffixation is phonologically conditioned, nothing has to be changed. The phonological (top) register of memory in states 6 and 7 will contain the |V| derivable from the final /i/ of the stem along lines already laid out. If the suffix were conditioned by the preceding morpheme, the power of the reader would have to be increased to a capacity to read to the previous morpheme boundary. This would not require a theoretical revision involving redefinition of the processor.

Anderson (1992, chapter 8) has suggested that morphological operations may be universally restricted to the periphery and heads of stems and phrases. In other words, affixal operations are restricted to the initial and final segment, phoneme or syllable, or accented syllable of the stem. Affixes may be added to either side of that segment, so that infixation can only occur inside the same segments to which prefixes and suffixes are added externally (or to the accented syllable). Clitics are considered phrasal affixes in the recent literature (Zwicky 1977; Carstairs 1981; Klavans 1980; 1985), because they, too, are limited to the positions immediately preceding and following the peripheral elements of phrases, that is, lexemes and free morphemes. However, clitics are also added before or after the heads of phrases. The LMBM MS-component, of course, must be constrained by limits which Anderson's observations impose since clitics, too, will be spelled out by the mechanism depicted in Figure 3.4. (Chapter 15 examines the question of clitics). Thus, the operation of the MS-mechanism in Figure 3.4 will be constrained to the heads and peripheral elements of phrases and lexical stems.

The existence of the spelling mechanism and the fact that it is capable of processing each step of a complex derivation like (3.11) does not mean that it does so in each act of performance in which such a form is uttered. It is probable that such a complex word as (3.11) is only partially assembled by the processes of L-and I-derivation and affixation each time it is spoken. This is because language as a whole depends upon large amounts of permanent, long-term memory; the large number of idioms and idiomatic exceptions to rules is eloquent testimony to this fact. Specifically realized tokens of this model, may receive partially assembled stems directly from the lexicon, as in *Avrupa-lı-laş-* "Europeanize" or *Avrupa-lı-laş-tır-* "cause to Europeanize". It is likely that actual performative derivations are considerably simpler than what is implied by (3.11). However, this does not undermine the fact that the processor described above is capable of such processing under optimal conditions. There is no reason, therefore, to constrain the competence model to producing anything less than (3.11) in toto. Certainly, it cannot be prohibited from generating constructions like *Avrupa-lı-laş-tır-* under less demanding circumstances, for this stem, too, represents a productive derivation in Turkish.

3.5 CONCLUSION

This chapter established a preliminary answer to the second question on the agenda of morphology outlined in section 1.3. The relation of the phonological, grammatical, and semantic representations of lexemes is direct, mutually implied, and immutable. However, bound grammatical morphemes have no semantic or grammatical content, but are independent phonological modifications of the phonological representation (only) of lexemes. That is, the morphological operations of the lexicon (L-derivation) and syntax (I-derivation) are distinct from the operations of the phonological operations of the MS-component that phonologically realize them (the Separation Hypothesis). The relatively close correlation between grammatical functions and their affixal markers is accounted for by the fact that the spelling mechanism responds to the features added by derivation rules. However, it is most commonly the case that an affix is not conditioned by one derivational feature alone, but rather by a derivational feature in conjunction with several inherent features.

The assumption that affixation is independent of derivation (the Separation Hypothesis) allows in some cases the omission of marking since the only direct mapping of meaning to sound is in the lexeme. If a grammatical relation is deducible without marking, as in the use of an adjective in a V-node with a Past Tense ending, for example, *they wet the rug,* no spelling operation is necessary and hence often none occur. The Separation Hypothesis also accounts for zero or, better, omissive morphology, without any ancillary theory of zero morphology. On the other hand, morphology may have reasons of its own for the application of a spelling operation. For no reason relevant to English morphology, stems borrowed from Greek ending on labials are extended by the suffix *-at: dram-at-ic, schem-at-ic.*

Such empty morphology, is also accounted for by the architecture of LMBM without ancillary theories of any sort.

The addition of morphemes whose sound and meaning are directly and isomorphically related is logically the most efficient way to symbolize categorial changes on lexemes. It is surprising, then, that this position succeeds so poorly in predicting sound–meaning relations among grammatical morphemes. Languages resort to isomorphic affixes no more often than they resort to asymmetrical morphology. This chapter has offered an explanation of this curiosity: what is logically simpler is not psychologically simpler, for the linguistic processor. Assuming that morphology is processed by a set of cognitive operations similar to those described in this chapter, the attachment of isomorphic affixes is no more efficient than asymmetrical stem modification. Morphological spelling is a more complex process than lexical selection. This may be taken as a warning to those arguing theoretical simplicity; such arguments must take into account the nature of the linguistic processor.

A striking entailment of the model illustrated in Figure 3.3 is that all bound morphemes are spelling operations which are both grammatically and semantically empty. No affix, therefore, should determine the grammatical or semantic output of a derivation. We should find no affix, for example, ranging over two or more Genders. If the output of an L- or I-derivational rule is marked with affixes distinguishing Gender or Number, this categorization must be accounted for either by the derivation rule, syntax, the lexicon, or phonology; it cannot be accounted for in the MS-component. Chapter 4 will demonstrate the remarkable accuracy of this ostensibly outlandish prediction.

NOTES

1. At least partially distinct. A common property of free grammatical morphemes that sharply distinguishes them from lexemes and unites them with affixes is their tendency to contract or cliticize, as in *do not : don't* or *I would have : I'd've*. Prototypical lexemes are never susceptible to contraction, another attribute that distinguishes them from grammatical morphemes (see chapter 15 for the details).

2. Chapters 6, 11, 12, and especially 16 will examine languages which, like English, express these same features as free morphemes, particles, auxiliaries, and the like.

3. Crucial arguments for morphemes as processes rather than items may also be found in Janda (1982) and references cited there.

4. Andrew Carstairs-McCarthy has pointed out (personal communication, 1992) that the outer limit on the number of features conditioning a

single affix is probably at least five, as illustrated in this chapter. In addition to the four verbal functions listed here, *-tis* also marks Active Voice, according to Meillet. Moreover, in the Greek participle form *lū-on* 'loosing', *-on* realizes Nominative, Singular, Neuter, Present, and Active. The actual number of columns is an issue aside from the argument for memory columns per se, so the five which appear here will serve purposes of illustration.

5. Beard (1987a) assumed this to be a possibility and proposed a concatenation constraint called the "Push-Down Principle". The more refined definition represented by (3.2–3.5) eliminates the necessity of that principle and any difficulty LMBM might have predicting affix order (see Don 1993: 90–93 for cogent criticism).

6. We will want to restrict this power, however, to allow the spelling mechanism to read only a small number of features ahead of the feature it is operating on. The discussion of this interesting constraint will be delayed for the moment, however.

7. Carstairs-McCarthy uses the term 'category' in the narrow sense of Matthews' (1972, 1991) to mean a set of mutually exclusive morphosyntactic properties or functions (see section 5.1).

8. A more vexing problem for LMBM is presented by the Fulfulde Future Active marker, *-ay,* which appears only before consonants and alternates with *-Vt* before V-initial suffixes, for example, *o-wall-ay-mo* "he will help him/her" versus *o-wall-at-am* "he will help me" and *o-wall-et-e* "he will help you (Sg)". The problem here is not the consonant alternation, which may be handled as stem allomorphy, but the vowel harmony, which seems to be conditioned by the peripheral affix rather than by the stem. At present this example is an isolated case which may involve a crystalized cluster, *-et-e.* Until more evidence is available, this ostensible exception can only be noted and set aside for later study.

9. Certainly, the memory will have to be slightly larger than that represented in Figure 3.4 in order to accommodate clitics. Clitics such as the English Possessive marker *-'s,* as in *the king of England's hat,* are notable for attaching to lexemes that do not contain their conditioning features. In the example just cited, *king,* not *England,* is the possessor. An account of this will be provided in chapter 15, where bound morphemes are examined in more detail.

10. In other words, "cumulative exponence" in Matthews' terminology is limited to two features in Turkish, while fusional languages allow as many as five cumulative features to be expressed by a single affix. This variation in the maximum number of short-term memory cells is LMBM's explanation of the typological difference between agglutinative and fusional languages. Notice that it correctly predicts a gradient between these two language types, rather than a sharp distinction.

11. Presumably, the acquisition process involves bidirectional exchange of information between the reader and spelling subcomponent such as would account for this identity. Figure 3.4 hence predicts that "acquisition of morphology" is in part a matter of successfully reaching an equilibrium between the spelling subcomponent and the reader such that the conditions that the reader selects are precisely those which the spelling operations require. Once acquisition is completed, however, only unidirectional communication between the reader and the speller is required.

12. This does not mean that general allomorphy rules are replaced by listings of every allomorphic variant; rules may operate across entries like those in the operations subprocessor of Figure 3.4. It simply means that allomorphy rules are located within the operations subprocessor. They are regularities found within the phonological conditions of rules like V25-V31.

13. In the Present and Future Tense paradigms, 1stPLURAL is marked with the ending *-(y)Iz*.

Chapter Four

The Empty Morpheme Entailment

4.1 THE NATURE OF MORPHEMES IN LMBM

If morphology consists of semantically empty operations modifying the phonological matrix *p* of lexemes only, it follows that such modifications cannot determine the grammatical subcategorization of derivates. Gender, Agency, and Diminution, for example, cannot be brought to a lexical derivation by an affix as in LMH theories. Hence LMBM and LMH explain the origin of [+ Neuter] in the German Diminutives of (4.1) in radically different ways.

(4.1) a. die Hand   das Händ-chen, -lein "hand"
       b. der Hahn   das Hähn-chen, -lein, -el "rooster"
       c. das Haus   das Häus-chen, -lein, -el "house"

LMBM predicts that the Gender of these derivations is controlled by derivation, not the suffixes *-chen, -lein,* and *-el*. In LMH [+ Neuter] is a lexical feature of the nouns *-chen, -lein,* and *-el*, and accrues to the derivates in (1) by virtue of affixation. Only when the phonological form of the lexical item is attached to the base can its feature inventory be copied onto the derivation. (2) illustrates feature percolation for *Mädchen* 'girl' as prescribed by (2.1).

(4.2)

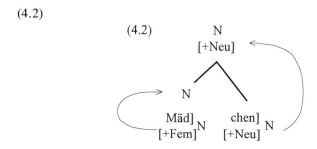

73

In other words, the suffix *-chen* provides the Neuter Gender to the underlying base along with the feature of Diminution. (4.2) illustrates the origin of derivational features not only under LMH, but under all traditional theories of morphology preceding it. The LMBM interpretation represents a bold, barely credible departure from that tradition.

4.2 SYNONYMY: THE LMH EXPLANATION OF CROSS-AFFIXAL GENDER CONSISTENCY

This chapter examines two critical entailments of LMH: that affixes are (i) directly associated with syntactic and lexical material and (ii) represent the heads of lexical derivations. As we saw in chapter two, derived words under LMH are structural configurations whose branches are one-way channels for the passage of lexical features upward to the maximal word-level projection. Principles like the Right-Hand Head Principle (Williams 1981; Di Sciullo and Williams 1987), or the percolation principles of Lieber (1981a), Selkirk (1982), and Sproat (1985), control the switching at junctions where conflicts between rising features crop up.

The ostensible source of Neuter in the German Diminutives of (4.1), then, is the Diminutive suffix, which is the head of the lexical construction. Di Sciullo and Williams (1987:26) "relativize" the head to "head relative to the feature F", so that derivates may not receive all their features from its affixes; some features may originate in the base if the affix contains no features of that category. For example, the Diminutive suffixes in Spanish do not contain class features (N, V, A) to pass on to the derivates they mark; hence, they may attach to any lexical class and the class feature of the base dominates:

(4.3)   a. Adjective: poco   poqu-ita   "little"
        b. Noun: chica   chiqu-ita   "girl"
        c. Adverb: ahora   ahor-ita   "now"

If an affix does not possess a feature, it cannot transmit it to the derived word. Only the features which an affix possesses can overwrite those of the base; otherwise, the features of the base dominate.

In German only Ns may be diminutivized. However, German *-chen* alternates predictably with *-lein*: only *-chen* occurs after nouns ending on /l/ and only *-lein* occurs after nouns ending in /x, ŋ, g/; both are free alternates elsewhere. The third German Diminutive marker, *-el,* also marks Neuter Diminutives in Southern dialects, as in *das Häus-el*.[1] The question for LMH, then, is how to explain that these three phonologically distinct lexical items coincide in Gender, given the fact that the chance is one in three that each of them is Neuter. The answer is that they are simply Gender-synonymous, as are so many other lexical items.

LMH theories predict that affixes are lexical items which combine with stems in essentially the same fashion that lexical bases unite to form a compound. In (4.4), for instance, the Neutrality of *das Essen* "food" might dominate the Femininity of *die Nacht* "night" in the compound *das Nachtessen* "supper", just as the suffix *-chen* dominates the base *Mäd-* in (4.1).

(4.4)

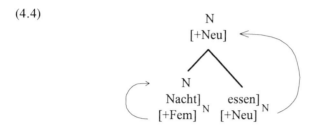

If, however, the affix chosen to mark Diminutives contributes Neuter to the Diminutive derivation in the same way that *Essen* contributes Neuter to *Nachtessen* in (4.4), Gender must be determined lexically, which is to say, idiomatically. Affix selection, like compound head selection, should be motivated by semantics, not grammar, since the nature of the lexicon is semantic. LMH thus claims that the three suffixes in (4.1), *-chen, -lein,* and *-el,* are simply accidental lexical synonyms.

There is, however, no a priori reason why all the suffixes marking Diminutives in (4.1), should be consistently Neuter if they are lexical synonyms. While some compounds containing synonymous head nouns share the same Gender (4.5), others do not (4.6).

(4.5) a. die Fleischbrühe   die Fleischbouillon   die Bohnensuppe
       "meat broth"   "meat bouillon"   "bean soup"
       b. die Hühnerbrühe   die Hühnerbouillon   die Fischsuppe
       "chicken broth"   "chicken bouillon"   "fish soup"

(4.6) a. die Vorspeise   das Zwischenessen   das Nachtmahl
       "hors d'oeuvre"   "between-meal snack"   "evening meal"
       b. die Nachspeise   das Abendessen   das Mittagsmahl
       "dessert"   "supper"   "dinner, lunch"

Zubin and Köpcke (1984a, 1984b, 1986) and Köpcke (1982) propose a lexical reason for patterns like (4.5) through (4.6) that could be extended to the suffixes of (4.1) if those suffixes were regular lexical items, as supporters of LMH claim. Zubin and Köpcke argue that semantic categories often reflect FOLK TAXONOMY through Gender, so that synonyms tend reflect the same grammatical Gender. Words associated with broader, less "imageable" concepts tend to be associated with Neuter. It follows from this that concepts associated with Neuter tend to be superordinate categories in the sense of Rosch et al. (1976) and Rosch (1977), while the sex-associated Genders, Masculine and Feminine, typify basic and subordinate level categories. Zubin and Köpcke include the following among their list of Neuter terms, which refer to the "broadest range of entities".

(4.7)   a. das Ding "thing"   d. das Geschöpf "creation"
        b. das Element "element"   e. das Mitglied "member"
        c. das Gebilde "product"   f. das Wesen "being"

If the test of these categories is either their referential range or imageability, many other categories not symbolized by Neuter must be added to (4.7), for example, those in (4.8).

(4.8)   a. die Sache "thing"   d. die Kategorie "category"
        b. die Welt "world"   e. der Kosmos "cosmos"
        c. die Art "kind, type"   f. der Teil "part"

It would seem that Zubin and Köpcke simply argue the point from converse accident. We would expect, *ceteris paribus*, approximately a third of the German vocabulary with low imageability to be Neuter accidentally. Since the category of broad concepts with low imageability is itself so vague, a statistical study showing a significant correlation between Neuter and these subordinate categories is impossible. We are left with the conclusion that grammatical Gender, as opposed to highly predictable Natural Gender, is lexically assigned in an arbitrary manner.

Not all affixes sharing the same function coincide in Gender as do the German Neuter Diminutives in (4.1). To anticipate a set of data that later will be scrutinized, we might consider the Locative derivations in Serbo-Croatian as examples. Synonymous Locative suffixes are sometimes Feminine, sometimes Masculine, sometimes Neuter, as in (4.9):

(4.9)   a. knjig-a "book"   knjiž-nic-a   [F]   "library"
        b. raž "rye"   raž-išt-e   [N]   "rye field"
        c. gus-k-a "goose"   gus-in-jak-∅   [M]   "goose pen"

Unlike the data of (4.1), which share two common threads, meaning and Gender, the affixes used in (4.9) share only one: meaning. The Feminine suffix *-nic-a,* the Neuter suffix *-išt-e* and the Masculine suffix *-jak* all mean "place of N", where N defines a base of any Gender. This counts as evidence, therefore, that the data of (4.1) is not grammatically or taxonomically determined but merely a lexical accident, as in the case of the heads of (4.5–4.6).

LMBM, however, disputes this claim: Gender cannot be predicted by any affix but only by the base or the L-derivation that the affix marks. In order to establish that affixes are the result of empty spelling operations and not listable items, LMBM must prove that Gender patterns are determined by grammar and not by semantics, by derivational operations and not by affixation. The latter proof is fairly straightforward, as contemporary models of language offer no other source of grammatical categories other than the lexicon, syntax, and derivation rules. If it can be proven that Gender-category parallels like those of (4.1) are not semantically determined, they can only be rule-determined. The task for LMBM, then, is to demonstrate that (4.1) does not represent lexical fortuity or the effect of affixation.

If the Gender associated with the three suffixes in (4.1) is not determined by derivation, it represents fortuitous lexical synonymy. The first step, then, is to disprove that we are dealing with lexical synonymy. This requires a test for lexical synonymy that may be applied to affixes whose meaning parallels their Gender.

4.2.1 The Nature of Lexical Synonymy under LMH

In order to determine whether the coincidence of Neuter and Diminution across all Diminutive affixes in German is a matter of lexical synonymy among discrete affixes, let us begin with an examination of examples (4.5–4.6) and those introduced by Zubin and Köpcke in order to arrive at a working definition of SYNONYMY. The plan of attack is the same as that of chapter 2: if data like (4.1) reflect lexical synonymy, they should reflect the properties of synonymy found among prototypical lexical classes. If lexical and morphological synonymy exhibit no conjoint properties, they represent two distinct phenomena.

Lexical synonymy is characterized by three notable attributes. First, it is approximate, not exact. Returning to the heads of the examples in (4.5), German *Suppe, Brühe,* and *Bouillion* refer to slightly differing kinds of soup. *Suppe* is distinguished from *Brühe* and *Bouillon* by its heavier ingredients. *Brühe* also means "gravy, sauce" as well as "bouillon", hence has a different natural function than *Bouillon*. The same applies to the examples of (4.6). *Speise* refers not to a whole meal but to a smaller amount of food, a snack, or hors d'oeuvre. *Mahl* may refer to a multicourse meal, while *Essen* has a much broader meaning whose reference may overlap both the others. There is little room to argue with the long history of synonymy research: absolute synonymy is rare, if it occurs at all.

Second, while some synonyms in such semantic fields as SOUP and

FOOD exhibit monotonic association with one Gender, such associations are occasional and inconsistent. Most synonymous affixes, therefore, should vary in their lexical categorization, and parallels between lexical categorization and semantics should occur only accidentally. Finally, in order to contribute its features to a compound, a lexical item must be present, phonologically expressed. This is an entailment of Principle I, chapter 1. There is no evidence among compounds of zero lexemes such that the rightmost element of a compound might be omitted without the loss of its meaning, e.g. *das Fleisch* "meat" : **die Fleisch-Ø* "meat broth".[2]

An account of data like *Mädchen*$_{Neu}$, *Mädel*$_{Neu}$, *Mädlein*$_{Neu}$ in terms of lexical synonymy depends upon the discovery of the following three fundamental attributes of lexical synonyms in the data:

(4.10)   a.   affix synonymy should be approximate, not absolute;
         b.   synonymous affixes should generally vary in their lexical categorization;
         c.   the affix must be present to project its features onto a derivate.

If the multiple exponence of grammatical functions such as Gender in (4.1) reflect lexical synonymy, they should conform to all three of these diagnostics.

4.2.2 The Nature of Morphological Synonymy under LMBM

Before testing the LMH hypothesis of lexical synonymy among affixes against the data, let us review the LMBM position with respect to the three diagnostics of lexical synonymy in (4.10), comparing its predictions against those of lexical synonymy. First, since Separation allows several affixes to mark a single L-derivation in different contexts, LMBM predicts absolute, not approximate, synonymy among morphological forms. The meanings of affixes and other morphological modifications are invariable, universal grammatical functions, not prototypical referential categories. "Synonymous" affixes should express specific grammatical functions like Diminutive and Neuter without categorial "fuzziness".

Morphological synonymy should result from derivationally determined Gender, which does not vary with suffix selection. Since derivation determines meaning and affixes are semantically empty, derivation should determine Gender and Diminution, and these categories should remain consistent across all suffixes marking the same derivation. If the Diminutive derivation adjusts the Gender features to Neuter, whatever affix is selected, it must reflect Neuter Gender.

Finally, since L-derivation and affix spelling are independent in an LMBM model, derivation does not depend on affixation and affixation is not totally dependent upon derivation. This additional power of the LMBM model makes the model capable of zero and empty morphology. Indeed, all morphological spelling is empty in the sense that morphological modifications themselves never determine "meaning" in any sense of the word, that is, in grammatical function or referential category. It follows that unlike compounding, derivational marking may be omitted under certain circumstances.

LMBM offers a sharp contrast to the predictions of LMH on affixal synonymy; as described in (4.11), it differs on all three of the points describing lexical synonymy in (4.10):

(4.11) a. affix synonymy should be absolute, not approximate;
   b. lexical categorization should vary with derivation, not affixation;
   c. derivational features should not be dependent upon affixation.

The two positions could not be more clearly distinguished. With these two positions and their predictions about the nature of affixal synonymy in mind, let us now examine some telling data on IE word formation.

4.3 Testing the LMH and LMBM Positions

To test the predictions of the Empty Morpheme Entailment of LMBM against the Lexical Synonymy Hypothesis of LMH, we will begin by examining two IE lexical derivations, which are marked in each language by several ostensibly synonymous suffixes. Beard (1988) pointed out that the abstract deadjectival nominals throughout the Western IE languages is consistently marked as grammatically Feminine.[3] The meaning (or lack of meaning) of the derivation in Table 4.1 is not only absolutely the same within each language but across languages as well.[4]

For the LMH position, the examples of Table 4.1 should follow the

Table 4.1 Deadjectival Nominalizations in Four IE Languages

Italian	*German*	*Russian*	*French*
la fals-ità	die Krank-heit	mjagk-ost' [F]	la moit-eur
la facond-ia	die Fähig-keit	slep-ot-a [F]	la différen-ce
la lucent-ezza	die Naiv-ität	tiš-in-a [F]	la modern-ité
la brav-ura	die Finster-nis	bel-izn-a [F]	la faibl-esse
la stupid-aggine	die Tief-e	sin' [F]	la avar-ice

pattern of (4.5). But the LMH predictions fail, since synonymy here is absolute, not the approximate synonymy of lexical items. If we assume the affixes have meaning that depends upon a referential category, the meaning of each of these affixes would be something like "the quality of being *A*". In fact, this meaning is predictable, given the assumption that the derivation rule controlling affixation simply reclassifies the base from A to N. But this does not affect the problem, which is that each of the affixes in the table have precisely, not approximately, the same function, as predicted by (4.11a).

Second, all the nouns of Table 4.1 are Feminine and change the category of the adjective to that of noun and nothing else in every case, regardless of the suffix used and regardless of its productivity. Therefore, if they are lexical items, their subcategorization is in every case identical, contra the prediction of (4.10b), as illustrated in Table 4.2:

Table 4.2   Lexical Categorization of French Deadjectival Suffixes

-esse	-eur	-ité	-ce	-ice
$\begin{bmatrix} +\text{Noun} \\ +\text{Fem} \\ \text{Adj}\_\_ \end{bmatrix}$	$\begin{bmatrix} +\text{Noun} \\ +\text{Fem} \\ \text{Adj}\_\_ \end{bmatrix}$	$\begin{bmatrix} +\text{Noun} \\ +\text{Fem} \\ \text{Adj}\_\_ \end{bmatrix}$	$\begin{bmatrix} +\text{Noun} \\ +\text{Fem} \\ \text{Adj}\_\_ \end{bmatrix}$	$\begin{bmatrix} +\text{Noun} \\ +\text{Fem} \\ \text{Adj}\_\_ \end{bmatrix}$

On the one hand, if the grammatical Gender of a lexical derivation is determined by that of the suffix, no reason exists for the consistent association of Femininity. We have already concluded that such a lexical pattern, while possible, would be accidental, as in (4.5–4.6). The consistency of the data in Table 4.2 suggests that the rule A → N itself, not the suffixes marking it, provides the Femininity.[5]

The claim that the lexical representations of these suffixes coincidentally associate Feminine with nominalization and are fortuitously synonymous, as in the case with the German words for soups in (4.5), is blocked two ways. First, these affixes are often capable of reflecting more than one Gender, yet consistently reflect Feminine only when associated with this derivation. The productive French suffix *-eur* listed in Table 4.1, for example, just as productively marks Masculine Subjective nominals, as in *le fum-eur* "smoker", *le lis-eur* "reader". Within LMH such cases would be treated as homonymous affixes of varying Gender, despite the problems with unfalsifiable theoretical affixal homonymy discussed in section 2.3.3. However, even were we willing to allow the proliferation of affixes that this assumption implies, it would be a truly remarkable coincidence that the homonym with the Gender that fits the abstract paradigm is chosen in every instance. Finally, the Gender predicted by the LMBM derivation rule is present even in the absence of any affix at all in Table 4.2, that is, in instances of zero morphology. Both of these problems deserve detailed examination.

4.3.1 Homonymous Affixes

French *-eur* and German *-nis* are two examples of suffixes from Table 4.1 that are not always Feminine; both *-eur* and *-nis* occur elsewhere as noun affixes bearing another Gender (recall also *-el* in fn. 1). Compare the functions of these suffixes in (4.12) and (4.13) with their functions in Table 4.1:

(4.12)   a. **Das** Erzeug-nis "product(ion)"
　　　　 b. **Das** Bekennt-nis "confession"
　　　　 c. **Das** Verhält-nis "relation"

(4.13)   a. **Le** lis-eur "reader"
　　　　 b. **Le** fum-eur "smoker"
　　　　 c. **Le** chant-eur "singer"

The suffixes *-eur* and *-nis* have no fixed Gender yet they do not pass on the Gender of the underlying lexical bases, which are verbal in both instances. Rather, the Gender of derivates expressed by these affixes clearly varies with derivational function.

The only alternative to the conclusion of LMBM, that the affixes are semantically empty, with the categorial status of their derivates determined by derivation, is that *-eur* and *-nis* represent independent homonyms: *-eur*$_{Fem}$, *-eur*$_{Mas}$; *-nis*$_{Fem}$, *-nis*$_{Mas}$. Treating the various functions of *-eur* and *-nis* as homonyms, however, runs into at least four problems: (i) an unjustified proliferation of affixes (ii) which are theoretically asserted contrary to all phonological evidence, (iii) circularity in the argument, and (iv) a lack of any basis for choosing between homonymy and an equally plausible theory of polysemy. Let us examine these problems one by one.

The extent of the proliferation of affixes occasioned by theoretical homonymy can hardly be exaggerated; in addition to the Masculine and Feminine uses of French *-eur*, this affix is also used adjectivally: *migrateur, migrat-euse* "migratory". If *-eur* is a lexical morpheme, then it is at least three, with lexical listings like those illustrated in Table 4.3.

Table 4.3　　French *-eur* as Homonyms

-eur$_1$	-eur$_2$	-eur$_3$
$\begin{bmatrix} +\text{Noun} \\ -\text{Fem} \\ \text{Agentive} \end{bmatrix}$	$\begin{bmatrix} +\text{Noun} \\ +\text{Fem} \\ \text{Abstract} \end{bmatrix}$	$\begin{bmatrix} +\text{Adj} \\ -\text{Fem} \\ \dots \end{bmatrix}$

(2.17–2.20) illustrate seven distinct functions of English *-ing,* ranging over inflection and derivation and including the recategorization of verbs into nouns, adjectives, and adverbs. German *-en* has many more functions. Beard (1985) points out that 80% of the 28 productive German suffixes have more than one function and even in an agglutinative language like Turkish, 35 of 65 productive suffixes have more than one function. Thus, the scope of the problem is significant and will result in doubling or tripling the number of affixes in each inflectional language. If such proliferation is justified, it must be accepted. To what extent then is it justified?

Phonologically, the homonymous suffixes of Table 4.3 are unitary and historically always have been; there is no synchronic or diachronic phono-logical justification for postulating homonyms. Section 2.3.3 introduced historical and synchronic evidence that *-er* and *-ing* represent two homony-mous suffixes in English. The historical evidence was earlier spellings of the Subjective marker as *-ere* and the comparative, *-re* and *-ra.* Synchroni-cally, at least one dialect of US English does not drop the velar before the comparative *-er* but does before the Subjective, so that the phonetic realiza-tion of *longer* and *singer* are [lɔŋ-er] and [siŋg-er], respectively. The suf-fixes of (4.12), (4.13), and Table 4.3 exhibit no such diachronic or syn-chronic tendencies.

Without some phonological support, the argument for homonymy be-comes circular. The only basis for concluding that the suffixes of (4.12) and (4.13) represent different homonymous morphemes is that they have different meanings. Differences in meaning, however, may not be used as an argument for concluding two independent lexical morphemes. The question here is whether the two different meanings indicate two discrete morphemes despite phonological identity. An argument designed to ex-plain two unexpected meanings of an ostensibly single lexical item cannot conclude from the assumption of the independence of the meanings that two lexical items exist.

Beard (1987a, 1988) discusses in detail the difficulty facing LMH in mounting a case for either homonymy or polysemy as a solution to the problem of mapping grammatical categories to phonological expressions. Without synchronic phonological evidence of individual affixes, it be-comes impossible to confirm or disconfirm the claim that such affixes enjoy the relationship in (4.14) rather than that in (4.15):

(4.14)   (4.15)

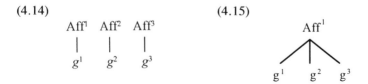

(4.14) illustrates homonymy while (4.15) illustrates polysemy. (4.14) distinguishes affixes in a purely theoretical sense, matched with grammatical functions that are empirically distinct. (4.15) represents the phonological identity of the affix, but misrepresents the identity of the grammatical functions, since the same functions will be represented as lexical accidents of other such affixes under morphological asymmetry. (4.14) loses both the phonological identity of the affixes Aff[1–3] as well as the identity of the functions, which are shared with other affixes. Without empirical evidence such as allomorphic variations, no empirical basis for choosing between these two solutions is available to LMH. In the absence of empirical motivation, no basis exists for arguing a preference for homonymy over a theory of polysemy; the selection of either approach must be made on a strictly ad hoc basis. So, in addition to requiring ancillary theories of purely theoretical homonymy and synonymy, there is no theoretical basis for LMH selecting either of the two.

LMBM theories posit only one derivation rule per derivation, for example, denominal adjective, deverbal Agentive, deadjectival nominal. The morphological spelling device (Figure 3.4) may then represent the suffix *-eur* as one operation with complex conditions on insertion along lines suggested in (4.16).[6]

(4.16)

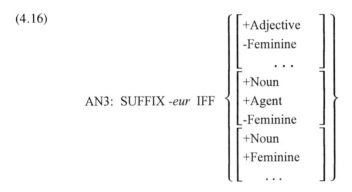

$$\text{AN3: SUFFIX } \textit{-eur} \text{ IFF } \left\{ \begin{array}{l} \left[\begin{array}{l} +\text{Adjective} \\ -\text{Feminine} \\ \quad \cdots \end{array}\right] \\ \left[\begin{array}{l} +\text{Noun} \\ +\text{Agent} \\ -\text{Feminine} \end{array}\right] \\ \left[\begin{array}{l} +\text{Noun} \\ +\text{Feminine} \\ \quad \cdots \end{array}\right] \end{array} \right\}$$

Since the LMBM model posits a single suffix *-eur*, it avoids the otherwise mysterious proliferation of pseudohomonymous lexical entries.

4.3.2 Zero Morphology

The second barrier to treating the suffixes of Table 4.2 as coincidental lexical synonyms is zero morphology. Whatever accounts for the change of class and Gender in Table 4.1, it cannot be the suffix, for the German and Russian examples at the bottom of their columns show no affixes. Moreover, Principle I prevents any definition of zero morphemes as objects without phonological description which may be listed in the lexicon. LMH simply fails in all respects to account for zero morphology; little more can be added to chapter 2's criticism. LMBM, however, predicts that the failure of MS-rules such as that depicted in (4.16) has no effect on the Gender of the derivation; class and Gender are provided independently by the deadjectival nominalization rule. Hence, forms like German *die Tiefe* "depth" and Russian *sin'* "blue(ness)"), from *sin'-ij* "blue", still receive regular Feminine features even though the MS-component assigns them no morphological marking whatever.

Even the exceptional behavior of some of these nominals does not deter LMBM. Although we find some zero nominals based on color adjectives in the Feminine in German (*die Röte* "red(ness)", *die Schwärze* "black(ness)"), and affixed Feminines in French (*la blanch-eur* "white-(ness)", *la roug-eur* "red(ness)), the Gender of these nominals is optionally Neuter in German and Masculine in French, with zero morphology.

(4.17)   a. **Das** Gelb, Grün, Rot, Blau, Schwarz, Weiß
         b. **Le** jaune, vert, rouge, bleu, noir, blanc

Again, however, whatever determines the Gender of these nouns, it cannot be the affix required by LMH, for no affix appears in these examples. LMH simply has no basis for postulating zero lexical items nor any justification for deriving them. LMBM, on the other hand, accounts for the Gender variation in (4.17), not on the basis of any affix, but on the basis of the semantic categorization of the base. A language-specific, optional condition on the L-derivation rule such as (4.18a) for French and (4.18b) for German readily accounts for the marked Gender of the nominalizations of the color adjectives in these languages.

(4.18)   a. IFF r = [COLOR] THEN g = [+ Masculine]
         b. IFF r = [COLOR] THEN g = [+ Neuter]

Since the selection of Gender in these nominals is determined by the semantic category of the underlying adjective, (4.18) represents conditions on the derivation of these nouns and has nothing to do with affixation—an account in complete accord with the evidence.

4.4 FURTHER EVIDENCE OF THE EMPTY MORPHEME ENTAILMENT

Having established a prima facie case for the Empty Morpheme Entailment, let us now examine a few more cases of this phenomenon in the IE languages. This section will first examine an obvious case where derivation and not affixation determines Gender: the Animate Subjective (Agentive) derivation and femininization. It will then return to the examples of the

Slavic Locative nominalization, which seem to reflect all three Genders (see (4.9)). Finally, it will examine the Perfective nominalizations in IE languages, which also appear to vacillate between all three Genders in a much more problematic way than the Slavic Locative.

4.4.1 The IE Masculine and Feminine Subjective Nominalizations

The most obvious piece of evidence in support of the Empty Morpheme Entailment is the distribution of Masculine and Feminine Subjective suffixes. For the sake of expediency, let us refer in this section to the subset of Animate Subjective derivations by their traditional term, ''Agentive nominalizations.'' To understand them, we will have to anticipate some of the contents of chapter 5, which deals with the nature of inflectional categories. Chapter 5 will distinguish the two common meanings of the traditional term Gender: NATURAL GENDER, which distinguishes male and female references, and NOUN CLASSES, arbitrary lexical subclasses of nouns including the nominal classes of Bantu and Niger-Congo languages. What has been referred to as Gender up to now in this book has not been Natural Gender but simply Noun Class. It is true that Noun Class is sometimes used to distinguish Genders; however, this function of Noun Class is not consistent, as the Russian examples in (4.19) demonstrate.

(4.19)   a. bol'š-aja   knig-a   ležal-a   na divane
          big-FEM   book-CLS2 lay   on sofa
          ''the big book was lying on the sofa''

          b. leniv-aja   devušk-a   ležal-a   na divane
          lazy-FEM   girl-FEMCLS2 lay   on   sofa
          ''the lazy girl was lying on the sofa''

          c. leniv-yj djadj-a   ležal-∅ na divane
          lazy-MAS uncle-MASCLS2   lay   on sofa
          ''the lazy uncle was lying on the sofa''

Let (4.19) pass for a tentative demonstration that Noun Class (CLS1, Cls2, and so on) and Gender are independent grammatical categories. The point is simply that the sex of a reference cannot be predicted by Noun Class because not all references belonging to the Feminine Noun Class 2 in Russian are female (4.19a). Moreover, it is possible for words referring to male objects to belong to that Noun Class 2 (4.19c).

The Agentive nominalization in Russian is marked by the suffixes listed in (4.20) and (4.21) among others. Notice that all the examples of (4.20) are Masculine and belong to Class 1, to which only Masculine and Neuter nouns belong (Neuter nouns end in /o/ or /e/; Masculine nouns end in bare consonants). Those in (4.21) are Masculine or Feminine and belong

to Class 2, identified by the final /a/ in the NomSg. Only Feminine nouns
and a subclass of Masculine nouns which may refer to females or males
belong to Class 2.

(4.20) a. upak-ova-   upak-ov-ščik "packer"
        b. pis-a-   pisa-tel' "writer"
        c. klevet-aj-   klevet-nik "slanderer"
        d. assist-ir-ova-   assist-ent "assistant"

(4.21) a. brod-i-   brod-jag-a "wanderer"
        b. vorot-i-   voroti-l-a "boss, bossy person"
        c. p'j-   p'j-an-ic-a "a drunk"

While it is difficult to predict which suffix will be used to mark the Agentive nominalization in Russian, the Gender is always predictable: Masculine. The reason for this is that this nominalization adds Animacy to verbs and Masculine is the default Gender expressing Animacy.

As unmarked Masculine nouns, the nominalizations in (4.20) may refer either to females or males. A special Feminine form, derived from the Masculine nouns of Class 1, refers exclusively to females. That variant always belongs to Class 2, whose Nominative ends in -*a*. Of course, if the derivate already belongs to Class 2, as in the case of (4.21), no morphological adjustment is required to mark Femininization, so that the 260-odd Pejorative Agentives and hypocoristics of Class 2, exemplified in (4.21), may refer exclusively to males or exclusively to females. Those of (4.20), however, require further stem modification, which (4.22) illustrates, to refer exclusively to females.

(4.22) a. upakov-ščic-a   "packer (Feminine)"
        b. pisa-tel'-nic-a   "writer (Feminine)"
        c. klevet-nic-a   "slanderer (Feminine)"
        d. assist-ent-k-a   "assistant (Feminine)"

In (4.22) the Gender value of (4.20) has been switched to exclusive Feminine, so the suffixation must reflect Femininity. Thus, Agentive derivates of the Masculine Declension Class 1 must be accorded a marker capable of expressing the Feminine Declension Class 2 (NomSg -*a*), hence the second suffix with a citation form ending in /a/.

If Gender in Agentive nominalizations were determined by the suffixes selected, we would expect an even distribution of such nominalizations across Masculine and Feminine, for Russian has Feminine Agentive suffixes. Belousov et al. (1989, 49–50), indeed, list 11 exceptional Agentives, which they claim are basically Feminine and not Masculine, including those in (4.23).

(4.23)   a. bolt-aj- "chatter" bolt-ušk-a "chatterbox"
            b. sid-e- "sit"   side-lk-a "a sitter" (= medical assistant)
            c. š'j- "sew"   šv-ej-a "seamstress"

The only motivation for assuming that these Agentives are Feminine, however, is social prejudice. Otherwise, nothing formal or categorial distinguishes them from the examples in (4.21).

If affixes were lexically defined in terms of arbitrary lexical items, there would be no reason why affixed Agentives, which by definition may be both Masculine and Feminine, are consistently Masculine, with corresponding Feminine forms derived from them. At best, we find some marginal forms which are both Masculine and Feminine simultaneously. If affixes were essentially idiosyncratic lexical items, some language should have some Agentive suffix that generates a basically Feminine form which could in turn be converted to a Masculine form by affixation. Since both Feminine and Masculine suffixes are available, the consistent choice of Masculine across such a wide range of possible suffixes must reflect the fact that the Agentive derivation, not the affixation, assigns Gender.

4.4.2 The Slavic Locative Nominalizations

The Locative nominalizations of Serbo-Croatian, Polish, and Ukrainian present ostensible problems for the Empty Morpheme Entailment. The grammatical gender of Locative nominals in these languages, in complete accord with the Lexical Morpheme Hypothesis, (i) is always marked by phonologically real affixes (ii) representing all three Genders, which (iii) ostensibly have only approximately identical meanings.

(4.24)   a. knjig-a "book"   knjiž-n-ic-a [F] "library"
            b. raž "rye"   raž-išt-e [N] "rye field"
            c. gus-k-a "goose"   gus-in-jak [M] "goose pen"

All the examples in (4.24) represent a productive Locative nominalization in contemporary Serbo-Croatian. Forms on *-nica* seem to mean "place **in** which" while those on *-ište* seem to mean "place **on** which", and the Masculine forms on *-in-jak* and other suffixes refer to places where animals are kept. LMH is seemingly substantiated by the variation in meaning, paralleled by the variation in Gender. However, closer examination demonstrates that patterns of meaning-Gender association persist which cannot be explained by affixes.

Unlike other IE languages, which exhibit a single Locative nominal referring to a location "in", for example, English *bakery,* Slavic languages have two Locative nominalizations, an *in*-Locative, meaning "place **in** which" and an *on*-Locative, meaning "place **on** which". Table 4.4 illustrates the distinction (see section 13.4.3 for an account of this semantic division).[7]

Table 4.4   "On" and "In" Locative Nominals in Serbo-Croatian

čekal- "wait"	čekal-išt-e "waiting area, hunting blind"
	čekao-nic-a "waiting room"
igral- "play, dance"	igral-išt-e "playground"
	igrao-nic-a "dance hall, casino"
radil- "work"	radil-ište "work site"
	radio-nic-a "workshop"
vežbal- "exercise"	vežbal-išt-e "training field"
	vežbao-nic-a "gymnasium"

Assuming with Žepić (1970) and others that the *in*-Locative means "small, enclosed place of N" and the *on*-Locative means "(large, open) place of N", either hypothesis predicts the data. Since two derivations are necessary, either the derivations or the suffixes could assign Gender appropriately. The *on*-derivation is consistently associated with the Neuter suffix *-ište*; the *in*-derivation, however, is associated with the range of consistently Feminine affixes exemplified in (4.25).

(4.25) a. igao "needle"   igl-ar-a, igl-ar-ic-a "pin cushion"
        b. pepeo "ashes"   pepel-jar-a "ash-tray"
        c. pil-a "saw"   pil-an-a "sawmill"
        d. račun-i- "calculate" račun-ic-a "arithmetic notebook"
        e. rafin-ir-aj- "refine" rafin-er-ij-a "refinery"

Even the idiomatic variations like *računica* "arithmetic book" reveal Feminine grammatical Gender. This distinction could be determined by derivation or affixation. However, scrutiny tilts the scales toward LMBM.

Most striking are those *in*-Locatives illustrated in Table 4.5 which, like the French examples in *-eur,* are marked with Masculine Agentive suffix *-ar* simply declined in the Feminine Class 2 paradigm: *-ara, -are, -ari,* and so on, instead of the Masculine Class 1, *-ar, -ara, -aru,* and so on.[8]

Table 4.5   The Serbo-Croatian Suffix -ar

mes-o	mes-ar	mes-ar-a
"meat"	"butcher"	"meatshop"
pek-	pek-ar	pek-ar-a
"bake"	"baker"	"bakery"
knjig-a	knjiž-ar	knjiž-ar-a
"book"	"book dealer"	"bookstore"

The femininization cannot percolate from any suffix here, for the only derivational suffix is *-ar*, which is no more Feminine than Masculine. Feminine not only emerges time after time as an *in*-Locative exponent, but in association with highly productive affixes, which otherwise express grammatical and natural Masculine Gender.

The exceptions to this pattern of Feminine markers on *in*-Locative nominalizations themselves form a subregular pattern. (4.26) illustrates an array of suffixes, *-ac, -n-jak, -in-jak, -ar-n-ik, -n-ik* (the Masculine variant of *-n-ic-a*) plus yet another unusual occurrence of the Agentive suffix *-ar* : *kokoš-ar*, which retains its Masculine Gender even while marking *in*-Locatives.

(4.26)   a. svinj-a "hog"   svinj-ac "pig sty"
          b. golub "dove, pigeon"   golub-ar-n-ik, golub-n-jak
                                       "dovecote"
          c. gusk-a "goose"   gušč-ak, gušč-ar-nik, gus-in-jak
                                       "goose pen"
          d. kokoš "chicken"   kokoš-ar-n-ik, kokoš-in-j-ac,
                                       kokoš-in-jak, kokoš-ar [!]
                                       "chicken coop"
          e. žab-a "frog"   žab-n-jak, žab-ljak "frog pond"

Some of the deanimate *in*-Locatives allow up to four suffixes, varying among speakers and dialects of Serbo-Croatian, yet all are Masculine.

The association of Masculine with *in*-Locatives based on Animate nouns in a Slavic language comes as no surprise in the LMBM framework, given the fact that Masculine is the default Gender for Animate nouns. Obviously, the common factor in (4.26) is that all the bases are Animate. Again we see a variation in Gender motivated not by the affixation, for the affixation is, as usual, quite varied, but by the lexical features of the base.

LMH would have to postulate an astounding lexical coincidence to account for the fact that, given the rich variation in the selection of suffixes to mark the Locative L-derivates in Serbo-Croatian, Feminine (Class 2) suffixes are consistently chosen unless the base happens to be Animate. In the latter case, regardless of the grammatical Gender of the base, Masculine (Class 1) suffixes are consistently chosen.

Exceptions to the subregularity reflected in (4.27), as might be expected under the assumptions of LMBM, follow the inanimate pattern.

(4.27) a. ovc-a "sheep"   ovč-ar-a "sheep pen"
        b. koz-a "goat"   koz-ar-a, koz-ar-ic-a "goat pen"
        c. krav-a "cow"   krav-ar-a "cowshed"

These examples exhibit the default, inanimate Feminine affixation of Locative nominalizations. However, the story does not end here. Milojević (1934) points out that terms like *konj-ar-nik* often occur in speech and Masculine forms with *-ar-nik* are acceptable to him as substitutes for all the Feminine exceptions in (4.27).

(4.28) a. ovč-ar-nik "sheep pen"
        b. koz-ar-nik "goat pen"
        c. krav-ar-nik "cow shed"

We can only conclude that Masculinity is productively associated with *in*-Locatives derived from Animate nouns, following the association of Animacy and Masculine Gender in inflectional usage. Otherwise, *in*-Locatives are assigned to Class 2 (Feminine) and *on*-Locatives are assigned to Class 1 (Neuter). The exceptions to this characterization account for no more than 1%–2% of attested forms and hence qualify as lexical exceptions. The forms of (4.27) are lexicalized idioms whose Femininity nonetheless varies in the contemporary language, with regular Masculinity predicted by the straightforward LMBM interpretation presented here. No evidence indicates that affixation is responsible for Gender and Noun Class; hearty evidence supports the LMBM hypothesis that the lexical base and derivation account for Gender and Noun Class.

4.4.3 The IE Perfective Nominalization

IE languages exhibit a rich variety of deverbal nominalizations based on argument and adverbal relations, for example, Subjective, Objective, Instrumental, Locative, and Measure. Among them we find the ACTION NOMINALIZATION, which is productively marked in German with *-ung,* a suffix always associated with the Feminine declension. (4.29) illustrates the action nominalization in German. The semantic interpretations are to be taken in the sense of "an instance of V-ing" where "V" refers to the meaning of the underlying base.

(4.29) a. mein-en "to mean" die Mein-ung "the meaning"
        b. land-en "to land" die Land-ung "the landing"
        c. erwerb-en "to acquire" die Erwerb-ung "the acquisition"

Other action nominalizations, that is, nominalizations with precisely the same grammatical function and distribution, appear in the Masculine.[9]

(4.30) a. blick-en "to look" der Blick "the look"
        b. schrei-en "to scream" der Schrei "the scream"
        c. erwerb-en "to acquire" der Erwerb "the acquisition"

Notice also the occasional appearance of pairs with the meaning under consideration here, consisting of a derivate with the suffix *-ung* in the Feminine and a Masculine derivate without a suffix (Fleischer 1975: 169):

(4.31) a. die Erwerbung : der Erwerb "acquisition"
        b. die Erweisung : der Erweis "proof"
        c. die Beschießung : der Beschuß "firing, bombardment"

If the action nominal derivation determines the Gender of the derivate, how is it possible that some of these derivates are Feminine, while others are Masculine?

The first point to make is, again, that whatever the origin of Masculinity in (4.30) and (4.31), it is not the suffix, for there is no suffix or it is optional. Therefore, LMH is embarrassed here, too.[10] If we wish a consistent universal theory of the origin of grammatical categories in word formation, we must further assume that *-ung* does not provide Femininity for the derivations which it marks, but is merely associated with the Feminine Noun Class due to its consistent selection by the MS-component as a Feminine marker. The situation is nonetheless serious for the LMBM position, too, for LMBM claims that these forms share one derivation in common and hence should share the same Gender. What account, then, is available within the LMBM framework for the Gender disparity in (4.29–4.30)?

The omissively marked action nominals are found throughout the IE languages, for example, English *to walk* : *a walk;* French *regarder* "look at" : *le regard* "the look, glance"; Russian *vypusk-at'* "to launch": *vypusk* (Mas) "a launch". German and Russian are presently replacing this omissive marking with a Feminine suffix. (4.32) exemplifies productive action nominalizations in German and (4.33), in Russian.

(4.32) a. präfigier-en "to prefix"   Präfig-ier-ung "prefixation"
        b. spezifizier-en "to specialize" Spezifiz-ier-ung "specification"
        c. prämier-en   "to award"   Präm-ier-ung   "award"

(4.33) a. pakova-t' "to pack"   pakov-k-a "packing"
        b. sortirova-t' "to sort" sortirov-k-a "sorting"
        c. planirova-t' "to plan" planirov-k-a "planning"

The differences in productivity between the Feminine forms in German and Russian suggest that the cause of the Gender disparity in these derivations may be historical, which is to say, lexical.

The Masculine forms are associated with a relatively large subset of subregular STRONG VERBS in the Germanic languages. That is, the base verbs comprise an exceptional set; hence, we should not be surprised that the nominals derived from them are also exceptional. The Masculine forms are historical remnants of an earlier version of the action nominalization rule, which assigned Masculine rather than Feminine Gender. The action nominalizations of strong verbs thus have become lexicalized and idiomatized, and synchronically are either listed independently in the lexicon or require a special subset of rules to derive them from the irregular subclass of verbs from which they are derived. The strong verb/weak verb distinction persists in many of the IE language families; it is only natural that the Ablaut-marked nominalizations of these verbs would also survive.

The question remains: how does grammar account for such a situation? Of course, we could simply list all the historical forms with their stems in the lexicon as idioms. That form is then simply mapped onto the terminal node by derivation, leaving the MS-component nothing to do. This would allow the derivation rule to operate while switching off the speller. However, since strong verbs must be lexically marked in any event, we could postulate a lexical marker specifying them as [+Masculine] or use the feature identifying its conjugational Ablaut type to predict its nominal form, as in [+/i/ > /u/]; often they are the same. Either type of lexical marking could trigger the action nominal L-derivation rule (a FEATURE SWITCH; see chapter 7) to switch on Masculine rather than Feminine Gender, under the assumption that lexical features take precedence over rule-determined features. The MS-component would then respond appropriately to these features.

The whole purpose of separating derivation from morphological spelling in LMBM is to allow the capture of even those derivational generalizations not reflected in affixation. LMBM would lose much of its appeal if it could not capture the derivational generalization of the grammatical function associated with the action nominals in the face of affixational irregularity. LMBM does just this even among exceptional classes and hence retains its advantage over LMH.

4.5 OTHER DETERMINANTS OF GENDER

It does not follow from the fact that derivation rules can determine Gender that they always do. Although in German the Diminutive derivation determines Gender (4.1), in general the Gender of Diminutives is determined by the base. Unlike the Locative derivations, which are determined by the combination of the Locative derivation plus the Gender of the base, the Gender of Italian (4.34) and Russian (4.35) Diminutives is determined exclusively by the Gender of the base:

(4.34)   a. il bimb-o : il bimb-ett-o   "baby" (Masculine)
          b. la bimb-a : la bimb-ett-a "baby" (Feminine)

(4.35)   a. komnat-a : komnat-k-a   "room" (Feminine)
          b. stol : stol-ik   "table" (Masculine)
          c. molok-o : moloč-k-o   "milk" (Neuter)

In neither case, however, can one say that the suffix itself provides Gender; it merely reflects Gender either transparently, as in the Italian and Russian cases, or by virtue of its association with Neuter declension paradigms, as in the case of German. The important point is that the Gender of expressive derivations must be accounted for by means other than the affixes assigned to them.

The Pashto deadjectival nominals seem to represent another violation of the Empty Morpheme Entailment. (4.36) illustrates that in Pashto the deadjectival nominals are sometimes Feminine, sometimes Masculine and sometimes both, if they are capable of receiving two different suffixes.

(4.36)   a. ārām "quiet"   ārām-i [F] "quietness"
          b. zṛə-vər "brave"   zṛə-vər-tiā [F] "bravery"
          c. zṛə-vər "brave"   zṛə-vər-tob [M] "bravery"
          d. klak "firm"   klak-vālay [M] "firmness"

If the suffixes *-tiā* and *-tob* were lexical items in an LMH model, the former classified as Feminine, the latter, as Masculine, examples like the pair *zṛə-vər-tiā* : *zṛə-vər-tob* would receive a simple and lucid account. While this account is not available to LMBM, another, more telling account is available to both models.

Remember that "Gender" now refers strictly to grammatical rather than natural Gender, and will be called "Noun Class" from chapter 5 on.

In Pashto, the Noun Class of inanimate nouns is determined phonologically. That is, no grammatical or semantic information is involved in the determination of Noun Class in the derivations in (4.36), hence no reference to Noun Class is required of these derivations in order for them to be assigned to the correct declension. Pashto has only two cases in each of two nominal declensions. Words ending on any vowel, with the exception of /u/ or the diphthong /əj/, are assigned to the "Feminine" declension; others are declined in accord with the "Masculine." So long as the MS-component supplies all the derivational affixes prior to inserting inflectional markers, the proper desinence can be assigned to the derived noun and any agreeing adjectives without reference to derivation or Noun Class on a purely phonological basis.

4.6 CONCLUSION

It is generally accepted in the scientific community that of two competing theories, the one that accounts for the data with the structure of the theory itself is preferable to one which requiring ancillary subtheories. We have seen here that lexical morphemes account for the phenomena of Gender-specific lexical derivations, but only by introducing ancillary theories of zero morphology, theoretical homonymy, synonymy, conversion, and others. In so doing, the lexical morpheme assumption either erodes or moves toward that of the Separation Hypothesis of LMBM. Whether ancillary subtheories accrue to it or the crucial, definitional distinctions between the two positions disappear— either way, LMH loses its appeal. LMBM, with its empty morphemes, on the other hand, accounts for the limited range of morphological phenomena explained by the lexical morpheme, plus the phenomena of derivationally determined Gender, including zero-marked Gender, without the addition of theoretical accretions. It would therefore seem to be the more elegant and explanatory theoretical framework of the two.

The Empty Morpheme Entailment is not an intuitive claim about morphological behavior; rather, it is quite startling. Without the separation of derivation from affixation, the generalization which it represents is not even visible. In the LMH framework, it is disguised as lexical synonymy and homonymy. The evidence therefore must strongly support it, evidence which must overcome our intuitive rejection of such a radical proposal. Yet the evidence does lavishly support empty morphemes in the strongest version, namely, that morphemes have neither semantic nor grammatical content. Where it does not seem to hold, in the case of action nominalizations, the alternative hypothesis does not hold either, for action nominalizations are frequently not marked by affixation at all.

To thoroughly demonstrate the viability of LMBM, we next need to clarify the derivational operations of the syntax and the lexicon. This presupposes an understanding of the categories involved in those operations, that is, the categories of the lexical and inflectional grammatical representations of lexemes. The next step then is to enumerate and define the G-categories of grammatical functions involved in I- and L-derivation. The following three chapters are dedicated to this task.

NOTES

1. The last suffix presents an interesting problem for LMH, for elsewhere this same suffix marks grammatically Masculine nouns: *der Heb-el* "lever", *der Schleg-el* "clapper," *der Deck-el* "lid, bookcover". The traditional account for these two functions of the phonologically identical suffix *-el* is that they represent two homonymous suffixes. However, morphological homonymy differs in significant respects from lexical homonymy, so we must return to this point and examine it in more detail (see section 4.3.1).

2. Dieter Kastovsky has pointed out (personal communication 1988) that colloquial German usage does allow such spontaneous clippings as *eine Weiß* (= *Weißwurst*), *eine Brat* (= *Bratwurst*). However, in these instances the stem of the head noun, *Wurst,* is simply stylistically optional, not universally omitted; it is still more common to use the entire compound. The null variant hence is not contrastive and thus is not a lexical or morphological marker. Since such usage is restricted to a few frequently used compounds, the phenomenon must be a spontaneous clipping, a performance process, not a grammatical one (Beard 1987b).

3. Every language, of course, has a few deadjectival nominals with Genders other than Feminine. Russian has perhaps a half-dozen such Neuter derivations (*bogat-stvo* "richness"; *zdorov-'e* "health"), and French has a similar number, not counting the color nouns, which are Masculine (*le chaud* "warmth"; *le froid* and *la froidure* "the cold"). The minute numbers and idiosyncratic usages of such exceptions, plus their high usage frequency, identify them as lexical exceptions.

4. Keep in mind that each example in Table 4.1 represents a significant class of derivations with the same suffix, most of which are productive.

5. The disparity between the regularity of derivational and spelling operations is not unusual. Derivation rules are much more regular than affixation rules because they are universal, while affixation rules are language-specific. Tables 13.2–13.3 and the surrounding text provide evidence and an explanation.

6. In chapter 3 we saw that while some of the MS-operations of Figure 3.4 are specifically N, V, or A spelling rules, some affix operations apply

to mixed classes. English *-er,* for example, may be added to verbs to mark Agentive nominalizations, as in *to warm : a warm-er* and to adjectives to mark Comparative Degree, as in *warm : warmer.* Chukchee has a "participle" suffix which accrues to N, V, or A stems (see 3.15) and will have no classification. Chapter 3 assumes that such affixational operations will be listed under mixed prefixes, as NA27 and NAV27 in the speller.

7. The base verbs in the Serbo-Croatian in Table 4.4 and the examples which follow are presented in their Past Tense stem form where this form serves as the base for Locative nominalizations; otherwise, the citation form is provided. The liquid /l/ is regularly replaced by /o/ unless followed by a vowel.

8. Some grammars suggest that forms like those of Table 4.5 are derived from the corresponding Agentives, for example, *mes-ar* "butcher": *mes-ar-a* "butcher shop". This is unlikely, however, since Agentives are not always available for Locatives, for example, *radi-o-nica* "workshop" from *radi-ti* "to work", whose Agentive is *rad-nik;* in addition, they are often irrelevant when available, as in *igl-ar* "needle-maker": *igl-ar-a* "pin cushion"; *ovč-ar* "shepherd": *ovč-ar-a* "sheep pen, barn". Such a derivational path would make the LMH position even more difficult given that /-a/ is not a derivational affix but a NomSg Noun Class 2 desinence and *-ar* is a productive Masculine Agentive suffix.

9. This suffix tends to mark a "Perfective" process nominalization. German, like other IE languages, also has an "Imperfective" process nominalization which uses the same suffix as the Infinitive, for example, *die Landung* "the landing" (countable event, as in Plural *die Landungen*) versus *das Landen* "landing", the process, which allows no Plural: **die Landen(e).* The same distinction often holds between the zero derived Perfective nominals, for example, *der Schrei* "the scream" versus *das Schreien* "screaming" (Fleischer 1975: 170). See section 8.2.6 for another comment on this distinction.

10. Lieber (1992: 160–61) uses the Perfective and Resultative Nominalizations as an argument for conversion, which she defines as "piecemeal" relisting of an item in the lexicon. If conversion is simply relisting, we would expect random Gender as well as random semantics. However, her examples all reflect precisely the same grammatical categories as do affixed nominalizations, for example, *der Ruf* "the call", *der Find* "the find", *der Band* "the bond, binding, bound volume", *der Klang* "the sound", *das Grab* "the grave", *das Band* "ribbon". All are Objective nominalizations of Resultative verbs or simple Perfective nominalizations with the exception of *das Band,* which is an Instrumental. Most are idiomatized but the ability of derived words to idiomatize is not at issue. An idiomatized L-derivation is equivalent to a newly listed lexical item with randomly shifting meaning. Lieber's examples are idiomatizations of consistent, universal L-derivations.

Chapter Five

Nominal Inflectional Categories

5.1 WORD FORMATION VERSUS INFLECTION

Chapters 2 and 3 responded to the first two questions in the agenda of morphology outlined in section 1.3: languages contain two basic types of indicators, lexemes and grammatical morphemes. Chapter 3 began examining the relation between the various representations of these indicators, the phonological, grammatical, and semantic representations. Much remains to be said on both these topics; however, this chapter and the next will move on to the third issue raised in section 1.3, the question of how many morphologies there are.

At this point, the Separation Hypothesis as described in (5.1–5.2) has been established as a fundamental property of LMBM grammars:

(5.1)   Lexical and inflectional derivation are discrete sets of operations.
   a. Lexical (L-) derivation accounts for the grammatical relations of word formation and is carried out in the lexicon.
   b. Inflectional (I-) derivation accounts for the grammatical relations of inflection and is carried out in syntax.

(5.2)   The affixational and other means of marking both L- and I-derivation occur in the morphological spelling (MS-) component, a single, integrated module operating over both types of morphological categories after lexical and syntactic rules have operated but before the operation of phonological rules.

This chapter and the next develop the first point by distinguishing L- from I-processes and then preliminarily indicating where and how they operate. We will not be able to return to the second point until chapters 14 and 15, which will complete the discussion of how the MS-component maps lexical and syntactic derivations onto P-structure begun in chapter 3.

Terminology

In describing derivational and inflectional categories, a terminological problem arises. The term ''derivation'' is generally used to distinguish the grammatical and phonological aspects of word formation from both these aspects of inflection. Hence, the question is usually cast in terms of a single distinction between derivation and inflection. The term ''derivation'' is used in this book in a different sense, to refer to the manipulation of grammatical categories in a lexeme aside from any phonological modification which marks such operations. Since the distinction between ''derivation'' in this sense and ''morphological spelling'' is crucial to the arguments of this chapter, to continue using ''derivation'' in the traditional sense would inevitably lead to confusion.

For this reason, ''word formation'' will be reserved hereafter as the term for traditional ''derivation'', the combined grammatical and phonological modification of lexemes at the lexical level. ''Inflection'' will refer to the combined inflectional operations in the same sense. The new terms ''L-derivation'' and ''I-derivation'' will refer strictly to operations on category features in the lexicon and syntax, respectively, that is, independent of any affixation. ''Morphology'' will be retained for its traditional meaning of all the semantic, grammatical, and phonological operations of morphology, while ''MS-component'', ''MS-rules'', ''MS-operations'' will refer to the specifically phonological modification of stems independent of derivation.

In review, then, the terminology henceforth will be as follows:

morphology	=	traditional morphology: inflection, derivation, affixation
word formation	=	traditional morpholexical derivation and affixation
inflection	=	traditional morphosyntactic derivation and affixation
L-derivation	=	(morpho)lexical category manipulation alone
I-derivation	=	(morpho)syntactic or inflectional category manipulation alone
MS-operations	=	phonological stem modifications and free morpheme selection aside from L- and I-derivation, as in LMBM models

The terms ''class,'' ''category'', and ''function'', on the other hand, will be used close to their traditional Neogrammarian and structuralist meanings:

class	=	lexical class: N, V, A
category	=	categories of grammatical functions: Case, Gender, Tense

function   =   the relations within grammatical categories, Matthews'
                   "properties" and "functions"; for example, (Accu-
                   sative of) Object, Feminine (Gender), Past (Tense).[1]

A grammatical category, therefore, is a category of grammatical functions
in the sense of traditional grammar and Lexical Function Grammar (Bresnan 1982a), the GRAMMATICAL RELATIONS of Relational Grammar, Marantz (1984), and others. Following Matthews' example, the initial letter
of both categories and functions are capitalized, as in Gender, Feminine,
Masculine. Semantic categories are fully capitalized, as in ACTOR,
PLACE, CAUSE.

5.2 DISTINGUISHING INFLECTIONAL FROM LEXICAL CATEGORIES

Previous morphological research has generated a substantial set of diagnostics for discriminating word formation from inflection. (5.3) represents the
core of those tests, selected from a longer list in Scalise (1988):

(5.3)   a. Word formation may change the syntactic class of the base; in-
           flection may not.
        b. Word formation markers attach to the base; inflectional markers
           attach outside derivational markers.
        c. Word formation is marginally productive; inflection is com-
           pletely productive.
        d. Word formation is subject to semantic idiomatization; inflec-
           tional morphology is grammatically consistent.

Unfortunately, these tests are unreliable. While word formation may
change the class of the base, as often it does not. Every major lexical class
has its non-class-changing derivations, for example, verbs, *to walk : to
walk the dog;* adjectives, as in *white : whitish*; and nouns, *violin : violinist*,
not to mention diminutives and augmentatives. Participles, on the other
hand, are generally considered an inflectional category, yet they may
change the class of their bases from verb to adjective.

The use of inflectional affixes inside word formation affixes is widespread. German, for example, possesses a class of derivational affixes
which require inflectional affixes before them in some contexts:

(5.4)   a. *frühling-s-haft* "spring-like," *bär-en-haft* "bear-like," *weib-
           er-haft* "womanly"
        b. *läch-er-lich* "laughable," *fürcht-er-lich* "fearful," *wein-er-
           lich* "whiny"

      c. *hoffnung-s-los* "hopeless," *staat-en-los* "stateless," *müh-e-los* "effortless"

Although these inflectional markers are referred to as FUGENELEMENTEN in the grammars because they lack any inflectional, which is to say, syntactic function, the fact remains that they are obligatorily drawn from the stock of German inflectional affixes and must be accounted for as such.

      (5.3b) becomes a reliable test of inflectional morphology if it is modified to something like (5.3b'), paraphrased from observations in Matthews (1972) and Anderson (1982):

(5.3)   b.' Word formation marking appears close to the base; inflectional marking is outside word formation marking *when it is syntactically engaged.*

(5.3b') clearly implicates the separation of derivation from morphological spelling. The same affixes (for example, English *-ing,* German *-en*) may be used to mark either L- or I-derivation, as we saw in section 2.3.3. However, when any affix is syntactically engaged, for example, when it marks coindexed lexical items, it cannot occur inside any affix marking L-derivation. (5.3b), then, is a useful test of nominal category markers when amended as (5.3b'); let us refer to this test as the PERIPHERAL AFFIX TEST and return to it further along.[2]

      Before examining this promising test, let us satisfy ourselves that the remainder of the diagnostics in Scalise's list lack sufficient promise to justify pursuing. Meijs (1975) and Beard (1977) showed that productivity (5.2c) does not distinguish inflectional categories. Word formation processes may be fully productive, as are the *able*-adjective and Agentive nominalization rules in English, while unproductive inflectional categories like the Abessive, Comitative, and Instructive Cases in Finnish abound.[3] Halle (1973) points out limitations on the productivity of the Russian 1st Person Singular. Finally, semantically idiomatized inflection exists widely alongside idiomatized word formation forms (5.3d). The Russian Instrumental marks Means, Agent, Manner. However, if the noun refers to a time period logically belonging to a set of four, it indicates Punctuality: *utr-om* "in the morning", *dn-em* "in the afternoon", *večer-om* "in the evening", *noč'-ju* "at night". Productivity does not distinguish lexical and inflectional derivation; differences in lexical and inflectional productivity are matters of quantity, not quality, thus cannot be used as a criterion to distinguish two types of morphology.

5.2.1 The Split Morphology Hypothesis[4]

In its strictest interpretation, the Lexicalist Hypothesis implies the total isolation of inflection, I-derivation, and affixation from word formation.

This position has been characterized as THE SPLIT MORPHOLOGY HYPOTH-ESIS. Perlmutter (1988: 95) has most recently defined the Split Morphology Hypothesis as in (5.5):

(5.5) a. Derivational morphology is in the lexicon
      b. Stems are listed in the lexicon. Consequently, suppletive stems are listed in the lexicon.
      c. Irregular and closed-class inflected forms are listed in the lexicon. Consequently, suppletive inflected forms are listed in the lexicon.
      d. Regular, productive inflection is extralexical.

In light of the separation of derivation and morphological spelling established in chapters 2 and 3, LMBM is forced to account for the effects of Split Morphology in two different theories: that of derivation and that of morphological spelling. Under LMBM as defined in chapter 3, however, L- and I-derivation are necessarily independent while sharing the same spelling operations in a single integrated MS-component (3.2–3.5). The current version of LMBM therefore predicts split derivation but integrated spelling. Is there any justification for this?

The problem with the argument for two spelling components as well as two derivational components is that it leads to massive, unfalsifiable reduplication of spelling rules. In section 2.3.3 we noted that the most productive suffixes in English, *-ing* and *-ed,* mark both lexical and inflectional functions, as in *John is painting* versus *John's painting, John walked* versus *John is tight-lipped.* We could add *-er* to that list if Comparison is inflectional: *cooler*$_A$ versus *a cooler*$_N$. All such identical spelling with duplicate functions at the L- and I-derivational levels will require paired sets of identical allomorphy at each level if Split Morphology includes morphological spelling. The Integrated Spelling model of chapter 3, on the other hand, captures the distinction between L- and I-derivation required by the Lexicalist Hypothesis, while explaining the overlap of L- and I-affixation in terms of a shared module.

Split Morphology, then, must be restricted to derivation. To allow it to carry over to spelling would entail massive duplication of those affixes, generally the most productive ones in a language, which mark both types of derivation in many languages. A natural question at this point is, how does this affect the Peripheral Affix Test. With Matthews' and Anderson's amendment (5.3b') this test works so long as the order of affixes mirror that of derivational features. This will be our assumption until chapter 15, where this assumption will be slightly modified.

5.2.2 The Free Analog Test

Syntax assigns the structural relations within phrases. It follows that I-categories should themselves be assigned to structural positions in phrases. In languages with rich morphology, V must be raised through several category levels beneath Infl as Modal, Aspectual, and Tense features accumulate under Infl to be marked by potentially long sequences of affixes. In morphologically impoverished languages like English, however, syntax maintains structural positions for auxiliaries, Case markers, and other free grammatical morphemes, which may occur independent of the lexemes they mark. This suggests a hypothesis about the relation of syntax and morphology which would allow us to test for inflectional categories.

In accord with Principle V, we continue to assume that the parameters of the components of grammar are universal. Let us assume more specifically that the grammatical categories such as Modality, Aspect, and Case are universal. Languages, then, differ as to their reliance on bound and free morphology to mark these categories. Isolating languages depend entirely on free grammatical morphemes like ADPOSITIONS (prepositions and postpositions), auxiliaries, pronouns, relator nouns. Inflecting languages depend upon stem modifications and upon declensional and conjugational endings to express the same categories. However, L-derivation rules under this hypothesis are never marked by free morphemes but only by bound ones, because the lexicon, where L-derivation takes place, cannot generate syntactic structure for its category functions.[5]

The fact that L-derivation operations are never marked by free morphemes or clitics is therefore an entailment of strict modularity and the Lexicalist Hypothesis.[6] Aside from the explanation of the absence of free word formation markers, there is another interesting entailment of this fact: any category marked by a free morpheme must be a syntactic hence inflectional category. This hypothesis, let us call it the FREE ANALOG TEST, provides a test of I-derivation which distinguishes it from L-derivation as reliably as (5.3b'). Those grammatical categories marked by free morphemes in syntactic positions in the more isolating languages must be controlled by syntax, since only syntax assigns structure. Assuming Principle V, that grammatical categories are universal, the same categories in morphology-rich inflectional languages ceteris paribus must also be inflectional.

5.3 THE NOMINAL CATEGORIES

The Free Analog and Peripheral Affixation tests together provide a reliable battery for discriminating affixes which mark I-categories from those which mark L-categories. We may now apply these two tests to those nominal categories traditionally considered inflectional. The results are often surprising.

5.3.1 Case

The only nominal category unquestionably controlled by syntax is Case. Case expresses relations between nouns, and nouns and verbs in a phrase. It may be marked by free adpositions or by simple affixation, as illustrated in (5.6).

(5.6)   Vanj-**a** pisal otkrytk-**u** Maš-**e** karandaš-**om** noč'-**ju**
        Vanya-NOM wrote postcard-ACC Masha-DAT pencil-INST night-INST
        "Vanya **wrote** a postcard **to** Masha **with** a pencil **at** night"

In the Russian phrase, *Vanya* appears in the Nominative to indicate its syntactic role as Subject while *otkrytk(a)* is in the Accusative to indicate that it plays the role of DO. *Maša* is in the Dative because it is the IO, and *karandaš* and *noč'* are in the Instrumental: the former because it represents the Means of writing and the latter because it represents the temporal Locus at which the letter was written.

How would we test the hypothesis that Case is inflectional? Certainly Case markers pass the Peripheral Affix Test, for they always occur outside all other morphological markers except clitics, which are themselves syntactic. They also pass the Free Analog Test, as the English examples in (5.7) demonstrate. Indeed, no language demonstrates the syntactic freedom of Case-marking adpositions like the PREPOSITION STRANDING of English:

(5.7)   a. **To** who(m) did you give it?
        b. Who(m) did you give it **to**?

The IO marker in (5.7) is just as independent of the noun whose Case it marks as the Dative Case marker in (5.6) is bound to the Russian IO. Since it must have a syntactic position in the phrase, the category it marks must be inflectional.

5.3.2 Grammatical Gender, Natural Gender, and Agreement

Gender is never marked by free-standing morphemes or clitics and its affixal markers consistently appear inside those of Number and Case. This implies that it is an L-category inaccessible to syntax. However, Gender is involved with Agreement, which unites several lexical items within a phrase. Gender thus represents a problem for any theory of morphological categories.

This section will examine Gender and two problems surrounding it. It will show that the term "Gender" is appropriate only for the grammatical category of Natural Gender, which includes just those nouns referring to sexed beings. Grammatical Gender is simply the same category found among the nouns of Bantu and Amerindian languages, and usually referred to as "Noun Class" (Corbett 1991: 43-49) or "Inflectional Class" (Aronoff 1993: 64–65). In the grammars of the IE inflectional languages it is also referred to as "Declension Class". These categories are similar in that they are arbitrary lexical subclasses of nouns which provide the basis for Agreement and for assigning nouns to declensions in languages which possess declensions. This section will show that Grammatical Gender and Natural Gender are not one and the same category and must be distinguished.

Following Aronoff, the term "Noun Class" will henceforth refer to "Grammatical Gender" and a neutral Arabic numerical system, 1, 2, 3, and so on, will distinguish the functions or "Classes" of this lexical category. This produces the ancillary dividend of consolidating the IE, Semitic, and Uralo-Altaic terminology with that describing languages with Noun Class and/or Number functions but not Gender, such as the Paleosiberian, Amerindian, and Bantu languages.

Halle (1990) has also recently argued that Natural Gender and Noun Class represent two discrete categories and presented an approach to morphology that accounts for this distinction. To his arguments we might add the observation that grammatical categories like Noun Class are arbitrarily determined by grammar, while in ordinary language "Gender" refers to natural classes of sexed objects. The current terms "Natural" and "Grammatical Gender" imply that these are two subcategories of the same category, which is not true. (5.8–5.11) are examples of the Nominative Case of Noun Classes 1, 2, 3, as well as what will be called Class 4, the purely derived Plural Noun Class in Russian.[7] The Agreement pattern specified to the right indicates that Class 1 is associated with Masculine and Neuter Agreement, Classes 2 and 3 are both associated with Feminine Agreement, while Class 4 motivates Plural.

(5.8)   a. Class 1   Moj-∅ star-**yj** brat-∅ upal-∅

"My old brother fell"   (M-Agreement)

b. Class 1   Moj-∅ star-**yj** stol-∅ upal-∅

"My old table   fell"   (M-Agreement)

c. Class 1   Mo-ë star-oe kresl-o upal-o

"My old chair fell"   (N-Agreement)

(5.9) a. Class 2   Moj-a star-aja sestr-a upal-a

"My old sister fell"   (F-Agreement)

b. Class 2   Moj-a star-aja čašk-a upal-a

"My old cup fell"   (F-Agreement)

(5.10) a. Class 3   Moj-a star-aja mat'-∅ upal-a

"My old mother fell"   (F-Agreement)

b. Class 3   Moj-a star-aja peč'-∅ upal-a

"My old stove fell"   (F-Agreement)

c. Class 3   Mo-ë star-oe znam-ja upal-o

"My old banner fell"   (N-Agreement)

(5.11) Class 4   Mo-i star-ye knig-i upal-i

"My old books fell"   (P-Agreement)

(5.8) exemplifies the Agreement pattern of nouns of Class 1 in the Nominative. The noun in (5.8a) refers to an object with Natural Gender, while the one in (5.8b) refers to an object with no Natural Gender at all, but which is nonetheless generally referred to as ''Masculine'' in the same sense as (5.8a). Classes 2 and 3 in Russian are the traditional ''Feminine'' Classes, although a small subset of Neuter nouns like (5.10c) share half the same Case endings with the Feminine nouns. While some of the referents of Class 2–3 nouns are naturally Feminine (5.9a, 5.10a), more, like (5.9b, 5.10b), are not. Some Classes, then, do not distinguish Natural Gender and so must be strictly accounted for independently of Natural Gender.

Number in the inflectional IE languages is marked by shifting Singular nouns to a Plural Class. Table 5.1 demonstrates this for Russian. In Russian the Plural Class is the same for all Singular Classes, hence constitutes

Table 5.1   Class 4 (Plural) in Russian

Case	Class 1 "table"	→ Class 4 Plural	←	Class 2 "price"
Nominative	stol-Ø	stol-y	cen-y	cen-a
Genitive	stol-a	stol-ov	cen-Ø	cen-y
Dative	stol-u	stol-am	cen-am	cen-e
Accusative	stol-Ø	stol-y	cen-y	cen-u
Locative	stol-e	stol-ax	cen-ax	cen-e
Instrumental	stol-om	stol-ami	cen-ami	cen-oj

an independent Class itself. The only Case which differentiates Class 1 and Class 2 is the Genitive. However, the Genitive Plural ending is determined phonologically. If the citation form ends in a consonant, the suffix *-ov* is added; if it ends in a vowel, that vowel is deleted. Class 1 Masculine nouns happen to end in consonants and all Class 2 nouns, in /a/. Thus, nothing in the Class of a noun contributes to the selection of its Genitive marking or any other Case marking in the Plural. The Plural is, therefore, simply another Noun Class.

Since adjectives agree with head nouns and verbs agree with the Subject in terms of Class as well as Natural Gender but do not belong to those categories themselves, it makes no sense to refer to Agreement in terms of "Masculine", "Feminine", "Neuter," and "Plural". On the other hand, for the MS-module to mark their Agreement with nouns, they must bear some categorial feature. While Class and Gender features are lexical in nouns, the Agreement features of the nonnominal classes are purely morphological, though they operate in syntax. For this reason, Zaliznjak (1964) distinguishes Agreement as an independent category and Corbett (1991: 150–154), citing him, distinguishes TARGET GENDER (= Agreement) from CONTROLLER GENDER (= Noun Class). Finally, Aronoff (1993) distinguishes INFLECTIONAL CLASS (= Noun Class) from GENDER (= Agreement).[8] Following their lead, let us simply stipulate that the Agreement patterns of (5.8–5.11) are M-Agreement, F-Agreement, N-Agreement, and P-Agreement, mnemonic yet neutral names. The next section establishes that Agreement must be a category in Russian and hence should be expected in other languages.

The Isolation of Gender, Class, and Agreement

The previous section established the hypothesis that Gender, Noun Class, and Agreement are independent grammatical categories rather than one category, Gender. Now this claim must be proved. Let us set out from the assumption that if these categories are not independent, any might be directly derived from any other. The range of possibilities are:

(5.12)   a.1 Gender is determined by Noun Class
        a.2 Gender is determined by Agreement

        b.1 Agreement is determined by Noun Class
        b.2 Agreement is determined by Gender

        c.1 Noun Class is determined by Agreement
        c.2 Noun Class is determined by Gender

Two types of evidence disproves any such dependence among these categories: (a) forms which exhibit one category in the absence of the other and (b) irreconcilable differences in the correlation of their functions.

The Independence of (Natural) Gender

The definition of Gender cannot be reduced to that of Noun Class because Gender is present in indeclinable nouns which belong to none of the four Classes. Borrowed nouns like Russian *šimpanze* "chimpanzee," *ataše* "attaché," and *kenguru* "kangaroo", which do not end on morphotactically appropriate sounds, do not inflect and thus belong to no Noun Class. They do, however, distinguish Gender.[9] The NomSg M-Agreement desinence of attributive adjectives in Agreement with Masculine nouns is *-yj*; for attributives in Agreement with Feminine nouns the ending is *-aja*. The Agreement patterns on the adjectives of (5.13) demonstrate that although borrowed indeclinable nouns like *šimpanze* have no Noun Class, both Natural Genders are nonetheless expressed in Agreement.[10]

(5.13)   a. Malen'k-**ij**   šimpanze$_{MasSg}$

         little-MAGRSGNOM chimpanzee

         b. Malen'k-**aja** šimpanze$_{FemSg}$

         little-FAGRSGNOM chimpanzee

Since the features of attributive adjectives are inherited from their head nouns, the features of Masculine and Singular must be present in *šimpanze* despite the lack of any Noun Class marking at all. The presence of Gender in the absence of Noun Class positively isolates Gender as a category independent of Noun Class.

Gender cannot be reduced to Agreement because Agreement follows Gender in cases of conflict between Gender and Noun Class. A Class 1 noun ending on a consonant usually exhibits M-Agreement while F-Agreement characterizes Class 2 nouns, all of which end on /a/ in the Nominative (5.14).

(5.14)   a. Aleksandr-$\emptyset_{MasCls1}$ prišёl-$\emptyset_M$

"Alexander   arrived"

        b. Aleksandr-$a_{FemCls2}$ prišl-a_F

"Alexandra   arrived"

However, M-Agreement co-occurs with all the Class 2 nouns referring to males (5.15a). Also, Class 1 may marginally control F-Agreement in colloquial Russian if the Subject noun belongs to Class 1 but refers to a female (5.15b).[11]

(5.15)   a. Sud'j - $a_{MasCls2}$ prišёl-$\emptyset_M$

"The-judge   arrived"

        b. ?Vrač-$\emptyset_{FemCls1}$ prišl-a_F

"The-doctor [a woman] arrived"

Gender and Agreement are thus related, in that Gender sometimes determines Agreement, but these two functional categories must be discrete, because Gender does not exclusively determine Agreement.

The Independence of Agreement

Evidence of the existence of a category of Agreement independent of Gender and Noun Class is the miscorrelation of their functions shown in (5.8–5.11). While Russian has four Noun Classes and four Agreement functions, they do not correlate one-one and neither may be predicted from the other. F-Agreement correlates with both Class 2 and Class 3. However, nouns like *imja* "name" and *vremja* "time," which effect N-Agreement, may also be assigned to Class 3. Although these nouns end in /a/, normally a Class 2 marker, they decline generally according to Class 3 and all Agreement is "Neuter" (see Table 5.2).

    The differences between Class 3 F- and N-Agreement nouns appear only in the Nominative-Accusative and Instrumental. However, Nominative and Accusative endings are identical within each subparadigm.[12] The differences in the Instrumental is a minimal variation predictable on the basis of the phonology of the stems. Thus Class 3 nouns ending on /en/ or /a/ (the "j" indicates sharpening of the preceding consonant expressed by the

Table 5.2   Noun Class 3 in Russian

Case	Feminine	Neuter
Nominative	dver'-∅	im-ja
Genitive	dver-i	im-en-i
Dative	dver-i	im-en-i
Accusative	dver'-∅	im-ja
Locative	dver-i	im-en-i
Instrumental	dver'-ju	im-en-em

vowel in the Cyrillic alphabet) (i) undergo the allomorphic switch in the Nominative and Accusative; (ii) receive the suffix *-em* in the Instrumental; and (iii) effect N-Agreement. All other Class 3 nouns receive the Instrumental suffix *-ju* and reflect F-Agreement. (5.16) demonstrates that Agreement differs among nouns of this Noun Class.

(5.16)   a. tvoj-a$_{\text{FAgr}}$ dver'$_{\text{Cls3}}$ byl-a$_{\text{FAgr}}$ . . .

"your door was . . ."

b. tvoj-e$_{\text{NAgr}}$ im-ja$_{\text{Neu/Cls3}}$ byl-o$_{\text{NAgr}}$ . . .

"your name was . . ."

Class 3 is not the only Noun Class associated with two Agreement classes. Class 1 similarly effects both M- and N-Agreement, depending, again, on the phonological status of the stem. Lexemes of Class 1 with citation forms ending in an /o/ effect N-Agreement while those ending in a consonant effect M-Agreement.

(5.17)   a. stol-∅   byl-∅ . . .
          table-NomSgCls1 was-MAgr
          "the table was . . ."

b. okn-o   byl-o
          window-NomSgCls1 was-NAgr
          "the window was . . ."

So Class 1 does not predict M- and N-Agreement; phonology does.
    Indeed, Agreement functions are assigned to impersonal verbs in the

absence of any overt Subject at all. Recall examples (2.8) from chapter two:

(5.18) a. *e* menja sbil-**o**   s   nog
me knocked-NAGR from legs
"Something knocked me off my feet"

b. *e* menja sbil-**i**   s   nog
me knocked-PAGR from legs
"Someone knocked me off my feet"

In Russian, the Animacy of the empty category in Subject position is reflected by verbal inflection. If Animacy is absent, N-Agreement is effected (5.18a); if present, the verb will express P-Agreement as in (5.18b). Thus syntactic contexts exist in which no Noun Class is possible but Agreement is required, further evidence that Agreement is independent of Noun Class.

(5.8b, 5.9b, 5.10bc) demonstrate that nouns without Gender commonly effect Agreement; thus, Gender cannot exhaustively determine Agreement. Further on we will see that Gender does effect Agreement in collaboration with Noun Class and other factors but Agreement and Gender cannot be conflated. Although Agreement may be predicted from a combination of factors arising from Noun Class, Natural Gender, and pronominal reference, (5.18) prevents the reduction of the definition of Agreement to that of either (or both) of the other two categories.

Another important distinction between Agreement, on the one hand, and Gender and Noun Class, on the other, is that Agreement is not an inherent category. Nouns may be semantically Masculine or Feminine and may be lexically assigned to one of the several Classes; however, As, Vs, and determiners generally exhibit Agreement. For this reason Agreement cannot be defined simply in terms of copying operations. (5.8–5.11) demonstrate that Agreement is a derived category, determined by a combination of factors including Noun Class, Number, and Gender. The categories realized on As and Vs, then, are not the same as those on Ns. Because Class and Gender historically have been referred to as "Gender," Agreement functions, too, have been named for the Genders. However, once Noun Class and Gender are separated, Agreement also must be distinguished.

(5.18) is also the second piece of evidence suggesting that Agreement is like Case, an inflectional (syntactic) rather than a lexical category. The facts that Agreement is marked in syntax without a lexical head from which it might copy features, and that it is derived from the purely lexical categories, Gender and Noun Class, indicate that Agreement interprets lexical categories for syntactic morphology and is hence a derived inflectional category.

The Independence of Lexical Noun Classes

Noun Class cannot be reduced to Agreement (5.12c.1) because of the same disjunction which prevents the reduction of Agreement to Noun Class. We saw in the Russian data in (5.16–5.17) that N-Agreement is associated with both Classes 1 and 3, while F-Agreement is associated with Classes 2 and 3 (5.9). Moreover, Class 1 is associated with both M- and N-Agreement, while Class 2 corresponds to F- and M-Agreement. Finally, Agreement now seems to be a derived inflectional category whose definition cannot be reduced to those of lexical categories since its operation is restricted to a different grammatical level, syntax, and to different lexical classes, V and A.[13] The definitions of M-, F-, N-, and P-Agreement could therefore never account for the four Noun Classes.

Noun Classes cannot be derived from Gender (5.12c.2.) first and foremost because it is common for languages to have more Classes than Genders. Russian exhibits four Noun Classes and only two Gender functions. The fact that many nouns in all four Noun Classes occur without Gender clinches the case (5.8–5.11).

Not only does traditional Gender yield three actual grammatical categories, Agreement, Noun Class, and (natural) Gender, the first seems to be a syntactic inflectional category, while the latter two are lexical. Agreement seems to be a mechanism interpreting Noun Class, Gender, and Number for syntax. Agreement is thus a derived category rather than a primitive one. It also seems that in fusional languages like Russian, the algorithm for interpreting the three lexical categories in syntax is relatively complex. It follows that Agreement is crucial for understanding the differences between inflectional and lexical categories and operations; hence, we must return to the issue further on. First, however, let us examine the final grammatical category related to syntax, Number.

5.3.3 Number

Number, whose common functions are Singular, Dual, and Plural, is another grammatical category generally taken to be inflectional. However, no language in the sampling upon which this work is based marks Number with a free morpheme; Number is always marked by a bound morpheme, usually located inside Case markers where the two are discrete, even though it is part of grammatical Agreement which holds across words in phrases.[14] The Russian phrase in (5.19) is illustrative:

(5.19) Molod-ye   mal′čik-i   igral-i   na ulic-e
        young-NomPAgr boy-NomPl played-PAgr on street-Loc
        ''(the) young boys played on the street''

In (5.19) the morphological marking reflects Agreement among N, V, and A forms. Hence there is no doubt that Number is reflected in Agreement.

Number is referential only among nouns, for only nouns referentially distinguish individuals and aggregations. What appears to be Number markings on adjectives and verbs is simple P-Agreement, since that Agreement reflects categories other than Number on verbs. In the German Present, for example, the suffix *-en* marks 1st and 3rd Person Plural: *wir sag-en* "we say," *sie sag-en* "they say"; however, it also expresses Honorificity as in *was sag-en* Sie? "What do you (Honorific) say." P-Agreement in Russian may express pure Animacy as (5.18) shows: *menja sbil-i s nog* "I was knocked off my feet (by someone)."

Adjectives and verbs may reflect Number in the absence of any phonologically realized nominal, that is, in head position (5.20), or in constructions with a phonologically null pronominal in Subject (5.21).

(5.20)   Molod-ye *e* igral-i   na ulic-e
         young-NOMPAGR *e* played-PAGR on street-CLS2SGLOC
         "The young ones played on the street"

(5.21)   *e* Sobral-i-s'   u Ivan-a
         e gathered-PAGR-REFL at Ivan-CLS1GENSG
         "They gathered at Ivan's"

However, this is no indication that the categories are nonnominal. In (5.20) and (5.21) Plurality refers to some phonologically unspecified assumption which would have to be symbolized by a pronoun, were it symbolized (for example, English *the young ones*). Hence we must assume a pronominal consisting solely of Gender, Number, and Noun Class features in Subject and head positions of such constructions, in other words, a phonologically null pronoun.

Number is thus a purely nominal concept, which may be reflected in adjectives and verbs but is not an inherent category of these classes. It is most commonly assumed that Number is an inflectional category. However, the remainder of this section shows that Number is a lexical (word-formational) category and not an inflectional one at all. Beard (1982) details four primary arguments for Number as a lexical derivational category; they are as follows.

1. Constraints on pluralization are always lexical constraints. A lexical stem of any Class is susceptible to all the Cases of that Class's paradigm, but thousands of Singular nouns may not be pluralized at all and in every language many Plural nouns have no Singular. Pluralis tantum nouns form an unsystematic lexical subclass referring to single objects (5.22).

(5.22)   a. pliers   b. pants   c. oats   d. measles
            tongs   shorts   grits   mumps

shears	trousers	greens	hives
scissors	slacks	collards	blues

Some of the referents of these nouns are composed of duplicate, mirror-image parts (5.22a). Moreover, forms of clothing with legs (but never those with sleeves) are often lexically marked for Plural. But this class also includes the names of some but not all diseases and foods. This sort of spotty systematicity has all the earmarks of a discrete lexical subclass.

2. In languages otherwise as divergent as Bulgarian, English, and Hindi, where the inflectional system has sharply atrophied, the Genitive ending is replaced by a free morpheme, for example, the Bulgarian preposition *na* (5.23a), the English preposition *of* (5.23ab), and the Hindi postposition *ká/ke/kí* (5.23b).

(5.23) a. gramatika na bəlgarskija ezik
"grammar of the-Bulgarian language"

b. panditon ká ghar
"the house of the pundits"

We now know from recent research on clitics that even the Possessive marker *-s* is no longer an inflectional ending in English, but is a phrasal affix, an enclitic.

The Plural marker, in contrast, remains a suffix in languages which have lost inflection, where it behaves like an L-derivational suffix. One may not say **the many king of Englands* but only *the many kings of England*. The Plural in both Bulgarian (5.24) and Hindi (5.25) remains marked by suffix rather than by adposition:

(5.24) a. kost "bone"   kost-i "bones"
b. sel-o "village" sel-a "villages"
c. agn-e "lamb"   agn-et-a "lambs"

(5.25) a. ghoṛ-ā "horse" ghoṛ-e "horses"
b. pothí "book"   pothíy-an "books"
c. rát "night"   rát-en "nights"

This attribute follows from the Free Analog Test: Number markers cannot have independent syntactic status as can Case markers because Number is a lexical category. Number follows the word formation pattern; Case follows the syntactic inflectional pattern.

3. Word formation endings are quite easily borrowed in languages which suffer the linguistic domination of another culture, as English suf-

fered French domination following the invasion of William the Conqueror. Inflectional endings, however, are rarely if ever borrowed.[15] Again, Plural markers follow the pattern of word formation. A wide range of Latinate plural endings such as *-i, -a, -ae, -es* (as in *alumni, data, alumnæ, bases*) in English have been borrowed just as word formation suffixes like *-ive, -ion, -ment,* and *-ible* have been borrowed. The Plural suffix *-s,* borrowed from English, has rapidly spread in German since World War II. So, in this respect, too, Plural behaves like an L- rather than an I-derivational category.

4. The relative pronoun in fully inflectional languages like Russian agrees with the noun which it modifies in Gender and Number. It agrees in Case, however, according to its function in the relative clause in which it occurs. In (5.26), for example, *kotorym* "which" reflects M-Agreement and Instrumental Case: M-Agreement marks the lexical Masculine Gender and Singular Number of the Accusative *student-a* "student" in the main clause, but the Instrumental Case is governed by the preposition *s* of the subordinate clause:

(5.26)   Ja znaju student-a$_i$,   s kotor-ym$_i$ ty včera govoril e_i
         I know student-MASSGACC, with whom-MASSGINST you yester-
         day spoke
         "I know the student with whom you spoke yesterday"

The pattern by now has become quite distinctive: Number behaves like lexically determined Gender rather than like syntactic Case.

The evidence supporting Number as a lexical rather than inflectional category is quite robust. The features of Number are lexically determined and constrained: they follow the historical patterns of lexical rather than inflectional categories; they exhibit the idiosyncrasies characteristic of lexical derivation; and they never behave like Case features. Since, however, Number, Gender, and Case are represented in inflectional languages by a single ending, it must be true that Number is determined by abstract rules whose output may combine with that of other rules to condition morphological expression. The "morpheme" marking [+ Plural, − Singular] in these languages is this: *transfer to Class X.*

5.3.4 A Third Diagnostic of Lexicality: The Arbitrariness Criterion

In IE languages like Russian and Latin, Noun Class, Gender, and Number are purely arbitrary grammatical categories and provide further evidence of lexicality which parallels that of the previous two tests. By "arbitrary" I mean that they may be set lexically to be invariable. For example, we saw in (4.7) and (4.8) an array of lexical items with similar meanings belonging arbitrarily to different Noun Classes, as in *das Ding* "the thing'', *die Sache* ''the thing''; *das Weltall* ''the universe''; *der Kosmos* ''the cosmos''; *die Welt* ''the world''. Speakers have no choice in the Noun Class of these nouns in their Singular form, for their Noun Class is set arbitrarily by the lexicon.

It is possible for speakers to change the Natural Gender of unmarked Masculine nouns, as in *der Lehrer* ''the teacher (Masculine)'' : *die Lehrerin* ''the teacher (Feminine)'' and the Number of Singular count nouns like *das Ding* ''thing'': *die Dinge* ''things'' by regular L-derivation rule. However, there are also nouns with fixed Gender such as *der Bruder, die Schwester,* and singularis tantum and pluralis tantum nouns, which are wholly inaccessible to L-derivation. The important point is that these categories cannot be varied by speakers except under a limited set of conditions determined by L-derivation.

Inflectional categories, on the other hand, are much more slippery; they are impossible to fix. All adjectives and all verbs are capable of agreeing with any type of noun. Moreover, there is no language for which adjectives have lexically fixed M- or F-Agreement and nouns are shifted between Classes 1 and 2 to match the Agreement function, although such languages are logically possible. Similarly, no language has six Cases and six Singular/Dual/Plural Classes corresponding to each Case so that a given noun, *n*, must switch Classes to take on a different Case. If lexical categories may be arbitrarily fixed but inflectional categories may not, we have a third test for lexical and inflectional categories.

To conclude, then, the assumption that Number, Gender, and Noun Class are controlled by the lexicon yet are reflected in syntactic Agreement leads to a paradox, given the Lexicalist Hypothesis: if these categories are determined by the lexicon, how does syntax access them? This is part of a larger question concerning the Lexicalist Hypothesis: if lexical and syntactic operations are modular and hence mutually inaccessible, how are lexemes copied into minimal projections? If the copying rule is syntactic, it must be able to recognize the lexical features of lexemes in order to distinguish the lexical features of Ns, Vs, and As so that it may select an item which fits a given minimal projection. If the rule is lexical, then lexical rules must be able to read the categories of syntactic projections. Both alternatives lead to violations of strict modularity.

5.4 A MODEL OF NOMINAL INFLECTIONAL CATEGORIES

The division of the five categories surveyed in the previous section into two inflectional and three lexical categories facilitates a solution to the problem of lexical-syntactic access. Case is a set of categories determined solely by syntax, and ostensibly has nothing to do with the lexicon.[16] Agreement, however, is a category which interprets the three lexical categories: Noun Class, Gender, and Number and, in fusional languages, incorporates them with Case in complex Agreement representations connecting syntactic positions.

We can account for this situation without violating the principle of strict modularity only if syntax is limited to reading the output of the lexicon and interpreting that output in terms of its own category, that of Agreement. This interpretation of Agreement requires that inflection serve as a syntactic interpretive mechanism capable of reading the content of each lexeme for the information relevant to syntax, then converting this information into a form that rules of Agreement can process. This operation must be part of the process that copies lexical items onto X^{Min} positions: those copies, too, must be syntactic to preserve modularity. The category of Agreement, then, is required of syntax, given the assumption of modularity and the fact that Number, Gender, and Noun Class are lexical, not syntactic categories. We may assume that this interpretive or translational device partially defines I-derivation. The following section presents an explicit account of this translation process for a segment of Russian nominal Agreement.

5.4.1 Mapping Lexical Category Features onto Inflectional Category Features

The evidence examined thus far suggests that the minimal projections in NPs with attributive adjectives may be diagrammed as in Figure 5.1. Figure 5.1 indicates the original grammatical functions with boldface and copies with italics. Regular print indicates lexical features. [Accusative] has thus percolated downward from the DP, while the lexical features for Feminine, [+ Feminine, − Masculine], and Singular, [− Plural, + Singular], have been interpreted as [F-Agreement] by I-derivation (broken line). The Agreement feature then migrates throughout the NP structure. The arrows indicate paths of feature copying and interpretation.

All features are available to all categories in the NP node except where they are blocked by category assigners like the Quantifiers described in Babby (1980b). Free migration or copying of features within the domain governed by X^{Max}, subject to subjacency, is permissible, since only features, not the actual affixes marking them, require assignment in syntax. If features migrate to positions where they are not expressed, the conditions on MS-operations will guarantee that markers are spelled out only in the appropriate positions since only featural combinations with corresponding MS realizations will be expressed phonologically.

Figure 5.1 demonstrates the effect of insertion of the Russian lexeme *devuška* "girl" into an N^0 node marked for Accusative with an attributive adjunct *mil-* "nice". It has been assumed since Chomsky (1965) that this process involves matching the syntactic and subcategorization features of

Figure 5.1

Elements of Grammatical Agreement in a Russian NP

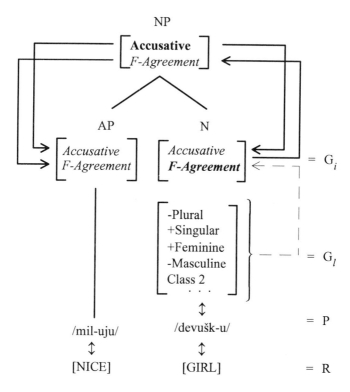

a lexical item with the features in the complex symbol in the minimal projection. This assumption presents profound difficulties. It leaves open, as mentioned previously, the question of whether the lexicon and syntax share the same categories. Either component operating on the same categories as the other compromises the most interesting aspect of the Lexicalist Hypothesis, modularity. The strong version of the Lexicalist Hypothesis requires that the operations of syntax be restricted to reading the output of the lexicon and interpreting that output in its own terms. Syntax should not have the ability to access lexical operations or structures, or operate on lexical categories. The question then is, how might inflection translate L-category features which it recognizes in lexical output into I-category features of Agreement.

5.4.2 Mapping Lexical to Syntactic Features

The mapping of the grammatical features of lexemes onto syntactic inflectional features of Agreement, as noted above, is not an isomorphic, one-

one copying process, but rather follows an algorithm. This is because conditions on Agreement patterns vary from language to language: from the virtual one-one mapping in Swahili to the complex fusional conventions of Russian. F-Agreement in Russian, for example, is effected by [+ Feminine, − Masculine] if Gender features are present, as they are in the Class 2 noun *sestra* "sister" and in the indeclinable *šimpanze* "chimpanzee". If Gender features are absent, however, as when the noun refers to an unsexed object like *čaška* "cup" (Class 2) or *peč'* "stove" (Class 3), the feature [Class 2] or [Class 3] triggers the same Agreement.

Table 5.3 represents an algorithm from Beard (1986) for translating Noun Class, Gender, and Number features from a lexical representation into inflectional terms for Russian predicates (Past Tense verbs and predicate adjectives). Formulas 1–3 in Table 5.3 account for the noun-verb Agreement of the (a) examples in (5.8–5.10) and (5.11). Formula 1 also stipulates that if the Number features of a noun are set for Plural or if a null *pro* is Animate, for example (5.18b), P-Agreement will be assigned in syntax. Later on P-Agreement will be marked by the MS-component, when it spells the suffix /-i/ onto the stem of the adjective or Past Tense verb. If the lexical features are set for Feminine or Masculine, F- or M-Agreement will be assigned, respectively, by formulas 2 and 3. The morphological expressions of Agreement are listed to the right of each operation stipulating the Agreement class. The marker for M-Agreement is the

Table 5.3   An Algorithm for Predicate Agreement in Russian

Lexical Conditions	*I-Derivational Operations*	*Spelling*
1. $\left\{ \begin{array}{l} [\text{+Plural, −Singular}] \\ \left[\begin{array}{l} \text{+Animate} \\ \text{+}pro \end{array} \right] \end{array} \right\}$	ASSIGN P–Agreement	**-i**
2. [+Feminine, −Masculine]	ASSIGN F–Agreement	**-a**
3. [+Masculine]	ASSIGN M–Agreement	**(None)**
4. $\left\{ \begin{array}{l} \text{Class } 2 \\ \left[\begin{array}{l} \text{Class } 3 \\ \text{/C/\#} \end{array} \right] \end{array} \right\}$	same as 2.	
5. $\left[\begin{array}{l} \text{Class } 1 \\ \text{/C/\#} \end{array} \right]$	same as 3.	
6. Elsewhere	ASSIGN N–Agreement	**-o**

omission of any modification of the stem; F-Agreement extends the lexical stem by the vowel /a/.

Formula 3 in Table 5.3 accounts for the facts of Markedness Theory, that only forms specifically marked [+ Feminine, − Masculine] receive F-Agreement markers; all others receive M-Agreement and its marker. Russian *student*, for example, must bear the featurization [+ Feminine, + Masculine], for either *on xorošij student* "he (is) a good student" or *ona xorošij student* "she (is) a good student" is grammatical. Notice that the new terminology allows us to avoid the confusion of claiming that a Masculine noun may have a Feminine referent; now we claim only that females may be referred to by Class 1 nouns with M-Agreement.

Formula 4 next assigns F-Agreement to nouns of Classes 2 and 3, which have not been assigned the same Agreement features by virtue of their Gender, as in the (b) examples of (5.8–5.10). Notice that, because we are situating the Neuter nouns like *imja* in Table 5.2 in Class 3, the assignment of F-Agreement to Class 3 nouns must be further specified to rule out those which end on vowels. Formula 5 next assigns M-Agreement to nouns of Class 1 ending on consonants. Formula 2 may not be conflated with 4, and formula 3 may not be conflated with 5, since Gender takes precedence over Noun Class in assigning Agreement. A Class 2 Masculine noun like *djadja* "uncle" has M-Agreement even though Class 2 nouns productively exhibit F-Agreement. Finally, all remaining nouns are assigned N-Agreement, whose expression is the suffix /-o/ spelled on the stem of the agreeing adjective or verb. This suffix also appears when the Subject is an N-Agreement noun, an infinitive, an Inanimate indeclinable noun, or an Inanimate null *pro*.

The algorithm of Table 5.3 actually accounts only for noun-verb Agreement; however, a similar or enriched algorithm for attributive Agreement is easy to imagine. It would account for such Agreement patterns as Russian *mil-uju devušk-u* "nice girl" in Figure 5.1, where the adjective ending *-uju* agrees with the noun ending on *-u*, not only in Gender and Number but also in Case.

The importance of the algorithm of Table 5.3 lies in its complexity and relevance to syntax. The complexity would be unnecessary if the categories Gender, Number, and Noun Class were syntactic or if the syntactic component could simply copy features directly from the grammatical representation of lexemes. Modularity predicts just such an interpretative device as we see in Table 5.3 in all languages. In Swahili it may interpret Noun Classes as Agreement features in a one-one fashion. In (5.27) the Subject and Object Agreement morphemes are identical copies of the Noun Class markers.

(5.27)   **wa**-toto   **wa**-li-**m**-piga   **m**-tu

CLS2-child 3PLSUB-PST-3SGOBJ-hit CLS1-man
"the children hit the man"

However, (5.28) indicates that lexical features are not inflectional nor are inflectional features lexical in Swahili, for the Subject Agreement morpheme is not identical with the Class marker.

(5.28)   **m**-tu   **a**-li-**wa**-piga   **wa**-toto

CLS1-man 3SGSUB-PST-3PLOBJ-hit CLS2-children
"the man hit the children"

This means that Swahili, too, will require a translational inflection, however simple the algorithm of the interpreter might be.[17]

5.5 CONCLUSION

This chapter has been rather long and complex for two reasons. First, previous interpretations of Gender have confused three different categories, two lexical (Natural Gender and Noun Class) and one syntactic (Agreement). No doubt this last ambiguous category contributed much to the confusion over the division of lexical and inflectional categories. Moreover, one word-formational category, Number, is still universally held to be inflectional despite a paucity of evidence supporting this position. The second complication examined in this chapter is the mapping of lexical to inflectional categories. Because LMBM supports a strong version of Lexicalism (and modularity in general), it strictly distinguishes lexical and inflectional information. The evidence reviewed in the first two sections of this chapter indicates that Gender, Number, and Noun Class are lexical categories while Agreement and Case are inflectional. Yet all four of the outstanding categories are expressed by Agreement. How can this be? The answer is that Agreement is a derived category, derived by inflectional operations based on an algorithm such as that in Table 5.3, which map lexical features onto syntactic positions, from which they migrate to agreeing positions by unconstrained automatic copying or "percolation" conventions.

Another important point of this chapter is that there is a level of grammatical computation which is neither semantic, syntactic, nor phonological, but which is nonetheless required of grammar. Aronoff (1993: 22–29) suggests that we call the level generated by algorithms like Table 5.4 MOR-

PHOMIC because it is a new, purely morphological, level for contemporary models of grammar. A similar level is required of the fusion, fission, merger, and impoverishment rules of Halle and Marantz (1993). However this level is named, the important point is that the evidence of this chapter offers signal support for Aronoff's conclusion and for Halle and Marantz's assumption; more evidence will emerge in chapters to come.

None of the innovations introduced in this chapter are model-theoretic; all are empirically motivated, yet all are perfectly at home in the LMBM model unfolding here. They bolster the strongest version of modularity: a lexicon containing only open classes, a syntax characterized exclusively by closed categories, and absolutely no interpenetration of either module by the other. The verbal categories reflect a similar picture. It is to this topic that we next turn.

NOTES

1. In choosing traditional terminology, I have not scrupulously respected Matthews' tri-level system, which distinguishes CATEGORY from PROPERTY from FUNCTION. This path has been chosen because Matthews' organization adds complexity to already complex subjects without bringing clarification relevant to the arguments in this book. Ultimately, morphological research will have to sort out his levels, so that "Case" is a category, specific cases, for example, "Nominative", "Accusative" are properties of that category, while "Subject", "Object", "Locus" are functions of the properties. The remainder of this book will refer to Case properties simply as "Cases" and its focus, their functions, will be called "functions". This is not to deny the distinction of properties and functions; only to admit the difficulty in defining them for every category at this point.

2. While the Peripheral Affix Test is useful in determining whether noun and adjective categories are inflectional, it does not apply to verbs, since verbs are never syntactically engaged with other classes. That is, other classes never agree with verb categories of Tense, Aspect, Voice.

3. These Cases appear only in idiomatized phrases in contemporary Finnish; their functions are productively marked by prepositions.

4. Booij (1993) examines split morphology in detail.

5. It follows from their reliance on free morphemes and their requirement of syntactic structure that isolating languages would also have no word formation. This, in fact, seems universally to be the case. Isolating languages like Vietnamese and Chinese reflect a minimum of unproductive word formation if any at all, other than analytic compounding. The syntax of these languages is CONFIGURATIONAL (Chomsky 1981), therefore, to

the extent that they use free morphemes they must provide syntactic nodes rather than paradigms for their grammatical markers.

6. This is a very odd difference between the derivational markings of word formation and inflection if derived words have structure as advocates of Word Syntax maintain. If Matthews and Anderson are correct, and derived words are AMORPHOUS, that is, astructural, the absence of free L-derivation markers in the face of free I-derivation markers is clear: the lexicon does not have the power to build structural trees, hence provides no positions for free morphemes or clitics.

7. Halle uses "Class 2" and "Class 1" to refer to the same declensions as are designated "Class 1" and "Class 2", respectively, here. Either numbering system is arbitrary; the system used here, however, occurs most widely in the literature. The derived Plural Noun Class 4 is not linguistically unusual: half the Noun classes of Bantu are derived Plural classes. In fact, the Plurals in both the IE and Bantu cases are probably not "Classes" in the sense defined here, but "declensions", where declensions are purely morphological paradigms at the MS level, the nominal equivalent of the conjugational paradigms described by Aronoff (1992b).

8. I have not followed Aronoff's terminology here because of the critical distinction I make between Natural Gender and Agreement, a distinction Aronoff does not take up. Because Natural Gender is directly related to sex, I will refer to it as "Gender" in order to gain the benefit of the term's mnemonic value. Beard (1986) provides the details of the Gender and Agreement distinction.

9. The consistent F-Agreement of Latin nouns on *-us* referring to trees, plants, cities, countries, and islands, as well as the equally consistent M-Agreement of the names of months and winds, do not qualify as Gender. These are examples of folk taxonomy discussed in section 4.1 in that they are lexical accidents which do not prevail in the face of conflicts like the Russian examples here. There is no conflict in a noun's ending on *-us* and having F-Agreement, since Class 2 nouns on *-us* exhibit F-Agreement across a relatively wide range of otherwise unrelated nouns. Moreover, no L-derivation generates Feminine plant names from lexical bases comparable to the Feminization of unmarked Natural Masculine agent nouns.

10. Contra Dressler and Doleschal (1990–91) LMBM handily accounts for Natural Gender in pronouns, which consist of nothing save grammatical categories (see chapter 15). Thus German *ja* "I" comprises only grammatical properties: $[+1, -2; \pm \text{Feminine}, \pm \text{Masculine}; +\text{Singular}, -\text{Plural}]$. First and Second Person pronouns are "shifters", to use Jakobson's term (Jakobson 1957), whose Number and Gender features may be manipulated by speakers.

11. See Corbett (1987) for a discussion of this controversial phenomenon and the literature on it. Because the poll conducted on this subject

showed native speakers evenly divided (51%–49%) on whether one may say, for example, *vrač*$_{\text{Mas}}$ *prišla*$_{\text{Fem}}$ "the doctor has arrived", when referring a female doctor, it will be considered a matter of acceptable ungrammaticality here.

12. The difference between the Nominative-Accusative and oblique endings derives from a historical shift to open syllables whereby syllables closed by nasals lost their occlusion, i.e. /en/ → /ē/. At a later stage /ẽ/ became /ja/ in Russian.

13. Corbett (1991: 106–16) surveys the full range of categories which may exhibit Agreement. As, Vs, numerals, and articles are the most commonly agreeing categories; however, Ps and complementizers also occasionally agree.

14. Dryer (1989) claims to have found independent morphemes marking plural in 48 of 307 languages he examined; however, his research, to the best of my knowledge, remains incomplete. He himself categorizes some of his Plural words as "numerals" and "articles" and many have meanings identical with those of quantifiers and classifiers in other languages, categories he does not distinguish from his Plural words. It is conceivable that Number is derivational in some languages, inflectional, in others; however, Dryer does not make this point.

15. I am grateful to Mark Aronoff for bringing this argument to my attention. It originates with Frank Anshen. Thomason (1988) argues that inflectional borrowing does occur. However, much of her argument depends upon the assumption that Number is an inflectional category and, as we are seeing here, that may not be the case.

16. Chapter 9 will demonstrate that the lexicon does have limited access to case functions such as Subject, Possession, Locus, Means, though not to the Cases themselves, in a way that does not undermine the statement here.

17. Andrew Carstairs-McCarthy (personal communication, 1992) in fact assures me that recent drift in Bantu languages has brought enough disparity between the lexical and declensional classes to require some sort of mapping principles for all of them.

Chapter Six

Verbal Inflectional Categories

6.1 VERBAL CATEGORIES

We have seen how LMBM models distinguish the derivational processes of word formation and inflection while treating the operations marking the output of these processes in a third component, a single, integrated morpheme spelling (MS-) component. Chapter 5 demonstrated the operation of these three components on nominal morphology; next we turn to verbal morphology. In so doing, we will open an issue equally proper to chapter five, the difference between spelling processes and free morphemes which often mark one and the same category across languages. Before proposing an account of this situation, however, we must first distinguish verbal inflectional categories from lexical categories as we did for the nominal categories.

6.1.1 A Survey of Verbal Inflectional Categories

This section extends the criteria for distinguishing nominal inflectional and derivational categories to verbal categories. This will require a list of the cardinal categories and the tests for inflectionality developed in the preceding chapter.[1] The cardinal universal verb categories are listed on the left-hand side of Table 6.1. Their properties and functions, as best they may be currently ascertained, are to the right in that list. Other categories (or properties) like Reversive (*undo*), Superior (*overdo*), Inferior (*underdo*), and Repetitive (*redo*) are lexical derivations. The Spatio-Temporal categories marked in IE languages by preverbs, for example, German *ein-* "in(to)", as in *einkommen* "come in", *aus-* "out", as in *ausgehen* "go out", *über-* "over", and as in *übergehen* "pass over", are a special problem which will require a more focused discussion than can be accommodated in the present work.

6.1.2 Delimiters

All languages also have a closed set of verbal specifier categories, referred to variously as DELIMITERS or DEGREE WORDS (Jackendoff 1977), listed in Table 6.2.

Table 6.1   The Cardinal Verbal Categories

VERB CLASS:	I, II, III, . . .
TRANSITIVITY:	Intransitive, Transitive, Bitransitive
MODALITY:	Potential, Desiderative, Obligative, Assertive, Hortatory, Monitory, Contingent, Necessitative, Dubitative, Emphatic
MOOD:	Indicative, Imperative, Subjunctive, Optative
ASPECT:	Perfective (Punctual, Semelfactive), Imperfective (Progressive, Durative, Iterative)
VOICE:	(Active, Passive, Antipassive, Applicative, Middle, Ergative) (Reflexive, Reciprocal)
TENSE:	Past (Recent, Distant), Present, Future (Recent, Distant)
PERSON:	First, Second
AGREEMENT:	F-, M-, N-, S(ingular)-; D(ual)-, P(lural)-Agreement

Table 6.2   The Functions of Verbal Delimiters

INTENSIVE	*a lot, very, very much, quite*
ATTENUATIVE	*(a) little (bit)*
EMPHATIC	*(!), do, indeed*
EXCESSIVE	*too, too much*
LIMITIVE	*just, only, barely, hardly*
SUCCESSIVE	*at last, finally*
DEFECTIVE	*almost*
REPETITIVE	*again*
COMPLETIVE	*already*

The categories of Table 6.2 exhibit properties of the lexicon and inflection. Some adverbs, such as *merely, barely, enormously, totally,* which are generally taken to be lexically derived words, correspond semantically to some Delimitive category. Even if a lexical adverb used in Delimitive functions does not perfectly correspond to the delimitive function it replaces, the result is that the semantics of the lexical item will shift, not in the direction of the delimitive function, but directly to that function. (6.1) illustrates two sets of adverbs which have assumed precisely a delimiter function.

(6.1) a. terribly, awfully, mighty, frightfully (= *very,* Intensifier) good
    b. absolutely, definitely, perfectly, really (= *indeed,* Emphatic) good

Apparently speakers of English enjoy considerable freedom in selecting lexical items to replace some Delimiters. This is possible only if this category has its own projection in syntax.

Since the semantics of these forms also fits the broad category Manner, one is tempted to interpret the functions in Table 6.2 simply as Manner adverbs. This does not work for two reasons. First, the categories in Table 6.2 constitute a small, closed set of categories, which may be specified only by another member of the category and hence cannot be a lexical adjunct. Furthermore, this self-specification is limited to one occurrence, that is, only one other member may specify these specifiers at a time and no third specifier is allowed, a situation which typifies specifiers but not adjuncts.

(6.2) Mary worked a. just a little
        b. quite a lot
        c. a very little bit

(6.3) Mary worked a. *certainly a little bit
        b. *a terribly lot (but, idiomatically, *an awful lot*)
        c. *greatly very much

(6.4) Mary worked a. *just only a little
        b. *quite very much
        c. *only too much

(6.2) demonstrates the relative freedom with which these Delimiters modify each other; they also specify verbs, adverbs, and adjectives. However, (6.3) shows that Manner adverbs, even those which elsewhere function as Delimiters, cannot specify Delimiters. (6.4) shows that Delimiter specification is limited to only one additional Delimiter which itself is unspecifiable. Manner adverbs, therefore, do not freely modify Delimiters as Delimiters freely modify Manner adverbs; thus, adverbs and Delimiters must represent distinct categories.

The second reason why the categories of Table 6.2 cannot be treated as lexical adverbs (in a universal theory of Delimiters, at least) is that Delimiters are marked by affixes in many languages. Yupik marks virtually all the Delimiter categories of Table 6.2 with inflectional affixes. (6.5) illustrates several that Menovshchikov (1967: 48–52) calls productive

"Aspect" markers (the suffixes -*ma* = Past Tense, -*na* = Near Future, and -*q* = 3rdSg.)

(6.5)   a. an- "go out"   an-**lata**-ma-q   "s/he went out
                              (Repetitive)   again"
        b. qava-"sleep"   qava-**vzeg**-na-quq   "s/he will barely
                              (Limitive)   doze off"
        c. kinəʁ-"dry up"   kinəʁ-**jaχtu**-ma-q   "it almost dried
                              (Defective)   up"

Intensification is marked prefixally in Classical Nahuatl: *coto-ni* "break" : *co-coto-ni* "break into pieces" (Sullivan 1988: 182), and Attenuation is marked by suffix in Tagalog: *mamula* "redden" : *mamula-mula* "redden a little" (Schachter and Otanes 1972: 340–41). If morphological categories are universal, then these categories should be closed, grammatically determined categories in English, too. The difference between English, on the one hand, and Yupik, on the other, lies in the fact that in English these categories are marked by free morphemes which may be replaced by a broader but still limited set of lexicalized adverbs.

6.2. LEXICAL AND INFLECTIONAL VERBAL CATEGORIES

According to the three diagnostics of chapter 5, the Free Analog Test, the Peripheral Affix Test, and the Arbitrariness Criterion, the Delimitive functions of Table 6.2 seem to be inflectional. The Peripheral Affix Test is compatible with this conclusion but equivocal. While Tense and Person markers do occur outside the Delimitive markers in (6.5), this is merely a matter of affix ordering if all these categories are inflectional. If DELIMITIVE is a category, then its functions (Table 6.2) are variable and not lexically fixed. The Free Analog Test unequivocally indicates that all the verbal and verbal specifier categories are inflectional except Verb Class and Transitivity. In fact, all the verbal categories except Transitivity and Verb Class seem to be inflectional by the criteria applied to nominal categories in the previous chapter. Let us begin our proof of this by examining Transitivity. Remember, we are excluding verbal Number and Gender since LMBM accounts for them as Agreement functions rather than as independent verbal categories.

6.2.1 Transitivity and Verb Class

According to the Free Analog Test, Aspect, Mood, Tense, Voice, and the category referred to as "Modality" in Table 6.1 are subject to the principles of syntactic rather than lexical derivation. Transitivity, however, is not. Apparently no language distinguishes Transitive from Intransitive verbs by freestanding morphemes and all languages have lexically fixed Transitive and Intransitive verbs. Moreover, all languages derive verbs from nouns and adjectives by simply reclassifying them as Intransitive or Transitive lexical items (see chapter 8). In English, Intransitive and Transitive variants of these derivations are not morphologically distinguished, for example *white → whiten* : *his face suddenly whitened* (Intransitive) versus *she whitens her clothes with bleach* (Transitive). In Russian the distinction is made by assigning the Intransitive and Transitive derivates to discrete Verb Classes with distinctive thematic markers, from *bel-yj* "white" one may derive *on po-bel-e-l* "he turned white", and *on po-bel-i-l bel'jë* "he bleached the laundry".

Yupik maintains a sharp distinction between all Transitive and Intransitive stems and a rule that transitivizes Intransitive stems. The Transitive markers, *-ta* in the Present and *-si* in the Past, precede Tense and Person markers.

(6.6) a. aglaʁ-[χ]a-χu-ŋa "I go"   a′. agla-**ta**-χa-m-kən "I take you"
          go-PRES-IND-3RDSG   go-TRAN-PRES-1STSG-2NDSG

       b. agla-ma-ŋa "I went"   b′. agla-**si**-ma-m-kən "I took you"
          go-PST-1STSG   go-TRAN-PST-1STSG-2NDSG

While the Peripheral Affix Criterion is inconclusive, its results are compatible with the conclusion that Transitivity is a lexical category.

Verb Class

Verb Class, too, is always marked by a suffix or thematic segment and never by a free-standing morpheme. Verb Classes determine stems and are always the first affix before or after the root. Recall the Russian examples *bel-ej-* 'be(come) white' and *bel-i-* 'whiten'. The *ej*-Class defines this set of stems as members of the First Conjugation, while the *i*-Class verbs belong to the Second Conjugation. While these markers may be replaced or deleted during conjugation, no verb morphology may precede them. The results of the Free Analog and Peripheral Affix Criterion offer a solid case for Verb Class and Transitivity as the only lexical verb categories.

All the remaining verbal categories are expressed by a free morpheme in some language and cannot be fixed arbitrarily for a lexical subclass. This demands constituent status for them in phrase structure, usually in the form of an auxiliary position, and supports the conclusion that they are syntactic and hence inflectional. Let us now examine Voice, Aspect, Tense, Mood, and the Modalities to see more clearly that this is true.

6.2.2 Voice

English is an excellent language in which to test the remaining verbal categories by the Free Analog Test. Rather than relying on a complex system of verbal affixes reflecting these categories, English relies on auxiliaries. Thus, rather than a Passive suffix or paradigm, English uses an analytic Aux + Past Participle construction to express Passive: *broke : has been broken.* Such a complex will require syntactic structure. In Latin, by comparison, Passive Voice is assigned its own conjugation:

(6.7) a. am-ō "I love"   a′. am-or "I am loved"
       b. am-ās "you love"   b′. am-āris "you are loved"
       c. am-at "he/she/it loves" c′. am-ātur "he/she/it is loved"

In fusional languages Passive may accumulate with Person, Agreement, and Tense for marking.

In accusative languages all Transitive and some Intransitive verbs are susceptible to passivization without any L-derivation which changes the meaning of the verb; passivization merely redefines the Object NP as the Subject of the verb. Passive is thus inflectional by the Arbitrariness Test. Since Passive seems to be a universal category of accusative languages, one which requires a syntactic position in some languages, we conclude that it is universally a function of an inflectional category.

6.2.3 Aspect

Aspect is a more problematic verbal category. Bybee (1985) is convinced that it has more lexical properties than Tense and Person but Yoruba marks the Imperfective with the independent particle *maa,* suggesting that syntax rather than the lexicon determines it (from Rowlands 1969: 92–94):

(6.8) a. nwọ́n á   wá— (l′-áago méjì)
           3RDPL FUT come (LOC-clock two)
           "they will come (at two o'clock)"

       b. á   maa wá (lójoojúmɨ)
           FUT IMP come (every day)
           "she will be coming (every day)"

English also provides evidence of free analogs sufficient to rest the case for inflectional rather than lexical Aspect: Progressive Aspect in English is expressed analytically, as in *was riding.*

Few verbs have lexically fixed aspect. Verbs meaning "work", "talk", "sit", "lie", "sleep" in Russian are consistently Imperfective without Perfective correlates. Even they, however, are subject to perfectivization, despite the fact that the semantic result is not quite that of Perfective, for example, *rabotat'* "work" : *po-rabotat'* "work a little". The fact that even semantically imperfect verbs are subject to perfectivization strongly suggests that Aspect is an arbitrary inflectional category available to all verbs regardless of meaning.

6.2.4 Tense

Since bound Tense markers usually occur between those marking the lexical category, Transitivity, and the inflectional category, Person Agreement, the Peripheral Affix Criterion is again equivocal for Tense. The Free Analog and Arbitrariness Tests, however, indicate that Tense is an inflectional category. Future presents the strongest case for Tense as an inflectional category. English marks this Tense with the Modal auxiliary *will* (*will go*) and the Slavic languages use either the null auxiliary BE (e.g. Russian *byt'* as in *budet xodit'* "will go") or the Desiderative, for example, Serbo-Croatian *hteti* "to want, will" as in *hoću ići* "I-will go").

Positive evidence for the inflectional status of Past is also available in the IE languages. Polish and Serbo-Croatian exhibit a complex Past comprising the copula BE plus a form which was historically a participle, as the following Serbo-Croatian example illustrates.

(6.9) a. on   je   doša -o - Ø
           he-EMPH 3RDSG come-PST-MAGR
           "HE arrived"

In (6.9) Past is marked by both the copula and the participial form of the verb. Both these elements will have to be assigned syntactic positions for the copula has a nonclitic form which requires a syntactic position. Serbo-Croatian is a *pro*-drop language and when *pro* is dropped, the verb raises to Comp:

(6.9) b. doša -o - Ø   je
           come-PST-MAGR 3RDSG
           "he arrived"

Pro is normally dropped in Serbo-Croatian; if it is not, the pronoun is interpreted as an Emphatic (6.9a). The Serbo-Croatian Past, therefore, will have to be treated syntactically. In English the Present and other tenses are marked by free morphemes in the Progressive forms: *is marking, was marking*. The only function of the auxiliary *be* here is to mark Tense; Voice is marked by the participles, for example, *is marked, was marked, will be marked*. Person, we will see below, is merely an Agreement function not requiring an Infl position.

Tense is never arbitrarily assigned by the lexicon nor semantically fixed on stems. It is marked analytically in many languages, however, so the conclusion that Tense is an inflectional category would seem to rest on firm ground.

6.2.5 The Modalities

Two attributes of the Modalities attract us to the idea that the auxiliaries expressing them are realized by the MS-component and not selected from the lexicon. First, like bound grammatical morphemes, they operate over a closed class of grammatical functions which seems to be universal. Second, the class of free morphemes that mark them, namely, the Modal auxiliaries, form a very small, closed class in all languages exhibiting them. The following set of core auxiliary functions expanded from Table 6.1 are commonly found in languages.

Table 6.3   Nonmodal and Modal Auxiliary Functions in English

1. NULL (BE, HAVE)	John **has been** at home
2. POSSESSIVE	John **has** a bottle of wine
3. FUTURE	John **will** work
4. CONDITIONAL	**Should** John work, . . .
5. DUBITATIVE	John **should** be working
6. EMPHATIC	John **does** work
7. OBLIGATIVE	John **must** work
8. POTENTIAL	John **can** work
9. CAUSATIVE	John **let/made** Jim work
10. DESIDERATIVE	John **wants** to work
11. NECESSITATIVE	John **needs** to work

Most of the functions in Table 6.3 are readily recognizable; however, a few deserve comment. First, the null auxiliary *BE* allows verbal and nonverbal categories to function as predicates; its purpose in this service is simply to host Tense, Person, and Number markers.

(6.10)	a. The book is on the mantle	PP is a predicate
	b. The book was long	adjective is predicate
	c. The book will be a hit	noun is a predicate
	d. The book must have been a hit	with a Modal Aux

In (6.10) the empty auxiliary *BE* simply provides the morphological necessities of verbhood (Tense) to a PP, an adjective, and a noun. It has no grammatical or referential force other than the expression of Tense.

The Possessive *have* is an auxiliary only in British English, where it may be inverted in questions and subjected to contraction, as are the Null *be* and *have* in US English. In upper-class British, questions in the form *have you any tea* are perfectly normal, as are answers with *have* cliticized: *yes, I've more than I can use.* Because only grammatical morphemes can be expressed as clitics, Possessive *have* must be a grammatical morpheme in British English. In US English, Possessive *have* is not a grammatical morpheme but a lexical item with the same phonological form. This is supported by the US norm: *do you have (*have you) any tea* and *I have (*I've) more tea than I can use.*

Notice that English does not represent all the functions in Table 6.3 by true auxiliaries, that is, by free forms which are raised in questions. Some of the forms in English are lexical: **made they John work, *wants John to work, *needs John to work.* The Causative, Desiderative, and Necessitative seem to be marked by designated lexical items in English, as is the case with the verbal Possessive in US English: **Have you a bottle of wine?* Russian uses regular adjectives to mark Obligative (6.11a) and Necessitative (6.12a) functions:

(6.11) a. ja   Ø dolžen rabota-t'
        I-Nom (am) obliged to-work
        "I should work"

        b. ja Ø dolžen Ivan-u   pjat'-Ø   rubl-ej
        I (am) obliged Ivan-Dat five-Acc ruble-GenPl
        "I owe Ivan five rubles"

(6.12) a. mne   Ø nužno   rabota-t'
        I-Dat (is) necessary to-work
        "I need to work"

        b. èto Ø   mne   nužno
        That-Nom (is) I-Dat necessary
        "That is necessary to me"

The short form in *-o* is simply the regular Neuter form for predicate adjectives, as (6.11b) and (6.12b) demonstrate.

If we assume that free morphemes require a syntactic position but bound morphemes do not, the syntactic positions for free morphemes must be provided under IP by the base along the lines of current Principles and Parameters (P&P) theory (see also Halle and Marantz 1993). These positions must contain function features like [Obligative], [Necessitative], and [Dubitative]. If these positions are available in the base, they are available to the lexicon and nothing prevents the lexicon from filling them, so long as the semantic representation of the lexical selection is compatible with the grammatical function. The present version of LMBM thus provides for the replacement of free grammatical morphemes by lexical items in isolative languages, without compromising its account of synthetic languages.

Another aspect of auxiliaries which allies them with inflectional operations is that all the functions marked by free auxiliary verbs in IE languages are marked by an affix or other morphological marking elsewhere. Languages as far removed from each other as Quechua, Turkish, and Veps express auxiliary categories with an affix attached to the stem of the main verb, as (6.13) illustrates.

(6.13) a. Quechua   pay ri-**na**-mi   "he **must** go"
                    he go-OBL-   OBL = OBLIGATIVE
                      VALIDATOR

        b. Turkish   hastaj-**mış**-ım   "I **should** be sick"
                    ail-DUB-1STSGPRES   DUB = DUBITATIVE

        c. Turkish   Ahmet gel-**ebil**-ir   "Ahmet **can** come"
                    Ahmet come-POT-   POT = POTENTIAL
                      3RDSGPRES

        d. Veps   hupi-**t**-da   "to **make** someone jump"
                    jump-CAUS-INF   CAUS = CAUSATIVE

However, we do not find these categories arbitrarily fixed for any set of verbs in the sense of the Arbitrariness Criterion.

The second reason why auxiliaries cannot be treated without reference to the affixal treatment of the same categories in other languages is that the functions marked by auxiliary verbs would seem to be dependent upon the main verb rather than upon the auxiliary itself. Two pieces of evidence support this claim. The first is the fact that while main verbs occur without Modal auxiliaries, auxiliaries do not occur without main verbs except in cases of tag deletion, where the verb is implicit and must appear in the main phrase. The amodal auxiliaries BE and HAVE merely support verbs, predicate nouns, and predicate adjectives by expressing the basic verbal categories, Tense, Voice, and Aspect. We could extend the criterion to include amodal Auxs by changing the claim: *predicates occur without Aux, but Auxs do not occur without predicates.* The reason for this is that auxiliaries semantically represent neither predicates nor arguments but semantic qualifiers which modify, that is, further specify the meanings of main verbs.

The second piece of evidence supporting the claim that auxiliaries are functionally dependent upon main verbs is that many of the Modal functions listed in Table 6.1 may be expressed without any auxiliary:

(6.14) a. John goes to NYC Friday
        b. John plays the piano
        c. (I can't go;) I work tonight

(6.15) a. John will go to NYC Friday (Future)
        b. John can play the piano (Potential)
        c. I must work tonight (Obligation)

Examples of implicit Modal functions expressed by verbs alone in (6.14) are accounted for if we follow the GB assumption that these Modal functions are introduced under Infl where they either block V-Infl raising, in which case a morphological auxiliary will be realized as in (6.15), or, as in case of (6.14), permit raising, so that the Modal feature accrues to the main verb, blocking independent phonological realization. There are other explanations but all point to auxiliary dependency.

6.2.6 Person

The category Person appears to be a nominal Agreement category, in that verbs bearing it reflect the Person of the Subject and, in some languages, that of the Object. Person is deducible from the Subject NP but is usually introduced under Infl (Agr node) in P&P theory. This is because the Subject NP is in [Spec, IP] and Agreement is usually passed from head to specifier, not vice versa. If there were a morphological way around this problem, Person could be removed as a verbal category and explained more intuitively as nominal one. Such a morphological treatment is possible with minimal tinkering on the current framework; indeed, it will be required of the theory of pronouns introduced in chapter 15.

Let us begin with Jakobson's (1932, 1957) assumption that verbs reflect First and Second Person and NONPERSON. Third Person is a default category, the ultimate unmarked Person category in Jakobson's terminology. This is why it is the phonologically unexpressed Person in virtually all languages with a null finite form of the verb. Since Third reflects Agreement with all lexical nouns in the Subject NP position, it does not even have to be listed as a property of Person since, in the absence of marking for First or Second Person, Third is the only alternative. All this is predicted from a system which posits only two Person functions, First and Second, plus the current theory of Markedness wherein " + " means "semantically and grammatically relevant" and " − " means "irrelevant" in the same sense, as shown in Table 6.4 (see also Adelaar 1977: 89; Anderson 1984; and section 6.3 below).

Table 6.4:   The Cross-Linguistic Range of the Category PERSON

[-1st, -2nd]	=	"Third" Person
[+1st, -2nd]	=	First Person Exclusive
[-1st, +2nd]	=	Second Person
[+1st, +2nd]	=	First Person Inclusive

This pattern in fact is what is found cross-linguistically. (Notice that the semantics of First Person Inclusive restricts it to the Plural Conjugation.)

The category Person is a set of Agreement functions reflected on auxiliary or main verbs. The Personal pronouns comprise a tightly closed class which express exactly the same properties as Person; moreover, only the 1st and 2nd Person pronouns control 1st and 2nd Person Agreement on verbs. 3rd Person Agreement is usually controlled by several pronouns plus all the nouns in the lexicon. This suggests that even Personal pronouns are grammatical markers rather than lexical items and that they must be accounted for by a theory of Person. Person features will then be required everywhere Personal pronouns may appear, that is, in every NP.

Current P&P grammars represent this fact as lexical fortuity, a derivative of the fact that Personal pronouns are syntactic nouns and accidentally (lexically) contain Person features. In an LMBM model, however, since Person is an Agreement category, it is inevitably inflectional. Let us imagine that "NP" is really a complex symbol containing [± 1st, ± 2nd]. Let us further assume that the lexicon has the alternative of inserting either a lexical item or the functions of the lexical categories which it controls into a terminal node, for example, [± Plural, ± Singular], via the algorithmic interpreter described in Table 5.3. A lexical item may be selected only for an NP node marked [− 1st, − 2nd] since no lexical noun is positively specified for either Person. An NP with any positive marking may be filled only with functions of the lexical categories Gender and Number. NPs with only category functions are then interpreted by the MS-component as personal pronouns at the same time that it marks verbs agreeing with those pronouns, in keeping with its duties of marking all closed categories.

Agreement is then accomplished by following the principle introduced in the preceding chapter of allowing all features to migrate everywhere in IP, just as they migrate throughout NP. Noun specifiers and adjuncts do not have Agreement categories, so they will acquire them when these features migrate in NPs. Verbs do not have nominal Agreement categories, either, including Person, so they will acquire them under free migration. "Head", "specifier", "complement" have no force under this interpretation. All features migrate everywhere. However, only those which condition MS-rules will be expressed; the rest will go unrecognized by the MS-component. Aspect and Tense features on NPs will not trigger any nominal affixation rules. Nominal Gender, Number, and Person features will be expressed in various combinations on verbs in some languages, but not in others.

Examples of feature migration will be presented later in this chapter and chapter 15 will further specify constraints on this process. Let this modest preview serve to show how a fully developed morphological theory eliminates Person as a verbal category altogether and represents it more convincingly as a nominal category.

6.3 STRUCTURAL ACCOUNTS OF VERBAL INFLECTION AND AGREEMENT

Much has been written about abstract inflection and Agreement since Chomsky (1981) introduced the functional categories Infl and Agr. The current assumption in P&P is that verbal Agreement categories are introduced under Infl by the functional category, Agr. P&P assumes that each of these features receives its own projection, which is filled with some morpheme during lexical insertion. V is then raised through those positions to Infl, AMALGAMATING with any bound morphemes occupying head positions intermediate between V and Infl. Affixes not accounted for by amalgamation combine with V by affix-hopping or lowering.

Nothing in the basic syntax of P&P is at odds with LMBM as it is unfolding here; however, inflectional categories must be represented in syntax as abstract function features of the appropriate syntactic category less any phonological expression. Versions of P&P which introduce affixes as lexical items directly into nodes, items which then move onto the auxiliary or main verb, are not compatible with LMBM. Affix movement is ruled out on two grounds: it fails to account for cumulative and extended exponence, as well as for phonologically context-sensitive affix selection. This section examines these two failures.

6.3.1 The Problems of Cumulative and Extended Exponence

Matthews (1972) has demonstrated how two fusional phenomena force the distinction of categorial features and the phonological means of marking them. His point is very simple: first of all, a single overt marker may mark two or three inflectional features as the simple ending *-tī* in Latin *rēxistī* "you (Sg) ruled" expresses 2nd, Singular, and Perfective, as (6.17) illustrates.

Matthews calls this CUMULATIVE EXPONENCE. If Perfective is intro-

(6.17)

Grammatical Representation: REG + PERFECTIVE + 2ND + SINGULAR

Phonological Representation: re:k   +   s   +   is   +   ti:

duced by Infl, and 2nd and Singular are introduced under Agr, "structure" loses its meaning. From two to five nodes under these conditions correspond to one phonological object actually requiring a structural position; moreover, that position is not a position in syntax but a purely morphological one.

Matthews also examined the obverse relation, the many-one relation, which he calls EXTENDED EXPONENCE, also illustrated in (6.17). The morphemes -*s*, -*is* and -*tī* are only used in the Perfective. The ending -*s* is the basic marker of the Perfective; however, -*tī* is the 2nd Singular ending on Perfective verbs, and -*is* is an empty morph used only with the 2nd Person Perfective forms. In this example, in fact, the extended exponence of Perfective -*s*, -*is*, and -*tī* overlaps the cumulative exponents of 2nd and Singular, -*is*, -*tī*. The features of Perfective, 2nd, and Singular in three nodes under Tense and Agr cannot be directly associated with their phonological expression and hence cannot be lexically listed. The selection of -*is* is conditioned by -*s* (or [+ Perfective]), and the selection of -*tī* is conditioned by -*s* and -*is*. Since -*s* is not the only Perfective marker in Latin, only if this suffix complex is spelled out after all the grammatical features they express are collected and attached to an appropriate verb stem can both the individuality of the morphemes and their noncompositionality in this context be explained.

The P&P analysis of extended exponence allows abstract morphemes in functional categories. Morphemes like BE-ING, which marks Progressive Aspect and BE-EN, which marks Passive Voice in English, have long been inserted as integral lexical items in Infl nodes. The result is structures like [BE-ING [[+ Pres] mark]], which are transformed into appropriate forms such as *is marking* by affix movement rules that lower the suffix to its proper position. Ignoring the morphemic boundary between *be* and -*ing*, while respecting that between the stem and -*ing*, however, remains a mysterious inconsistency. But there is an even greater problem facing the assumption that affixes are lexical items copied to one position then moved to another: CONTEXT-SENSITIVE AFFIX SELECTION.

6.3.2 The Problems of Context-Sensitive Affix Selection

Context-sensitive affix selection is a ubiquitous attribute of morphology representing an insuperable barrier to all forms of LMH. To understand this, let us examine two well-known theories of affix-lowering. Chomsky (1981 and elsewhere) argued for a description of passive sentences requiring movement.[2] Since this example of movement to an affix position is probably the most familiar one, it makes sense to begin our discussion with it.

Lowering to an Affix-Filled Position

Chomsky (1981) proposed that passive constructions are derived from active ones by raising the Object NP to the [Spec, IP] position. The version of GB assumed under this notion of passive assigns cases and θ-roles independently. The Nominative is assigned by Agr and the Accusative by V, both under government; the θ-roles of both the Subject and Object are assigned by the verb. In the case of passive constructions, passive morphology in the guise of the suffix *-en* is added to the verb and, following Burzio's Generalization, is assigned both the external θ-role and the Accusative Case borne by the verb. This allows the verb to assign the θ-role, Theme, to the NP in Object position but not Case. The Object NP then must remove itself to a Case-marked position, the only one available being the Subject position. The Object NP is thereby forced to move to Subject position to receive Case, the Nominative assigned by Agr.

Jaeggli (1986: 592) defines Case and θ-role absorption as "assignment to a bound morpheme". Baker, Johnson and Roberts (1989: 219), following Zubizaretta (1985) and Roeper (1987), extend this claim and argue that the morpheme *-en* itself is the external argument, originating under I as a lexical item (6.18).

(6.18)

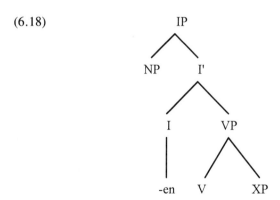

In order to be Case-marked Accusative by the verb so that it is visible for θ-assignment in LF, *-en* lowers onto the verb, producing (6.19). According to this scenario, *-en* is selected from the lexicon by the same mechanism as the lexical stem to which it will ultimately accrue. That mecha-

(6.19)

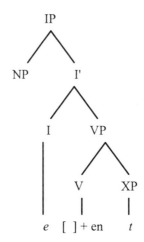

nism is syntactic, since it selects syntactic categories, although it may be sensitive to lexical (sub)categories. The problem is that *-en* is only one of several means of marking the Past participle in English; consider the examples in (6.20):

(6.20)   a. Bill was driv-**en** to work
         b. the Jim Beam was wast-**ed**
         c. the song was su**ng**
         d. the ball was hit-**∅**

(6.20) is representative of the wide range of affixes which must be inserted under I in (6.18) above. All are conditioned by lexical classes (Halle and Marantz 1993). Before *-en* may be lexically selected, for example, the selector must know that the stem belongs to the subclass of "strong" verbs containing stems like *drive, give, write*. The implication is that affixation must apply subsequent to stem selection since bound morphemes presuppose the inflectional classes of N, V, and A stems (recall also section 2.3.4).

The English participial suffixes are selected by idiomatic lexical subcategories; the Russian Past Passive participle suffixes, however, represent a case of purely phonological context-sensitivity. Russian exhibits three all but wholly predictable suffixes, *-n*, *-en*, and *-t*, which are assigned according to the following well-known algorithm:

(6.21)   a. verb stems ending on /a-/ or /aj-/ select the suffix *-n*;
         b. those ending on any nonsonorant consonant other than /j/, or on a front vowel, select *-en*;
         c. those ending on anything else select *-t*.

In other words, the assignment of participle suffixes represents phonologically principled behavior for which any adequate description of Russian grammar must account. (6.22) illustrates a sampling of the output of this algorithm.

(6.22) a. sdel-aj- "do, make"   sdela-**n** "done, made"
        b. napis-a-"write"   napisa-**n** "written"
        c. prines-"bring"   prines-**en** "brought"
        d. okonč-i-"finish"   okonč-**en** "finished"
        e. vymoj- "wash"   vymy-**t** "washed"
        f. obt[e]r-"wipe"   obter-**t** "wiped"
        g. vern-u-"return"   vernu-**t** "returned"

The crucial facts of Russian Past Passive participle morphology, then, are these: it involves several phonologically incompatible affixes which are perfectly predictable, and each is phonologically context-sensitive to the right edge of individual lexical stems. Since this selection is regular but morphologically conditioned, it must be carried out by a rule-oriented component other than syntax. Since the selection of affixes which express a function is often phonologically based, it must also be carried out in a component whose rules are context-sensitive where the context may be phonological (or lexical or morphological). The lexical selection mechanism responds to lexical category alone. Since it is not phonologically or morphologically context-sensitive, it cannot account for the distribution of such affixes. Affix selection is also dependent upon the outcome of lexical stem selection. This means, first, that lexical insertion must precede affix selection, a circumstance which forces independent operations for stem and affix selection. Second, suffixes cannot be introduced higher or lower than the verb stem, for they will find their conditions only at the right edge of the P-representation of specific lexical verbs.[3]

Defenders of syntactically selected affixes might regroup around the claim that -*en* represents an abstract morpheme, a morphosyntactic feature equivalent to [+ Passive] which has the requisite qualities of passive morphology. However, this places the morpheme in the class of grammatical categories to which the very Case it absorbs belongs, for [+ Passive] is a morphosyntactic property in just the same sense [+ Accusative] is. There is no non-ad hoc reason why [+ Passive] would be incompatible with this feature but not with other Case properties. LMH would seem to have no alternative to copying affixes directly to the position they occupy in surface structure.

Lowering an Affix to a Filled Position

Pollock (1989) notes that verb-to-Infl movement in French is restricted to Tensed clauses. In finite clauses like (6.23a) the verb passes over the Negation marker *pas* but not in nonfinite clauses like (6.23b):

(6.23)   a. Pierre ne dort pas
              "Pierre is not sleeping"
          b. Ne pas dormir rend la vie difficile
              "Not sleeping makes life difficult"

Pollock assumes that both (6.23a) and (6.23b) are derived from a structure roughly that of (6.24): When Infl (Pollock's T) is set for

(6.24)

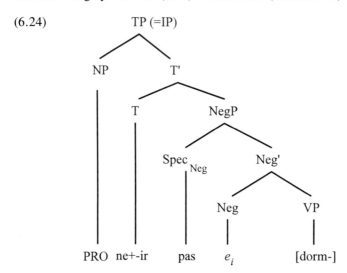

[− Tense], the verb is not raised to Infl so the suffix must be lowered to the verb. Affix movement in such clauses is accomplished according to (6.25), which Pollock (1989: 391) proposes for reorganizing his VPs after verb-raising and feature amalgamation have occurred:

(6.25)   [PRO + ne + -ir + pas + [dorm-]] ⇒ [PRO + ne + pas + [dorm- + ir]]

The problem in this analysis, again, is that Infinitives take an assortment of endings determined arbitrarily by Verb Class: *-er, -ir,* and *-re*. Pollock does not discuss how any one of these endings is originally selected for insertion in a position other than the one that contains the conditions which select them.

The difficulty with all forms of affix movement, then, is the assumption that morphemes are essentially free lexical items, an assumption we have seen to be unworkable time and again in previous chapters. Chapter 2, in fact, demonstrates that affixes do not share a single definitional property with lexemes; not even the necessary phonological representation of lexemes is an attribute shared with grammatical morphemes. What is marked by a phonological form in one language is marked by relative word position, subtraction, prosodic modification, or omissive marking in another. Bound grammatical morphemes are manipulated by rules sensitive to the phonological and grammatical representation of lexemes. It follows that grammatical morphemes must be inserted in their surface position, after the insertion of lexemes and following any movement of lexemes or syntactic categories in syntactic structure.

6.4 AN LMBM ACCOUNT OF VERBAL INFLECTIONAL CATEGORIES

Section 6.2 established that all but two verbal categories are inflectional, which by our account means that most verbal categories are manipulated in syntax. Section 6.3, however, made it clear that I-derivation cannot manipulate the morphological spelling which expresses the functions of these categories in speech. Now that we have isolated verbal category functions which are the morphological domain of syntax, we need to determine exactly how these functions are manipulated in syntax. The problem has been delineated above: some languages mark these features with free morphemes, like auxiliaries, which are independent of the main verb and capable of movement, while others mark them with bound morphemes, such as affixation and other spelling operations on the stem of the main verb. We need to ask, then, how we might explain verbal inflection features in such a way that morphosyntax may manipulate their markers in isolative languages in a way different from the way they are manipulated in synthetic ones. This issue will be the focus of the next section.

6.4.1 Inflectional Categories as Syntactic Positions

The problem of affix movement examined in the previous section does not affect LMBM since LMBM permits no phonological material expressing grammatical features in syntax; the phonology of grammatical morphemes is added postsyntactically by the MS-component. The problem facing an LMBM model is to explain raising the verb to positions in Agr, Infl, and Comp. In the process of being raised, a verb may pick up the Tense, Negation, Aspect, Agreement features but no phonological material. If LMBM could find a means of minimizing V-Infl raising in isolative languages with many auxiliaries while maximizing it in synthetic languages with few auxiliaries, LMBM could treat all grammatical aspects of verbal inflection by the same set of universal principles.

Current P&P syntax introduces features such as Tense, Aspect, Negation, Causation in their own projection, T(ense)P, AspP, NegP, CausP, under IP (Chomsky 1989; Pollock 1989; Ouhalla 1990). The advantage of this approach is that if category features are assigned their own nodes, those nodes may be filled with auxiliaries in isolative languages like English, while in synthetic languages like Turkish, they may be collected in the V^0 position during VP-Infl raising as an ordered list of features such that of (3.8). A list of features such as that shown in (3.8) is required for appropriate morphological spelling of complex derived words in synthetic languages. To understand how this would work, let us begin with an example of current work on the expanded IP.

(6.26) illustrates Aux-Comp movement in such French phrases as *n'avoir pas eu d'enfance heureuse . . .* "not to have had a happy childhood . . . ." Ouhalla considers auxiliaries to represent a distinct subclass of verbs which mark Aspect in isolative languages. As the Aspect marker *avoir* rises head-head to C, it acquires Tense ([-Tense] in this case), Negation, and Agreement categories.

(6.26)

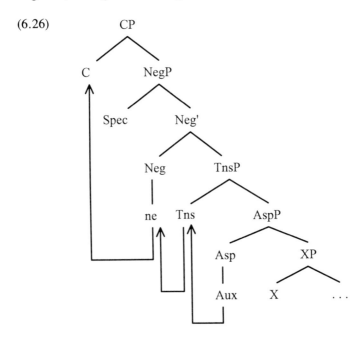

P&P still depends on LMH, assuming that *ne, pas, -oir* and suppletive *eu* are phonologically and grammatically base-generated. The base *av-* is selected from the phonological variants of AVOIR, such as *av-, eu-,* during lexical insertion because it subcategorizes Tense and the syntactic context (IP) includes [−Tense]. However, nothing is lost if we assume that no phonological material is involved at all, that only inflectional features accumulate on V^0 as it is raised to Infl. Rather than amalgamating the Negation marker, *ne,* as Ouhalla's example implies, under LMBM the feature

[+ Negation] will be combined with [− Tense] under Infl. This is all the information required by the MS-component to procliticize *n'*- to *av-*, suffix *-oir,* and encliticize *pas* to *avoir,* assuming precise morphological descriptions of these grammatical markers as operations on lexemes.

The Chomsky-Pollock-Ouhalla approach to Infl is to provide syntactic positions in base structure for each auxiliary category, since they are often marked by independent, moveable auxiliaries. The ability of an item to move and bear its own inflectional affixes is good evidence that it has syntactic status. Many languages, however, express the same categories represented by auxiliary verbs in isolating languages like English as affixes on the main verb. Turkish is such a language. (3.8), reiterated for convenience here as (6.27), displays the verbal featurization required for the spelling of Turkish *gel-e-me-di-m* ''I could not come'':

(6.27)   **Infl**

$$
g_{I} = \begin{bmatrix} \text{-Plural} \\ \text{+1stPerson} \\ \text{+Past} \\ \pm \text{Negation} \\ \text{+Potentiality} \end{bmatrix} \quad \begin{array}{l} \leftarrow \text{Number Switch} \\ \leftarrow \text{Person Switch} \\ \leftarrow \text{Tense Switch} \\ \leftarrow \text{Negation Switch} \\ \leftarrow \text{Mode Switch} \end{array}
$$

$$
g_{L} = \begin{bmatrix} \text{Subj ---} \\ \text{+Verb} \end{bmatrix} \quad \text{\small BASE GRAMMATICAL REPRESENTATION}
$$

$$
\updownarrow
$$

$$
p = \quad \text{/gel/} \quad \text{\small PHONOLOGICAL REPRESENTATION}
$$

$$
\updownarrow
$$

$$
r = \quad \text{[COME]} \quad \text{\small SEMANTIC REPRESENTATION}
$$

While surface structure demands structural Infl nodes (NegP, PotP) for English, none are justified in Turkish; Turkish needs only an independent Infl and VP. If Turkish were provided with independent XPs for each function by the base as Chomsky and Pollock argue, no great damage would ensue. In particular, the result would not be any ''explosion of functional categories'' promised by Iatridou (1990: 552). The point to remember is that the number of verbal grammatical categories is fixed at some number which speakers have no difficulty maintaining in memory or accessing (Table 6.1 represents a considered estimate).

LMBM, however, is just as amenable to Iatridou's alternative as it is to Pollock's original suggestion. Iatridou prefers a weaker position, ''according to which languages vary with respect to the functional categories they instantiate and that therefore evidence for AgrP (or CausP, BenP, etc.)

will have to be found in each language separately'' (Iatridou 1990: 553). This approach would ostensibly leave the contents of IP a set of parameters which must be learned for each language, the range of options restricted by the closed class of functions and the morphological options for marking them, that is, free or bound morpheme, vis-à-vis each function. The option finally selected by syntactic theory will be of no concern to morphology. Of concern to morphology is that no phonological material be involved in the amalgamation of functional categories during raising.

The omission of phonological material in auxiliary positions through which the VP passes on its way to Infl does raise a problem for LMBM. LMH provides a convenient constraint on raising. If a position is filled with a bound morpheme, that morpheme is amalgamated with the verb. If, however, the position is filled with a free morpheme, that morpheme blocks VP raising so that free auxiliaries are not amalgamated with verbs and verbs are not raised beyond a free auxiliary. Under LMBM, only grammatical functions are base-generated and the phonological distinction between free and bound grammatical morphemes is available only postsyntactically, in the MS-component. It follows that LMBM must provide another means of constraining VP raising so that it stops only where a free morpheme will eventually mark a function but continues through functions which will be marked by bound morphemes.

6.4.2 Raising as Bracket Erasure

Let us examine a potential common origin for the Turkish example in (6.27) above and its English counterpart to see if LMBM can account for raising to Infl. We begin with a consideration of (6.28), which is in all its syntactic essentials the universal structure of (6.27) but is enriched as well by the morphology discussed in this and the preceding chapters. The headings Infl, Neg, and Mod in (6.28) are all redundant; they are included here only for the sake of clarity. They simply represent the functions listed beneath them, that is, [+ Past], [+ Negation], [+ Potential].[4]

Under P&P all auxiliaries originate in V. The lexical item *can,* therefore, must move over NegP and AdvP in order to account for the English order in *I could not do it.* In addition to the syntactic problems pointed out by Iatridou and Ouhalla, there are morphological problems facing this account of the English word order. First, adverbs are adjuncts and not VP specifiers as indicated in (6.28). The variation in their order thus may be determined by whether they are adjoined to IP or VP and whether they are right-adjoined or left-adjoined. Second, the evidence for NegP is very weak; there is no convincing evidence of [Spec, NegP], and Negation markers behave morphologically throughout the world's languages like ordinary particles and affixes. This last comment means, among other things, that the position of the Negation marker may be predicted in terms of the

(6.28)

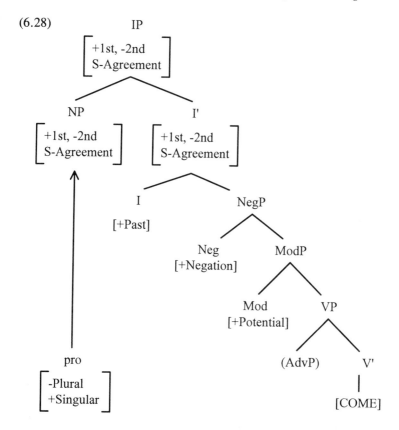

lexemes and free grammatical morphemes to which it attaches without reference to structure. In Russian it must be procliticized to the auxiliary or
main verb; in English *not* must follow the auxiliary or its trace: *could$_i$ John
e$_i$ not come* : *couldn't John come*. The morphological rules are so simple
that it makes no sense to add the sort of complexity to syntactic theory
proposed by Pollock in order to account syntactically for the positioning
of the Negation particles.

Morphologically, it also makes sense to introduce *can* under ModP as
a feature [+Potential] along with the other mutually exclusive Modal features, allowing it to be raised to Infl, accumulating the Agr features above
it.[5] It will collect [±Negation] from Infl or elsewhere, the morphology of
not accounting for its positioning and optional contraction. These adjustments suggest that (6.29) is just as plausible a source for the phrase under
consideration as (6.28).

The treatment of [+Negation] as a specifier is encouraged by the fact

(6.29)

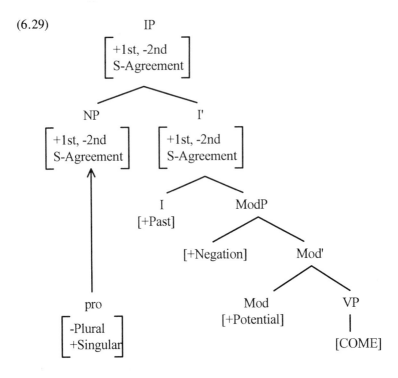

that in many languages its position varies with consequences on scope. We have already seen in the Turkish example (3.9) that it may be placed before or after the Potential feature with effects on scope. (3.9) is reproduced here as (6.30) for convenience.

(6.30)   a.   Ahmet gel-**me**-yebil-ir-∅
             Ahmet come-NEG-POT-PRES-3RD
             "Ahmet can [not come]" ("It is possible that Ahmet won't come")

         b.   Ahmet gel-e-**me**-z-∅
             Ahmet come-POT-NEG-PRES-3RD
             "Ahmet [can not] come"

The English particle has two positions which may be occupied simultaneously:[6]

(6.31)   he couldn't (very well) **not** go

Since the auxiliaries form a closed class, their spelling must be handled by the MS-component under LMBM whether they are free or bound morphemes. In an LMBM framework, then, raising must occur before bound or free morphemes are inserted. Iatridou's position, that constraints on VP raising are language-specific, is sympathetic to LMBM's problem, but we cannot leave it at that; we must explain why these constraints are language-specific and which language-specific factors determine VP-raising.

Let us begin our search for an answer to this question with the observation that if the differences between languages which mark verbal categories with free auxiliaries and those which mark them with affixes is language-specific, as Iatridou suggests, the component in which to seek the parameters is the MS-component. The reason for this is that grammatical and syntactic categories are universal; however, affixation and other marking expressing the functions of these categories are language-specific. If auxiliaries are free markers in a class with affixes, and the distribution of free and bound markers is language-specific, the MS-component is in fact the only grammatical module which could provide an account of raising.

What then could be the role of the MS-component in VP raising? The first question is, what is VP raising once we have removed NegP and Adv as immovable projections and removed auxiliaries from VP. With these independently motivated changes in (6.21), head-head raising becomes simple BRACKET ERASURE (Beard ms.) As the ModP or VP rises upward through the Agr nodes, the brackets are collapsed, that is, erased along the way. Affixes are added to the V stem to mark that erasure and provide recoverability for the grammatical features.

Since Chomsky and Halle (1968), the assumption has been that bracket erasure is the responsibility of phonology (see also Kiparsky 1982). The MS-component is a neighbor of phonology in LMBM, perhaps a subcomponent, so let us assume that bracket erasure is carried out by the MS-component. This fits well with the assumption that the function of that component is to translate syntactic structure into phonological forms. The MS-component carries out cyclic allomorphic adjustments necessary for postcyclic phonology by replacing syntactic and lexical bracketing with phonological material visible to P-rules.

If the MS-component erases brackets, it will control VP-Infl raising. If VP-Infl is a matter of bracket erasure at MS-level, it cannot involve movement around other categories but only the telescoping of projections containing purely functional category features and is so distinguished from other types of movement. Negation has been incorporated into the complex symbol I', although we have noted that it may be projected in other categories as well. The important point is that it is not a bounding category of any sort. In English and Turkish adjuncts are attached before IP or after

ModP but not between these two. In other languages, for example, Chukchee and Yupik, they are optionally incorporated into the verb complex as
it is raised. It is reasonable to assume, therefore, that VP-Infl movement
may be accurately interpreted as the erasure of nested syntactic brackets
by the MS-component.

  If this type of verb movement can be reduced to bracketing erasure,
the MS-component will control where this "movement" ends and whether
complex Infl features are realized as an auxiliary or as affixes on the lexical
verb. The effect of erasing the brackets between the function [+ Potential]
of the category Modal and between the latter and Infl in (6.29) for English,
then, is illustrated in (6.32).

(6.32)

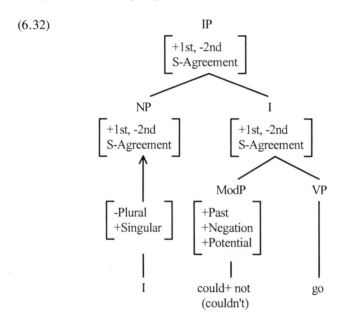

  A push-down stack in an MS-component like that of Figure 3.4 might
account for the English word order on the basis of the features (6.32) by
operating cyclically on its features from the bottom up in the following
way. [+ Potential] is read and held in memory until the reader reaches
[+ Past]. A maximum of four memory columns of the speller in Figure 3.4
will suffice to accomplish this. The reader then passes on to [+ Negation]
following [+ Potential] and holds that feature in memory, too. The assumption is that *not* is a particle attached to *could* and thus requires no
syntactic position (section 12.4.1 presents the reason). Finding no operation specified for [+ Potential, + Negation], it passes on to [+ Past], where
it finds an operation, the insertion of *could + not* or *couldn't*, conditioned

by [+ Potential, + Negative, + Past]. LMBM thus predicts that the position of both the Negative particle and clitic is ordinarily determined by the morphological spelling of the auxiliary rather than by syntactic structure.

There is another marked set of Negation operations for English, one of which suggests that syntax may determine the position of *not*. If the Modal has been moved to Comp, Negation either follows the Modal as the current hypothesis of Negation placement predicts, or remains in trace position (6.33b).

(6.33)   a. Couldn't I *e* come?
         b. Could I *e* not come?

Verb-Comp movement still represents a problem for LMBM, since in (6.33b) only Mod seems to move while in (6.33a) the entire feature inventory seems to move. In fact, the morphological speller outlined in Figure 3.4 handles this situation with ease, assuming that it is capable of reading features in one position and responding phonologically to them in another. The facts of cliticization such as English Possessive constructions like *the king of England's hat* forces this power on any workable model of morphological operations. The MS-component must be able to read the feature inventory collected in (6.33) and write all the phonological markers for them in Comp or write one there and the other on trace. In fact, the LMBM approach has an advantage here: even though the feature [+ Negation] is spelled out on trace in (6.28a), it remains adjacent to [+ Potential] in the feature inventory, where it is required for uniform semantic interpretation. Chapter 15 will provide more details of long-distance spelling.

The Turkish result of VP-Infl bracket erasure in (6.28) is somewhat different, as (6.34) illustrates. (6.34) illustrates the rise of the Turkish lexical verb *gel-* to Infl caused by the erasure of brackets between V and Infl, presenting the G-representation of (6.34) for morphological spelling. The order of the features provided by syntax (6.27) is that required by the morphological speller and improves on current P&P theory in one respect. Current theory defines the domain of Agr inside that of Infl; however, virtually all languages mark Agreement outside Tense. The correct order automatically falls out of the proposal here, that Person and Agreement features are inherited from NPs.

6.5 CONCLUSION

Much research on the order of complex auxiliaries and their features remains to be conducted and much of that work lies in the realm of syntax; however, the story outlined here makes eminent sense and suggests an extremely promising direction for future cooperation in morphological and

(6.34)

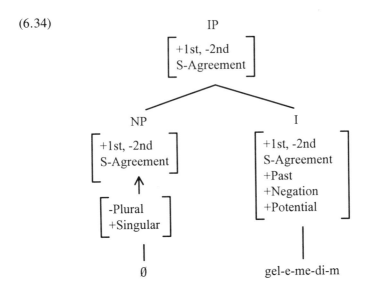

syntactic research. Chapters 5 and 6 have established that it is not only possible but necessary to distinguish the categories of lexical derivation from those of inflectional derivation. These two chapters have developed three tests for that distinction. The Free Analog Test assumes universal morphology and controls for grammatical functions which are expressed by a free morpheme in some language. Since free morphemes must be assigned structural projections, they must be controlled by syntax; so, if inflectional morphology is that morphology relevant to syntax, those functions assigned syntactic projections must be a part of inflection.

The Peripheral Affix Test is the traditional assumption that, if L-derivation applies in the lexicon and I-derivation in syntax, the former applies first and hence its markers will tend to appear inside inflectional markers. This test is equivocal at best for verbs. Since other classes do not agree with verbs, it is difficult to determine the syntactic relevance of verbal categories. Finally, the Arbitrariness Test assumes that the categories of the lexicon are arbitrary with respect to syntax and hence less accessible to speakers. Speakers may not shift a noun from Class 1 to Class 2 except by a derivation rule; shifting an adjective from M-Agreement to F-Agreement, however, is an option available on all adjectives. Noun classes would therefore seem to be lexical but Agreement, inflectional.

Applying these tests to the major categories of verbal functions, this chapter concluded that only Verb Class and Transitivity are lexical. All other categories, Voice, Aspect, Tense, Mood, Modality, and Person, are consistently marked morphologically outside the markers of Verb Class and Transitivity; moreover, they are never arbitrarily (lexically) fixed and are marked in some language by a free grammatical morpheme. Since syntax is the domain of inflection, these categories will have to be accounted for in syntax, while Verb Class and Transitivity will have to be derived lexically.

Finally, this chapter pointed out the similarity of verb-Infl raising and bracket erasure. This suggests the possibility that one of the functions of the MS-component is to erase brackets and mark their positions with morphological expressions. If this is the case, a more integrated theory of Aux may be developed, one in which Infl categories are raised until the raising process reaches a node which the MS-component invests with a free morpheme. From that point on, the raising process incorporates the sub-Infl features under the free morpheme. The advantages to this approach are striking. First, it obviates verbal affix movement. Affixes and other stem modifications are built onto verbal lexemes at one point only, after all category features are accumulated under the appropriate stem. The features may then be selected for the specific verb or auxiliary stem and marked by the MS-component presented in chapter 3, following the principles outlined there. Second, the marking processes, which were determined to be operations and not items in chapters 2 and 3, are not treated the same as lexemes. Thus we continue to maintain the strictest distinction between open and closed classes, items and operations on items. Chapter 15 will add more detail to this suggestion.

NOTES

1. The list of categories examined here were taken from the grammars of a random selection of languages, mostly Indo-European, Caucasian, and Paleosiberian languages, but including some South American and African languages, and languages of the Pacific rim (see pp. 206–7 for a complete list).

2. Chomsky (1992) obviates the necessity of NP movement in the explanation of passive constructions. However, this example remains typical of movement and thus still provides valid insights into the previously overlooked morphological problem discussed here.

3. See also Carstairs (1990) for a discussion of an even wider range of phonologically conditioned suppletion.

4. Notice that S[ingular]-Agreement is derived from lexical features by a transducer like that in Table 5.3 and that Person features originate under the NP node as suggested above. Constraints on their migration will be discussed in chapter 15.

5. Notice, again, that the problem facing LMH is knowing to select the

suppletive *could* rather than *can* in the absence of [+ Past] in the conditioning position. The lack of any fine-grained account of conditional selection recurs time and again in examining LMH in the light of a fully developed theory of morphology.

6. It is also possible to explain double Negatives in English as a case of reanalysis such that [*not*[*come*]] is reanalyzed [*not come*]. However, Turkish is not a marked case in allowing the position of Negation in verbal word forms to vary, and so variable positioning of Negation will have to be accommodated at least in agglutinative languages.

Chapter Seven

The Types of Lexical Derivation

7.1 THE LEXICAL DERIVATIONAL CATEGORIES

In addition to inflectional morphology, most grammatical theories contain a set of operations, called DERIVATION or WORD FORMATION rules, which map underlying bases to lexically derived forms. The LMBM model emerging here distinguishes L-derivation rules from I-derivation rules by defining the former as lexical operations, the latter, as categorial operations in syntax. All L-derivation rules are not the same, however, and require further analysis. This chapter will distinguish four different types of L-derivations found among the languages of the world. The goal here is to respond to points four and five of the morphological agenda of chapter 1, to establish a set of constraints on the possible number and nature of L-derivation rules and the categories over which they operate in natural languages. Let us begin with the first of the four types of derivation rules proposed in Beard (1988) : (i) feature value switches, (ii) expressive derivations, (iii) transposition, and (iv) functional L-derivations.

7.2 FEATURE VALUE SWITCHES

The most common type of L-derivational rule required of a description of natural languages is a simple SWITCH, or TOGGLE, which resets the ± or other values of grammatical features. This type of rule no doubt operates both in syntax and the lexicon, determining the values on the features of the I-categories discussed in chapters 5 and 6 as well as the values of inherent lexical features. This chapter will only consider the latter.

7.2.1 Feature Value Switches and Gender

Languages which maintain Natural Gender generally have a rule which derives Feminine correlates from unmarked Masculine nouns, for example German *Lehrer* "teacher" (unmarked Masculine) → *Lehrer-in* "female teacher" (marked Feminine), and Russian *student* "student" (unmarked

Masculine) → *student-ka* "female student" (marked Feminine). Let us assume that MARKED Masculines, such as German *der Bruder*, and Russian *brat* "brother", whose Gender cannot be changed, are lexically subcategorized as [− Feminine, + Masculine] to distinguish them from UN-MARKED Masculines like *student*, which bear the features [+ Feminine, + Masculine]. This marking allows derivational rules to distinguish those Masculine nouns which may be femininized from those which may not. It also characterizes the semantic potential of unmarked Masculines to refer to both females and males. If unmarked Masculine nouns have both their Feminine and Masculine values set at " + ", [+ Feminine, + Masculine], as proposed in chapter 5, German, Russian, and other Gendered languages must share a rule of femininization such as (7.1):

(7.1)   [+ Feminine, + Masculine] → [+ Feminine, − Masculine]

In other words, this rule optionally resets the value of [+ Masculine] in the context [+ Feminine] to [− Masculine].

The notion of MARKEDNESS is central to the morphological enterprise. Jakobson (1932, 1939) defined markedness thus: for any category A, a marked term of that category signifies the presence of A while the un-marked term makes "no statement of A". Others, Battistella (1990) for example, have noted that more often the phenomenon involves a binary set of functions, A and B. Rather than the opposition we find in nature, the unmarked grammatical form A′ refers indiscriminately to A and B, while the marked grammatical form, B′, refers exclusively to B. The unmarked form is then the default form, used in situations where the category but not the functional distinction is relevant. For example, the Russian Masculine noun *student* may refer to any sexed being who studies. The category "Gender" is relevant here but the term may refer equally to females if the male/female distinction is irrelevant, complicated by Plurality, or un-known.[1] Since the M-Agreement form is the default form for Gender, in-discriminate Gender is realized as M-Agreement.

In Beard (1986) I point out that Natural Gender cannot be handled by a single feature, that is, [± Feminine]. This would predict two Gender functions in grammar where there are, in fact, four. In Slavic, moreover, the four predicted functions correspond referentially and grammatically to the plus-and-minus marking system applied to two property features as in (7.2):

(7.2)   a. [+ Feminine, + Masculine]
         b. [+ Feminine, − Masculine]
         c. [− Feminine, + Masculine]
         d. [− Feminine, − Masculine]

The presence of the Gender properties [Feminine] and [Masculine] in a lexeme indicates the grammatical relevance of the corresponding semantic categories, FEMALE and MALE, respectively, to a lexical item (see also section 6.2.6). Thus, inanimate nouns such as Russian *stol* "table" and *kniga* "book" will not possess this binary pair of features at all, since Gender is irrelevant here. Agreement in these cases, according to the algorithm of Table 5.3, defers to Noun Class. The value setting, then, may be defined as a referential and grammatical indicator of sex specificity, the sex to which the lexeme may refer.

The relation, however, is not isomorphic; if the grammatical representation of the lexeme contains Gender features with values set as in (7.2a), the lexeme may refer to both sexes. If the values are set as in (7.2b) or (7.2c), the lexeme may refer either exclusively to females or exclusively to males, respectively. (7.2d) is at first puzzling, for it indicates the Gender marking of a lexeme referring to an object whose Gender is grammatically relevant but whose reference is not sex-differentiated. Russian has just such a class of nouns. To understand the relevance of Gender to them, we must understand another ostensible category, animacy.

Animacy is marked only among Masculine nouns in the Singular but among Masculine and Feminine in the Plural, as Table 7.1 illustrates.

Table 7.1   Russian Animacy Marking in the Accusative

		NOUN CLASS 1		NOUN CLASS 2	
		Inanimate "garden"	*Animate* "grandpa"	*Inanimate* "book"	*Animate* "old woman"
SINGULAR	*Nominative*	**sad**	ded	knig-a	bab-a
	Genitive	sad-a	**ded-a**	knig-i	bab-y
	Accusative	**sad**	**ded-a**	knig-u	bab-u
PLURAL	*Nominative*	**sad-y**	ded-y	**knig-i**	bab-y
(CLASS 4)	*Genitive*	sad	**ded-ov**	knig	**bab**
	Accusative	**sad-y**	**ded-ov**	**knig-i**	**bab**

Table 7.1 shows that both the inanimate Class 2 noun *kniga* "book" and the animate *baba* "old woman" have their own Accusative marker, the ending *-u*. The Class 1 nouns, however, distinguish the animate *ded* "grandfather" from the inanimate *sad* "garden" in that the latter selects its Nominative marker in the Accusative while the animate noun selects its Genitive marker, *-a*. In the Plural Class 4, all animate nouns, Feminine and Masculine, select their Accusative marker from the Genitive, since Class 4 does not distinguish the Genders in Russian.[2]

Animacy, in fact, is not a category in Russian (and thus the term no longer will be capitalized) since animate nouns are precisely those nouns with Natural Gender noted in their lexical representation.[3] One class of nouns in Russian, however, select the Genitive ending in the Accusative and thus must be animate, yet do not distinguish the Genders referentially:

(7.3) a. Class 1 (M-Agreement): xomjak "pica", pavlin "peacock", žuk "bug"
     b. Class 2 (F-Agreement): sobaka "dog", ptica "bird", lisica "fox"
     c. Class 3 (F-Agreement): myš' "mouse", lošad' "horse"

Although some of these nouns belong to Class 1, some to Class 2, and a few to Class 3, none reflect either Gender in their Agreement but all reflect animacy, as (7.4) and (7.5) illustrate:

(7.4) a. ja videl *xomjak$_{NomSg}$/xomjak-a$_{GenSg}$
      "I saw a pica"
     b. ja videl *xomjak-i$_{NomPl}$/xomjak-ov$_{GenPl}$
      "I saw picas"

(7.5) a. ja videl sobak-u$_{AccSg}$/*sobak-i$_{GenSg}$
      "I saw a dog"
     b. ja videl *sobak-i$_{NomPl}$/sobak$_{GenPl}$
      "I saw dogs"

Of course, Russian has marked Masculine and Feminine nouns referring strictly to male dogs (*kobel'*) and strictly to females (*suka*). But *sobaka* refers to neither sex; it is sex neutral, just as (7.2d) predicts. In fact, all these nouns conform to the description of (7.2d): they do not agree by Gender, but they refer exclusively to Gendered beings as reflected in their animacy. Thus Gender in general is just as relevant in these terms as it is in *ded* and *baba* above, determining their animacy; however, Gender specificity is referentially and hence grammatically irrelevant, for male and female references are not distinguished by Agreement.

Because Gender always overrides Noun Class in cases of Agreement conflict, we cannot conclude that the animate nouns of (7.3) are specified for Gender, even though semantically they are sexed and sex is relevant to animacy. This is precisely what we would expect, however, if these nouns possessed the features Feminine and Masculine, but the values of both were set to indicate that these specific features are grammatically irrelevant, in other words, if they contain [−Feminine, −Masculine]. For this reason the Agreement algorithm of Table 5.3 excludes this setting from Gender

Agreement assignment and allows Noun Class to determine Agreement when Gender features with this setting are present.

7.2.2 Feature Value Switches and Number

The next question to consider is whether the definitions of binary features and the plus-minus markedness symbolism just developed for Gender apply to other binary morphological category functions. Are there, for example, nouns that are both Plural and Singular which may be distinguished from nouns that are neither Plural nor Singular? Assuming that only two semantic categories, say, INDIVIDUAL and AGGREGATION, correspond to these two grammatical categories, we find neither a one-one correlation between the semantic and the corresponding grammatical concepts nor the two-four relationship of Gender.

Let us begin with the observation that the marking system just postulated for Gender projects four similar functions for the two Number properties:

(7.6)   a. [+ Plural, + Singular]
       b. [+ Plural, − Singular]
       c. [− Plural, + Singular]
       d. [− Plural, − Singular]

The [+ Plural, − Singular] and [+ Singular, − Plural] combinations predict the most obvious classes of nouns, Plural and Singular count nouns. However, the remaining two combinations of features and values hardly suffice to account for all the Number phenomena found cross-linguistically. (7.7) is a complete catalogue of Number phenomena we must account for:

(7.7)   a. Singular count nouns
       b. Plural count nouns
       c. Singularis tantum (mass) nouns
       d. Collective
       e. Pluralis tantum
       f. Dual nouns
       g. Trial or Paucal nouns

Although the categories of Number phenomena in (7.7) seem too numerous for the two-property system of (7.6), we have not taken the Number derivation rules into consideration. So, let us examine each of the examples in (7.7) for their semantic and grammatical implications to see how well in fact they fit the predictions of (7.6), given the interpretations of the relation of features to the specificity symbols '' + '' and '' − '' introduced in the previous section.

First, Plural nouns are derivates of Singular nouns (and vice versa in some languages, for example, Kiowa). Hence Singular nouns may be represented as [− Plural, + Singular], which means that Number is semantically relevant and the reference must be an individual, not an aggregation. [+ Plural, − Singular] describes Plural count nouns in the same way. We must assume an L-derivation rule (7.8) to generate Plural count nouns from Singular ones in IE languages:

(7.8)   [− Plural, + Singular] → [+ Plural, − Singular]

IE languages have no rule whose operation is the reverse of (7.8), that is, which would convert Plural nouns into Singular ones. Thus we may assume that the features [+ Plural, − Singular] describe Pluralis tantum nouns like *scissors, pliers, pants, oats, measles,* and so on. These Plurals are Plural "always" because English lacks a singularization rule. Other languages, for example, Kiowa and some Bantu languages which have lexically plural count nouns, do have such a rule.

The feature [+ Plural, + Singular], then, must define true collective nouns, nouns which refer to a group of objects which may be perceived as an aggregation of individuals or as a single aggregation, such as a team, a group, an organization. The grammatical means of marking this situation varies from language to language in dependence on the morphological means available. The British mark the noun Singular but effect P-Agreement on verb, as in *the team are agreed.* The richly morphological Slavic languages still maintain a collective rule by which collectives may be derived much like Plurals. Serbo-Croatian exhibits perhaps the most productive means for deriving collective nouns among the IE languages, as Table 7.2 demonstrates.

Table 7.2   Serbo-Croatian Plurals and Collectives

Singular	Plural	Collective	Gloss
dugm-e	dugm-et-a	dugm-ad	"button"
bur-e	bur-et-a	bur-ad	"barrel"
gran-a	gran-e	gran-j-e	"limb"
snop	snop-ov-i	snop-lj-e (snop-j-e)	"bundle"
drv-o	drv-et-a	drv-eć-e (drv-et-j-e)	"tree"

The reference of the collectives in Table 7.2 is Plural but their morphology is Singular; that is, all effect Singular Agreement even though their semantic reference is Plural or, better, Singular and Plural. It is better to say "Singular and Plural" because these nouns are used when one wishes to refer to a plurality of objects as a singular group. The situation here is quite comparable with the unmarked Masculine, which refers equally to males and females yet displays only unmarked M-Agreement. S-Agreement is the default Number marking.

We are left with one morphological characterization, [− Plural, − Singular], and four Number subclasses to account for: Dual, Trial, Paucal, and mass nouns. Let us begin with the latter, nouns which have no Plural, for example, *air, contemplation, running, envy, happiness, breakability.* The explanation of the fixed Singularity of this subclass depends upon the question of what prevents the pluralization of these terms. Let us examine a typical example, *breakability,* to find an answer.

Breakability cannot be pluralized because it does not refer to a countable object; rather, it refers to a quality. Indeed, it is derived from an adjective, which in turn comes from a verb, the two origins of the majority of Singularis tantum nouns, and classes which cannot refer to countable objects. It therefore makes no sense to speak of Number in connection with these nouns, derived or underived. If the concept of Number is simply irrelevant to these nouns, the situation is that of the ungendered nouns like *stol* "table" and *kniga* "book" discussed in the previous section, nouns which possess no Gender features. Both analogously and intuitively, therefore, mass nouns would seem to have no Number features at all. (This conclusion, however, will be adjusted in the next chapter.) As in the case of ungendered nouns, we would expect the Agreement of nouns without Number to revert to Noun Class and to default (unmarked) Number, which, as Jakobson long ago observed, is always Singular (S-Agreement).

The only nominal subclasses which possess Number but are neither Singular nor Plural are Dual, a very common Number across languages, and Trial, and Paucal, which are exceedingly rare except where Paucal replaces Dual. However, the system predicted by (7.6) licenses only one more category. Does the existence of three more Number functions destroy the symmetry of (7.6)? Not so long as no language exhibits more than four Number functions, all of which may be interpreted in terms of (7.6). Fijian is a language often said to possess a Trial; however, Dixon (1988: 52–57) argues that Proto-Fijian Trial has become Paucal today, that reflected in the pronominal system only. The Paucal pronominals in Fijian evolved from compounds in Proto-Fijian based on the number for "three," similar to English constructions like *we three, you three, those three.* When these compounds assumed the sense of Paucal, however, they lost their tie with the numerical and became a paradigm unto themselves. Many of them may now be suffixed to nouns in Possessive constructions. However, since Fijian has no trial verb Agreement, it is difficult to argue that Trial is a grammatical rather than lexical property.

The more interesting thing about Fijian, however, is that its pronominal system has only four Number functions: Singular, Dual, Paucal, and Plural. (7.6) would probably allow [+ Singular, + Plural] to be semantically interpreted as Paucal but this would preclude the possibility of Collective nouns in Fijian. Does Fijian in fact, then, have Collectives? Dixon (1988: 175–76) does describe a set of derivations which he claims has a "collective sense"; however, these derivatives do not have the properties of grammatical Collectives such as those of Table 7.2.

(7.9)   a. kau "tree"   vei-kau "forest"
        b. ?aa "thing"   vei-?aa "everything"
        c. tamata "person"   vei-tamata "everybody"
        d. vale "house"   vei-vale "every house"
        e. vanua "place"   vei-vanua "every place"

Collectives do not refer to the entire membership of the category referred to by the base; they refer to a subset of that category perceived as an individual object. Crucial to the definition is that the reference be in some sense both Singular and Plural. Of the examples in (7.9), only (7.9a) has a potentially Collective meaning, but Dixon notes that it is a dialectal isolate, thus a potential lexicalization. The evidence therefore weighs against Fijian having a genuine Collective, so that its four Number functions comply with the constraints of (7.6); they simply map onto semantic categories differently.

Even with the marginal Trial (and highly questionable Quadral and Pental) and Paucal forms, Number phenomena generally conform to the licensing principles of the two polar binary features of (7.6) plus ± . While the semantic interpretation of these grammatical categories may vary from language to language, the number of Number-related phenomena in any given language is usually four or fewer. There may be semantic motivation for the two features themselves; that is, languages may have Plurality and Singularity because INDIVIDUALS and AGGREGATIONS exist in the world. However, the grammatical system expresses its independence from semantics by the plus-minus value system of markedness which generates four grammatical functions corresponding to the two natural categories. The semantic and grammatical categories therefore are neither the same nor are they isomorphically related.

Only in LMBM models with their separation of derivational processes from marking operations is it possible to express value switches as the universal type of L-derivation which they seem to be. LMH models represent Gender, Number, and other categories as G-representations in lexical items, for example:

(7.10) a. -in: [N___, + Feminine, Class 2] (German)
        b. -s: [N___, + Plural] (English)

The implication of lexical listings like (7.10) is that the distribution of the categories Feminine and Plural is as idiomatic as their phonological expression. Another implication is that we should find as many Singular affixes as Plural, and as many Masculine affixes as Feminine in the lexicon. However, Singular and Masculine markers are rare across languages relative to Plural and Feminine markers. The phonological representations of Plural and Feminine markers do vary from language to language and are idiomatic; the categories, however, neither vary nor are they idiomatic. An LMH model thus has no way of distinguishing genuinely idiomatic phonological representations of affixes from the regular morphological effects of markedness.

The rules for deriving the functions of Gender and Number, in conclusion, seem to be universal; only affixation rules vary from language to language, so they must be accounted for in language-specific MS-components. It is true that different features allow different switching combinations. The major Gender rule switches [+ Feminine, + Masculine] to [+ Feminine, − Masculine] while the major Number rule switches [− Plural, + Singular] to [+ Plural, − Singular]. Different languages also allow different switching rules, so that some but not all languages have a Collective noun rule which switches [− Plural, + Singular] to [+ Plural, + Singular]. However, the parameters are set by the interpretation of markedness outlined above, parameters which LMBM can capture without any extension of the model, since the rules and the categories upon which they operate are independent of rules which phonologically realize their expressions.

7.3 EXPRESSIVE DERIVATIONS

Another type of L-derivation exhibited widely in the world's languages is the EXPRESSIVE DERIVATIONS, which reflect at least five functions universally: the Diminutive, Augmentative, Pejorative, Affectionate, and Honorific. The expressive derivations do not change the meaning or lexical class of the lexemes over which they operate; they generate nouns from nouns, verbs from verbs, and adjectives from adjectives. Rather, they express prejudices of the speaker as to whether the referent is smaller, larger, more likable, or more threatening than other members of its semantic category. The categories of expressive derivations are therefore not like other grammatical categories. While Augmentative and Diminutive nouns do express such functions as LARGE(X) and SMALL(X) of some semantic category SIZE, they do not seem to map onto grammatical functions because expressive derivations are always optional and subjective. A speaker may refer to a person of normal size with a Diminutive in one context and an Augmentative in another for emotional effect. Such relativity does not typify other types of L-derivation; one may not, by contrast, refer to a baker as a *bakery* or as *baking* depending one's mood.

A Pejorative noun variant indicates that the speaker dislikes the reference; an Affectionate form reflects the speaker's favor. Most often the Affectionate and Pejorative forms conflate with Diminutive and Augmentative forms, respectively. For example, Russian *sobač-ka*, from *sobaka* "dog", can refer to a small dog or to any other dog toward which the speaker feels a particular affection. However, Russian also provides forms which are exclusively Affectionate (7.11) and others which are exclusively Pejorative (7.12).

(7.11)   a. vino "wine"   vin-co "a nice little wine"
         b. djadja "uncle"   djadj-uška, djadj-enka "my sweet uncle"
         c. zima "winter"   zim-uška "a nice little winter"

(7.12)   a. kniga "book"   kniž-onka "damned book"
         b. rek-a "river"   reč-onka "damned river"
         c. lošad' "horse"   lošad-ënka "damned nag"

None of the examples in (7.11) imply smallness nor do those in (7.12) imply any variation in size. It follows that Affectionate and Pejorative must be taken as independent functions of expressive L-derivations.

Expressive L-derivations apply recursively. Expressive rules in Russian are seldom applied more than once; *dožd', dožd-ik, dožd-ič-ek* "rain" is exceptional in this respect. According to Shepardson (1983), however, Swahili can express up to five grades of Augmentation, as (7.13) illustrates:

(7.13)   a. kʰapu "basket"
         b. kapu "large basket"
         c. ji-kapu "larger basket"
         d. m-kapu "very large basket"
         e. m-ji-kapu "huge basket"

Such recursivity reflects the fact that expressive categories are not binary but gradient, capable of marking degrees. This seems to be determined by the semantic categories with which they are paired. Functional L-derivations are generally restricted to one occurrence; forms like **bakeryery* "a place of bakeries" are universally blocked.

Dressler and Kiefer (1990), in criticizing LMBM for having no story on expressive derivations, argue that these forms are not L-derivations at all. That is, at least some expressive derivations do not form a definable set of universal categories, as do other types of L-derivation. Basing their arguments on data from motherese and "the language of love", such as *Hund-i* "doggie", *Katz-i* "kitty", *Maus-i* "mousy", in Viennese German and Hungarian, they conclude that these derivations do not have grammatical functions but purely (morpho)pragmatic ones; they merely reflect context in language-dependent ways.

On the one hand, the premise of Dressler and Kiefer is not entirely accurate: the semantic functions SMALL(X), LARGE(X), and the like do recur in languages, including Hungarian and Viennese German, taking on the caste of grammatical categories. This argument would be stronger if there were more cross-linguistic variation in the meanings of expressive derivations. On the other hand, LMBM is in fact the only morphological theory that provides a model of morphological performance (= "morphopragmatics"; Beard 1981: chapter 10, 1987b) that distinguishes it from competing morphological theories, yet does not as it stands account for expressive derivation. Certainly, LMBM could simply stipulate the expressive functions as competence or performative rules, but that would not result in an adequate account. If Dressler and Kiefer are right, then, LMBM is the only model in a position to account for expressive derivation.

The discussion of expressive derivations has been rather terse. This derives from the fact that, despite the enormous literature on the subject, mystery still enshrouds these forms. Given the wide range of human attitudes, why are the expressive categories restricted to those which reflect only five or so attitudes of the speaker? It is only clear that the categories of expressive L-derivations are distinct from those of other types of L-derivation in at least three ways. First, they change neither the fundamental lexical meaning nor the lexical class of the base. Second, they reflect subjective attitudes of the speaker rather than a fixed relational function. Finally, because they are gradable, they also apply recursively.

7.4 TRANSPOSITION

Kuryłowicz (1936) pointed out a crucial distinction among word formation rules that depends on derivation rather than affix spelling: some lexical rules apparently have semantic content ("lexical" in his terminology), while others do not. For example, an explanation of the derivational relations in (7.14) will require an account of the origin of such grammatical relations as Subject, Object, Instrument, Locus, plus the change of class

V → N. An explanation of the derivations of (7.15), on the other hand, requires only the latter, a rule, X → Y, which reclassifies the bases.

(7.14)   a. recruit → recruit-er
           b. recruit → recruit-ee
           c. mix → mix-er
           d. bake → bak-ery

(7.15)   a. annoy → annoy-ance (V → N)
           b. new → new-ness (Adj → N)
           c. annoy → annoy-ing (V → Adj)
           d. dry → to dry (Adj → V)

Of course, the term "semantic" is used much more explicitly here than is Kuryłowicz's term "lexical". "Semantics" refers to a level of cognitive processing distinct from lexical, syntactic, and phonological processing. For this reason we will refer to the difference between (7.14) and (7.15) as a difference in derivations reflecting a change in lexical class only (7.15) versus a change in lexical class, plus a change in grammatical function (7.14). This means, for instance, that converting the adjective *dry* into a verb consists in assigning it to a Verb Class and providing it with Transitivity features. Continuing Kuryłowicz's line of reasoning, Marchand (1967) named asemantic reclassification rules TRANSPOSITIONS and argued that they represent a major type of derivation rule which cannot be explained in the same terms as semantic (grammatical function) rules.

If the functional and classificational features of L-derivations are handled by distinct sets of rules, we would expect a distinct set of L-derivation rules which provide only functional features without reclassifying. Indeed, such rules do exist:

(7.16)   a. fish-ery, heron-ry, dean-ery, cream-ery (N → N + Locus)
           b. Russi-an, Venezuel-an, Georgi-an (N → N + Origin)
           c. violin-ist, pian-ist, mathematic-i-an (N → N + Agent)

Thus the derivational side of word formation, L-derivation, must account for the addition of functional categories to the base and the transposition of the base, and it must handle these two aspects of derivation independently.

There are many questions touching upon transposition and its relation to other types of derivation. Let us begin our examination of the issue with a question: should we expect transpositions to exist? The evidence which we have examined thus far indicates that semantic categories are in fact quite distinct from lexical and grammatical ones. Semantic categories vary across different lexical classes depending on the structure of the given phrase. For instance, if one wishes to refer to a semantic category as a THING, it might be expressed as a noun, *sorrow*. The same concept may be expressed as a PROPERTY or STATE by another category, for example, *sad* and *to mourn*. In cases where a lexical item of a given class referring to some semantic category does not exist for class C the grammar needs to provide rules for transferring that semantic category from its original lexical class to C, for example, *sorrow → sorrowful, sad → sadness/ sadden, mourn → mourning/mournful*.

The assumption of semantic-syntactic isomorphism upon which contemporary theories of grammar have long rested seems to fail in a growing number of cases. Beard (1991, 1993), Napoli (1989), and Pustejovsky (1991) discuss gross misalignments between the semantic and syntactic structures. Napoli (1989), for example, demonstrates that propositional structure is found in many places throughout syntactic structure, not just in the VP. Propositional structures are found in AP + PP structures like *John is [good as a coach]* and in small clauses like *paint [the barn red]*. If argument structure does not consistently map only syntactic predicates, semantics must also have its own means of deriving argument structure from syntactic structure algorithmically rather than isomorphically.

Pustejovsky (1991) posits decompositional lexical features to account for the presence of conceptual categories at the semantic level absent at the syntactic and morphological levels. *John began a new novel*, for example, may mean either "John began reading a new novel" or "John began writing a new novel". Pustejovsky argues that only if the lexical entry for *book* contains two functional features, as in (7.17), can we explain these two semantic interpretations.

(7.17) $Telic(x) = \lambda y, e^T[read'(x)(y)(\ e^T)]$
         $Agent(x) = \lambda y, e^T[write'(x)(y)(e^T)]$

Again the clear distinction between N and V breaks down at semantic level.

Were semantic categories and lexical classes not autonomous, transpositions would be unnecessary, for there would be no reason why semantic categories and functions could not directly correspond to grammatical ones. Only if lexical classes and semantic categories belong to independent, heteromorphic domains would grammar require a mechanism for shifting semantic categories vacuously between lexical classes. If the domains of semantics and grammar are autonomous, however, we would expect a lexical class like V to express several semantic categories, for example, EVENT, STATE, CONDITION, QUALITY. At the same time we would expect any given semantic concept category, say, ANNOY, to be expressed by several lexical classes, *annoy, annoying, annoyance*, depending upon syntactic context. Transpositions are predicted, therefore, by the

same assumptions of modularity upon which this book is based. Chapter 8
examines them in detail.

7.5 FUNCTIONAL L-DERIVATIONS

The functional L-derivations have received more attention than any other
type in the recent literature. Advocates of Word Syntax have attempted to
demonstrate that the range of meanings within this type of derivation is
constrained by the subcategorization frames of lexical items, that is, by
their argument structure or grammatical function. Word Syntax studies
have focused on thematic relations (Agent, Patient) of argument structures
for which verbs subcategorize. They argue that these relations must be
inherited by derivates or compounds from their underlying bases and that
such inheritance precludes any further use of them by syntax in the phrase.
For example, the Agentive sense of *driver* by these accounts arises from
the Agent relation in the argument structure of *drive*: [Agent __ (Theme)].
Once an argument role is linked to an affix by derivation, as [Agent] is
linked to *-er* in this case, it is unavailable for further lexical or syntactic
service. The failure of *man-driver* to be interpreted as ''a man who drives''
derives from the fact that the Agent argument of *drive* has been assigned
both to the suffix *-er* and, in the compound attribute, to *man*. *Truck-driver*
is acceptable because *truck* is assigned the otherwise unassigned Theme
role of the argument structure.

7.5.1 Word Syntax Constraints on Functional Derivations

Recent trends in linguistics have focused on constraining grammatical
models so that they do not overgenerate; however, undergeneration is just
as serious a theoretical fault as overgeneration. This section demonstrates
how Word Syntax theories too tightly restrict the generation of functional
derivations, an L-derivational type which includes synthetic compounds.

Roeper and Siegel

Roeper and Siegel (1978: 208) argue that ''all verbal compounds are
formed by the incorporation of a word in the first sister position of the
verb'', the FIRST-SISTER PRINCIPLE. According to this principle, verbs like
(7.18) should be available to compound only with nouns which may serve
as the first argument in their subcategorization frames. Consider a hypo-
thetical entry for the verb *build* represented in (7.18).

(7.18)   [build] [$_{Adv}$] [$_{Instr}$] [+ word] [$_{Loc}$] W $\Rightarrow$ build [+ word] [$_{Loc}$] W

Only if the [$_{Adv}$] and [$_{Instr}$] frames are first deleted, making them unavailable
for assignment in syntax as well as the lexicon, can an item assigned to the

Locative position in (7.18) be incorporated into a synthetic compound. Thus the Adv and Instr arguments are unavailable to the derived compound *factory-built*. As evidence of this, Roeper and Siegel cite the unacceptability of *factory-built by hand,* where *by hand* represents an Instrumental argument, which is closer to the verb than the Locative in (7.22). By the same reasoning, *hand-built in a factory* is acceptable.

However, even if speakers of English generally agree with Roeper & Siegel's judgment of the acceptability of *factory-built by hand,* the cause of the unacceptability cannot be the First-Sister Principle.[4] Semantically felicitous similar examples abound in the data:

(7.19)   a. home-made hurriedly by hand, sun-baked (too) quickly, fire-
                brewed naturally by Boy Scouts
          b. mountain-grown, garden-tested, field-harvested, night-stalker

The examples in (7.19) demonstrate two facts, both indicating that the First-Sister Principle is far too restrictive. First, first sisters are generally ignored in the production of this type of compound (7.19a). Second, adjuncts, which are not part of subcategorization frames, freely occur in compounds (7.19b). It is highly dubious that verbs subcategorize for an Instrument; however, no one would claim that verbs subcategorize for Locus adjuncts, yet (7.19b) represents the Locative relation, which must be adjunctive.

Roeper and Siegel discover some interesting language-dependent facts about English: a strong preference for an incorporated noun of a compound to stand in Object, Instrumental, or Locative relation to the verb if the verb is transitive.[5] Roeper and Siegel did not prove, however, that the First-Sister Principle restricts English compounds or that it restricts compounds language-independently.

Selkirk

Selkirk (1982) offered a nontransformational account of the same synthetic compounds described by Roeper & Siegel. Operating within the framework of Bresnan's LFG model, she offers the following two principles (7.20) and (7.21) to explain the range of relations between the head and complement of compounds.

(7.20)   The SUBJ argument of a lexical item may not be satisfied in com-
          pound structure.

(7.21)   All non-SUBJ arguments of the head of a compound *must be satis-
          fied* within the compound immediately dominating the head.

The NO-SUBJECT CONSTRAINT (7.20) rules out compounds like *girl-swimming, weather-changing*. Hoeksema (1987: 124), however, points out that the corresponding derivations in Dutch allow subject incorporation freely among unaccusative and ergative verbs.

(7.22) a. aard-beev-ing   "earthquake"
            earth quak-ing
        b. klank-verander-ing   "sound change"
            sound chang-ing
        c. kosten-stijg-ing   "cost increase"
            cost increas-ing

Indeed, synthetic compounds with Subjects based on unaccusative verbs are permitted in English, for example, *student rioting, guest lecturing, visitor parking*. (7.20) thus strictly rules out compounds incorporating Subjects of Transitive verbs.

(7.21) restricts non-Subject arguments of a compound to those locally satisfied by a sister argument. For instance, **tree-eating of pasta* is ruled out by the fact that *pasta* would be a non-Subject argument (Object) of *eat*, not satisfied in the compound as it is in *pasta-eating in trees*. However, it is not perfectly clear that (7.21) constrains constructions like *tree-eating of pasta*. In fact, all such constructions sound odd in American English since the Genitive marker *of* is itself highly restricted in English deverbal nominals. The contemporary equivalents without *of*, like those in (7.23), sound much better.

(7.23) a. Tree-eating pasta (is frowned upon in this neighborhood)
        b. Street-peddling your art (is degrading)
        c. Field-stripping rifles can get you down

Of is productive only in Latinate nominalizations where (7.21) does not hold.

(7.24) a. garage storage of automobiles
        b. home maintenance of electronic equipment
        c. overseas distribution of widgets

It is clear that Objects are privileged modifiers in N + V compounds; however (7.23) and (7.24) demonstrate that other relations are not precluded. Selkirk arbitrarily limited her study to compounds based on Germanic suffixes such as *-ing* and *-er*. If her principles are to be of any general interest, however, they should hold for all suffixes used for the same class of derivations.

One might want to argue that (7.24) represents N + N compounds, as in *garage + storage*. But then nothing precludes an identical account of compounds like *pasta-eating* which would analyze this compound as $[[\text{pasta}]_N[\text{eating}]_N]_N$. In fact, Booij (1988) has proposed just such an account. Argument structure is then assigned at semantic level under the assumption that the deverbal noun inherits the argument structure of its base. Booij's approach, then, permits the concatenation of any two nouns, derived or underived, as in *water + fall, pasta + eating, home + maintenance*. Argument structure will be assigned to compounds just as it is to all semantic constructions, based on the subcategorization of the head. In the case of derived heads like *eating* and *maintenance*, this structure is inherited from the underlying base. The process is simple and purely semantic, and gives the same results as deriving the compound and simple derivates independently. Thus, the cost of Booij's solution would be null, yet it buys a system that applies to Latinate as well as Germanic compounds, nominal and verbal, simple and compound derivations alike.

Baker's View of Noun Incorporation

Baker (1988a) attempts to explain noun incorporation in terms of the principles of contemporary P&P theory. Baker claims that noun incorporation is a syntactic process and not lexical. He then sets out to prove that noun incorporation is constrained by the Empty Category Principle (ECP), which restricts empty categories to positions which are strictly governed, that is, those for which verbs are subcategorized. If Objects are moved syntactically, they leave a trace, which under ECP must be governed by the verb. Since the verb governs only the Object and Indirect Object, the ECP allows only these two categories in incorporated verbs. Subjects and adjuncts should not be incorporable. In order to explain the incorporation of nouns governed by adpositions meaning ''to/for'' in some languages, Baker claims that such adpositions in fact are empty markers of Indirect Objects.

Like Roeper and Siegel's and Selkirk's approaches to nominal compounds, Baker's hypothesis is based on the assumption that only a very small number of relations are permitted in verbal compound derivations. However, many more relations are reflected in the incorporated noun than even the Patient, Location, and Instrument allowed by Mithun (1984). Even though the Object relation dominates all others among the spoken tokens of verbal compounds, thriving polysynthetic languages with verbal compounding provide substantial evidence that many more grammatical relations besides Objects may be incorporated into complex verbs.[6]

Takelma: (Sapir 1922: 68) Adv + MEANS	(7.25)	dāᵃ-ts.!elei-sgalaw-i'n (dāᵃ: "ear; beside") beside-eye-looked.at-1Sg/3Pl (or: aside-with.the.eye-looked.at- ɪSɢ/3PL) "I looked at them askance"
Chukchee: (Skorik 1977: 241) OBJECT + TIME + DURATION	(7.26)	mən-nəki-ure-qepl-uvičven-mək 1IMP-night-long-ball-play-1P1 "Let's-night-long-ball-play"
Nahuatl: Sapir 1911 MEANS	(7.27)	ni-k-tle-watsa in nakatl I-OBJ-fire-roast DEF meat "I fire-roasted the meat"
Takelma: Sapir 1922 SOCIATIVE + LOCATIVE	(7.28)	nãx-i-heᵉl-agw-n pipe-hand-sing-SOC-ɪSG "I-pipe-hand-sing" ("I sing with my pipe in my hand"
Takelma: Sapir 1922 ALLATIVE/ILLATIVE	(7.29)	ha-t'gāᵃ-gwidìk'ʷ into-earth-threw.3SG/3SG "He-to-earth-threw-it" ("He threw it into the open")
Chukchee: Skorik 1977:241 GOAL + Adj	(7.30)	mət-majŋ-ə-gətg-ə-lqən-mək 1PLPST -big - lake- go -PL "We-big-lake-went" ("We went to the big lake")
Tiwi: Osborne 1974: 47 Adverb + OBJECT	(7.31)	ji - məni -ŋilimpaŋ-alipi-aŋkina 3SG-1SGACC-sleeping-meat-steal "He-sleeping-meat-robbed-me" "He stole my meat while I was asleep"
Classical Nahuatl: Sullivan 1988: 219 ILLATIVE	(7.32)	te - tla -ix -co -maca SUB-OBJ- face-LOC-give "someone-something-in(to)-face- give" "to tell someone his faults to his face"
Classical Nahuatl: Sullivan 1988: 218 MANNER	(7.33)	cuauh-tza'tzi "eagle-screech" "to screech like an eagle"

Most of the incorporations above differ in no material way from English verbal compounds. English does not allow more than one noun or adjective to be incorporated; this, however, would seem to be a language-dependent constraint. Otherwise, English compounds behave the same way as the forms of (7.25–7.33): the first sister need not be incorporated nor the first argument satisfied within an incorporation or compound, as (7.34) indicates.

(7.34) a. Manner: cold-roll (aluminum), spray-paint (the wall), freeze-dry coffee), quick-freeze (beans)
   b. Locus: mountain-bike (the trails), road-test (the bike), desert-train (soldiers), sky-write (a message), back-stab (a neighbor)
   c. Means: fire-brew (beer), hand-knit (a sweater), machine-wash (clothes), computer-test (anything)

In summary then, these compound forms incorporate a far greater range of grammatical relations than the ECP allows. Possible relations include Object, Recipient, Goal, Means, Sociation, Comitation, Manner, and the Locatives: Allative and Illative, Punctual Time (Temporal Locus) and Duration. Locatives corresponding semantically to English *in, on, to, from* are incorporated without adpositional markers, while others, those meaning "under, over, into", Sociative "with", and so on, are usually incorporated with some marker.

The ECP does seem to predict the absence of Subject relations in compounds based on transitive verbs, for example, *boy-carry, snake-swallow, sun-burn*. As the last example suggests, however, the case even here is difficult to prove. Consider the sentences in (7.35), for example.

(7.35) a. The girl sun-burned her arm
   b. Mary student-directed the play
   c. The company doctor-tests all its drugs

All these sentences superficially seem to contain compound verbs based on transitive verbs plus a noun standing in Subject relation to that verb; however, other interpretations are possible. (7.35a) may also paraphrase *the girl burned her arm in the sun* if the relation in the compound is Locative. (7.35b) might be motivated by an Essive relation: *Mary directed the play as a student*. If, however, the meanings of the compounds in (7.35) do reflect various non-Subject grammatical relations, those relations are not Direct and Indirect Object and thus still recommend relaxing the constraints on incorporation and considering it as verbal compounding.

7.5.2 *Toward Loosening Constraints on Functional Derivations*

Those familiar with traditional morphological research will immediately recognize in the relations exemplified by (7.25–7.33) the thematic relations of recent GB research, the grammatical functions of LFG, and the functions of the traditional grammatical category, Case. Case, as chapter 11 will show, is a category whose properties include Nominative, Accusative, Genitive, Dative, Ablative, Locative, and Instrumental. These properties, in turn, express a set of relations referred to here as GRAMMATICAL FUNCTIONS. The use of the Nominative is usually restricted to marking the Subject of the sentence, for which reason Jakobson considered it the ultimately unmarked case (see also Falk 1991). The Instrumental, however, has several functions in IE and other languages; common among them are Means (*hit with a hammer*), Manner (*dance with grace*), Agent (*hit by John*), and Sociation (*work with John*). The Accusative marks the Direct Object but also Duration (*work all night*) and Measure (*weigh five pounds*). The Genitive marks Possessivity (*the honor of the man*) and Possession (*a man of honor*), Object of Quantification (*much of the time*), Partitivity (*some of the milk, the arm of the chair*), and other relations. English, as these examples demonstrate, marks the same relations with a tightly closed class of prepositions.

Any hypothesis which restricts functional L-derivations and compounding to these relations runs afoul of three problems. The first is that thematic relations, deep cases, or case functions are typically considered semantic. Chapter 9 will establish that they are in fact grammatical and independent of conceptual relations. The second problem is that most case functions are associated with prepositions, which are held to be lexical items in current GB theory. If these functions are grammatical rather than semantic, prepositions must be grammatical function markers rather than lexical items—an idea which has enjoyed some popularity in this century but which remains unsettled. Chapter 10 will mount a new case for this notion. Third, the set of property functions marked by prepositions and cases must represent an integral category. If prepositions are grammatical function markers in a class with case endings, the same functions marked by prepositions in English, such as Indirect Object, Means, Locus, Origin, should be marked by pure cases like Dative, Instrumental, Locative and Ablative in other languages.

A universal hypothesis restricting functional L-derivations to grammatical functions must treat prepositions and case endings as morphological variations marking the same set of category functions. Chapter 11 will attend to this question and chapter 12 will demonstrate how syntax will handle an expanded system of case which includes Ps as case markers in a P&P grammar. Finally, chapter 13 will demonstrate that functional L-derivations, simple and compound, derive from one set of grammatical (case) functions which must be base generated and accessible to both syntax and the lexicon. Before embarking on this complex enterprise, however, chapter 8 will next examine the type of L-derivation that most saliently supports grammar-semantics autonomy: transposition.

7.6 CONCLUSION

The overview of the data and literature on word formation in this chapter revealed four basic types of operations for which the lexicon appears to be responsible. First, the lexicon must have a set of rules which toggle the values on binary and nonbinary features of lexical items; rules which switch Masculine nouns to Feminine ones, Singular nouns to Plural. Second, languages seem to contain a set of expressive derivations which ultimately reflect the attitude of the speaker toward the size and merit of the referent. Much more remains to be said about this class of derivations, but at this point it remains a mysterious type. Third, languages have a set of functional derivations which operate over grammatical functions like Subject, Object, Locus, Means, Manner, Possession, Possessive, Origin and the like. These functions are very similar to those of Case inflection and hence the possibility that the two sets of functions are identical will be examined in Chapter 13. Finally, the lexicon can also change the lexical class of a lexeme by simply providing a stem with the lexical subcategorization features of a new class. We are curious to know whether the lexicon can provide all its classes with the subcategorization of all other classes, the zero hypothesis. This issue will be the topic of the next chapter.

NOTES

1. The Masculine form is also used when the term refers to a position of authority or prestige. Hence, office secretaries are referred to as *sekretar'* (Masculine) and *sekretar-ša* (Feminine) depending upon the sex of the referent in Russian; however, a Party secretary in the former Soviet Union was referred to only by the grammatically Masculine *sekretar'*, regardless of sex (Meier 1988).

2. In Czech and Serbo-Croatian, however, Masculine and Feminine are distinguished in the Plural and, as this hypothesis predicts, they do not distinguish animacy in the Plural.

3. This account explains why no Slavic or other IE language possesses a special affix or other marking for animacy (Beard 1986).

4. It is not clear why Roeper and Siegel chose a semantically anomalous example in this case. Goods analytically are not built by hand in factories, thus the grammatical issue is confused with a referential anomaly. The unacceptability of the latter term therefore could be a matter of semantics, not grammar.

5. Mithun 1984 discovered the same three functions dominate verbal compounds in verb incorporation languages.

6. Baker (1988b) revises current P&P theory to allow verbs to govern Instruments, but this move still leaves the rule of verbal compounding materially overconstrained.

Chapter Eight

Transposition

8.1 Lexical Transposition

Chapter 7 introduced four types of L-derivation operating exclusively on the abstract category features of lexical items without determining the phonological spelling of affixation. Discussion of two of the types of rules, feature value switches and expressive derivations, has been completed. This chapter outlines a theory of transposition. The next six chapters will then deal with the most complex and widely discussed type of L-derivation, the functional derivations.

Szymanek (1988: 31–39) has laid a foundation for the study of transpositions in an LMBM framework. According to Szymanek, the important distinction between the types of derivations has not been pursued in the literature because "most investigators focus on the form and distribution . . . of *individual* affixes found in a language, instead of first trying to establish what categorial functions may be expressed on the level of word-formation in this or that language, and only then concentrating on the formal means used to achieve this" (Szymanek 1988: 31). The first question pertaining to transpositions which needs to be raised is to what extent does the operation of transposition need to be constrained in UG. The ideal would be no necessary universal constraint, so that each class, N, A, V, may be shifted to either of the other two. In order to determine whether this is the case, we must examine each lexical class for a rule that maps it onto the other two without grammatical effect beyond adjusting its lexical class features.

Let us begin this examination of the data with the optimal assumption:

(8.1) *The lexicon may transpose any member of any major lexical class (N, V, A) to any other major lexical class by providing it only with the lexical G-features of the target class and neutralizing (but not deleting) the inherent G-features of the base.*

"Neutralize" means that the value settings of the grammatical features of the base are set at some value which the MS-component recognizes but does not respond to, for example, [+Transitive] → [0Transitive]. This prevents their conditioning affixation on bases which have not undergone transposition.[1]

To prove (8.1) true, we must find the output types listed in (8.2), demonstrate that any limitations on them are language-specific, and explain how adverbs fit the picture.

(8.2)　a. N → V　　c. N → A　　e. V → N
　　　　b. A → V　　d. V → A　　f. A → N

(8.2a–8.2b), for example, imply that, subject to any language-specific constraints, any noun or adjective may be provided with the lexical features defining a verb and nothing more by the lexicon. While other verbal derivations may also be available in a given language, all languages with L-derivational morphology should evidence this type of verbal transposition. According to chapter six, the only verbal lexical categories are Verb Class and Transitivity. Verbal transposition is hence defined as the addition of these features to a nonverbal item. The rule may also add the features [+V, −N], but no motivation for these features appear in the morphological data. So far as morphology is concerned, any lexeme containing the features for Verb Class and Transitivity belongs to the class which is marked in current syntactic theories as [+V, −N].

(8.2c–8.2d) compel the lexicon to maintain a rule that provides nouns and verbs with the distinctive lexical feature(s) of adjectives. The obvious distinctive adjectival category is Gradability, the Comparative and Superlative degrees. Section 8.2.2 will demonstrate that the major constraints on purely adjectival behavior are predicated on this category. This assumption implies that adjectival transposition will generate adjectives which are either [+Gradable] or [−Gradable]. Again, morphology does not motivate further featurization, so that the current syntactic features [+V, +N] are simply equivalent to [+Gradable]. Nonadjectives lack this feature altogether.

(8.2e–8.2f) require an L-rule which provides verbs and adjectives with the features of substantives—Number, Noun Class, Gender, and animacy. Number is ostensibly the critical category. Even isolating languages which do not morphologically mark Number, Indonesian for example, exhibit a sensitivity to Number. An Indonesian noun may be reduplicated to indicate Plurality, even though specific pluralizing morphemes are not available. However, chapter 7 raised evidence suggesting that mass (singularis tantum) nouns possess no Number features, so that the addition of Number features to nouns cannot serve to distinguish them from the other two lexical classes. The most likely alternative to Number as the distinguishing feature of nouns is Noun Class. In synthetic languages this class chooses declensions; in analytic languages like Chinese and Vietnamese it chooses lexical classifiers. There are, however, some languages—English is one of them—which seem not to classify nouns. There is ostensibly no one category distinguishing all nouns as Transitivity distinguishes verbs and Gradability defines (qualitative) adjectives.

A solution to this question within the P&P model of GB grammar is that the features Number, Gender, and Noun Class are the parameters of nouns. All nouns possess the features Number and Noun Class and those referring to animate beings possess Gender features. However, since not every noun reflects all these features morphologically, that is, since these features are not grammatically relevant for all nouns, not all possess ± values for them. Rather than a mass noun not possessing the features Plural and Singular, as was suggested in chapter 7, they simply do not possess any values for these features. The ability of speakers to force Plurality on mass nouns speaks for this approach, as in *two beers, three meats, the sands of time*. If the absence of Tense and Comparison features in nouns explains the inability to force these categories on nouns, the presence of [Plural, Singular] would account for these examples.

Whether values are added to Number features becomes another parameter of Number; they are not added to mass nouns, whose marking becomes [0Plural, 0Singular]. The parameters of the lexical class "noun" include Number and Noun Class as always potentially relevant whereas Gradability, Transitivity, and Verb Class are never potentially relevant. In learning a language, then, children must simply learn whether these categories are relevant to the target language and how that relevance is expressed morphologically. The assumption hereafter will be that the features [0Plural, 0Singular] and [0Noun Class] are obligatorily added to nominal transpositions and values must be added to one or the other. [0Feminine, 0Masculine] are added conditionally in some languages and values are both added and set under relatively complex conditions.

Let us now examine the derivational data of English and a few other languages for evidence of each of the six potential types of transposition. Hopefully, such an examination will also bring more insight into the nature of transposition.

8.2.1 N → V

The N → V shift reveals problems in determining whether an L-derivation is a functional derivation or transposition caused by the separation of derivation and affixation. Specifically, since affixation is not isomorphically determined by derivation, its presence or absence cannot serve as proof of derivation of any type. A test for recognizing transposition more reliable than affixation must be developed before the data can be tested for (8.2).

Clark and Clark (1979) provide an in-depth analysis of a set of denominal verbs whose specific semantic content is difficult to determine. (8.3) illustrates the much larger corpus which they submit.

(8.3)	a.	hammer	to hammer	e.	shell	to shell
	b.	brush	to brush	f.	husk	to husk
	c.	saddle	to saddle	g.	ship	to ship
	d.	frost	to frost	h.	cap	to cap

Clark and Clark argued that these verbs are derived without the addition of any grammatical categories and concluded that the variation in meaning is purely semantic. If these derivations are transpositions, that fact must be determined primarily on the basis of semantic, not affixational, evidence; however, Clark and Clark arbitrarily selected their set of unsuffixed forms from a larger set of asemantic verbalizations, many of which are suffixed, as (8.4) demonstrates.

(8.4)	a.	crystal	to crystallize	a′.	clot	to clot
	b.	scar	to scarify	b′.	mark	to mark
	c.	carbon	to carbonate	c′.	salt	to salt

An adequate theory of L-derivation must account for both affixed and unaffixed variants, since both are based on the identical derivations (section 2.3.1). The productive meanings of the verb *crystallize* (8.4a) is "come to have crystals" and "cause to have crystals" just as *clot* means "come to have clots" and "cause to have clots". The meaning of *scarify a table* is to "cause the table to have scars"; to *mark a table* means to "cause the table to have marks" (8.4b). (8.4c) reflects the same pattern. Hence no derivational basis exists for Clark and Clark's distinction of "zero-derived" verbs and derived verbs exhibiting affixation.

In accord with the predictions of LMBM, affixes provide no more evidence as to the nature of verbalizations than does the zero affixation. The most common isolable semantic functions in these derivations, which we usually associate with grammatical functions, are BECOME(XY), CAUSE(XYZ), often combined with other functions. They are marked by three productive suffixes, *-ize, -ify,* and *-ate,* but there is no positive correlation between the suffixes and the functions. Whatever types of derivation are reflected in (8.4), they are unrelated to affixation for affix selection is conditioned by the base. The presence or absence of affixation thus cannot distinguish transpositions from functional and other types of derivations.

Let us now examine the semantic categories involved in these verbalizations for some indication of whether they reflect transposition or functional derivation (or both). The two categories associated with the semantic concepts BECOME(XY) and CAUSE(XYZ) are most likely to be involved in transposition. BECOME(XY), the semantic interpretation of the Inchoative verbal function, may be read into all verbalizations. CAUSE(XYZ) is obviously associated with Causative, which is detectable exclusively in the Transitive verbalizations. (8.5) illustrates the Intransitive pattern; (8.6) exemplifies the Transitive one.

(8.5)   a. to crystallize "become crystal"
        b. to vaporize "become vapor"
        c. to materialize "become material"

(8.6)   a. to deputize "cause Y to be(come) a deputy"
        b. to vaporize "cause Y to be(come) vapor"
        c. to prioritize "cause Y to be(come) a priority"

The two recurrent semantic functions in these derivations are necessarily and sufficiently associated with Transitivity, an interesting fact, since aside from Verb Class, Transitivity is the only inherent lexical category of verbs found in chapter 6. Intransitivity and Transitivity are, therefore, precisely the features we would expect transposition to assign to a noun in order to simply reclassify it as a verb. The fact that Inchoative always accompanies Intransitive derivation while Causative is restricted to the Transitive version suggests that we are dealing with semantic categories predictable from grammatical functions, which are, in turn, predictable from transposition. If deadjectival verbs are simply assigned the feature [±Transitive] by transposition and the value then set at either " + " or " − ", we can account for the basic semantic categories of all the verbalizations examined thus far. If the verbalization bears the feature [− Transitive], semantic conventions assign the semantic function BECOME (XY). If the verbalization bears the feature [+ Transitive], semantic conventions assign it both BECOME(XY) and CAUSE(XYZ). (8.7) exemplifies the sort of mapping convention or CORRESPONDENCE RULE which will be required to interpret [− Transitive] in semantics.

(8.7) *If the output of a verbal transposition is marked [− Transitive], assign it the predicate structure [BECOME(XY)] and coindex Y with the R-representation of the base.*

(8.7) takes some liberties with the more precise formalizations developed in Jackendoff (1990) but serves our purposes here. The effect of this correspondence convention is to account for the argument relations in the semantic representation of a newly transposed Inchoative verb on the basis of Transitivity.

(8.7) must be accompanied by another such convention to interpret the effect of Transitivity for semantics. (8.8) is a reasonable facsimile of that principle; it merely adds [CAUSE(XYZ)] and appropriately adjusts argument structure.

(8.8) *If the output of a verbal derivation is marked [+ Transitive], assign it the predicate structure [CAUSE(XY$_i$[BECOME(Y$_i$Z)])] and coindex Z with the R-representation of the base.*

The point is that, given information about the Transitivity of the transposed verb, information provided by an unconstrained transposition rule such as (8.1), and a simple toggle which sets the values for that feature, the more elaborate semantic interpretations of "*X* BECOMES N" and "CAUSE *X* TO BECOME N" are wholly predictable. Moreover, these semantic readings may be derived without introducing the categories Causative and Inchoative at the grammatical level.

The examples in (8.3), however, contain meanings even more specific than those predicted by (8.6) and (8.7). The examples of (8.3) may still be counted as transpositions rather than functional derivates if the remaining intension may be predicted from the R-representation of the base noun. For example, verbs derived from nouns which are lexically INSTRUMENTS, such as, *to hammer, to brush, to knife, to paddle, to comb,* have very predictable meanings: "to use *X, X* = some instrument, in accord with its natural function."[2] Kiparsky (1983: 14–15) argued that when verbs are derived from nouns referring to instruments, some inherit the specific meaning of the underlying noun, while others do not. *To pencil* is an example of the former; one can pencil something (in) only with a pencil; *he penciled his name in with a ball-point pen* is unacceptable. The verbs in (8.9) are examples of the latter in that they do not imply the use of the specific instrument referred to by the base noun, as the Instrumental PPs demonstrate:

(8.9)   a. He brushed his coat with his hand
      b. I paddled the canoe with a copy of the New York Times
      c. He combed his hair with his fingers

Kiparsky took this loss of specificity in the verbs in (8.9) to signify that they have become lexicalized and hence must be listed in pairs with their corresponding noun, as in the case of *brush$_N$* and *brush$_V$*.

Kiparsky's data, however, yield another analysis more in keeping with their high productivity. If the R-representation of lexical Instrumental nouns possess features which specify their natural function (Pustejovsky's TELIC FEATURE; section 7.4), it becomes possible to predict the specific sense of Kiparsky's verbs from their base. Let us begin with the natural assumption that the definition of the noun *hammer* would be roughly [INSTRUMENT$_i$ POUND(XY$_{USE}$Z$_i$) . . .], that is, "an instrument used to pound Y," where POUND(XY$_{USE}$Z) is the natural function of *hammer*.

(USE is the telic function of the category INSTRUMENT.) The definition of *to brush,* similarly, would be [INSTRUMENT$_i$ WIPE(XY$_{USE}$Z$_i$) $_{PURPOSE}$GO (U$_{FROM}$Y)] or, "an instrument used to wipe objects for the purpose of removing some U from them." Of course, the complete definitions will further specify the physical properties of hammers and brushes; however, for our purposes, only the natural function specifiers are relevant.

Assuming further that the derivation process in this instance is a semantically vacuous transposition, the simplest explanation of Kiparsky's pairs is that, since the definition of a noun contains its natural function, all features denoting anything other than the natural function may be ignored when the noun is used in verbal contexts. The predicted meaning of the verbal derivation, then, is the natural function of the noun. Thus, *(to) hammer* will mean "pound," *(to) brush* will mean "wipe (with the intent of removing)," and so on. Indeed, since the meaning of the derivation is the natural function of the base, no grammatical functional derivation can be involved. However, so long as all other semantic features survive transposition, they should define the default instrument, so that *he hammered in the nail* means, ceteris paribus, that he pounded it with a hammer.

While the absence of affixation cannot be taken as proof of no functional derivation, the presence of affixation can provide oblique evidence of functional derivations. The assumption is that affixes and other morphological marking are conditioned primarily by grammatical, not semantic functions. Grammatical functions similar to the semantic functions which Clark and Clark found among bare verbs are marked overtly among deverbal nominals in a consistent though not isomorphic manner. It is possible to distinguish these grammatical functions from semantic functions. Consider the following Instrumental deverbal nominals.

(8.10)   a. relaxant, stimulant, irritant, lubricant, contaminant, defoliant
         b. mixer, trimmer, mower, lighter; softener, whitener, developer
         c. (a) lift, catch, cover, swing; (a) rinse, wash, stain, seal, soak

The category marked by *-ənt, -er,* and the omission of any overt marker in (8.10) seems to be the grammatical function Means, because it maps two intuitive referential categories, INSTRUMENT and CHEMICAL AGENT, onto the base verb.[3] While English has at least two affixes which mark the deverbal Instrumentals and allows null marking as well, liquid agents and solid tools are consistently distinguished only among Latinate stems. While the native suffixes do not distinguish the semantic categories, they do, however, distinguish the Means function from other functions like the Locus, as in *bakery, hatchery, fishery.*

This characterization of a single grammatical function and two semantic categories must be approached cautiously, however, since the same suffixes are also used to mark the Subjective L-derivation: *resident, runner, cook.* If we consider this a case of polyfunctionality, why should we not draw the analogy here and conclude that Liquid Means and Solid Means are grammatical categories on the same level as Subjective and Means? In other words, how do we choose between the hypothesis that Means is a grammatical function which maps two semantic categories into grammar, and the hypothesis that Liquid Means and Solid Means are two functions operating at the grammatical level? This question cannot be fully answered in this chapter, for it depends upon the central issue of the following chapter: the question of where to draw the line between grammatical and semantic functions (section 9.4.1 offers a conclusive resolution of this particular problem).

Before proposing a test for transpositions within an LMBM model, let us examine some other languages with denominal verbalizations similar to the English ones discussed above. Within LMBM it is possible that some of the semantic categories mentioned by Clark and Clark, for example, AGENT, INSTRUMENT, LOCATION, SOURCE, and GOAL, are grammatical functions and represent functional L-derivations which are simply not overtly marked because of the impoverishment of English morphology. In order to determine whether affixation might provide more clues where it is more readily available, let us turn to a language with a more richly endowed overt marking system: Yupik.

Menovshchikov (1967: 16–21) sharply distinguishes noun-verb conversion in Yupik from overtly marked derivation. What he calls denominal conversion is an operation of limited productivity, which simply adds the Conjugation marker *-qu* to any noun. Otherwise, his examples are remarkably similar to the English null derivations described by Clark and Clark, as (8.11) illustrates.[4]

(8.11)　a. mysuna　comb　　mysuna-qu-q "he combs"
　　　　　　　　　　　　comb-PRES-3RDSG
　　　　b. pama　pump　　pama-qu-q "he pumps"
　　　　　　　　　　　　pump-PRES-3RDSG

The examples of (8.11) are lexically INSTRUMENTAL nouns whose verbal meaning is that of their natural function, as in the case of Kiparsky's examples (8.9). Yupik does overtly mark some distinguishable relations between derived verbs and their underlying nouns; most fit the description of nominal case functions and hence seem to be grammatically determined. Appendix B categorizes all those Yupik verbalizations listed in Menovshchikov (1967), Menovshchikov (1980), and Menovshchikov and Vakhtin (1983) according to the categories of Appendix A and the preceding chapters. The Yupik derivations exhibit as well a few parallels with the semantic categories of Clark and Clark: GOAL is particularly salient, along with a related category, PURPOSE. INSTRUMENT is notably absent but is present in the zero-derived forms of (8.11); moreover, this same category receives overt marking in Chukchee, another highly synthetic language spoken in the same general area (taken from Appendix C):

(8.12) a. rəpe-ŋə "hammer"   rəpe-tku-k "to hammer"
        b. walə "knife"   walə-tku-k "to cut"
        c. wəlpə "shovel"   wəlpə-tku-k "to shovel"

Again, affixation does not contribute to determining whether we are dealing with transposition or functional derivation. How do we then determine whether the examples in (8.12) are generated by the same sort of operation involving the same category, semantic INSTRUMENT rather than grammatical Means, as in (8.10)?

In fact, there is a difference between the Instrumental nominals of (8.10), on the one hand, and the verbalizations in (8.11) and (8.12), on the other. The difference points to a distinction between functional derivation and transposition. The difference is that the category Means cannot be derived from the base in (8.10), while in (8.11) and (8.12) there is no other source for it. In other words, the input of the rule which generates (8.11) and (8.12) must be restricted to lexical instruments in order for the output to have the semantic function, USE(XY). As explained above, in connection with Kiparsky's examples, the precise meaning of these derivates can be predicted perfectly only if they are transposed, if no grammatical is function added by the rule. This is not the case with (8.10), where the bases are verbs which do not generally have the conceptual feature INSTRUMENT or USE(XY) in their R-representation.

It follows, as in the case of (8.9), that nothing other than the inherent verbal category features are added by grammar to the derivation of (8.11) and (8.12). The specific semantic output of the derivation is most accurately predicted by the input, that is, the semantic representation of the base. Not only does this suggest that (8.11) and (8.12) both represent transposition, it suggests a test for transposition. If the semantic variation of the output of a lexical operation is predictable from the R-representation of the input, lexical functions cannot be invoked to account for the variation. Transposition predicts the addition of Verb Class and Transitivity only. Before wording a statement of the Transposition Test, let us apply this corollary to a more difficult set of Yupik data.

Perhaps the most problematic meanings in the Yupik data of Appendix B to explain is "eat N" and "make N." These L-derivational interpretations are not functions found among the universal L-derivational functions of Appendix A. Yet the suffixes which mark them are generally consistent according to Menovshchikov, implying that they express semantically specific lexical functions. Consider the examples listed in (8.13) and (8.14).

(8.13)   a. iqałjuk "fish"   iqałjux-tu- "eat fish"
         b. əłqwaq "sea cabbage"   əłqwaχ-tu- "eat sea cabbage"
         c. ukaq "perch"   ukaχ-tu-"eat perch"

(8.14)   a. pana "spear"   pana-ŋłja- "make a spear"
         b. məŋtəʁa-q "house"   məŋtəʁa-ŋłja- "build a house
         c. anja-q "canoe"   aŋja-ŋłja- "make a canoe"

The input of (8.13) must be a noun referring to an edible object belonging to the semantic category FOOD, and the input of (8.14) must be a constructed object belonging to the semantic category ARTIFACT. The fact that the input is constrained to control the meaning of the output indicates strongly that transposition is at work here. How then do these examples acquire such specific meanings and why are those meanings distinguished by affixation?

Let us assume that FOOD and ARTIFACT are not primitive categories but that FOOD must be represented as roughly $[\text{THING}_j \text{ ACTOR}_i \text{ EAT} (\text{XY}_j)]$ and ARTIFACT, as $[\text{THING}_j \text{ ACTOR}_i \text{ MAKE}(\text{X}_i\text{Y}_j)]$. If so, the meaning "eat N," where N must belong to the category FOOD, is accounted for on the same basis as that which predicted the precise INSTRUMENTAL meanings of the examples in (8.11) above. That is, if the semantic input to the derivation rule which generates (8.15) is constrained to nouns containing, say, $[\text{THING}_j, \text{EAT}(\text{XY}_j)]$, and if transposition assigns no grammatical function to the derivation, the semantic component has no alternative but to search the R-representation of the base noun for a meaning for the new transposition. The most obvious natural function associated with food is the predicate EAT(XY). The same interpretation of (8.15) accounts for the meaning "make N" among denominal verbs based on nouns referring to artifacts.

Leaving aside for the moment the question of why distinct affixes mark the same derivation in (8.13) and (8.14), let us now articulate our universal test for discriminating transposition from functional L-derivation:

(8.16) *A derivate whose meaning differs from that of its base by either (i) the inherent grammatical category of the derived lexical class and/or (ii) a semantic feature present in the base itself is a transposition.*

If we apply (8.16) to all the Yupik data of Appendix B, we discover that some of the types there are in fact functional L-derivations. Specifically, the categories Goal, Purpose, Similitude, and Possession are accounted for neither by the inherent grammatical features of verbs nor by the semantic categories restricted to the input. The remaining forms are predictable under the assumption that these verbs are nouns simply shifted to the verbal lexical class, their semantic interpretations left to logic and the semantic categories of each individual base item.

The final question pertaining to transposition, then, is this: why does Yupik and Chukchee affixation distinguish the semantic classes of the bases of transpositions? Given strict modularity and the location of the MS-component in grammar, we would expect the MS-component to be conditioned by the G-representation of the lexical base and not by its R-representation. Should we weaken the principle of strict modularity and allow some semantic relations to condition affixation? The type of semantic discrimination among transpositions varies with the availability of affixes. That is, in morphologically impoverished languages like English, it does not occur. Only in languages like Chukchee and Yupik, which have a superfluity of affixes, are the various base meanings of transpositions distinguished.

Beard (1981) offers another explanation that remains a reasonable hypothesis in these cases. Let us say that at the grammatical level in morpheme-rich languages, speakers have a choice of several affixes for marking transpositions. Given the highly organized nature of language, it is most unlikely that the superfluous affixes will be used randomly.[5] Having no grammatical basis for choosing between the excess affixes, speakers resort to semantic conventions not unlike derivation rules, but use them at the level of performance. This interpretation does not weaken the modularity of the MS-component by allowing it to operate on semantic categories, because the level of regularity is not grammatical. Nor does it materially strengthen the theory, for it applies only as a last resort and only in cases of affixational superfluity. It makes the easily disconfirmable predictions that only nouns containing appropriate natural functions will be subject to semantically motivated affixation, and that they are subject to such affixation only in morphology-rich languages.

8.2.2 N → A

The obvious candidate for transposition from noun to adjective is the relational adjective (RAdj). RAdjs differ from qualitative adjectives (QAdjs) in that the latter are not subject to (i) comparison, (ii) predication, (iii) modification by delimiters like *very,* (iv) adverbalization, and (v) lexical nominalization. Table 8.1 illustrates these two subclasses with the RAdj *federal* and the QAdj *pleasant.* The striking differences in these two types of adjectives demand that we consider them independently.

Relational Adjectives (RAdj)

The RAdj *federal* in Table 8.1 is lexical but the majority of RAdjs are derived from nouns (Levi 1978). (8.17) is a representative sampling of derived RAdjs.

Table 8.1   A Comparison of RAdjs and QAdjs

federal tax (RAdj)	*a pleasant tax (QAdj)*
1. *this tax is federal	this tax is pleasant
2. *this tax is more federal than...	this tax is more pleasant than...
3. *this tax is very federal	this tax is very pleasant
4. *to tax federally	to tax pleasantly
5. *the federality of this tax	the pleasantness of this tax

(8.17)   a. industrial output   c. senatorial leadership
         b. cellular structure   d. budgetary item

Levi noted that RAdjs often are semantically paired with a plain noun in attribute position. Those in (8.17), for example, semantically match those in (8.18).

(8.18)   a. industry output   c. senate leadership
         b. cell structure   d. budget item

The rule for English is that Latinate nouns are subject to affixation; Germanic nouns and, optionally, Latinate nouns are used without morphological marking, as in (8.18). This situation parallels that of the denominal verbs for, recall, only Latinate denominal verbs are affixed. There is also a semantic parallel. Like the denominal verbs, it is impossible to establish a single meaning for this class of derivates or even to associate a set of meanings with the set of affixes in the conditioned fashion required by the theory presented in chapter 3.

Some languages morphologically distinguish QAdjs from RAdjs. Chukchee, for example, marks all QAdjs with a special prefix *nə-* and the citation suffix *-qIn*, as in (8.19) from Skorik (1961: 268, 422):

(8.19)   a. n-ilg-əqin "white"
         b. nə-korg-əq en "happy"
         c. n-erme-qin "strong"

RAdjs are not prefixed and are suffixed with *-kIn*, as in (8.20):

(8.20)   a. məčəkw-əken mumkəl "shirt-RAdj button"
         b. emnuŋ-kin gənnik "tundra-RAdj animal"
         c. lʔeleŋ-kin ewirʔən "winter-RAdj time"

The distinction would therefore seem to be a universal one, which may have morphological as well as syntactic consequences.

Levi (1978) and Warren (1984) argue that the RAdj functions may be reduced to a small number of high-level semantic functions, which Levi labels CAUSE, HAVE, MAKE, USE, BE, IN, FOR, FROM, ABOUT, and the categories ACT, PRODUCT, AGENT, and PATIENT (Levi 1978: 279–84). The resemblance of Levi's categories and Clark and Clark's eight categories mentioned in the previous section, AGENT, EXPERI-ENCER, GOAL, SOURCE, LOCATUM, LOCATION, and INSTRU-MENT, is remarkable. If these categories are grammatical functions, we must consider the possibility that RAdjs are functional L-derivations rather than transpositions. If, on the other hand, these categories are semantic, we would expect to find no correspondence between the affixes used to mark RAdjs and the categories themselves, the situation we found among the denominal verbs.

The evidence suggests that Clark and Clark, Levi, and Warren are correct: none of these categories are even conditionally associated with any specific affix. There are no RAdj rules such that function F^1 of Levi's set is expressed by -*al* under conditions C^1, by -*ory* under conditions C^2, by -*ar* under conditions C^3, and so on. In the absence of any correlation with affixes, there is no reason to believe that we are dealing with 13 different derivations. While LMBM does not require a one-one relation between derivation and affix, it does require a conditioned relation of some sort: one-many, many-one, with describable conditions allowing us to make a case for each derivation.

Like the English denominal verbs examined in the preceding section, the RAdj affixes seem to be conditioned not by the L-derivation features but by inherent features of their bases. They simply indicate the fact that the Latinate noun has been converted to an adjective by transposition or functional derivation, for both QAdj and RAdj functions receive the same affixation:

(8.21)   a. criminal law : *the law is very criminal
         b. criminal lawyer : her lawyer is very criminal

(8.22)   a. biological journal : *the journal is very biological
         b. biological response : the response was very biological

(8.23)   a. generative grammar : *the grammar is very generative
         b. generative operation : this operation is very generative

The (a) examples in (8.21–8.23) exemplify RAdj functions of the same forms which otherwise represent QAdjs, indicated by the ability of the (b) forms to predicate and take the Intensifier *very. A criminal law* is a law which deals with crime. A *Criminal lawyer* usually refers to someone who practices criminal law and hence the adjective would be a RAdj. *Criminal lawyer*, however, may also refer to someone characterized by his or her crimes, in which case the adjective must be a QAdj since in this sense it may be predicated and intensified. The same distinction holds in the examples in (8.22-8.23). Nothing therefore prevents the conclusion that RAdjs are N → RAdj transpositions which provide the base with no grammatical features other than those of the lexical class A or, at least, RAdj.[6]

Qualitative Adjectives (QAdj)

RAdjs have virtually none of the properties of QAdjs, a fact which suggests that we have assumed the habit of referring to two different categories as "adjectives". RAdjs notably lack the capacity to compare, which has been represented as the availability of the feature [±Gradable] elsewhere in this book. If transposition is to operate without universal constraint, there should be evidence of N → QAdj transposition which provides this feature. However, all QAdjs exhibit a fair number of grammatically predictable meanings which are often distinguished morphologically. The two most common mean "Like N" and "Having N":

(8.24)   a. a friend-ly person ("like a friend") Similitudinal
         b. a blue-eye-d bandit ("having blue eyes") Possessional

(8.24) exemplifies Similitudinal and Possessional QAdjs. The two functions which distinguish them, Manner and Possession, are conspicuous grammatical functions in inflection. Manner is a function of the Instrumental case in Russian: *on voet volk-om* "he howls like a wolf." The Possessional is a Genitive function in Serbo-Croatian: *čovek plav-ih oč-iju* "a man of blue eyes = a man with blue eyes". The point is that the derived QAdjs in (8.24) all reflect relations which count as grammatical category functions elsewhere in grammar; therefore, they must be considered grammatical functions among L-derivations, too. It follows that (8.24) may represent the output of functional derivation rather than transposition.

Beard (1993), however, showed that this characterization of Similitudinal and Possessional QAdjs is incomplete and that the QAdjs in (8.24) may in fact count as transpositions. In order to explore this hypothesis, it is necessary to understand more clearly the nature of QAdjs and the relation of semantic theory to lexical classes and morphological categories. This is scheduled for the next chapter. Suffice it to close this section with the observation that the evidence for transposition generating RAdjs is solid and robust. We must either find evidence for QAdj transposition somewhere in the data or eventually provide a reason for why this type of transposition might be ruled out.

8.2.3 $A \rightarrow V$

The discussion of $N \rightarrow V$ transposition leads us to expect to find exactly two variants of the $A \rightarrow V$ transposition, one Intransitive, corresponding to the predicate [BECOME(YZ)], and the other, Transitive, corresponding to [CAUSE(XY$_i$) [BECOME(Y$_i$Z)]], where Z is the property indicated by the base adjective. For example, *John dried the clothes* should mean that John caused the clothes to become dry, [CAUSE(JOHN, CLOTHES) [BECOME(CLOTHES, DRY)]].[7]

All languages with morphology, even morphology as degenerate as that of English, maintain two deadjectival verbalizations with precisely these attributes. They are often morphologically unmarked and undistinguished, as in the case of the following English examples.

(8.25)   a. The channel narrowed
        b. Their clothes dried
        c. The pie cooled

(8.26)   a. They narrowed the channel
        b. They dried their clothes
        c. They cooled the pie

Since all the examples of (8.25) are Intransitive and all those of (8.22) are Transitive, and both behave otherwise like the $N \rightarrow V$ transposition, we are safe in concluding that nothing more than Transitivity distinguishes them from their bases.

Other languages exhibit the same two basic deadjectival verbalizations. Zaitseva (1978: 48, 64, 116), for example, finds examples like (8.27–8.28) in Veps, marked with distinguishing morphology:

(8.27)   a. must "black"   must-nü-da "to become black"
        b. kova "hard"   kov-idu-da "to become hard"
        c. čoma "pretty"   čom-idu-da "to become pretty"

(8.28)   a. must-išta-da "to make (something) black"
        b. kov-išta-da "to make (something) hard"
        c. čom-išta-da "to adorn, decorate (something)"

Finally, (8.29) and (8.30) illustrate exactly the same relations in Indonesian (Korigodskii et al. 1961).

(8.29) a. hitam "black"   meng-hitam "to become black"
        b. tipis "thin"   men-ipis "to become thin"
        c. gelap "dark"   meng-gelap "to become dark"

(8.30) a. meng-hitam-kan "to blacken (something)"
        b. men-ipis-kan "to thin (something) down"
        c. meng-gelap-kan "to darken (something)"

The derivation of verbs from QAdjs by assigning the base nothing more than Transitivity seems to be a universal phenomenon of inflectional languages.

The operation of A → V transposition is illustrated in (8.31). (8.31) is based on the assumption that the feature distinguishing all adjectives, RAdjs and QAdjs, from other lexical classes is Gradability. RAdjs are then represented as [-Gradable] and other lexical classes do not even possess this feature. As in chapter 5, " + " and " − " are symbols indicating semantic and grammatical relevance.

(8.31)

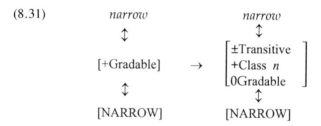

(8.31) implies that *narrow* transposed is capable of grammatical transitivity and belongs to a specific Verb Class, that is, possesses a subcategorization frame, the distinguishing feature of verbs.[8] It may also reflect Tense, Voice, Mood, and Modality, but these are all inflectional features assigned under Infl. The adjective feature, [0Gradability], has been neutralized, so that the lexical property of QAdjs is no longer grammatically active, though MS can distinguish the transposed verb from its adjective base.

The base features are required for what is apparently the only grammatical constraint on A → V transposition: the adjectival input to transposition is constrained to QAdjs. In addition to the properties distinguishing RAdjs and QAdjs illustrated in Table 8.1 above, QAdjs universally undergo verbal transposition while RAdjs like those in (8.32) universally do not.

(8.32) a. oceanic : *oceanicize/*oceanify
        b. canine : *caninate/*caninify/*caninize
        c. dental : *dentalate/*dentalify/*dentalize

The obvious explanation of this, assuming RAdjs to be transpositions as described in the previous section, is that RAdjs are all derived by transposition from nouns (Levi 1978). RAdj → V transposition would be grammatically and semantically indistinguishable from a corresponding N → V transposition.

Some of the examples in (8.31) might seem acceptable verbs, potential though unattested. *Felinize,* for example, might be derived in the sense of "make feline". However, the ability of any adjective in (8.31) to verbally transpose should vary with the degree to which it may be used acceptably in the predicate as a QAdj. That this is the case is illustrated by the examples in (8.21–8.23), *criminal, biological,* and *generative.* Those examples demonstrate the difference between the RAdj and QAdj functions of these forms. On the basis of (8.31) we would predict that the (a), (b), and (c) constructions in (8.33), those based on [− Gradable] RAdj senses, would be ungrammatical, while the (a′), (b′), and (c′) forms, based on [+ Gradable] QAdj senses, would be grammatical in English.

(8.33) a. *criminalize the law "make it criminal (not civil) law"
        a′. criminalize lawyers "make lawyers criminal"
        b. *biologicalize the journal "make it a biological journal"
        b′. biologicalize its response "make the response biological in nature"
        c. *generativize the grammar "make it a generative grammar"
        c′. generativize the operation "make the operation generative"

The prediction is borne out: the QAdj verbalizations are grammatical while those with RAdj bases decidedly are not.

There are certainly further restrictions on this transposition. Most words which have been previously derived seem to be blocked from transposition:

(8.34) a. *to friendly, *manly, *womanly, *fatherly
        b. *to childish, *boyish, *Finnish, *Danish
        c. *to starry, *dusty, *healthy, *sandy (but: to muddy)

How much of this restriction is derivational, how much semantic, and how much morphological is a question for future research. The evidence seems to indicate that these restrictions are language-dependent, since open-ended derivations involving what seem to be transpositions in other languages are not difficult to find. The following example from Turkish has been cited earlier:

(8.35)   Avrupalılaştırılamıyacaklardansınız
Avrupa-lı -laş - tır - ıl - a -mı- yacak -lar- dan -sın -ız
Europe-an-ize-CAUS-PASS-POT-NEG-FUT/PART-PL-ABL-2N D-PL
''You (all) are among those who will not be able to be caused to
become like Europeans''

Everything which should be possible in transposing adjectives to verbs, therefore, seems to emerge in the data.

8.2.4 A → N

One of the most untroubled examples of transposition is the deadjectival nominals of the type (8.36). The affixation varies greatly but the reference of the input and output is identical; the only difference is that the adjective represents the reference as a (natural) property rather than as a category.

(8.36)   a. rare   rar-ity
          b. able   abil-ity
          c. new   new-ness
          d. important   importan-ce
          e. long   leng-th

This transposition is also restricted to QAdjs. Every pure QAdj, i.e. which compares, occurs in predicate position, and accepts intensifiers like *very,* also has a corresponding noun which does no more than express the quality associated with the adjective as a noun. A *rare gem* is a gem characterized by the quality of RARITY, an *able person* is one with ABILITY, and so on. The only information necessary to interpret the relation between the base and the derivate is the name of that quality, a feature of the base, and the fact that the adjective has become a noun. The reference of the noun is the same as that of the adjective, only its grammatical guise is different: the adjective presents the reference as a natural property of the noun which it modifies and hence its semantic form is a one-place predicate. The adjective *red,* for example, refers to the color red, REDNESS; however, it attributes REDNESS to some referential term as a natural property, for example, *red car.* Transposing the adjective to a noun results in the semantically obvious: the transposed noun expresses the covert referential quality in the adjective, as in the case of *redness.*

RAdjs are not subject to this transposition because they are transposed nouns themselves, as discussed above, and are transparent terms already. Undergoing A → N transposition after having undergone N → A transposition would be semantically and grammatically vacuous. However, the transposition of ostensibly underived RAdjs is also ruled out.

(8.37) a. federal   *federality/*federalness
        b. rural   *rurality/ruralness (only in QAdj sense)
        c. cardiac   *cardiacity/*cardiacness

The reason for this is that RAdjs are a purely derived class. Examples like
(8.37) represent Latinate suppletive RAdjs for the native nouns illustrated
in (8.38).

(8.38) a. federal   ?country$_1$
        b. rural   country$_2$
        c. cardiac   heart

Even here, an RAdj $\rightarrow$ N transposition would simply duplicate the input.

8.2.5 V $\rightarrow$ A

The obvious candidate for deverbal adjectival transposition is the participle; however, the participle, rather than a single derivation, is a set of
derivations. Russian has four: (i) Present Active, (ii) Present Passive, (iii)
Past Active and (iv) Past Passive, as Table 8.2 illustrates. Lexical transposition, however, has only the power to adjust Transitivity and Verb Class;
the Tense and Voice functions in Table 8.2 are inflectional, hence syntactic
categories, to which the lexicon has no access under LMBM. Participles
therefore cannot be considered lexical transpositions.

There are, however, two classes of deverbal adjectives which are morphologically and semantically quite similar to participles but which differ
in significant respects: the so-called PARTICIPIAL ADJECTIVES. There are
two of these found consistently across languages, distinguished by the Active and Passive Voices. The English Active deverbal adjective is exempli-

Table 8.2   The Russian Participles of *(s)delaj-* "do, make"

	Active	Passive
Present Tense	delaj-ušč-ij "doing"	delaj-om-yj "being done"
Past Tense *Imperfect*	dela-vš-ij "doing (Past)"	. . .
Perfect	s-dela-vš-ij "having done"	s-dela-nn-yj "done"

fied in Table 8.3. We saw in chapter two that the suffix *-ing* is the most productive suffix in English, marking both lexical and inflectional derivations. Table 8.3 demonstrates that it is used to mark an inflectional Present Active participle and a lexical Active adjective which differs only by properties distinguishing lexical from syntactic derivations in general.

Table 8.3   Active Adjectives and Participles

Affixes	Active Adjective	Active Participle
Distinct	is (very /un)product-ive is (very /un)repent-ent is (very /un)compliment-ary	(not) produc-ing (very much) (not) repent-ing (very much) (not) compliment-ing (very much)
Same	is (very /un)surpris-ing is (very /un)excit-ing is (very /un)mov-ing	(not) surpris-ing (very much) (not) exciting (very much) (not) mov-ing (very much)

Table 8.3 reveals that the lexically derived adjective is only sporadically marked by an affix which distinguishes it from the syntactically derived participle. Suffixes other than *-ing* are added to some Latinate stems while *-ing* marks both participles and native L-derivates. Participles, however, are distinguished by their incompatibility with the adjectival prefix *un-* and intensifiers like *very*; they require *not* and *very much/many* or *a lot*. Furthermore, the participle but not the adjective accepts a base complement: *the man (not) annoying his friend* but **the man (un)annoying his friend*. Finally, the adjective but not the participle compares and, suffix permitting, nominalizes (*more productive, productivity* : **more producing (it), *producingness*). The suffix *-ing* does not allow any further affixation other than the Plural marker *-s,* permitted when it is used as a nominalizer, as in *winnings, beatings, killings,* and *-ly,* when it is used to mark adjectives, as in *surprisingly, annoyingly, movingly.* Thus the suffix usually blocks deadjectival nominal transpositions like **annoyingness, *movingness, *surprisingness.*[9]

The evidence initially points to a transpositional relation between the verb and the Active deverbal adjectives. The problem with this hypothesis is that languages which exhibit this deverbal adjective generally possess another adjective which may be derived from verbs without the addition of any grammatical function except, ostensibly, Passive, for instance, *John is very annoyed.* This adjective refers to a state while the other refers to a proclivity, as in *John is annoying.* The Passive participle and its corresponding adjective is the participle-adjective correlation most discussed in the literature (Siegel 1974; Wasow 1977; Bresnan 1978; Emonds 1985; Levin and Rappaport 1986; Milsark 1988; Sproat 1985: 306–312; Brekke 1988; Borer 1990). Table 8.4 demonstrates that the evidence for this division is the same as that for the Present participle and Active adjective except that Passive adjectives do not differ morphologically at all from the corresponding Passive participle. Even the most idiosyncratic of affixes are used without exception to mark the I- and L-derivations based on the same verb stem and function. Again, the lexical adjectives are distinguished from the participles by all the characteristics discussed in relation to the Active participles of Table 8.3.

Table 8.4   Passive Adjectives and Participles

Adjectives	*Participles*
is (very/un) impress-ed	(not) impress-ed (very much)
is (very/un) mov-ed	(not) mov-ed (very much)
is (very/un) bent	(not) bent (very much)
is (very/un) swoll-en	(not) swoll-en (very much)

The Unconstrained Transposition Hypothesis (8.1) has now fallen into a quandary. To maintain this hypothesis, we must accept both the Active and Passive adjectives as transpositions. If we reject both, the strong hypothesis fails because no other deverbal adjective exhibits the grammatical and semantic emptiness required of transposition. The only other universal deverbal adjective is the Passive Potential, for example, *breakable,* which ostensibly contains the two grammatical functions indicated by its name. If we accept the Active and Passive participle adjectives as the deverbal adjectival transpositions predicted by our hypothesis, we must explain the two versions.

The solution to this quandary again raises issues of semantics which have thus far not been broached. (Recall also the outstanding obligation to explain QAdj transpositions in semantic terms in the next chapter.) The explanation here again begins with the fact that adjectives impute natural properties to referential terms and are not themselves referential terms. Thus *red* does not refer to REDNESS as an independent object as does *redness* but rather infers it to be a property of some object. For this reason, properties are one-place predicates in symbolic logic, for instance RED(X), the semantics expressed in *X is red.* Deverbal adjectives, however, may inherit two-place predicates from their base verbs. *Annoy,* for example, has the argument structure ANNOY(XY). The deverbal adjective from *annoy* may logically link with the either argument of the base but not with both.

The only means of converting the one-place argument structure required of adjectives from two-place verbs is to generate two distinct forms, each of which assigns one of the verbs arguments to its head. Deverbal adjectives do exactly this; one form assigns the first (Subject) argument of the base verb to its head noun as, for example, *the annoying boy,* and another assigns the second (Object), as in *the annoyed boy.* The transposition of V to A, therefore, requires an operation that binds one argument internally so that it will not be assigned externally. If the first argument is bound, the second may be assigned. In this case the MS-component provides the morphology of the Passive participial that we see in examples like *(the) annoyed (boy)*, for obvious reasons.[10] If the second argument is bound, the first may be assigned, resulting in an Active adjective, as in *(the) annoying (boy).* This account does not appeal to category functions, only to the structures of verb and adjective subcategorization and the pressures they bring to bear on V $\rightarrow$ A transposition.

Despite the persuasiveness of this argument, the fact that two of the most powerful grammatical functions, Subject and Object, are involved in these adjectives taints it with the suspicion that these adjectives are functional derivations rather than transpositions. Throughout the history of Western language study they have been referred to as "Agentive" and "Patientive" adjectives and they have never been described as transpositions (see Szymanek 1988, for example). Since Subject and Object are extremely salient functions, they go a long way in explaining the striking productivity of these adjectives. We will not close the question, therefore, but will return to it when the functional L-derivations are examined in chapter 13. It is unfortunate that two issues surrounding adjective transposition must be left open; however, a little patience at this point will lead to a much broader understanding of the constraints on L-derivation and the variation in their productivity.

8.2.6 V → N

While adjectives support only one argument position in the propositional structure of their R-representation, nominals are capable of expressing two, a fact which emerges in denominal verbal transpositions like (8.39b).

(8.39)   a. John is the chauffeur of the family = [CHAUFFEUR(JOHN, FAMILY)]

   b. John chauffeurs the family = [CHAUFFEUR(JOHN, FAMILY)]

   c. John's chauffeuring (of) the family = [CHAUFFEUR(JOHN, FAMILY)]

Since (relational) nouns are capable of supporting two arguments, no need arises for two forms of nominal transpositions.

Kuryłowicz (1936) found only one deverbal nominal transposition, the Action Nominals. However, Guilbert (1975) for good cause divided the French action nominals into Perfective and Imperfective types, since differences in meaning can be reduced to the basic differences in reference of these two Aspects. Now, aspect in transpositions presents the same problem as Passive: it, too, is an I-category proper to syntax, not to the lexicon. It is not clear, however, that Aspect is involved in action nominals. Take, for example, the nominals in (8.40) and (8.41), similar to the French Perfective and Imperfective action nominals described by Guilbert:

(8.40) a. a statement
        b. a walk
        c. a swing

(8.41) a. the stating (of the facts by the mayor)
        b. (John's) walking (through town)
        c. the swinging (of the bat by the player)

The non-Resultative readings of the nominals in (8.40) refer to the action of the verb in terms of countable instances of that action, very much like the Perfective Aspect, as in *has stated*. The meanings of the nominalizations in (8.41) are very similar to the Progressive and Iterative senses of the Imperfective, for example, *is stating, has been stating*. The major difference between (8.40) and (8.41), however, may also be reduced to the differences in the derivate's capacity to express Number, specifically, whether the Number features inserted in the nominalization have been provided with values (recall section 7.2.2). If no values are added to the Number features, the MS-component can only mark the nominalization as a singularis tantum noun.

English also has Gerundives like those in (8.42) which differ from the nominalizations of (8.41) in that their Objects do not require the case marker *of*.

(8.42) a. John's reviving the play   a'. the play's being revived by
                                                 John
        b. John's having revived the   b'. the play's having been
           play   revived by John

The gerundives in (8.42) clearly reflect Tense and Voice. (Polish gerundives similarly reflect Aspect.) These derivations, as Chomsky suggested two decades ago, seem to be syntactically derived. They parallel rather perfectly the participles and verbal adverbs of English and other languages. Russian, for example, maintains four participles which fit perfectly the English gerundive paradigm: Present Active, Past Active, Present Passive, Past Passive, but no Modal forms including Future (Table 8.2). Quechua has a similar set of gerundives (Muysken and Lefebvre 1988). All these forms share in common some but not all of the verbal categories within a nonverbal syntactic classification of N and A. These forms suggest that, parallel to the lexical transpositions discussed in this chapter, languages universally have access to something like a syntactic version of transposition. However, it would take us too far afield to pursue this question here. Suffice it to conclude this section on the note that available evidence indicates that English and other languages have the capacity to transpose verbs into nouns, adding only the features defining nouns as a class: Number, Gender, and/or Noun Class.

Each underived lexical class would therefore seem to transpose into every other class (the issues of N → QAdj and V → QAdj remain open). This is visible only within the LMBM framework where L-derivation may be examined independent of affixation, which is always less predictable than derivation. No further universal constraints are needed on the operation of transposition other than to limit it to (i) neutralizing the features of the base and (ii) adding the inherent lexical features of the new class. Once the inherent features are added, feature switches set their values according to the switching principles of the given language. This means that we expect to find no more and no less than Transitive and Intransitive transposed verbs, Gradable and Ungradable adjectives, Subjective and Objective deverbal QAdjs, and all possible combinations of Number, Gender, and Noun Class in transposed nouns cross-linguistically.

8.3 ADVERBS

We are left with the mysterious adverb. The manner adverbs, marked by the adjective suffix *-ly* in English, seem to transpose readily from adjectives and verbs but not from nouns. Denominal adverbs seem to bear additional grammatical or semantic content, as in *clockwise* (Manner), *southward* (Goal), *aboard* (Locus), *nightly* (Iterative), hence appear to be the results of functional L-derivation rather than transposition. Moreover, other classes do not productively derive from adverbs. This suggests that adverbs constitute a class that invites a special word or two.

The term "adverb", in fact, has been used to cover obviously different kinds of things, as Jackendoff (1977), Emonds (1985), and Bierwisch (1988) have pointed out. First of all, with Jackendoff we will exclude from consideration a tightly closed class of DELIMITERS (degree words) like *very, just, right, already, again,* already discussed in chapter 6. Next we have to separate the exclusively deadjectival Manner adverbs, for example, *quickly, suddenly, healthily,* from the temporal-spatial pronominal adverbs like *here/there/hence, then, now,* again a paradigmatic closed class which is apparently grammatically determined. These forms behave more like pronominals than a major lexical class, since they may anaphorically replace nouns in adverbial cases such as Locative, Ablative, and Allative.

Adjectives and verbs readily convert to adverbs, though adverbs do not readily convert to these categories in IE languages. The manner adverb from adjectives is well known; however, verbs also productively generate adverbal participles just as they generate verbal adjectival ones.

(8.43) a. John pricked his finger baiting his hook
         b. Walking home from work John met his son

In (8.43) the *ing*-variant of the verb tells how John pricked his finger and how he met his son. In neither instance does the deverbal form modify a noun and in both it modifies the main verb; hence, we are dealing with an adverbal and not an adjectival participle. Moreover, the adverb relation of (8.43) is probably grammatically empty and simply reflects the default adverb function, which is semantically interpretable as MANNER(X).

The reason for the lack of deadverbalizations is that the open classes of adverbs — adjectival, verbal, and denominal adverbs — constitute a derived class; there are no nonpronominal lexical adverbs. The Temporal-Spatial adverbs form a closed class which exhibits defective derivational patterns in most IE languages, for example, *the then judge, today's newspaper.* Directional adverbs of this class, such as Russian *tuda* "thither", and *ottuda* "thence", are not subject to such derivation, a hallmark of pronominal paradigms. Since the adverb is itself a derived category, it presents no lexical basis for L-derivational rules and hence no lexical classes are derived from adverbs.

The manner adverbs are all derived from adjectives. In English they are derived by a special suffix *-ly friend-ly : quick-ly);* in French by the otherwise nominal suffix *-ment (gouverne-ment* "government" : *vite-ment* "quickly"). In the Slavic languages they are marked by the absolutely unmarked NeuSg suffix *-o.* In Yupik they are marked by the suffix of the Comparative case, whose fundamental function is Manner. In German and Turkish adjectives may be used without modification as adverbs. Adverbs rarely exhibit agreement and hence are either reduced to some neutral inflectional form, or are modified in an arbitrary way. This suggests that lexically active adverbs are adjectives serving as nonnominal adjuncts and therefore would not be expected to participate in transposition (see also 12.2.1).

8.4 CONCLUSION

This chapter has established a logical basis for a type of lexical derivation long observed in the data: transposition. This type of derivation simply provides members of one lexical class with the lexical features of another while neutralizing those of the base. Importantly, no grammatical or semantic function is provided by transposition. The importance of discussing transposition at this point is that it allows us in future chapters to exclude from consideration all operations which simply change lexical class (N, V, A). The derivation of a deverbal Locative nominalization like *bake* → *bakery* thus involves three distinct processes: the addition of the case function [+ Locus], the transposition of the verb to the noun class by providing it with the distinctive features of nouns, and the adjustment of the values on these features by feature value switches. Having previously defined affixation and other morphological modifications of the base in purely phonological terms, the common traits of lexical and inflectional derivation should now be assuming a new clarity.

NOTES

1. Don (1993) is rightly critical of earlier recensions of LMBM for ignoring this problem.

2. The possibility that a derived verb like *to hammer* might come to mean "to brush" or "to raise cows" is extremely remote and is clearly determined by idiosyncratic conditions extraneous to grammar. They therefore need not be considered part of the principles of derivation.

3. Jackendoff (1987: 386) provides an example which exemplifies the distinction of SOLID and LIQUID. This distinction, which must also underlie the difference between INSTRUMENT and CHEMICAL AGENT, prevents combinging these two semantic categories at the semantic level.

4. Throughout this book the Chukchee and Yupik examples are simply transliterated from the Cyrillic as presented in the works cited.

5. Lass (1990) points out that superfluous affixes ("junk") are always put to use. It seems reasonable to expect that, since superfluous affixes must be put to use, they would be put to use systematically. If all grammatical functions are assigned an affixes, the only types of systematicity remaining are semantic and phonological.

6. Beard (1991) provides a more detailed analysis of RAdjs, which suggests that they in fact may not be adjectives at all but rather attribute nouns required by some languages but not others to agree with their heads. The Latinate RAdjs in English by this interpretation are grammatically irrelevant reminders of the fact that Latin was such a language.

7. Obviously, this is something of an oversimplification, in that DRY has the attributes of a natural property which are not expressed in this formulation: [POSSESS(X,DRYNESS)]. More will be said about these attributes further along. Presently, however, this formulation serves to distinguish Intransitive from Transitive deadjectival verbalizations.

8. A rule detailing subcategorization frames in the sense of Chomsky (1981) would be somewhat more complicated than the simple insertion of [+ Transitive]. Transitivity is probably a binary category comprising two features, [± Intransitivity, ±Transitivity], which account for Transitive, Intransitive, Ergative and Middle voice. The rule in (8.31) has been simplified here to expedite discussion.

9. Beard (1993: fn. 14) notes that these adjectives are QAdjs and that these suffixes are often forced when appropriate derivation is desired.

10. Apparently the MS-component ignores the fact that the adjective and participle come from two different modules, and instead, marks the common argument structure phonologically. Other languages ignore the common argument structure and distinguish the lexical and inflectional derivational origins. Bashkir, for example, marks the Past participle with *-KAn* (*köt-kən xəbər* 'expected news') and the Passive adjective with *-(O)q*, as in *ton-*''clarify'' : *ton-oq* ''transparent'').

Chapter Nine

Grammatical Categories and Semantic Relations

This chapter will argue that the functions which underlie nominal inflection (Case and adpositions) constitute a set of categories which are independent of those of general cognition (semantics).[1] In this respect, these functions do not differ from the lexical classes, N, V, and A, which are also determined solely by grammar. They may differ from purely lexical categories such as Gender and Number, since these are determined by the lexicon, which does contain semantic material, and hence may respect semantic categories more than syntax.

The nature and number of the grammatical category functions are particularly critical to LMBM. Of the four types of L-derivation discussed in chapter seven, the functional L-derivations constitute the largest set in languages with word formation. Section 7.5.1 demonstrated, however, that the constraints on this class of L-derivation afforded by subcategorization and the ECP are much too stringent. LMBM, therefore, needs to propose a more relaxed yet adequate set of constraints. Chapter 13 will propose that functional L-derivations are ultimately constrained by the set of nominal inflectional functions examined in this chapter. That is, all languages possess a single set of relational primitives which determine the range of nominal inflectional relations, including those of Case systems and adpositions and those of functional L-derivations.

If the relations of inflection and L-derivation are grammatical primitives, they cannot be analyzed further. They must simply be enumerated and defined. Few question that they are special. Talmy (1978: 2) notes that the adposition *through* specifies (i) some motion (ii) along some line (iii) through some medium, but never specifies the medium (for example, air, water, land), the motion (flying, swimming, walking), the speed (running, walking). Slobin (1985: 1173–74) claims that such grammaticizable notions must constitute "a privileged set for the child" learning language in that "they are embodied in the child's conceptions of 'prototypical events' that are mapped onto the first grammatical forms universally." Talmy's conclusions derive from linguistic investigations similar to those underlying this research; Slobin's result from massive cross-linguistic typological investigations. The question is whether these functions represent merely a quantitatively or a genuinely qualitatively distinct set.

Appendix A represents a preliminary catalogue of Case and adposition functions. While Appendix A may not be complete, at most one or two additional functions cannot be semantically subsumed under one of the functions already listed there. Appendix A lists functions which are either innately available to children prior to acquisition or are phylogenetically fundamental, deriving from some ancestral protolanguage. Since these functions are primitive, they need not be further defined grammatically; however, they must be distinguished from cognitive or conceptual categories, particularly those which bear a strong resemblance to them. And, if they are discrete from conceptual categories, we must provide a means of mapping them onto conceptual categories.

9.2 The Object of Our Investigations: Grammatical Functions

This chapter will examine some of the functions collected in Appendix A in order to assess whether they are grammatical or semantic. Some of the same terms (Subject, Object, Agent, Patient, Instrument, Goal, Origin) are often applied at both levels. If these categories are similar enough to be covered by the same terms, the question naturally arises whether two sets exist. Jackendoff (1990) has established that there is a set of theta roles which are purely semantic. Are the Case functions then simply the full set of theta roles and thus not grammatical phenomena at all? Or do Case functions belong to the autonomous level of morphological categories Aronoff (1993) deduces? If we could reduce all or even most of them to an independently motivated semantic set, the theory of grammar would be significantly simplified. If functional L-derivation is based on a large set of grammatical functions independent of semantic functions, the burden of proof to demonstrate this falls squarely upon advocates of this position.

Let us first isolate the object of investigation. The list of grammatical category functions in Appendix A was originally compiled from the lists of Case functions in the major traditional grammars of the classical IE languages, Sanskrit (Coulson 1976; Speijer 1886; and Whitney 1967), Greek (Kühner & Gerth 1963; Smyth 1920), and Latin (Bennett 1914; Hale and Buck 1966; Woodcock 1959). That list has since been compounded by case functions found in grammars of contemporary IE languages and corroborated across a wide variety of randomly selected non-IE languages including Amharic, Archi, Arabic, Bashkir, Basque Buryat, Cherokee Chukchee, Dakota, Fijian, Finnish, Georgian, Hausa, Hebrew, Hungarian, Japanese, Koryak, Indonesian, Kiowa, Lezghian, Menomini, Nahuatl, Navajo, Palauan, Quechua, Swahili, Tamil, Tiwi, Turkish, Veps, Yakut, Yupik, Yoruba, and any other languages mentioned in this book. The combined Case-adposition systems of all these languages seem to be constrained to the set of functions represented in Appendix A.

The list of functions in Appendix A contains 44 basic relations. If we count the semantic subcategories represented by "a" and "b" (for example, 12a, 12b) independently, and add the directional variants of the spatial functions forming triads like those expressing the functions "on" : "onto", "off of"; "under" : "(to) under", "from under", the number of functions listed in Appendix A approaches that of the 68 functions posited by Hjelmslev (1935). Hjelmslev claimed that each of his functions is justified by the fact that each is represented by a Case in some language in the world. That justification generally carries over to Appendix A, although some discrepancies between Hjelmslev's list and Appendix A remain to be adjudicated.

That these functions have been utilized successfully by language learners in acquiring a wide range of IE and non-IE languages speaks not only to the accuracy of the compilation in Appendix A but to the universality of this set of functions. Were we misled by the categorization of IE languages to perceive similar functions in other languages where they do not exist, students learning those languages from grammars based on these functions should face inordinate difficulty in communicating with native speakers of those languages, because the systems of categorization would be mismatched. Indeed, there is no reason for grammarians to have used the identical set of functions in their accounts, because it would be a simple matter to define any other set of functions for grammars, if distinct sets were warranted.

9.3 GRAMMATICAL FUNCTIONS: SEMANTIC OR GRAMMATICAL?

If the functions of Appendix A are grammatical and not semantic functions, they must interpret semantic functions like $_{Path}TO([_{Thing}], [_{Place}])$ in Jackendoff's (1990) terms via algorithms similar to the one posited for the mapping of L-features onto Agreement features in Table 5.3. This account has intuitive appeal. Jackendoff (1983: 82–83) has argued that the number of semantic types is unlimited since new types may be created by simply constructing a type from a token, $t \rightarrow T$. If the number of semantic predicate types is unlimited, some sort of grammar would have to be invoked to reduce a potentially uncontrollable number of predicates to a learnable set, efficiently manipulable for purposes of speaking. The fact that the functions under investigation belong to a closed class is the first piece of evidence that they are grammatical. They are either arbitrarily selected from a much wider range of semantic categories by universal grammar (Talmy 1978, 1983, 1985) or they represent a unique set of windows between syntactic and semantic categories. Assuming now the set of functions in Appendix A, let us proceed to examine the arguments for their being peculiarly grammatical functions rather than cognitive categories.

9.3.1 Szymanek's Cognitive Grounding Principle

Szymanek (1988) made the first attempt to define and classify the categories and functions of L-derivations based on contemporary principles of cognitive categories. Szymanek bases his analysis of L-derivational functions on The Cognitive Grounding Principle (9.1):

(9.1) *The basic set of lexical derivational categories is rooted in the fundamental concepts of cognition.*

This principle makes eminent sense: certainly the categories of grammatical functions are cognitive to the extent that language is a cognitive process and thus all its categories and operations must be cognitive. It does not follow from this, however, that grammatical functions are no more than the superordinate, high-level cognitive concepts; they could be a special set determined by a discrete module, grammar, which requires special mapping to conceptual level.[2] What then is Szymanek's specific claim?

Three terms of (9.1) present problems of interpretation: "basic", "is rooted in", and "fundamental". The qualifier "basic" in (9.1) leaves room for derivational functions which are not rooted in cognitive concepts. Thus, Szymanek does not deny the existence of discrete semantic and grammatical functions; he only claims that the latter "are rooted in", are justified by the former, however indirectly. All of the asymmetric relations between grammatical and semantic categories mentioned in the previous section are described by Szymanek. It is not clear, therefore, that Szymanek's operator, "is rooted in", differs in any respect from the one proposed here: "is mapped algorithmically from".

Szymanek lists 25 "fundamental concepts of cognition" taken from the evidence in the literature:

(9.2) OBJECT (THING), SUBSTANCE, PERSON, NUMBER, EXISTENCE, POSSESSION, NEGATION, PROPERTY, COLOR, SHAPE, DIMENSION, SIMILARITY, SEX, SPACE, POSITION, MOVEMENT, PATH, TIME, STATE, PROCESS, EVENT, ACTION, CAUSATION, AGENT, INSTRUMENT

What (9.2) lacks is a basic principle motivating this list over some similar one. In particular, Szymanek mentions no attempt to control the influence of prior knowledge of language on the selection of these categories.

Using the term DERIVATIONAL CATEGORY in the same sense as "grammatical category function" is used here, Szymanek (1988: 119) notes the following implication of (9.1):

(9.3) *A lexico-semantic class whose generalized meaning is directly accountable for in terms of any one or more of the fundamental concepts of cognition is a possible candidate for the status of a derivational category.*

Szymanek's claim, then, is that there is some reliable correlation between an eventually definable list of categories like those of (9.2) and the L-derivational categories of Appendix A. The first observation is that to the extent that the correlation may be an indirect mapping, the claim is not at odds with the position here. However, under LMBM, grammatical category functions are arbitrary and independent, specialized cognitive categories mapped algorithmically onto general cognitive categories, not directly, as (9.3) implies.

Gender, for example, is a lexical category whose extensions are the SEX of its references. Evidence abounds for a level of grammar at which there are two and only two properties of Gender. Feminine and Masculine do refer to FEMALENESS and MALENESS; however, markedness relations of grammar allow the two grammatical properties to distinguish four functions. The Slavic languages possess nouns which are both Feminine and Masculine and those which are neither Feminine nor Masculine, yet which refer exclusively to sexed beings (section 7.2.1). The same complex relationship characterizes the relation between Number and AGGREGATION (section 7.2.2). These lexical categories, Gender and Number, which are cognitively grounded, nonetheless reflect uniquely grammatical behavior distinct from that of general cognitive categories. Let us follow the evidence further.

9.3.2 Grammar-Semantics Asymmetry

The disjunction between Gender and the two semantic functions of SEX is reminiscent of the disjunction between derivation and affixation. There, too, we found one-many, many-one, and many-many relations. There is no better proof of distinct but indirectly related levels requiring mapping algorithms than this type of disjunction. Let us now consider three other cases of such a disjunction between the semantic and grammatical levels: CONCRETE/ABSTRACT terms, TIME/PLACE relations, and the [POSSESS(*XY*)] function.

A Many-One Relation: CONCRETE versus ABSTRACT

Conceptual distinctions just as obvious as Gender and Animacy exist but never emerge as categories in any inflectional or derivational system. The failure to distinguish concrete from abstract objects as lexical or inflectional categories is a compelling example of two prominent cognitive categories absent among grammatical functions. Abstract nouns are treated as metaphors of concrete ones by grammar: *John was struck by the idea* versus *John was struck by the bat*. No language exhibits Nominal or Agreement Classes distinguishing concrete and abstract references, nor do we find them among L-derivations.

It is sometimes claimed that some of the Noun Classes of Bantu languages are restricted to abstract nouns. Class 6 of Swahili (9.4), for example, comprises predominantly abstract nouns and all those of Class 7 (9.5) are abstract (Brauner and Herms 1986: 137–38, 153).

(9.4)   a. u-kubwa "largeness"
       b. u-moja "unity"
       c. u-koloni "colonialism"

(9.5)   a. ku-andika "writing"
       b. ku-soma "reading"
       c. ku-ondoka "departing"

It is incorrect, however, to describe these declensions as marking some category "ABSTRACT". Class 6 also contains concrete nouns like those in (9.6).

(9.6)   a. u-kurasa "page"
       b. u-so "face"
       e. u-wanja "stadium"

The more important reason that these declensions cannot be considered markers of the semantic category ABSTRACT is that they mark pure transpositions: Class 6 is the Class of deadjectival and denominal transpositions; Class 7 is that of deverbal ones. Thus they mark an operation which is purely grammatical, since it transfers lexical items from one grammatical class to another. These classes are independent lexical classes, not determined by abstractness or transposition, but used to mark subsets of Swahili transpositions. Such lexical categories as Noun Class thus cannot be taken as marking the much wider semantic superordinate category ABSTRACT.

Another Many-One Relation: TIME versus PLACE

Assuming the functions of Appendix A to be primitive universal cognitive relations, we would expect to find grammatical functions paralleling the semantic functions TIME(X) and PLACE(X). TIME and PLACE are superordinate categories containing such base level categories as SINCE,

UNTIL, FREQUENCY, DURATION, PUNCTUALITY, for TIME, and UNDER, OVER, BEHIND, BEFORE, for PLACE. That TIME and PLACE, and their subcategories are discrete cognitive categories is demonstrated by the fact that all vocabularies maintain distinct lexical items referring to places and times. Lexicons do not contain words polysemous as to minutes and homes, hours and neighborhoods, days and villages, or months and regions. Distinct proadverbs like *when* and *where* are common, though by no means universal (Brown 1985). The conclusion can only be that temporal and spatial concepts must be cognitively and semantically quite distinct.

TIME expressions, however, are consistently metaphors of Spatial grammatical expressions in Case and adposition systems cross-linguistically. The English prepositional system accurately reflects the Case systems in other languages where the locational and directional Cases mark time expressions, as in *on top : on Friday, in town : in July, from here to there : from 1975 to 1980.* Occasional distinctions made by adpositions like *since, until, ago* consistently break down: *I can't wait until Boston, we haven't stopped since Charlotte.* However, no language has a specifically Temporal, Punctual, or Durational Case.[3]

Richmond is five hours from here is a grammatical sentence, yet massive algorithmic mapping is required to render its semantic interpretation: "Richmond lies a distance from our spatial location which would require five hours to traverse." This is because a common semantic distinction is missing in grammar, forcing the grammatical structure to metaphor but allowing it to be much more compact than the corresponding semantic structure. If all such relational categories were semantic, or isomorphic with corresponding semantic categories, grammars would not consistently fail to develop the TIME/PLACE distinction among their grammatical categories while without exception maintaining it in their lexicons. Since no language apparently has a Case dedicated primarily to point of time, we may conclude that PUNCTUALITY is a theta role with no corresponding grammatical function and therefore must map metaphorically onto the nearest correlate, Locus, or arbitrarily onto some other Case.[4]

A cogent question for this proposal would be, how do we distinguish PUNCTUALITY as a metaphor of the grammatical function, Locus, from the alternative hypothesis: a single Locative Case with two functions, Locus and Punctuality. As grammatical categories, cases often express several functions. For instance, the Genitive expresses Possession, Partitivity, and Origin in IE languages; the Instrumental, Means, Sociation, and Manner. Each Case, however, has one function which defines it, without which it cannot retain its name. Genitive, for example, is assigned to the Case which expresses Possession; Instrumental is assigned to the Case which expresses Means (often called "Instrument"). Hjelmslev (1935) pointed out that in languages with a superfluity of affixal means, multiple functions expressed by one Case in affix-poor languages are expressed by their own Case. In Finnish, for example, the IE Genitive Case functions, Partitivity and Origin, are assigned distinct cases, the Partitive and Ablative. Now, if the Partitive and Originative functions are expressed by their own Case in some language, then they must be grammatical functions rather than alternate semantic interpretations of the same function.

It follows from Hjelmslev's observation that any language which has a Case whose cardinal function is Punctuality establishes a Case function, Punctuality. In fact, the research upon which this book is based revealed no language with demonstrable temporal Case; hence, we conclude that PUNCTUALITY is a metaphorical interpretation of the grammatical function, (Locative of) Locus.

A One-Many Relation: POSSESS(XY)

The relationship of TIME and PLACE functions to their corresponding Case function is that of many semantic to one grammatical category as (9.7a) illustrates:

(9.7) a.   Locus

PLACE   TIME

b. $G_1, G_2, \ldots, G_n$

R_x

If the relation between the functions of semantic and grammatical planes may be many-one, a one-many relation like that in (9.7b) should also be possible. Recall that both relations characterize the morphological asymmetry addressed by the Separation Hypothesis.

Szymanek (1988: 99–101) first discovered evidence of this relation between cognitive and grammatical categories in Polish. The Polish phrases in (9.8) contain Possessional (9.8a-9.8c) and Possessive adjectives (9.8a'-9.8c').

(9.8)   a. pomysł-**ow**-y pisarz   a'. pisar-**sk**-i pomisł
           "writer with ideas"   "writer's idea"
        b. posaż-**n**-a panna   b'. panień-**sk**-i posag
           "doweried girl"   "girl's dowery"
        c. ość-**ist**-a ryba   c'. ryb-**i**-a ość
           "bony fish"   "fish('s) bone"

Oddly enough, all the examples in (9.8) express the same predicate argument structure: (9.8a) POSSESS (WRITER, IDEA); (9.8b) POSSESS

(GIRL, DOWERY); (9.8c) POSSESS(FISH, BONE). However, the forms to the left are Possessional QAdjs while those to the right are Possessive RAdjs: the NP head in (9.8a-9.8c) is the first argument of POSSESS(XY) while in (9.8a$'$-9.8c$'$) it is the second.

Szymanek does not provide a reason for two L-derivations corresponding to one semantic function in this case. However, in light of the discussion of transitive V → A transpositions in section 8.2.5, the reason is clear: since adjectives have only one argument position and POSSESS(XY) has two, the only way to express the verbal predicate adjectivally is via two distinct adjectives. At the grammatical level two functions must correspond to the one at semantic level, exactly the prediction of (9.7b).[5]

Jackendoff (1990: 59ff.) provides another example of the disjuncture between semantic and grammatical functions. The definition of the English verb *buy* requires two sets of semantic relations which Jackendoff expresses as (9.9):

(9.9) X buy Y from Z
  a. Y changes possession from Z to X
  b. money changes possession from X to Z

Exactly how Jackendoff accounts for this in his theory of Conceptual Semantics is not directly germane to the point here. The important point here is that semantically, the predicate BUY(XYZ) involves two sets of opposing directional (FROM-TO) relations: the direction of the purchase and the direction of money. Grammatically, however, no language seems to represent both those relations consistently; rather, all languages seem to use an Exchange function for the money, expressed by the preposition *for* in English: X bought Y from Z for U. The reason is that X and Z have two semantic roles apiece, a violation of the Theta Criterion. The Theta Criterion, which is not violated in the syntactic phrase, therefore, must apply at the grammatical level to a set of functions distinct from those determining the semantic level.

9.3.3 The Inaccessibility of Case Functions to Semantic Systems

If the set of grammatical functions is closed it should not be possible to add or subtract from Case and adposition functions. This seems to be true; the functions in Appendix A may only be (i) omitted, (ii) realigned, or reassigned primary and secondary status, or (iii) subspecified. Notice that the functions listed in Appendix A are divided into PRIMARY and SECONDARY FUNCTIONS. One of the characteristics of primary functions is that in languages with a large number of cases, the primary functions tend to be marked by Case alone, while the secondary ones are marked by double Case endings or a Case ending plus an adposition, as is the case with the

Sanskrit examples in Appendix A. In the IE languages, the Sociative function is always marked by a Case ending plus a preposition, as with the Russian example (9.10a), and hence behaves like a secondary function. In Yakut, however, a Turkish language of strong Mongolian admixture spoken by about 220,000 people in Central Siberia, according to Korkina et al. (1982: 132), Sociative is expressed by a primary Case, as in (9.10b) without any adposition such as that required in Russian (9.10a).

(9.10)　a.　so starik-om
　　　　　　with an.old.man-INST
　　　　　　"with an old man"
　　　　b.　oкonnor-duun
　　　　　　an.old.man-SOC
　　　　　　"with an old man"

　　　While such shifting of functions between primary and secondary service characterizes the historical development of languages, no relation not contained in the catalogue of functions in Appendix A can be expressed by a Case ending or adposition, thus *becorner* "around the corner from" is impossible despite the presence of *beside* "on the side of", and *abottom* "on the bottom of" is not acceptable although *atop* is. No matter how much pragmatics might demand a grammatical function meaning, "on friendly terms with", it is impossible to derive any preposition *afriend* on the model of *atop* to be used as in *John worked afriend Mary*, let alone such a Case relation.

　　　The category of TERTIARY FUNCTIONS in Appendix A suggests that the functional system may be open, susceptible to a slower but qualitatively similar type of derivational expansion as are the major lexical classes. Closer examination of the these functions, however, reveals that they represent nothing more than further subspecification of primary and secondary functions. Most of the English tertiary markers are listed in (9.11).

(9.11)　a. atop　　　g. alongside　m. since
　　　　b. astride　 h. except　　　n. including
　　　　c. aboard　 i. save　　　　o. toward
　　　　d. amid　　 j. but　　　　　p. until
　　　　e. among　 k. opposite　　q. during
　　　　f. beside　 l. near　　　　 r. besides

Astride, aboard, atop subspecify the function Adessive, marked in English by *on*; that is, they mark the Adessive in specific contexts. The tertiary prepositions may be substituted for *on* if the prepositional subject straddles the object, is on a ship, or is on a tall object, respectively. Crucially, the tertiary marker may be replaced by the secondary one, though not vice versa: *aboard/on the ship, astride/on the fence, atop/on the building* vs. **aboard/ *astride/ *atop /on Friday, television, the field.*

Of course, the claim that the tertiary functions subspecify primary and secondary functions does not entail any tertiary function sharing the distribution of the function it subspecifies. *Among* and *amid* ostensibly subspecify Inessive, marked in English by *in*. Some languages, for example, Russian, use their Inessive marker regularly to mark this function: *v derev'jax* "in/among the trees". *Among, amid* are used in English to subspecify "innerness" in relation to non-Singular objects: *I heard her voice, in/among the trees, amid/in the laughter.* Sometimes *in* and *among* may be used interchangeably, as in *John was in/among the bushes;* however, their distribution is more usually complementary: *Sue is unique *in/among her friends* : *Sue is in/*among the house.*

As cognitive categories and functions change with the industrialization of society, we would expect grammatical functions to follow their lead if there were a direct connection between the two levels. This does not seem to occur, however. One of the universal changes in our consciousness in past centuries is the emergence of the cognitive category of PROFESSION or OCCUPATION. One's profession has become a basic means of identification yet the category semantically nearest to PROFESSION is the Subjective nominalization. *My husband is a wonderful baker* is ambiguous; it may mean that my husband bakes as a profession or that he simply likes to bake more than other people. The Subjective nominalization merely marks the fact that the referent is identified by his or her baking. No grammar distinguishes professional from avocational activities, yet cognition presumably does, since no industrialized society fails to make the distinction in practice or speech.

It follows from all this that the number of the primary and secondary functions cannot be altered synchronically or diachronically, as can the stock of lexical classes. Only the stock of morphological markers may be expanded to subspecify the 44 universal functions; that is, after all, how adpositions themselves arose, as subspecifiers of Case functions (Kuryłowicz 1949). Appendix A therefore predicts the ultimate limits of the semantic range of Case paradigms, including that of the catalogue of adpositions.

9.3.4 A Summary and Interim Conclusion.

If grammatical functions are a privileged set of cognitive categories occupying a distinct grammatical level, and if a level of semantics exists outside grammar, the trimodular model of morphology expressed in Table 9.2 follows. Level 1 is pure phonology; levels 2–4 represent closed grammatical categories of an autonomous morphological level, described for verbs by

Aronoff (1993); while level 5 represents the open categories of semantics or general cognition. The double lines in Table 9.1 indicate boundaries between phonology, syntax, and semantics which certainly require algorithmic mapping. Single lines represent module-internal boundaries, across which information may be exchanged although module-internal rules may be required. Level 4 represents the level of I-derivation (syntax). Morphological spelling and phonology occupy all higher levels and semantics occupies the lower one. The motivation for including the Case properties such as Nominative, Instrumental, and Locative inside the MS-component will become evident in chapter 11. Morphology, then, maps lexical and syntactic categories onto semantics, on the one hand, and onto phonology, on the other. It also maps lexical and syntactic categories onto one another.

Table 9.1   The Relation of Morphology to Semantics and Phonology (Russian)

1. Unstressed: /o/ → [a] → [ə], C'[+Vowel] → C'i			*Postcyclic Phonology*
2. -∅, -o; -a	-om, -oj, -ju	-e, -i	*Spelling/Allomorphy*
3. Nominative	Instrumental	Locative	*Grammatical Properties*
4. Subject	Means, Manner	Locus	*Grammatical Functions*
5. THING ACTOR	USE(XY) LIKE(XY)	PLACE(X) TIME(X)	*Semantic Categories and Predicates*

Table 9.1 illustrates the algorithmic nature of the correspondence rules which map conceptual functions like USE(XY) onto grammatical functions like Means. Later we will see how Case properties like the Instrumental map functions like Means onto specific affixes, such as the Instrumental desinences. In Russian the Instrumental of Class 1 nouns is marked by the ending *-om* at P-level, while Class 2 nouns are marked by *-oj,* and Class 3 nouns, by *-ju.* Allomorphy will make these selections, guided by the Case paradigm. The suffix /-om/, however, is pronounced [om] only if accented [otc-óm] ''father''. If it is unaccented and follows a nonpalatalized consonant, postcyclic rules reduce /o/ it to [ə] [ļés-əm] ''woods''. Finally, /o/ reduces to [i] if unaccented and preceded by a palatalized consonant [učíţi]-im] ''teacher''. Levels 1–3 account for these allomorphic and phonological variations.

The effect of Table 9.1 is to expand grammatical functions to a whole range of closed-class grammatical relations and claim that they must be assigned not at S-structure or by the lexicon but by morphosyntax (Aronoff's ''morphomics'') at D-structure. Morphology does not distinguish structural from adverbal categories, marking both with phrase position, Case desinences, and adpositions. The categories of levels 3 and 4 of Table 9.1, then, represent a complete complement of grammatical functions, discrete from the broader and looser class of predicate argument relations of level 5, which represents the level of theta roles.

9.4 THE BOUNDARY BETWEEN GRAMMATICAL AND SEMANTIC CATEGORIES

To more clearly understand the boundary between the grammatical and semantic functions outlined in the previous sections and illustrated at levels 4 and 5 in Table 9.2, we need to examine some typical cases of interaction between the two. Also, a measure for testing and establishing the boundary between the two is necessary. Jackendoff (1990: chapter 11) outlines the various current accounts of this mapping in terms of correspondence rules, which explain the relations between theta roles and various syntactic roles or surface cases. The morphosemantic asymmetry documented above, and that described by Jackendoff, is incompatible with the simple assumption that semantic functions map isomorphically onto grammatical functions. This section examines two instances of multiple semantic categories mapping onto a single grammatical one. The first case involves a functional L-derivation; the second, one of the outstanding transpositions predicted by chapter 8.

9.4.1 -Er/-ənt *and Means*

Let us examine first a problem of L-derivation located on the boundary of grammatical and semantic functions and introduced in section 8.2.1 of the preceding chapter. Examine the Modalic (Instrumental) L-derivations of (8.10). Those referring to tools are reproduced in (9.12) and those, to substances in (9.13).

(9.12)   a   . . .
       b. mixer, trimmer, mower, lighter
       c. lift, catch, cover, swing

(9.13)   a. relaxant, stimulant, irritant
       b. softener, whitener, developer
       c. rinse, wash, stain, soak

The suffix -ənt distinguishes chemical agents from tools; however, -er (9.13b) and affix omission (9.13c) do not. Thus two of the affixational operations here suggest a single conditioning grammatical function while the remaining one suggests two. There are three competing accounts of

(9.12–9.13): (i) CHEMICAL AGENT and TOOL are semantic categories which directly determine L-derivation (9.14); (ii) Chemical Agent and Tool are grammatical functions which map isomorphically from corresponding semantic categories CHEMICAL AGENT and TOOL (9.15); finally, (iii) CHEMICAL AGENT and TOOL are semantic categories which both map onto a common grammatical function, Means (9.16).

(9.14)

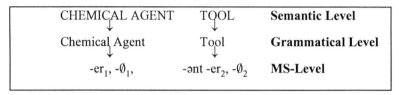

(9.15)

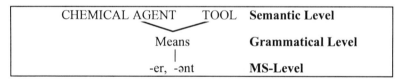

(9.16)

CHEMICAL AGENT ⌣ TOOL	**Semantic Level**
Means	**Grammatical Level**
|	
-er, -ənt	**MS-Level**

The problem for both (9.14) and (9.15) is that the maintenance of direct lines between meaning and sound proliferates theoretically motivated synonymous affixes. Remember from chapter 2, rarely does phonological evidence support synonymy in such situations. In the case of affix omission marked by $-\emptyset$ above, it is impossible to demonstrate whether this marker is an allomorph of *-er* or *-ənt*. The suffix *-ənt* does not escape this cloud either, for although it is restricted to marking only chemical agents among the Modalic derivations, the same suffix also marks Subjective nominalizations based on Intransitive Latinate verbs (*resident, immigrant, participant*) as well as Subjective adjectives (*indulgent, persistent*). The proliferation of purely theoretically synonymous zero morphemes despite the postulation of dual categories is a particularly grievous violation of the assumption of isomorphy.

(9.16), on the other hand, is supported by two tests of grammatical status which CHEMICAL AGENT and INSTRUMENT fail but which Means passes. The test is a lexical variant of Hjelmslev's test for Case functions mentioned above: no language seems to possess an affix which is dedicated to expressing chemical agents, not even English. Notice in (9.14–9.16) that English has two semantically distinguishable Means functions and that precisely two phonological expressions, -*ənt* and -*er*, mark them. Since affixes mark grammatical functions, if the two functions were grammatical, we would expect one affix to mark the one function and the other to mark the other. Indeed, if affixes distinguished semantic functions, we would expect the same. Rather than this, however, one affix marks both functions and only one actually distinguishes chemical agents from tools. We could avoid the conclusion that this distinctive usage is accidental except for the fact that the distribution of -*ənt* is restricted to Latinate stems. Its distribution vis-à-vis -*er* and -∅, then, is purely accidental, a reflection of the Latinate-native distinction in English.

Remember that chapter 8 concluded that whether a noun is a mass noun or count noun is a function of whether its Number features are provided with ± values. Number is irrelevant to mass nouns like *wind, hatred, and contemplation;* hence, we may conclude that their Number features lack value even though they might be present. This implies that the assignment of values to Number features is an option of transposition that depends ultimately upon the reference a speaker has in mind at the moment of derivation.

Let us now assume the grammatical function Means underlies the functional derivation of (9.12) and (9.13). Since this derivation applies to verbal bases and its output is nominal, Number features, [Plural, Singular], must be assigned by transposition. Next, the values of these features would be set by feature switches either at [− Plural, + Singular] or [+ Plural, − Singular], depending on whether the reference is Singular or Plural. However, as section 7.2.2 concludes, values may be omitted if Number is irrelevant to a reference as in the case of mass nouns. If the feature value switches were not to operate, they would generate the correct grammatical representation for semantic pairing with a SUBSTANCE, a mass noun. Hence (9.14) and (9.15) predict some consistent distinction between the markers for instruments and chemical agents, while (9.16) predicts a set of suffixes conditioned by the one grammatical function, Means, which may combine with Number values to form a count noun or, without Number values to form a mass noun. Spelling differences then are determined by purely lexical factors in the base such as the Latinate-native distinction, in accord with the Empty Morpheme Entailment of chapter 4.

9.4.2 Another Transposition: N → QAdj

Chapter 8, which dealt with transpositions, promised an answer to the question of the denominal qualitative adjective transposition in this chapter. The reason why the discussion of this transposition was delayed was that the output of this transformation receives two semantic interpretations which require additional semantic paraphernalia to comprehend. Now that we have examined some of the differences between the grammatical and semantic levels of morphology, we may return to the question of the N → QAdj transposition. This transposition dramatically illustrates differences between grammatical and semantic processing and hence the necessity of maintaining two distinct levels.

Possessional and Similitudinal Adjectives

The two most productive and widely distributed denominal QAdjs are the Similitudinal adjective (SAdj), whose semantic function is [LIKE(XY)], and what Jespersen called the Possessional adjective, which selects the Object argument of [POSSESS(XY)] and hence will be referred to as O(bject of) P(ossession) Adj.[6] (9.17) is a random sampling of SAdjs; (9.18) is a sampling of OPAdjs for English.

(9.17)   a. spongy   e. quail-like
         b. girlish   f. despotic
         c. friendly   g. Nixonian
         d. elephantine   h. McCarthyesque

(9.18)   a. bearded   e. fashionable
         b. sorrowful   f. modular
         c. stylish   g. dusty
         d. dramatic   h. scrofulous

These two are by far the most prominent denominal adjectivizations in languages throughout the world. Huasteca Nahuatl is a Uto-Aztecan language spoken by a population of about 350,000 in Mexico. In the discussion of Huasteca adjectives and adjective derivation in Beller and Beller (1979), these two categories clearly dominate.

Table 9.2   Nahuatl Possessional and Similitudinal Adjectives

Base	*Possessional*	*Similitudinal*
popo "smoke"	tla-popo-ka "smoky"	
soki "mud"	soki-titla "muddy"	
saka "grass"	saka-titla "grassy"	
te "rock"	te-yo "rocky	te-tik "hard"
čil "chili"		či-čil-tik "red"
toma "tomato"		toma-wak "fat"
kama "mouth"		kama-wak "humid"

Hebrew exhibits the same semantic patterning across its denominal adjectives (Glinert 1989: 486–490). The sampling of adjectives in Tables 9.2 and 9.3 illustrate the fundamental attributes of SAdjs and OPAdjs. The Possessional forms have the basic meaning "characterized by having X" where X varies over the meanings of input nouns. The Similitudinal forms have the meaning "like or similar to X" where X is the same variable. The effect of the SAdj, then, is to compare the noun modified by the adjective with the base of the adjective, always another noun.

Table 9.3   Hebrew Possessional and Similitudinal Adjectives

Base	*Possessional*	*Similitudinal*
kol "voice"	kol-ani "vociferous"	
leset "jaw"	list-ani "(big-)jawed"	
tarbut "culture"	me-turbat "cultured	
koxav "star"	me-kuxav "starry"	
tipeš "fool"		me-tupaš "foolish"
idyot "idiot"		idyot-i "idiotic"
enoš "man"		enoš-i "human"

Two peculiarities of these two L-derivational categories must be accounted for. First, most languages seem to have an intermediate category of adjectives bearing an identical affix which expresses both the SAdj and OPAdj meaning. In English we find examples like those of (9.19), which may be used in either the sense of "like N" or "similar to N", as in *a sandy beach* versus *sandy hair*.

(9.19)   a. icy, dusty, rusty, fuzzy, sandy, lacy
         b. arched, bowed, pointed
         c. nodular, annular, columnar

Notice that the Hebrew prefix *me-CuCaC* also may be combined with nouns to generate QAdjs with both meanings: *me-kukav* "starry" versus *me-tupaš* "foolish".

The second peculiarity characterizing these two adjectivizations is that SAdjs often express a combination of the semantic attributes of the SAdj and an S(ubject of) P(ossession) Adj.

(9.20)   a. Nixonian ethics
         b. friendly smile
         c. Napoleonic personality

The semantic interpretation of these forms cannot be explained in terms of either of the functions, LIKE(XY) or POSSESS(XY), underlying the

SAdjs; it can only be explained in terms of a combination of both. That is, *Nixonian ethics* is not ethics like Nixon but ethics like Nixon's, i.e. ethics like Nixon possesses where *Nixon* is the Subject, not Object, of the Possession. This attribute suggests that the two derivations are related and not the discrete Possessional and Manner derivations widely assumed. The nature and relationship of these two derivations can only be explained semantically. To do that, however, we must first understand the semantic demands on adjectives.

A Semantic Explanation of OPAdjs and SAdjs

In Beard (1991) I point out that without decompositional semantics, the scope ambiguities of adjectives in attribute phrases like *criminal lawyer* and *moral philosopher* cannot be explained. The ambiguity of such phrases over the years has been referred to as OPAQUE versus TRANSPARENT readings, NARROW SCOPE versus WIDE SCOPE readings, BRACKETING PARADOXES, and most recently MORPHOSEMANTIC MISMATCHES (Stump 1991). We can predict the meanings of attribute phrases if we assume that (a) the R-representations of lexical items decompose into semantic features, and (b) attributive adjectives compose not with the entire semantic feature inventory of the noun, but only with one of its semantic features.

To see how featural composition predicts the multiple meanings of attribute phrases, consider the following semantic interpretation of *old friend* in (9.21):

(9.21)   old   friend

$$[\text{OLDNESS}\{[\text{---}]\!\!\!-\!\!\!-\!\!\!-\!\!\!\begin{bmatrix} \text{ACTOR}_i \\ \text{FRIENDSHIP}([\ ]_i, [\ ]) \end{bmatrix}$$

(9.22)   a. [OLDNESS{[ACTOR$_i$ FRIEND SHIP([ ]$_i$ [ ]$_j$)}] 'old actor in a friendship'
         b. [ACTOR$_i$ OLDNESS{[FRIENDSHIP([ ]$_i$ [ ]$_j$)}] 'actor in an old friendship'

Featural composition forces the semantic features of an attributive adjective to compose with a single feature of the R-representation of head noun rather than with all the head noun's features. *Old* may compose with ACTOR or FRIENDSHIP in (9.21). The result will be either (9.22a), ''an old member of a friendship'', or (9.22b), ''a member of an old friendship''. If the adjective composes with a single features of its head, a natural question arises: may individual features of the adjective compose with the selected feature of the head? According to Beard (1993), this option is not only possible, but accounts for the characteristics of OPAdjs and SAdjs so that they may be generated by functionally empty transpositions. Let us examine the OPAdjs (Possessional adjectives) first.

OPAdjs

The primary function of QAdjs is to specify properties of the nouns with which they are associated, as in *red car*. Natural properties are qualities or parts inherently possessed by the objects of which they are predicated, that is, a *red car* inherently and inalienably possesses redness in some broad, generic sense of the term (Givón 1970). A knife possesses a blade as a definitional part in the same sense. This explains the preponderance of denominal adjectives reflecting a possessional relation between the underlying noun and the modified noun, as in *joy-ous rabbi, sorrow-ful moment, wealth-y fellow*: the stereotypical motivation for adjectivizing a noun is simply to convert it to a property specifier.

The relation specified by OPAdjs is not just any relation of possession. While a *twin-engine(d)* boat is an acceptable use of the compound OPAdj, a *twin-engine(d) man* is not, even if the man does in fact possess two matching engines which he keeps in his garage. The possession of OPAdjs is specifically that of an inherent property which must be listed in a complete definition of the noun's denotation. Because this relation enjoys special status among lexical definitions, it must be assigned primitive symbolization. Beard (1991) suggests curly brackets: Q{[ ]}, where Q refers to the semantics of any qualitative adjective. Thus, instead of the normal predicate symbolism of propositional logic, for example, BLACK([ ]), the relation of inherent property is always marked by the curly bracket convention, BLACKNESS{[ ]}. The property is stated as a noun so that qualities like that expressed by *black* may be categorized together with concrete properties which share the same relation, for example, WING{[ ]}. WING bears the same semantic relation to *crow* as does BLACK; namely, both are inherent, definitional properties of a crow.

Assume now a definition of *rust* roughly that of (9.23) and that of (9.24) for *knife*. The derivational semantics of *rusty* would now be RUST → RUST{[ ]}, where RUST is simply reclassified from a referential term to a qualifier. (9.23) provides a residual external argument position {[ ]} on *rust*, correct for the external argument of the derived adjective; *a rusty object* is "an object having a brownish-red substance which corrodes it" under the condition that the object is made from the material iron (or steel). (9.23) provides a built-in selection restriction, [CONTAIN([ ]$_j$, [IRON v STEEL]), which limits the feature selected to a concept referring to an object made of iron or steel. Transposition with featural composition

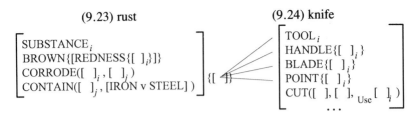

(9.23) rust   (9.24) knife

allows RUST to compose with KNIFE as a natural property as well as with [HANDLE{[ ]}, BLADE{[ ]}, POINT{[ ]}], that is, as a predicate of the category specifier [TOOL], [RUST{[TOOL]}], or with any other feature. A rusty knife probably would have a rusty blade, [RUST {[BLADE]}], but the rust could be restricted to the handle, [RUST{[HANDLE]}], or even the point, [RUST{[POINT]}], without anomalous denotation.

The conclusion is that OPAdjs are simply Ns represented as inalienable properties of other Ns. Since this is the definition of a QAdj, the derivation of OPAdjs is the simple provision of Ns with the capacity to serve as an inherent property, as in the transposition in (9.26a).

(9.26)   a.   [+F] → [0F, +Gradable]

(9.26a) stipulates that any major class lexical item may be transposed into a QAdj by providing the item with the ability to compare. Since gradability is the grammatical equivalent of "natural-propertihood", the semantic correspondence rule for QAdjs would be (9.26b) since the semantic structure of a QAdj is X{[ ]}.

(9.26)   b.   [+Gradable] = {[ ]}

In other words, any R-representation which is grammatically gradable functions semantically as a property (whether it is derived or not). The next question is whether this rule can also account for SAdjs (Similitudinal adjectives).

SAdjs

The adjective *rusty* can also mean "LIKE rust" in color only, as in *rusty hair*. The specific feature of comparison selected by a SAdj is not always a color feature. *Muddy* in *muddy argument* implies unclarity; *icy* in *icy hand* implies coldness. How can such semantic diversity be explained by transposition?

In Beard (1993), I propose that the semantic component does not dis-

(9.27) [RUST]   [HAIR]

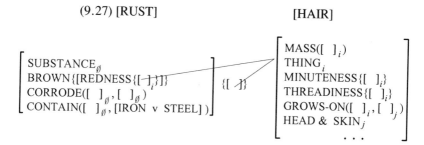

tinguish the external argument position of an attribute from its internal ones. (9.27) shows how the features of the noun underlying the QAdj *rusty* could compose with *hair,* a noun which violates the IRON material constraint on predicates of *rust* and thus is incapable of composing with the external argument position. The selection restriction [CONTAIN([ ]$_j$, [IRON v STEEL])] prohibits the R-representation of *rust* as a whole from composing with any of the features of *hair*; however, it does not prevent its composing with one of the natural properties of *rust,* as in [BROWN {REDNESS{[ ]}}]. If the R-representation of *hair* composes with just that feature, ignoring all others, the correct semantic interpretation, ''like rust specifically in color'' is appropriately composed.

The semantic interpretations of *rusty knife* and *rusty hair* presented here require no theory of L-derivation. They fall naturally out of decompositional semantics, which allow a noun to serve as an argument of an attribute or of any property of that attribute. Without introducing any new operation or principle, not only the differences between two ostensibly discrete L-derivations dissolve, the derivations themselves reduce to transposition. This also explains why these two are such prominent denominal adjectivizations: they are the missing N → QAdj transposition discussed in chapter 8. The suffixes on these derivations merely mark their change of status to qualifiers and do not bear any semantic value themselves. They are therefore more and more often omitted altogether in English:

(9.28) a. chestnut, straw, raven hair
        b. midget, giant, drawf plants
        c. rose, fuschia, tangerine briefs

(9.29) a. strong-arm(ed) tactics
        b. long-nose(d) pliers
        c. spice(d), ice(d) tea

Two Mysteries Resolved, A New One Revealed

The conclusion that both these ostensible L-derivations are in fact the effects of the same semantic process is now supported by the two puzzling aspects of their behavior mentioned above. Recall first the universal tendency of these QAdjs to exhibit the effects of SAdjs and SPAdjs simultaneously: *Nixonian ethics, friendly smile, Napoleonic personality* (9.20). A *Napoleonic personality* is not a personality like Napoleon nor a personality which inalienably possesses Napoleon; rather, it is a personality like that which Napoleon possessed. Let us assume that the concept NAPOLEON contains some feature referring to a special natural property, say, a kind of arrogance which distinguished Napoleon from other historical figures. We will simply call this property [N-HUBRIS{[ ]}] and assume that it is conceptually recognizable. The appropriate reading of phrases like *Napoleonic personality* is consistently achieved by transfer of that feature to the inventory of the head noun, PERSONALITY, so that it inalienably possesses the hubris possessed by Napoleon.

(9.30)   Napoleon   personality

$$\left[\begin{array}{l} \text{ACTOR}_{\emptyset} \\ \text{N-HUBRIS}\{[\ -]_j\} \\ \cdots \end{array} \right] \!\!- \ [\text{F}]$$

The result of the composition in (9.30) would be: [N-HUBRIS{[F]}] where [F] is the feature of PERSONALITY which [N-HUBRIS {[ ]} selects, probably its category specifier. Indeed, PERSONALITY may be a category itself; if so, composition would produce [N-HUBRIS {[PERSONALITY]}]. The only location of information on [N-HUBRIS] would be the lexical entry for *Napoleon*. By this interpretation, a Napoleonic personality is one which inalienably possesses this trait of Napoleon as a natural property, just as rusty hair is hair with the redness of rust as a natural property. No special semantic interpretation is required beyond that required of metaphoric compositions like *rusty hair;* only the N → QAdj transposition.

The single transpositional origin also explains the second puzzling aspect of SAdjs and OPAdjs: that a single suffix often marks both derivations, as in English *sandy beach* and *sandy hair* illustrated in (9.31).

(9.31)   a. icy, dusty, rusty, fuzzy, sandy, lacy
          b. arched, bowed, pointed
          c. nodular, annular, columnar

Indeed, if these two L-derivations do result from a single transposition, a new question arises: why do two sets of endings ever distinguish the SAdj from the OPAdj reading? This suggests that the two derivations are functional despite the lack of any need to resort to functions in order to explain the two readings.

In chapter 8 we saw that languages do contain Possessional and Similitudinal functions in inflection. If these functions are available for inflection, they are available for derivation; indeed, chapter 13 will argue that the two sets of functions are identical. Beard (1993) argued on this basis that there are in fact two origins of Similitudinal and Possessional adjectives: transposition and functional derivations based on the Similitudinal and Possessional functions. The former triggers a single marking, if any, the latter tend to trigger two. The competition for a distinction and no distinction in the MS-component would account for the affixational confusion. Moreover, if these adjectives simultaneously have two derivational origins, their productivity is less a mystery. The interesting point for this chapter is that even though grammatical and semantic categories interact here, each level has its own, clearly distinguishable role.

9.5 CONCLUSION

This chapter has explored some of the functions of Appendix A which seem to determine I-derivations and functional L-derivations, and concluded that they are, indeed, grammatical rather than semantic. Time and again we have seen major differences between these functions and similar ones in semantics, so that the line separating grammatical and semantic functions must be maintained. Algorithms like those seen operating between the lexicon and syntax in chapter 6 also determine the mapping of semantic to grammatical functions, in ways reminiscent of Jackendoff's correspondence conventions. We did examine closely one area where the output of grammatical and semantic functions seem to coincide, that is, the generation of Possessional and Similitudinal QAdjs.

Having distinguished grammatical category functions as properties of grammar, we must next explain how they operate in syntax and morphology. Up to this point we have casually referred to functions marked by adpositions in the same terms as those expressed by Case desinences. Adpositions, however, are widely held to constitute an independent, governing lexical class. If we are to move on to the argument that this set of functions underlies both nominal inflection and functional L-derivations, we must next show that we are not confusing lexical with grammatical functions, that adpositions do not bear semantic functions assigned by the lexicon. To do this we must examine the case made by Emonds, Klima, Jackendoff, and van Riemsdijk for adpositions as lexical items, then demonstrate that adpositions are Case markers like nominal desinences. The next two chapters will carry out these two tasks in that order.

NOTES

1. Marantz (1984:3–4), who subscribes to a similar view, ascribes it to Pāṇini.

2. No distinction will be made between the COGNITIVE and CONCEPTUAL level. The two terms will be used interchangeably here.

3. Hjelmsslev (1972:147) mentions a Postessive Temporal Case in Tabassaran, for example, *sa-β vadzā-lan* "after a month" (he does not explain the *sa-β*) but the incident is so isolated and the language so little studied, the evidence is unreliable.

4. In Russian PUNCTUALITY is marked for some lexical categories by Locative (*v mart-e* "in March"), for others by Accusative (*v p'jatnic-u* "(on) Friday", and by the Instrumental for two sets of four nouns referring to periods: *utr-om, dn-em, večer-om, noč'-ju* "in the morning, afternoon, evening, at night" and *let-om, osen'-ju, zim-oj, vesn-oj* "in the summer, fall, winter, spring". Genitive expresses PUNCTUALITY in complex temporal expressions: *ja rabotal tret'-ego oktjabrj-a 1990-go god-a* "I worked the third-GEN of October-GEN 1990-GEN".

5. This leaves open the question of why only this two-place semantic predicate is expressed at the grammatical level. This question will be answered further on in this chapter. Here the interesting fact is that, of an infinite number of potential two-place predicates, only this one is reflected in I- or L-derivation.

6. More specifically, as we will see below, the operator for the OPAdj is what Fillmore (1968: 61–81) called "inalienable possession"; that is, the reference must be an inherent or definitional possession of the nominal argument, not simply a legal or casual possession. In this sense, BEDROOM is a possession of HOME but not of HOMEOWNER.

Chapter Ten

The Syntax and Morphology of Adpositions

INTRODUCTION

We have embarked on a program to demonstrate a major constraint on the largest set of L-derivation rules, the functional derivations. That constraint is a closed set of about 44 Case functions, which the preceding chapter proved to be grammatical and not semantic, and which must be memorized independently of the system for marking them (The Separation Hypothesis). Interest in this set derives from the fact that it defines both the range of nominal Case functions which, as this chapter will show, includes the range of adpositional meanings, and that of the functional L-derivations. In other words, the next three chapters make possible a theory of grammar which conflates the functional ranges of all Case systems, adpositions, and simple and compound functional L-derivations, while maintaining the distinction between the operations of syntax and the lexicon.

The first step along this route is the proof that adpositional and Case functions coincide. To prove this, we must first demonstrate that Ps are not lexical items but are themselves grammatical morphemes which mark Case. Since Jackendoff has defended the contrary position most astutely, his defense will be the focus of the refutation here, although the evidence from Dutch adduced by van Riemsdijk (1982) will not be ignored. This chapter, then, has two goals. First, it will examine the LMH case for a lexical governing class, P (prepositions and postpositions = ADPOSITIONS), mounted by Klima (1965), Emonds (1972), Jackendoff (1973, 1977), and van Riemsdijk, and demonstrate the problems with these arguments. The second goal of this chapter is to lay a foundation for chapter 11, which will argue that Ps are in fact phrasal affixes (clitics) or pronominal free morphemes which mark Case in a way comparable to that of Case endings.

10.1 PREPOSITIONS AND VERBS

In contemporary generative models of language, the lexicon contains four major lexical classes: N, V, A, and P. According to Chomsky (1981: 48;

1986: 2), van Riemsdijk & Williams (1986: 43), Gazdar et al. (1985: 21) among others, these four categories are the result of the interaction of two binary features, one nominal [± N], one verbal, [±V]. Usually these four categories are divided into pairs, the nominal N(oun) and A(djective) and the nonnominal V(erb) and P(reposition) in accord with Table 10.1.[1]

Table 10.1   The Major Categories of GB Theory

		+ *Verbality* –	
Nominality	+	Adjective	Noun
	–	Verb	Preposition

Table 10.1 provides four subclasses from two classes, essentially following the interpretation of markedness theory in previous chapters:

(10.1)   a. [+ Noun, – Verb]
          b. [+ Noun, + Verb]
          c. [– Noun, + Verb]
          d. [– Noun, – Verb]

But Table 10.1 also produces problems with the " ± " toggle. The previous binary polar categories referred directly to semantic categories, FE-MALE/MALE, INDIVIDUAL/AGGREGATION. The symbols " + " and " – " then indicate whether either, both, or neither of the grammatical functions corresponding to them are semantically relevant, that is, referential. These definitions do not apply to (10.1). For (10.1) to work, " ± " must signify "possesses the properties of category C". At least, this works for adjectives, which cross-linguistically possess the morphological features of verbs in predicate function and nouns in attribute function. (Many languages, like Chukchee and Japanese, conjugate predicate adjectives, while others, like Greek and Serbo-Croatian, decline attributive adjectives like nouns.)

But if " – " signifies that Ps bear none of the properties of N and V, the same is true of Delimiters (degree words), conjunctions, and particles, so the designation does not distinguish P. If, however, " – " indicates that P shares properties of N and V which are not the same as those shared by A, it is difficult to imagine what those properties are. Under P&P, P and V assign Case and theta roles but N does not; N is assigned Case and theta roles. The lack of definition for the lexical class P as [– Noun, – Verb] is a serious shortcoming in justifying P as a lexical class.

10.2 Prepositions as a Major Lexical Class

The idea that Ps might constitute a lexical class originated with Klima and Emonds, but Jackendoff and van Riemsdijk have presented the most explicit cases for this position. It is worth noting that Emonds (1985) and Jackendoff (1990) still embrace this position in its entirety. Although Emonds (1985: 157) claims that P is more grammatical than lexical, he offers no alternative account and leaves Ps in the lexicon as a minor governing category. Thus the interpretation of P as a lexical category has not been superseded by recent research, so Jackendoff's position remains the appropriate focus of a rebuttal.

Jackendoff attempts to show that Ps are similar to Vs in heading identical phrase structures; if this is so, the argument goes, Ps must represent a major lexical class. The basic structure of Jackendoff's argument is illustrated in (10.2):

(10.2)   a. If two linguistic phenomena are substantially similar, they must be coclassified.
          b. Verbs are classified as a major lexical class;
          c. prepositions are substantially similar to verbs.

          d. Prepositions must represent a major class.

Jackendoff takes the first two claims as premises and tries to demonstrate the third in two steps. First, he shows that Ps, non-*ly* adverbs, and verbal particles constitute a unitary class (P).[2] Next, he demonstrates that the maximal projection of this class, PP, is identical to VP. He does not consider similarities between Ps and Ns although, if Table 10.1 is accurate, Ps must equally resemble (or not resemble) Ns; rather, he focuses exclusively on the similarities between Vs and Ps. Jackendoff also does not question the presumption of Table 10.1 as a means of determining the major lexical and syntactic categories. Thus the structure of the argument itself is weak at several points.[3] Although the argument from analogy inherent in (10.2) is a suitable strategy, this chapter will use the same strategy to reach the opposite conclusion by examining a wider range of phenomena phonologically and functionally similar to Ps.

10.2.1 Distributional Tests for a Unified Class, P

In order to prove that Ps, non-*ly* adverbs, and verbal particles constitute a single major class, P, Jackendoff applies five tests of categorical identity and shows that all these types pass four of the tests indifferently. The first test is the strict subcategorization of "verbs such as *put*," which subcategorize a NP and PP (Jackendoff 1973: 346).

(10.3)   a. *Irving put the books

b. Irving put the books $\left\{\begin{array}{l} \text{on the shelf} \\ \text{there} \\ \text{away} \end{array}\right\}$

The second distributional test is the Subject-verb inversion, which raises (a) PPs, (b) non-*ly* adverbs, and (c) particles.

(10.4)   a. Into the opera house raced Harpo
         b. There goes Chico
         c. Off came Harpo's false beard

The third distributional test is compatibility with the *with*-imperative. (10.5) shows that the same three categories pass this test, too.

(10.5)   a. Into the dungeon with the traitors!
         b. Outdoors with these noisy machines!
         c. Off with his nose!

The fourth distributional test is compatibility with the Delimiter *right*, that is, *right* in the sense in which it can precede the same three categories.[4]

(10.6)   a. The collapse came right after Ricardo's arrival.
         b. The eager dwarves reached right inside
         c. The scenery caved right in under Gummo's weight

Jackendoff claims that the derivation of this and the preceding three construction types is simplified if ordinary PPs, non-*ly* adverbs, and particles are all classified as PPs. Such a classificatory unification is supported by the phonological and semantic identity of many of the items involved.

Jackendoff admits that all his data do not pass a fifth distributional test: ''prepositional phrases (except those consisting of a single intransitive position) can appear in the focus position of cleft sentences . . .'' (Jackendoff 1973: 352).

(10.7)   a. It was there/in the house that they had the ceremony
         b. It was *away/out the back way that he drove

(10.8)   a. It was *there/*in that the cat was
         b. It was *away/*out that he went

Jackendoff proposes that if this is the only test running counter to the general trends of the data, it should be treated as exceptional; however, he offers no explanation of this exceptional behavior.

A more satisfying account of Jackendoff's four successful test constructions, however, appeals to semantics. Each of his test examples is based on specifically spatial (locational-directional) functions: Goal, Origin, or Locus. All Ps with nonspatial functions consistently fail the same tests, even when semantically nonanomalous, unless they may be assigned a spatial semantic interpretation. Compare (10.3–10.6) with (10.9–10.12), respectively.

(10.9)   a.   John put the apples with the oranges (Sociative + semantic TO)

          b. *John put the apples with a shovel (Instrumental)

          c. *John put the apples from the shelf (Origin)

(10.10)   a.   By the rack with him! (Goal + Proximate)

          b. *By the blade with him! (Means)

          c. *From the rack with him! (Origin)

(10.11)   a.   In the room stood my sister, Mary (Inessive Locus)

          b. *With enthusiasm worked the dynamic duo (Comitative)

          c. *By ear played the dynamic duo (Manner)

(10.12)   a.   He did it right in the classroom (Inessive Locus)

          b. *He did it right with his hands (Means)

          c. *He did it right for the president (Purpose)

          d. *He did it right from fear (Cause)

Notice that even some spatial relations fail Jackendoff's tests (10.9c, 10.10c), usually because of some impinging semantic factor. Proof that the critical level for Jackendoff's tests is semantic derives from examples like (10.9a), where the phrase *with the oranges* is a Sociative, not Goal phrase.[5] Sociative does not combine with Goal as do other secondary functions; *John went with Harry* cannot mean "John went to Harry to be with him". (10.9a) has exactly this interpretation, however, and since that interpretation cannot be derived from the grammatical function, it must be semantic. The verb *put* requires specifically a GOAL relation of its second Object, so that function, $[_{Path}TO([\ ])]$, must originate in the verb itself.

The fact of the matter, then, is that functions expressing semantic GOAL regularly pass Jackendoff's four distribution tests. However, not even the preposition *to,* the grammatical Goal marker in English, always passes the tests:

(10.13)   a.   John sent a letter right to Bill

          b.   John gave the letter right to Bill

(10.14)   a. *John wrote a letter right to Bill
           b. *John dedicated his book right to Bill
           c. *John devoted his life right to Bill

A close examination of such examples reveals that the English Delimiter *right* applies only when the grammatical function which it modifies corresponds to some semantic category, let us say, DESTINATION([ ]), where DESTINATION must be defined in terms of physical movement, like GO([ ]). This operator must be a purely semantic concept if *to* marks a grammatical function, Goal, for the distributions of Goal and DESTINATION([ ]) do not always coincide.

Any successful theory of these test constructions must appeal to semantic functions but need not appeal to any particular syntactic class or grammatical function. Any class capable of reflecting the appropriate semantic relation, that is, Adv or N marked for an adverbial Case, suffices even if it does not ordinarily serve that purpose. To begin with constituent structures which restrict these positions to PPs, a theory will have to assume ancillary ad hoc constraints in the form of surface filters or something similar to prevent the nonspatial PPs from surfacing in these positions. An approach appealing to selection restrictions would appear more cogent at this juncture.

10.2.2 Structural Parallels with VPs

On the other side of Jackendoff's argument lies the symmetry between the structure of PPs and other lexical classes, particularly that of the VP. This assumption predicts the possibility of PPs reducing to plain Ps, P + NP, or P + PP. What we actually find is that elevating P to the position of a major governing lexical class on the basis of a comparison of P with V requires mutually incompatible definitions of "government", "transitivity", "head", and "complement" for P and V. The remainder of this section examines each of the predicted structures of (10.15) to demonstrate this.

Jackendoff illustrates prepositional intransitivity paralleling that of verbs with examples like (10.15).

(10.15)   a. The cat came in
           b. John went out
           c. Mary came over

Jackendoff argues that the final items in (10.15) must be considered Ps because they are phonologically identical to the Ps used in ordinary PPs (*in the house, out the door, over the hill*) and because they satisfy the four (now discredited) distributional criteria discussed above for an item's inclusion in the class, PP.

The use of the term "transitivity" itself implies for Jackendoff only that Ps in some sense take an Object. Jackendoff's proof is difficult to maintain if we move away from this superficial interpretation of Transitivity to a more sophisticated one. Transitivity implies much more than governing an Object; it implies support for movement such as Passive NP raising and directional L-derivations such as the Transitive → Intransitive Reflexive derivation illustrated in (10.16):

(10.16) a. He shaved his brother   He shaved (himself)
         b. She dressed her son   She dressed (herself)
         c. They washed the baby   They washed (themselves)

That (10.16) reflects a genuine L-derivation is confirmed by the fact that these forms are morphologically marked in other languages, as in Russian *on breet brat-a* "he shaves (his) brother" : *on breet-sja* "he shaves".

Transitivity also implies the possibility of Causative derivation, illustrated in (10.17).

(10.17) a. The plane flew   He flew the plane
         b. The dog walked   He walked the dog
         c. The boat sank   He sank the boat

This derivation, too, is productive and morphologically marked in other languages, as in Turkish *uç-mak* "to fly" : *uç-ur-mak* "to fly something".

In some cases the phonology and semantics of the "intransitive" P are indeed identical with those of the "transitive" (10.18–10.19).

(10.18) a. He came in the house   He came in
         b. He came through the woods   He came through

(10.19) a. He is inside   He is inside the house
         b. He stood outside   He stood outside the office

However, neither Ps nor their complements are subject to any of the transformations to which verbs are subject or any L-derivation at all. No language marks the relations (10.18) and (10.19) morphologically as Russian and Turkish mark the verbal relations (10.16) and (10.17); yet, according to Jackendoff, the syntactic behavior of the Vs and Ps in (10.17) and (10.18–10.19) are syntactically identical.

There is a further difficulty facing the claim that Ps may be transitive. In Case languages like Russian, only a few Vs necessarily subcategorize

Case, roughly, 50. Yip, Maling & Jackendoff (1987) suggest that the number of verbs subcategorizing lexical Case in Icelandic may be considerably larger, perhaps in the several hundreds, even excluding those whose semantics predict an oblique Case function for the DO. The point here, however, nonetheless holds even for Icelandic, since in the unmarked case Icelandic assigns Accusative to the DO. The vast majority of Vs, including neologisms generated in discourse, conventionally associate the Accusative with the DO and the Dative with the IO. It follows that verbs with Accusative DOs and Dative IOs form an open, unmarked class.

Ps do not behave this way; there is no default Case for Ps. Each P is associated with one or two, occasionally three Cases which are never predictable. English has but one Case, Accusative, visible only among pronouns, so it is possible to claim that Ps assign configurational Case in English. Russian, however, has six Cases, and the Case associated with any given P is unpredictable. *Na* "on, onto" requires the Locative when indicating Locus and Accusative when indicating Goal, but in either instance, *nad* "above, over" requires the Instrumental. Other Ps require the Genitive and Dative. In fact, since P is a closed class, it would be logically impossible to have a productive, default Case for them to govern.

Emonds (1985: 227) and Bierwisch (1988: 39) argue that Dative is the default Case for German Ps when Accusative or Genitive is not assigned lexically. They conclude that Dative is assigned structurally to Ps in the same way that Accusative is assigned structurally to the DOs of verbs unless the verb is lexically marked to assign an oblique Case. The situation in German, however, is a function of the fact that the IE oblique Case system has been reduced to Genitive and Dative, so that German now has only four Cases: two direct and two oblique. As we would predict on the basis of the Russian data, Genitive is also unpredictably associated with several German prepositions, for example, *wegen, während, trotz, (an) statt*. More importantly, new Ps, developing primarily from APs, such as *inmittens, seitens, oberhalb, längs, mittels* are consistently associated with the Case of APs, the Genitive. Thus by one measure Dative is the default Case for Ps and by another, Genitive is.

If we claim that P is a governing class, we will have to define a context-sensitive type of government and transitivity exclusively for P which is distinct from that of V and restrict Intransitive Ps to those signifying semantic spatial relations. While the DO and IO Cases for transitive verbs are wholly predictable, the Cases associated with Ps are universally lexical. Lexical parallels between P and V simply do not sustain scrutiny.

10.2.3 Prepositions Subcategorizing PP Complements

A second possible PP structure predicted by Jackendoff's assumptions is P–PP: a head P with a PP complement. Jackendoff distinguishes Ps with complement PPs from those with adjunct PPs on the basis of examples like (10.20):

(10.20)   a. Chico raced away from Mrs. Claypool
          b. Otis T. Flywheel raced away in a battered Ford

In (a) the sequence P–PP can be preposed but in (b) it cannot; this proves that in (b) *away in a battered Ford* does not form a constituent. The adjuncts in (10.21), according to Jackendoff, do constitute P–PP constructions.

(10.21)   a. Harpo rode the horse out of the barn
          b. Up into the clouds shot a riderless broomstick
          c. Sam disappeared down into the darkness

Again, all the examples corresponding to the P–PP configuration must express a physical, directional function, so an account of (10.21) cannot end with subsuming everything under the rubric of PP. A nonspatial P–PP is not even possible in English, for example, *onto* but **onfor, *foron, *forwith, *withfor; out of* but **by of, *with of, *for of, *on of*.[6] *Out by* is acceptable due to the Locative reference and the fact that *out* is probably a Delimiter. The point is, once again, a complete explanation of these distributional data is impossible without an appeal to semantics.

If Jackendoff's interpretation of (10.21) is correct, the definition of "head" and "complement" will have to be radically revised. The heads of obvious major categories can occur independently without their complements but not vice versa, as is shown in (10.22–10.24).

(10.22)   a. The house on the hill is pretty
          b. The house is pretty
          c. *On the hill is pretty

(10.23)   a. The bag is full of flour
          b. The bag is full
          c. *The bag is of flour

(10.24)   a. The man thought of his mother
          b. The man thought
          c. *The man of his mother

The P–PP constructions of (10.21) do not follow this pattern at all, however.

(10.25)   a.   Harpo rode the horse out
           b.   *Harpo rode the horse of the barn

(10.26)   a.   *Sam disappeared down
           b.   Sam disappeared into the darkness

(10.27)   a.   Up shot a riderless broomstick
           b.   Into the clouds shot a riderless broomstick

Sometimes the head can stand alone (10.25a, 10.27a), sometimes not
(10.26a); sometimes the complement can appear without the head (10.26b,
10.27b), sometimes not (10.25a). In the overwhelming majority of cases,
either the head or the complement may stand alone in the phrase as in
(10.27), suggesting two independent adjunct phrases modifying the verb.
The radically different behavior of PP heads and complements forces exclusive definitions of them, as does that of adpositional ''Transitivity'' and
''government''.

10.2.4 Prepositional Specifiers

Jackendoff's syntactic evidence for P as a major class includes parallels
between the specifiers of PPs and other phrasal categories, such as those
in (10.28):

(10.28)   a.   5 miles farther down the road than we expected
           b.   too far along the road for us to see him (Jackendoff 1977:
                 206)

Assuming *down* and *along* are the heads of their phrases, Jackendoff argues that PPs exhibit the same specifier relations found among NPs, VPs,
and APs. Closer examination, however, suggests that what Jackendoff proposes as specifier + head constructions are, like the P + PP constructions,
two independent adjuncts. Their structural independence is confirmed by
the fact that the two APs may be moved about in the phrase independent
of each other.

(10.29)   a.   John ran 5 miles farther *down the road* than we expected
           b.   John ran *down the road* 5 miles farther than we expected
           c.   John ran 5 miles farther than we expected *down the road*

Compare (10.29) now with the potential positional variations of adverbs
and PPs in (10.30).

(10.30) a. John ran quickly *down the road*
        b. John ran *down the road* quickly

The semantic dependency, therefore, does not map isomorphically onto structure and, once again, must be explained semantically, not structurally.

The same counterargument raised in the second point of section 10.2.2 may also be applied here; namely, the prepositional complement is perfectly natural without its presumable head.

(10.31) a. John ran down the road
        b. John ran five miles farther than we expected
        c. John ran farther (than we expected)
        d. John ran five miles

Structurally, the specifier, complement, and head—all may occupy the head position in headless constructions without any structural or semantic difficulties. Hence, if we concede headhood to *down* in (10.28), we will have to define "head", "specifier", and "complement" uniquely for Ps.

10.2.5 Toward a Semantic Account of P + PP

The evidence considered here suggests that the two major phrases of (10.28), *down the road* and *5 miles farther than we expected*, are syntactically independent adjuncts. However, the latter phrase falls semantically within the scope of the former. This situation is not at all at odds with recent research. Napoli (1989), as mentioned in section 7.4, demonstrates that configurational approaches to predication theory are not ineluctable because the relation of semantics to syntax is much looser than even the homomorphism commonly assumed by P&P; rather, predication theory is wholly independent of syntactic theory. Napoli raises a host of arguments which indicate that Ps are often semantic modifiers which introduce complex predicates. Lexical items which have a P as part of their lexical entry, as in *look after*, and lexical items which have a PP as a sister assign theta roles to the "Objects" of the Ps. Still other Ps, for example, the Passive *by*, are empty role markers (Napoli 1989: 129–136).

Very similar to the situation here, Napoli claims that two adjacent PPs may represent a predicate and Subject role player (Napoli 1989: 95).

(10.32) a. We think of John as a friend
        b. John is thought of e as a friend

In order to account for preposition stranding in English, *of John* must be treated structurally as a PP. This means that the two PPs in (10.32), *of John* and *as a friend* together form a proposition at semantic level: FRIEND([-

JOHN]). It follows that the semantic level must be capable of determining propositional structure from a broader variety of constructions than IPs and NPs. Relevant to the arguments here, semantics must be able to find propositional structures in two sister PPs.

Recall also the arguments for featural composition in section 9.4.2 and Beard (1991, 1993), which explain morphosemantic mismatches such as [*nuclear physic*[*ist*]], [*moral philosoph*[*er*]], and [*criminal law*[yer]], as well as all other attribute scope ambiguities. Attributes do not compose with their heads as whole, but feature by feature, so that the features of an attribute selects one feature of the head with which to compose as a proposition. The same sort of disjuncture between syntax and semantics seems to characterize the relation between the syntax and semantics of the adjuncts in (10.28). If two PPs or other adjuncts adjoin the same verb, the semantic component is free to set their scope vis-à-vis each other as it sees fit, regardless of their structural relations. To set out definitive proof here would take us off course. However, only an exclusively semantic interpretation of the scope relations in (10.28) is compatible with their relative stability in the face of the structural variation illustrated in (10.29–10.31).

10.3 PREPOSITIONS AS A LEXICAL CLASS

Surface Case is associated with Ps but association does not itself prove that Ps govern Case. Fillmore (1968), Napoli (1989), and others have argued that the phonological matrices of Ps, like surface Case endings, are determined by a deeper set of relations. The 44 nominal category functions of Appendix A represent an attempt to more closely define this set of relations. This section proposes that the set of functions in Appendix A underlies all Case-related phenomena, both declensional endings and Ps, the latter comprising a class of inflectional morphemes. Section 10.2 demonstrated that Ps do not behave syntactically like a major or minor governing class. This section will demonstrate that they do behave like grammatical morphemes.

10.3.1 Prepositions and Case Assignment

The first type of evidence which suggests that Ps simply mark Case functions is their frequent optionality. In languages with rich Case systems like German, Russian, Latin, and Sanskrit, a single function frequently may be expressed either by a Case alone or by a Case accompanied by a P (10.33–10.37). However, the reverse is never true: Ps do not occur without Case marking on the nouns which they accompany in inflectional languages.

(10.33)   **Latin Accusative of Goal**

      a.   Alesi-am proficiscitur "sets out to Alesia" (Accusative)

    b. ad Alesi-am proficiscitur "sets out to Alesia" (*ad* + Accusative)

    c. *ad Alisi-a proficiscitur "sets out to Alesia (*ad* + citation form)

(10.34)   **Sanskrit Sociative Instrumental**
    a. bāla-ih "with (the) children" (Instrumental)
    b. bāla-ih saha "with (the) children" (Instrumental + *saha*)
    c. *bāla saha "with (the) children (citation form + *saha*)

(10.35)   **English Dative of Recipient**
    a. give the ball to him (*to* + Accusative)
    b. give him the ball (Accusative)
    c. *give the ball to he (*to* + non-Accusative)

(10.36)   **English "Bare NP Adverbs"**
    a. work (for) five hours ((*for* +) Accusative of Duration)
    b. work (on) Friday ((*on* +) Accusative of Punctuality)

(10.37)   **Russian Accusative of Translation and Perlation**
    a. pere-xodit' (čerez) ploščad' "walk across the-square"
    b. pro-xodit' (čerez) ploščad' "walk through the-square"

In (10.33–10.37) the identical function may be marked by Case alone or by P + Case but not by P alone. If theta roles were only assigned by those governing classes which subcategorize theta roles, they could not be assigned in the absence of the governing class. In (10.33–10.37), however, even though the P in each instance is removed, its Case function remains unaffected. This could be possible only if these Ps are optional Case markers, not assignors, alternating here, as grammatical morphemes often do for purely morphological reasons, with zero.

Nothing is gained by terminological erosion which would allow Case affixes in the lexical class P. Jackendoff (1977: 236) is willing to call *-ing* a P and Cole (1985: 120) categorizes all declensional suffixes as syntactic Ps. This leads to the unsupportable conclusion that Case affixes both govern and mark Case. Even within Jackendoff's framework, Ps govern the Accusative, which is marked, for example, by *-m* and vowel laxing for *he,* as in *see him, with him.* If it is true that Case endings mark lexemes for Case and that elsewhere Ps are phrasal markers of the same relations, the difference between Case endings and adpositions is only morphological, not lexical or syntactic. Of the two possible explanations of the mutual, universal functions of Ps and Case endings, (i) both assign Case and (ii) both mark Case, only the latter shows promise of holding.

If Ps are Case markers rather than a governing class, we would expect their complements to be governed by verbs. It is widely agreed, in fact, that this is often the case. *Smell, reek, stink (of)*, their synonyms and antonyms then lexically govern the Genitive in exactly the same sense as do the Russian verbs of anticipation, *iskat' kogo* "seek someone", *ždat' čego* "wait for (of)-something", *ožidat' čego* "expect something". *Listen (to)* governs the Dative just as *helfen* "help" does in German. The evidence again encourages our treating Ps as phrasal Case markers in the sense that traditional Case endings are phrasal head markers.

10.3.2 Prepositions as Grammatical Morphemes

Chapter 2 showed that the uncontroversial major class items, N, V, A, share an array of attributes which affixes do not. Stereotypical lexical items belong to (i) open classes which do not form grammatical paradigms. They are (ii) phonologically fully specified; zero and empty lexemes are ruled out. They are (iii) susceptible to lexical and inflectional derivation. They (iv) belong to one and only one class and may change class only via L-derivation. Lexemes are (v) listable items, not operations or processes more akin to phonological rules. Grammatical morphemes, on the other hand, form paradigmatic closed classes characterized by omissive and empty marking, and are not susceptible to L-derivation. Any number of lexical classes may serve as input to a MS-operation. Next, we examine Ps with respect to all five of these attributes; Ps resemble grammatical morphemes and not lexemes on all grounds.

1. Open and Closed Classes. Verbs belong to grammatically unordered open classes. Semantic relations like *give : get, sell : buy, send : receive* may be recorded in the lexicon, but they are irrelevant to grammar for they comprise categories not directly marked by morphemes. Each verb has a meaning directly and idiomatically associated with its P-representation. Ps, however, belong to tightly closed classes which form paradigms with their functions, paradigms which exhibit the morphological asymmetry discussed in chapters 2 and 3. This means that several Ps may refer to one function and any one P may refer to several such functions. Yet both the phonological expressions and the set of prepositional functions form closed classes. A fragment of a paradigm of Ps is illustrated in (10.38–10.40) and diagrammed in Figure 10.1.

(10.38)   a. She jumped in the car
          b. She is in the room
          c. She arrived in January

(10.39)   a. She jumped on the table
          b. She is on the field
          c. She arrived on Friday

(10.40)   a. She jumped at Tom
          b. She is at home
          c. She arrived at 5 o'clock

Figure 10.1

A Fragment of a Prepositional Paradigm

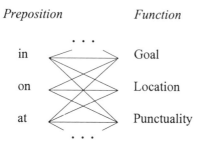

Preposition   Function

    in   Goal

    on   Location

    at   Punctuality

We have already seen that directional functions are subject to the conventions of markedness. When we combine the markedness and paradigmaticity exhibited by Ps, the picture of P as a grammatical morpheme emerges.

2. Zero and Empty Forms. We have already seen examples of zero Ps in (10.33-10.37), where a theta role is present in the absence of a corresponding phonological expression. Empty Ps also abound. *Of* is a notorious empty P, marking relations between NPs which are expressed in the NPs themselves:

(10.41)   a. the mother of the girl
          b. a victim of fate
          c. the king of England

In each of these phrases, the relation between the two NPs is fully specified in the semantic representation of the head N. Thus mother refers to the relation between a mother and child, a relation specified in the R-representation of the lexeme, [MOTHER([ ])]; hence, *of* emptily links the head NP with its Object. Null and empty lexemes do not exist but null and empty morphemes are common.

3. Susceptibility to L-Derivation. Verbs can be productively derived in most languages, as in Russian *uč-i-* teach'', *uč-en-nyj* ''taught'', *uč-en-nik* ''pupil'', *uč-en-ie* ''teaching'', *uč-i-tel'* ''teacher'' and English *bake* : *bak-er, bak-ing, bak-er-y, bak-able*. Ps cannot be productively derived: **to-able, *with-ery, *between-er, *after-ee, *along-ate*. This derivability accounts for the fact that Vs, like other major lexical classes, constitute open classes. If Ps were productively, synchronically derivable, they would have to belong to an open class. The evidence of section 9.3.3 pointed in just the opposite direction. Let us reconsider some of it in light of the current discussion.

The only classes of derived Ps even ostensibly productive are those generated from nouns and adjectives via prefixation.

(10.42)   a. atop, along, astride, aboard
          b. behind, before, beside, beneath, below

The class might be open but restricted by grammatically irrelevant semantic factors. But instances of derivations such as those in (10.42) are sporadic and unpredictable. *Abottom, *ashort, *astand are impossible even though the underlying forms belong to the same class as those of (10.42) and the output is semantically transparent: *abottom the building, *ashort the mark, *astand the podium.

(10.42), in fact, cannot represent lexical derivation since the underlying base cannot corefer with other tokens of itself locally (10.44) as transparent lexical derivations can (10.43).

(10.43)   a. He is **short**$_i$ but his **short**$_i$ness is not a factor
          b. John **rose**$_i$ to the top in a **rise**$_i$ which now is legendary
          c. Everything **break**$_i$able **break**$_i$s

(10.44)   a. *It is **long**$_i$ but there is nothing **along**$_i$ it
          b. *His **stride**$_i$ is obvious when he is **astride**$_i$ a horse
          c. *He is **atop**$_i$ a tall building whose **top**$_i$ is in bad condition

It is simply impossible to expand the class P synchronically as we can V.

4. Single Class Membership. We have seen that Ps are not susceptible to productive L-derivation; not only do Ps fail to undergo lexical derivation themselves, they often mark lexical derivations as prefixes.

(10.45)   a. between-class (break)   f. overeat
          b. after-dinner (mint)   g. in-house (doctor)
          c. on-line (service)   h. outdistance
          d. upstage   i. underestimate
          e. downplay   j. throughway

These derivations cannot be interpreted as compounds, as Lieber (1981a, 1983) and Selkirk (1982) suggest for two reasons. First, languages like

Serbo-Croatian require interfixes between the lexical stems of a compound as in (10.46):

(10.46) a. dug-o-nog-an ''long-legged''
         b. konj-o-goj-stvo ''horse-breeding''
         c. vod-o-pad ''waterfall''

However, none ever occurs between a preposition and the stem:

(10.47) a. nad-zem-ni kamen '' aboveground stone [tombstone]''
         b. među-grad-ski saobraćaj ''interurban traffic''
         c. posle-diplom-ske studije ''postdiploma [graduate] studies''

Second, in nominal derivations containing P, the lexical class of the constituent on the right changes, as in [[*between*]$_P$[*class*]$_N$]$_{Adj}$, [[*after*]$_P$[*dinner*]$_N$]$_{Adj}$. The word formation theories of Lieber and Selkirk predict that the rightmost member of an English compound determines the class of the compound. They cite examples like *overdose, underdog, outbuilding*, in which the left member is P, the right member is N, and the compounds are all N. However, Selkirk (1982: 14) inadvertently includes the adjectives of (10.48a) in her compound noun list and Lieber (1983: 261) claims that the adjectives of (10.48b) are noun compounds.

(10.48) a. inland, uptown
         b. between-class, over-ground

Neither Lieber's nor Selkirk's percolation principles account for the majority of P + N compounds in English which are, like (10.48), adjectives rather than nouns.

Evidence like this brings into question whether Ps belong to one class. Assuming that the right-hand members of these forms, whether derivations or compounds, are their heads, how is it that *drop out, stand in, hold over* may be verbs or nouns but never prepositions? There are distinctive differences between Ps, verbal particles, and prepositional prefixes. Like the suffixes *-ing* and *-ed*, they seem to be a part of complex words of all lexical classes rather than limited to one.

5. Items or Processes. An interesting aspect of Ps and Case endings is that both generally appear to be listable items. Even in Semitic languages, characterized by inflectional revowelling, Case is generally marked by affixes and real Ps rather than by revowelling. Ps, however, do contract and cliticize, an attribute of grammatical morphemes (as in English auxiliaries). In French *a* + *le* contract to *au*, *de* + *le* reduce to *du*. Russian possesses asyllabic Ps: *v* ''in'', *s* ''with, from'', *k* ''toward''. If we grant listed status to such items, therefore, we again introduce behavior which will be unique for Ps, for uncontroversial lexical items, N, V, and A stems, never contract or cliticize synchronically.

A common trait of listed items is their ability to serve as labels outside grammatical contexts, as in *stop, slow, walk*. This is possible because they have a naming function which is determined by the lexicon and not by grammar. If Ps were listed items, they should be capable of labeling. It is true that spatial Ps are used as labels, for example, *on, off, in, out, up, down*. However, only those with clear adjectival functions are used in this way. Notice that *on* and *off* can only be used in peculiarly idiomatic adjectival senses as labels. Ps marking primary functions, for example, *of, for, with, by, to, from*, are never so employed.

10.4 THE PRIMARY AND SECONDARY GRAMMATICAL FUNCTIONS

This section will examine the primary and secondary division of Case functions introduced in chapter 9. It will show that the primary functions are distinguished from the secondary ones by the fact that they are simple and include all the NP grammatical functions such as Subject and Object. The second subset of functions are all adverbal and most are complex; that is, they are usually compounded with one of the primary functions, most often Locus, Goal, or Origin.

10.4.1 Adpositions and the Primary Case Functions

In order to understand how adpositions may be treated as phrasal Case markers supplementing affixal Case markers rather than as major class lexical items, we must first examine the set of category functions which Ps express. The set of functions in Appendix A is divided into two major subcategories, referred to as the ''primary functions'' and ''secondary functions''. The 44 functions enumerated in Appendix A do not include the complex functions which can be formed by combining secondary location functions with the primary Goal, Locus, and Origin functions. These compound functions are reflected in such compound PPs as *from under* [Origin-[Subessive]], *from over* [Origin[Superessive]]; *in(to)* [Goal[Inessive]], *on(to)* [Goal[Adessive]] (= Allative), and so forth. (10.49) represents the primary functions of Appendix A with examples from English.

(10.49) a. Subject [Nominative]   **She** hit the ball
         b. Object [Accusative]   She hit **the ball**
         c. Possessivity [Genitive]   the honor **of the woman**
         d. Possession [Genitive]   a woman **of honor**
         e. Measure [Accusative]   It weighs **five pounds**
         f. Material [Genitive]   the woman **of steel**

g. Partitivity [Genitive]   a part **of it**
h. Distinction [Ablative]   bigger **than life**
i. Absolute [Abl, Dat, . . .]   **With the weather changing**, . . .
j. Means [Instrumental]   She works **with her hands**
k. Route [Instrumental]   She came **by Sunbury**
l. Manner [Instrumental]   She works **like a dog**
m. Essive [Instrumental]   She works **as a doctor**
n. Duration [Accusative]   She worked **five hours**
o. Iteration [Accusative]   She works **every day**
p. Accordance [Ablative]   She plays **by ear**
q. Purpose [Dative]   She works **for Mary/for money**
r. Exchange [Dative]   She bought the book **for $5**
s. Cause [Ablative]   She acted **from fear**
t. Sociation [Instrumental]   She works **with John**

----

u. Locus [Locative]   She works **at home/at noon**
v. Goal [Dative, Accusative]   She goes **to Boston**
w. Origin [Ablative]   She is **from Philly**

These primary functions are marked by Case alone in the Sanskrit, without a supplemental adverb, and are the most likely functions marked by Case ending alone in inflectional languages in general. The secondary functions require a supplemental adverb in Sanskrit and are in general more likely to be marked by double Case endings or adposition + Case elsewhere.

The primary functions are marked in English by word order (Subject and Object) and the clitic Ps *of, to, for, from, than, with, by, like, at, in* and *on*. These constitute the Ps in Jackendoff's system which have no "Intransitive" correlate with the ostensible exception of *by, in* and *on*. However, *by* may be used adverbally only in its secondary Proximate or Prolative senses: *he stood by, he passed by*, but not as an Agentive or Means marker, as in **John was hit by*. Moreover, *in* and *on* are basically secondary functions fundamentally distinguished from the primary Locus marker, *at*. *In* and *on* are used only subregularly to mark the primary functions of spatial and temporal Locus, for example, *on Friday, on top, in May, in bed*. So the list of English primary function markers is probably *of, to, for, from, than, with, by* (marking Agent and Means), *like*, and *at*, none of which are used as verb particles, adjectives, or prefixes. The IO Goal function expresses properties of NPs, not PPs, as do adpositionally marked Subjects and Objects in other languages. The adpositions marking primary functions pass Jackendoff's distribution tests for P only if they may be semantically interpreted in terms of spatial semantic functions.

Other interesting attributes of primary functions distinguish them from secondary ones. First, only primary functions may be represented by omissive (zero) marking. Indeed, only those relatively high on the functional hierarchy can escape overt marking, for example, Subject, Object, IO Goal, the Genitive functions, Manner, and Means. At the other end of the phonological visibility pole, only secondary function markers (adpositions) may be independently accented. The primary function markers are usually asyllabic or monosyllabic affixes or clitics. Second, only secondary functions may be semantically complex. Secondary compound functions all comprise exactly two functions, one of which is a primary function. Most complex secondary functions are based on one of the three primary spatial functions separated in (10.49) by the broken line: Locus, Goal, Origin. Two combine with [Negation], and other combinations are found in some languages.[7] In *the ball is under the table, under* marks [Locus [Subessive]] while in *the ball rolled under the table* it marks [Goal[Subessive]]. However, only if the secondary function is Origin is the complex function overtly distinguished in most languages: *the ball rolled from under the table. From under* expresses the complex function [Origin[Subessive]].

Third, the prepositions marking secondary but not primary functions are available as prefixes for L-derivations. Table 10.2 illustrates this overlap.

Table 10.2   Preposition-Particles and Derivational Prefixes in English

Forms	*Preposition-Particle*	*Prefix*	*Function*
a. by/along	He came by/along	by-pass, by-way	Prolative
b. before	I've seen that before	fore-play, fore-tell	Anterior
c. behind	I am so behind	hind-sight, after-burner	Posterior
d. above/over	He flew over	over-fly, over-stew	Superessive
e. below/under	He just went under	under-pay, under-eat	Subessive
f. across/over	He just came over	cross-walk, overpass	Translative
g. between	She is in between	between-class/-scenes	Intermediate
h. near/by	He came by	by-law, by-stander	Proximate
i. in	He came in	in-house, in-state, input	Inessive
j. on	His hat is on	on-line, on-shore	Adessive

Although this description of the distinction between primary and secondary grammatical functions is rather programmatic, the importance of the distinction does emerge. The point is that the secondary functions are for the most part complex spatial, hence adverbal, functions. No doubt because of their functional complexity, they tend to be marked with dual Ps, double Case endings, or a combination of P + Case. It is odd that only the secondary Ps double as affixes; however, this is consistent with their doubled marking at the inflectional level. Let us now examine the secondary functions a bit more closely.

10.4.2 Adpositions and the Spatial (Locative + Directional) Functions

The three primary spatial functions of (10.49) have been set off with a broken line because they are special. Although they are commonly marked by a simple ending of their own Case—Locative, Dative, and Ablative, respectively—as are the primary functions, they are closely linked to the secondary spatial functions because of their related semantics. They will be referred to simply as the PRIMARY SPATIAL FUNCTIONS and treated specially. The Locus, Goal, and Origin functions combine freely with all but about five of the secondary functions (40–44, Appendix A). The secondary spatial functions are in fact subcategories of these functions which combine with them to form complex functions as Table 10.3 illustrates.

Table 10.3   Four Sets of Combinatory Locative-Directional Case Functions[8]

[Goal[Posterior]]	It went **behind** the camera
[Locus[Posterior]]	It stood **behind** the camera
[Origin[Posterior]]	It came **from behind** camera
- - - - - - - - - - - - - - -	- - - - - - - - - - - - - - - -
[Goal[Anterior]]	It went **before** the camera
[Locus[Anterior]]	It stood **before** the camera
[Origin[Anterior]]	It came **from before** the camera
- - - - - - - - - - - - - - -	- - - - - - - - - - - - - - - -
[Goal[Subessive]]	It went **under** the camera
[Locus[Subessive]]	It stood **under** the camera
[Origin[Subessive]]	It came **from under** the camera
- - - - - - - - - - - - - - -	- - - - - - - - - - - - - - - -
[Goal[Superessive]]	It went **over** the camera
[Locus[Superessive]]	It stood **over** the camera
[Origin[Superessive]]	It came **from over** the camera

There are several more such triplets which need not be illustrated here since they behave identically. A few other adverbal categories do not form systematic triples like those in Table 10.3, for example, the Prolative, expressed by the English preposition *along*: *He walked **along** the river*, and the Perlative, as in *he came* **through** the forest. However, those functions which do combine to form complex functions are all subcategories of Goal, Origin, Locus and, in Dutch at least, Perlation, as in van Riemsdijk's example *Hij is net er-onder door gekomen* = he has just there-under through come "he has just passed under it". That is, to be *behind, before, under,* or *over* something, one also has to be *at* it semantically, whether this particular concept is expressed by a preposition or not.

The secondary spatial prepositions, therefore, refer to more specific loci vis-à-vis their complement, for instance, *the camera* in Table 10.3; the primary spatial functions, *at to, from, through,* are the most general spatial relations. To go under the camera implies that one goes to a position under the camera. In other words, the single preposition *under,* with verbs of motion, expresses a complex function, [Goal[Subessive]], where the secondary relation always falls under the scope of the primary one, semantically interpreted as $[_{Path}TO[_{Place}UNDER([\ \ ])]]$. The complexity of the antonym, [Origin[Subessive]], is expressed phonologically under markedness conditions as we saw in section 10.2.3: *from under the camera.* Any theory of adpositions must explain these morphosemantic relations and do so within the theory of markedness.

10.5 CONCLUSION

This chapter criticizes the description of adpositions as lexical items and sets the stage for an alternative interpretation of adpositions. Jackendoff's distributional tests for a governing lexical class, P, were shown to discover a superordinate semantic spatial category, not a lexical or syntactic category. The case for a governing lexical class, P, therefore, does not hold.

The range of possible meanings for P is determined by the same set of grammatical functions found cross-linguistically in Case systems. These comprise two distinct sets: primary and secondary functions. The primary-secondary distinction is important, for it underlies all of the attributes which led Jackendoff to conclude that Ps are lexical. Only secondary Ps with spatial meanings may appear "intransitively" or function as verb particles. Moreover, Jackendoff's approach has nothing to say about the same Ps operating as derivational prefixes; it predicts that derivations like *in-house, between-class, inland* are compounds. Such constructions cannot be compounds, however, since they do not belong to the class of their ostensible heads. Rather, they must be L-derivations without overt affixation in which Ps serve as prefixes. If Ps form a closed class and function as prefixes, they must be grammatical morphemes generated by the MS-component in an LMBM model rather than listed lexemes. The next chapter will define Ps as Case markers which vary from language to language as bound lexical or phrasal affixes or free grammatical morphemes.

NOTES

1. Recall from section 1.1 that in *De Lingua Latina* (47–45 BC), Marcus Varro categorized the parts of speech according to whether they reflected Case or Tense, in a way quite similar to the current generativist ± mechanism. Varro, however, reached a different conclusion as to the major parts of speech:

1. nouns and adjectives [+Case, −Tense]
2. verbs [−Case, +Tense]
3. participles [+Case, +Tense]
4. adverbs, conjunctions, etc. [−Case, −Tense]

While the system has its appeal, it drives Varro to mix primitive categories (N, V, A) with a purely derived one (Participles).

2. This chapter continues to use the term "adverb" in its usual sense despite the attempt in chapter 8 to obviate them from grammar in favor of one class, A. The residue of adverbs, aside from those marked by *-ly* in English, will be reduced to A in chapter 12.

3. The rebuttal of Jackendoff's argument structure is due Ellis (1987).

4. Jackendoff also does not explain the special status of *right* in testing Ps, why this particular Delimiter provides a more reliable test than others, for example, *just, only, sorta, really,* and so forth. It is not the case that *right* typifies the entire class.

5. This example and several others in this chapter are due Ellis (1987).

6. Dutch does have a complex P corresponding to *for* with (van Riemsdijk 1982: 58–60):

De cognac is [voor [bij de koffie]]
The cognac is for with the coffee
"The cognac is to go with the coffee"

Such constructions are relatively rare and are not freely constructed from primary Ps like *for* and *with* and their counterparts in other languages. English *without* no longer reflects the meanings of its constituents. A complete explanation of complex function behavior must await future investigations.

7. The Privative, expressed by *without* in English, may be explained as a complex secondary function based on a primary function, Sociative, marked by *with* in English: [Negative[Sociation]]. This might explain the appearance of *with* in *without*. Notice, however, that the scope relations are reversed; hence, the parallel cannot be taken for granted.

8. The grammatical [Goal[ ]] function maps onto two semantic functions, $[_{Path}TO([ ])]$ and $[_{Path}VIA([ ])]$ in English (Jackendoff 1990: 78–79).

The ball rolled under the table is thus ambiguous as to whether the ball stopped under the table of continued through to the other side. The Case paradigm of Caucasian languages like Archi, however, distinguish between Goal and Vialic, so that distinction must also be grammatical.

Chapter Eleven

Case, Case Marking, and Paradigms

11.1 ADPOSITIONS AND CASE

Since Chomsky (1981) first introduced Case Theory, more and more of GB theory has come to depend upon it. It is curious, then, that no attempt has been made to define abstract Case or morphological case. The result of this omission is that, with the exception of the Nominative, Case has the status of a stipulated diacritic whose only origin is the idiomatic contents of the lexical listings of Vs and Ps.

One property of abstract Case as it is applied in contemporary GB theory is its ability to be assigned independent of its functions, the (also undefined) theta roles. Traditional treatments of Case assume that Cases cannot occur without expressing function; the expression of function is the very purpose of Case. If we combine the insights of the previous chapters in this work with those of the greater part of Case research, a remarkably different picture of Case emerges: Case is present only to mark grammatical functions, where the means of marking may be affixational or adpositional. Chapters 9 and 10 established that Case functions are grammatical and not lexical. This chapter and the next will demonstrate that adpositions are grammatical markers in a class with Case desinences.

Attempts to integrate adpositions and Case systems persistently recur; Kuryłowicz (1949), Fillmore (1968), J. Anderson (1971, 1977), Cook (1989), and Starosta (1978), are a representative sampling of these attempts. Case Grammars, as recent versions are called, are all semantically based since their authors assume that the functions, or deep cases, are semantic. Inasmuch as these deep semantic cases are introduced in the base component of grammar, the grammars fall into the class of semantically based models which attempt to obviate grammar in favor of semantic structure. This notion will not distract us; chapter 9 provided assurances for a level of grammatical functions distinct from the level of semantic predicate structure. We may now reopen the issues of how Case functions are intro-

duced under the assumption that they represent grammatical and not semantic properties.

11.2 The Morphological Paradigm

An important aspect of inflectional morphology which has been ignored
by all grammatical theories until recently is the PARADIGM. It is common
to define the paradigm as simply the complete set of the phonological
forms of an inflectible lexical item, associated with their functions. Anderson (1992: 134), for example, says that "an item's paradigm is the complete set of surface word forms that can be projected from the members
of its stem set by means of the inflectional Word Formation Rules of the
language." Jensen (1990: 116) claims that "[a] paradigm is a set of all the
inflectionally related forms of a single lexeme." Carstairs (1987: 48–49),
expands on these definitions, introducing the concept of a PATTERN: "a
paradigm for a part of speech N in a language L is a pattern P of inflexional
realizations for all combinations of non-lexically-determined morphosyntactic properties associated with N such that some member of N exemplifies P (that is, displays all and only the realizations of P)." Taking Carstairs' insights as a point of departure, I would like to argue here that
paradigms are more than a set of surface forms for a lexical item and that
the concept of pattern introduced in Carstairs' definition of paradigms is
crucial to understanding them. To understand paradigms we must therefore
understand the nature of their pattern.

11.2.1 The Paradigmatic Pattern

The first point to be made about the inflectional patterns of synthetic languages is that they cannot be explained exclusively in linguistic terms;
paradigms depend crucially upon deductive logic to work. The second
point is that Case is a purely morphological—not syntactic—set of categories which are necessitated by the fusion of fusional synthetic languages.
It is thus a product of the MS-component and is of no consequence to
syntax. Each of these points will be argued independently in sections
11.2.1 and 11.2.2.

The paradigm is first and foremost a means of mapping one linguistic
level, that of grammatical functions, to another, the phonological (P-)
level. Recall levels 2–4 of Table 9.2, reproduced in Figure 11.1. The paradigm maps a multiplicity of morphological markers such as those in Figure
11.1.2 onto a multiplicity of grammatical functions such as those of Figure
11.1.4. The questions raised by this picture of mapping, then, concern
what makes up level 3 in Figure 11.1 and why such a level is necessary.

In order to get at an answer, let us examine one Case, the Genitive, in
a highly fusional inflectional language, Russian. The Russian Genitive

Figure 11.1

The Grammatical Levels of a Case Paradigm

GRAMMAR
{
2. *allomorphy (Russian)*: /-∅/, /-o/, /-a/, . . .
3. *grammatical properties*: Nominative, Instrumental, Locative, . . .
4. *grammatical functions*: Subject, Means, Manner, Locus, . . .
}

marks a wide variety of grammatical functions between verbs and nouns, nouns and nouns, quantifiers and nouns, and adjectives and nouns, as (11.1) illustrates:

(11.1) a. vystuplenie **Ivan-a** "Ivan's appearance" (nominal Subject)
   b. poraženie **Ivan-a** "Ivan's defeat" (nominal Object)
   c. dom **Ivan-a** "Ivan's house" (Possessive)
   d. čelovek **izvestn-ogo talant-a** "man of known talent" (Possession)
   e. dva **vedr-a** "two buckets" (quantifier Object)
   f. On vypil **molok-a** "he drank some milk" (Partitive)
   g. prišel **perv-ogo maj-a** "arrived the first of May (Punctuality)
   h. polon **molok-a** "full of milk" (Adjective complement)

The functions of the Genitive in (11.1) are not isomorphic with their forms and thus cannot be identified in isolation. In order to identify a Genitive function, speakers must appreciate the conditions under which the genitivized noun occurs. To know, for example, that *Ivana* serves as simple Subject to the verb underlying *vystuplenie* in (11.1a), the speaker must know that the head noun is a deverbal nominal rather than some other type of noun. In order to interpret (11.1c) as a Possessive relation, the speaker must know that the head noun is an object which may be possessed and not a deverbal nominal, and so on. In short, to interpret the referential extension of a phrase with a Genitive qualifier, the speaker must have independent knowledge of a complex set of syntactic, lexical, and morphological conditions in which Genitive phrases may appear and deduce the Genitive. Figure 11.2 illustrates most of the conditions required of such a deductive process.

Because the functions of the Genitive are conditioned by the syntactic context of the NP, the relation of Case functions to Case illustrated in Figure 11.2 must be expressed as an algorithm. For each function labeling an NP-node there must be a deductive mapping from syntax to Case, similar to the algorithms mapping from the lexicon to syntax already discussed:

Figure 11.2

The Genitive in Russian

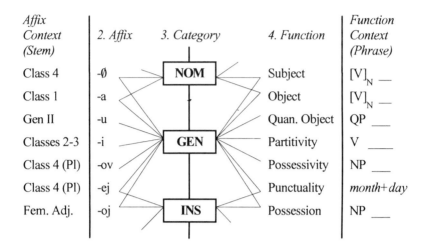

Affix *Context* *(Stem)*	*2. Affix*	*3. Category*	*4. Function*	*Function* *Context* *(Phrase)*
Class 4	-∅	NOM	Subject	$[V]_N$ —
Class 1	-a		Object	$[V]_N$ —
Gen II	-u		Quan. Object	QP ___
Classes 2-3	-i	GEN	Partitivity	V ___
Class 4 (Pl)	-ov		Possessivity	NP ___
Class 4 (Pl)	-ej		Punctuality	*month*+*day*
Fem. Adj.	-oj	INS	Possession	NP ___

(11.2)   a. IFF Subject and within domain NP THEN Genitive;
        b. IFF Subject and within the domain [-INFL] THEN Dative;
        c. IFF Subject and within domain [+ INFL] THEN Nominative.

(11.2) represents the knowledge required to determine which Case the Subject function will be mapped onto within a morphological paradigm. It exemplifies the sort of operations which must take place between the levels of grammatical function (Figure 11.2.4 = Figure 11.1.4) and phonological realization (Figure 11.2.2 = Figure 11.1.2): functions are mapped onto phonology via a set of mediating properties. The Subject of a phrase in Russian, for example, is marked by Genitive if it occurs within the domain of NP, Dative, if the verb is an infinitive, and Nominative if the verb is finite (see Greenberg and Franks 1991 for the treatment of Dative Subjects in Russian):

(11.3)   a. rabota Ivan-a ''the work of Ivan-GEN''
        b. Ivan-u rabotat' ''it is for Ivan-DAT to work''
        c. Ivan-∅ rabotaet ''Ivan-Nom works/is working''

Mapping to a Case, however, does not predict the exact desinence assigned to each Case; it only gets the speaker from function to an intermediate point, Case. Since the number of affixes marking a given Case varies with the number of Noun Classes in fusional languages, a second algorithm is required to map the Case, Genitive in this instance, to its surface phono-logical form. Russian has four Genitive suffixes, not counting omission ([y] ~ [i] is phonologically determined):

Table 11.1   Genitive Desinences in Russian

Base	Class	Gloss	GenSg	GenPl
stol	[Class 1]	"table"	stol-a	stol-ov
okn-o	[Class 1]	"window"	okn-a	okon-∅
cen-a	[Class 2]	"price"	cen-y	cen-∅
dver'	[Class 3]	"door"	dver-i	dver-ej

The desinential multiplicity illustrated in Table 11.1 requires a second complex algorithm to predict the exact suffix for any given Case, once Case has been determined by (11.2). Table 11.1 also shows that this algo-rithm comprises an independent set of conditions: Noun Class, Number, Gender, and stem phonology:

(11.4)   a. if Genitive and Noun Class 1, suffix /a/;
        b. if Genitive and Noun Class 2 or 3, suffix /i/;
        c. if Genitive and Noun Class 4 (Plural),
            (i) and the stem ends on /j/ or nonsharp consonant, suffix /ov/,
            (ii) and the stem ends on a sharp consonant, suffix /ej/;
            (iii) otherwise, null.

In other words, the same sort of deductive processing operates between the levels of allomorphy and grammatical categories (levels 2 and 3 in Figures 11.1 and 11.2) as between the categorial and functional levels (levels 3 and 4 Figures 11.1 and 11.2). To return then to Carstairs' term, the pattern of a fusional paradigm is produced by a double set of logical conditions for mapping many functions onto many affixes, where the conditions on the functions are independent of and incompatible with those on the affixation. If the level of grammatical functions is syntax, and allomorphy is essen-tially phonological, the function of morphology, that is, its categories and their properties, is to interpret the output of syntax for phonology.

The question then is: Why such a complex mapping system? The mor-phological conditions on the Case markers, that is, the various declension classes that choose different markers for the same Case, could map a set of Case markers, m_1, m_2, . . . m_n, directly onto a given function, f, as (11.5) illustrates.

(11.5)

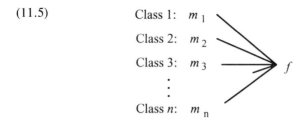

However, if each Case function were assigned four markers, one for each Noun Class (ignoring phonological conditions such as those of Class 4), the Genitive functions in Russian alone would require 7 x 4 = 28 markers. This explosion in the number of declensional markers, by Carstairs-McCarthy's Paradigm Economy Principle, would license an equal number of potential declensions.

Carstairs (1987) has described a principle of Case paradigms which limits the number of declensions to the number of endings in the paradigm slot with the largest number of endings. THE PARADIGM ECONOMY PRINCI-PLE maintains parity between the maximum number of declensions and the maximum number of endings marking any Case of a declension. An increase in the number of endings marking the category of the nominal paradigm with the largest number of endings, by this principle, concurrently licenses an identical increase in the number of possible declensional paradigms. Thus, 28 markers for any given Case licenses 28 full declensional paradigms. With six Cases in the Russian declensional paradigms, 28 markers for one Case would license a maximum of 28 paradigms with 6 x 28 or 168 endings, assuming the extreme case where all paradigm slots contain the maximum number of endings. A central function of paradigms, therefore, is to keep the number of Case markers in check, for Case markers increase exponentially and their number licenses an equal number of paradigms.

In order to maintain a manageable number of efficiently accessible markers, a system must group functions together with their conditions, and endings together with theirs, in such a way that an organism capable of deductive logic can map either efficiently onto the other. The declensional paradigm accomplishes this by arbitrarily associating sets of functions with sets of markers, as (11.5) illustrates. A Case K, then, is an arbitrary grammatical property which associates a set of conditional grammatical functions with an equally arbitrary set of conditional markers (MS-operations), as illustrated in (11.6).

K, then, forms a set with such other Cases as Dative, Accusative, Instrumental, Locative, Ablative, called a DECLENSION or CASE PARADIGM.

(11.6)

$$
\left.\begin{array}{c}
C_1 : f_1 \\
C_2 : f_2 \\
C_3 : f_3 \\
\vdots \\
C_n : f_n
\end{array}\right\} K \left\{\begin{array}{l}
m_1 : \text{Class 1} \\
m_2 : \text{Class 2} \\
m_3 : \text{Class 3} \\
\vdots \\
m_n : \text{Class N}
\end{array}\right.
$$

11.2.2 Paradigms in Nonfusional Languages

According to (11.6) Case K connects two sets of deductive conditions across modules, a set of nominal functions and a set of MS-operations. It follows that grammatical functions but not necessarily Case must be assigned in syntax. The Accusative is associated with the NP_{Obj} position, not with specific verbs, for it is the default Case for Object NP, automatically assigned unless the verb is subcategorized for an oblique Case.[1] Chomsky's new Minimalist Program, which distinguishes Subject and Object functional categories, is therefore a move in the right direction (Chomsky 1992). Case is simply a means of converting these syntactic functions into phonological terms occasioned by the vast modular differences between syntax, the lexicon, and phonology.

Not only is it impossible to justify Case in syntax, Case is a necessary concept only in fusional languages, which accumulate several functions under one Case and mark each Case with several endings as does the Russian Genitive. Given function F, in condition C only Case K markers may be assigned. If either the functions or the Case marking lack independent conditions, Case becomes redundant. To see this, let us examine an example of "Case" in a nonfusional, agglutinative language, Bashkir. Bashkir's Case endings are not conditioned to attach only to stems of a given Noun Class. The Bashkir Genitive marker -$QY\eta$ is suffixed to all stems to mark the Genitive and varies only with the postcyclic phonological laws of vowel harmony, consonant truncation, and assimilation. No reference to Case at all is required to account for this situation (see Figure 11.2).[2]

There is no way to prove that the suffix -$QY\eta$ marks the Genitive, which in turn denotes the Genitive functions. -$QY\eta$ may be simply defined as a multifunctional morpheme which directly expresses these functions, that is, replaces GEN in the box of Figure 11.2. Bashkir has only one set of conditions which determine the distribution of functions. Because the selection of endings is unconditional, endings may be explained as directly denoting the functions. While there is no way to reduce either of the two

Figure 11.3

The Nominative in Bashkir

Affix *Context* *(Phrase)*	*2. Affixes*	*3. Category*	*4. Functions*	*Function* *Context* *(Stem)*
-QYŋ		**GEN**	Partitivity	NP + NP
			Material	NP + NP
			Possession	Indefinite
None	-∅	**NOM**	Subject	NP
			Object	NP
			Goal	IntrVOM
-NY		**ACC**	Punctuality	AdvP

deductive systems of Figure 11.2, there is no way to justify the use of more than one in Figure 11.3.

The same argument applies to languages like English which mark the direct functions (Subject and Object) with word position and the adverbal functions directly with adpositions. While English adverbal functions collect and overlap just the way they do in Figures 11.2 and 11.3, referring to *of,* for instance, as the Genitive marker would be unjustifiably redundant. An adequate description of English *of* need refer only to the fact that *of* marks the nominal function Material (among others) under conditions C_{Mat}, while other markers *(from, out-of)* mark this same function under other sets of conditions, as in *made from wood, made out-of wood.*[3] No reference to an intervening category is required for a complete, explicit definition of the form-function relations here.

If we are looking for linguistic universals, we wish to account first and foremost for grammatical functions and the syntactic conditions which determine any variation in their marking. Case is not a universal principle but a parameter of synthetic languages and a purely morphological one at that. Case is not a property of nonfusional languages at all; it is a paradigm-2atic set required to map sets of functions onto nonisomorphic sets of function markers. Where functions are mapped onto a set of Cases, each of which is in turn expressed by a unique affix or adposition, Case becomes irrelevant even to morphology. Since I-derivation is a property of syntax, the evidence of this section implies that a theory of I-derivation must ignore Case and account only for inflectional functions. We are therefore searching henceforth for the relation between grammatical functions and function markers; Case becomes a minor, language-dependent issue.

11.3 AFFIXES AND ADPOSITIONS

There are two ways to achieve an integrated universal theory of grammatical function marking: either we must demonstrate that Case endings are in a class with adpositions, the lexical class P, or we must demonstrate that adpositions are grammatical morphemes in a class with Case endings. This section will examine the claim that Case endings are governors in the sense Ps are in current P&P theory. Given the case against Ps as a governing lexical class mounted in the previous chapter, the outcome of this exercise is all but a foregone conclusion. However, we will work through the arguments in order to close all doors on the possibility that adpositions assign grammatical function. The exercise is also worth working through for the additional light it will bring to our understanding of the ways in which Case functions are marked. In order to maximize the relevance of the discussion to our ultimate goal of describing the relation of Case functions to their markers, let us examine a relatively isolating language, English, a highly agglutinative synthetic language, Lezghian, and a fusional synthetic language, Russian.

In Lezghian, a Caucasian language spoken in southern Russia, Case functions are mapped onto 17 Case endings and combinations thereof. Notice in the list of Lezghian Cases in (11.7), taken from Talibov (1966), that many functions are marked by complex desinences comprising 2–3 endings which correspond to English PPs often comprising 2 and 3 prepositions.

(11.7) **Lezghian Noun Declension II**

    1. Nominative   *sev* "bear"
    2. Ergative   *sev-re* "bear"
    3. Genitive   *sev-re-n* "of the bear"
    4. Dative   *sev-re-z* "to the bear's"

    5. Locative I   *sev-re-v* "at/to the bear('s)"
    6. Goal I   *sev-re-v-di* "toward the bear"
    7. Ablative I   *sev-re-v-aj* "away from the bear"

    8. Locative II   *sev-re-x^h* "behind the bear"   II = Posteriority
    9. Goal II   *sev-re-x^h-di* "to the bear"
    10. Ablative II   *sev-re-x^h-aj* "(out) from behind the bear"

11. Locative III   *sev-re-k* "under the bear"   III = Subessive
12. Goal III   *sev-re-k-di* "(to) under the bear"
13. Ablative III   *sev-re-k-aj* "(out) from under the bear"

14. Locative IV   *sev-re* "in the bear"   IV = Inessive
15. Ablative IV   *sev-re-j-aj* "out of the bear"

16. Locative V   *sev-re-l-aj* "on(to) the bear"   V = Adessive
17. Goal V   *sev-re-l-di* "to the bear"
18. Ablative V   *sev-re-l-aj* "off of the bear"

The remaining primary and secondary functions in Appendix A are distributed across these same forms, some marked with, others, without an ancillary adposition. It is true that this paradigm seems defective among the Goal functions; however, this does not detract from the unmarked pattern by which the same functions expressed by endings alone in Lezghian are marked by adpositions alone or endings plus adpositions in other languages.

The P&P representation of the Lezghian word expressing "(out) from under the bear" is roughly (11.8). Its structural and functional representation is equivalent to its correlates in English and Russian, as (11.9) and (11.10), respectively, show. The single Ablative Subessive (Sbs) denominal adjectival in Lezghian shares an identical function with P + N complement combinations in English and Russian.

The first problem with this approach is that forms like *sevrekaj* are single words, functionally adjectival but with nominal bases. Inflectional categories such as those of Case declension are the hallmarks of lexical classes, our very means of determining the lexical class of a stem. The classical definition of "noun" is *those lexical items subject to Case inflec-*

(11.8)

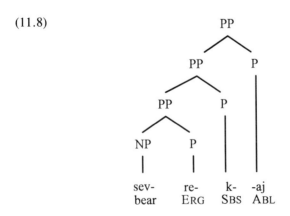

(11.9)

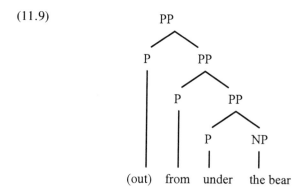

(11.10)

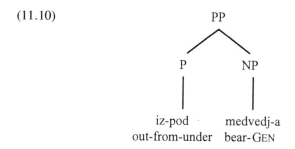

tion. It follows that inflectional morphology cannot change the lexical class of a stem. This, in fact, is the strength of the Lexical P Hypothesis: it assumes that the lexical class P is the head of PPs, hence may account for the change of class in its complement NP.

Extending the lexical class P to include inflectional endings, however, is a violation of Lexicalism, because Case desinences then become the only unquestionably inflectional endings capable of changing lexical class. Even this characterization is not consistent for now the inflectional endings in (11.8) become members of the governing class P, while those of (11.10) are markers of the government induced by the governor *is-pod.* Adding to these inconsistencies is the fact that the first four Lezghian Cases in Table 11.2, Nominative, Ergative, Genitive, and Dative, do not change the category of the stem, while all others do.

Classifying Case endings as P also leads to violations of the Case Filter and Theta Criterion since forms like *sevrekaj* in (11.8) are in fact assigned three Cases, Ergative, Subessive, and Ablative, by their three endings. The traditional term for this form is "Ablative III", which takes its place alongside "Ablative I", "Ablative II", and so on. But these are only met-aphorically single, discrete Cases; in reality, all are complex Cases, reflecting recombinant functions remarkably similar to the recombinant Ps of (11.9) and (11.10).

The parallel recombinancy of these grammatical functions, in fact, raises the question of whether the differences between the English, Russian, and Lezghian constructions represent structural disparities of any significance. In current P&P models, P must govern and stand as head of the PP in order to explain the change of lexical class from N to A. But which is prior, preposition, Case, or neither, is an empirical issue. Now, given the possibility of Case without P but not P without Case, the conclusion that P assigns Case would certainly be post hoc at best. If Case and adpositions are at all interdependent, this possibility suggests initially that Case is basic and adpositions are secondary. However, if Case is a purely morphological phenomenon restricted to fusional languages while the functions that Case marks are universal, Case must presuppose functions. The best working hypothesis, therefore, based on the all the foregoing evidence, is that Ps are a phrasal type of Case marker, while desinences are a bound version of the same thing, and that both are driven by grammatical (Case) functions. That is, Case is determined by Case functions where it can be justified at all.

11.4 ADPOSITIONS AS GRAMMATICAL MORPHEMES

In order to make the case for adpositions as Case markers, LMBM must mount a unified theory of spelling which accounts for adpositions and affixes as morphological variants of the same type of operation. Chapter 10 established that adpositions are grammatical morphemes and not lexemes. Section 11.4 examines the morphological evidence that adpositions are functional markers in a class with inflectional endings and not function assigners. It shows that adpositions behave like inflectional morphemes in that they may be omitted, and may exhibit flexible ordering, just as do inflectional morphemes but not lexemes. This will clear the way for the unified theory of Case marking in chapter twelve.

11.4.1 Optional Adpositions

The hypothesis that all Ps, regardless of accent, are phrasal Case markers is initially borne out by PPs in which adpositions are optional but Case is not, reviewed in the previous chapter (10.33–10.37). We saw in that chapter that in such instances the function remains identical when a P but not the Case it ostensibly governs is omitted. This implies that if we must choose between the adposition or Case as the direct marker of function, the inevitable choice is Case. In instances such as Latin *(ad) Alesi-am profiscitur*, which means ''set out to Alesia'' with or without the preposition (10.33), the adposition seems to be a secondary Case marker which reinforces Case marking or specifies a Case function. In other words, given the multifunctionality of most Cases, adpositions would seem to be secondary accretions added to discriminate individual functions of a multifunctional Case.

11.4.2 Stable Adpositions, Variable Cases

The Slavic languages offer another piece of evidence that adpositions are function markers rather than Case governors. The secondary spatial Cases, those marked by complex, systematic affixation in Lezghian (11.7), distinguish Goal and Locus variants in an interesting way in Serbo-Croatian. The secondary spatial functions Subessive, Superessive, Anterior, and Posterior are marked by *pod, nad, pred,* and *za,* respectively. The Locus variants, however, are associated with the Instrumental, while the Goal variants are marked by the same prepositions plus the Accusative, a traditional Goal Case in IE languages.

(11.11) a. ležati **pod** kamen-**om**   a'. ići **pod** kamen-**∅**
           "lie **under** the rock-INS"   "go **under** the rock-ACC"
      b. ležati **nad** kamen-**om**   b'. ići **nad** kamen-**∅**
           "lie **over** the rock-INS"   "go **over** the rock-ACC"
      c. ležati **za** kamen-**om**   c'. ići **za** kamen-**∅**
           "lie **behind** the rock-INS"   "go **behind** the rock-ACC"
      d. ležati **pred** kamen-**om**   d'. ići **pred** kamen-**∅**
           "lie **in front of** the rock-INS"   "go **in front of** the rock-ACC"

The interesting aspect of this paradigm is that the Case but not the preposition changes with the function. It is difficult to claim that the preposition governs Case in these instances since the P does not change with the Locus-Goal functions. Either Cases determine preposition selection or some third factor controls both the Case ending and preposition. In the current framework, based on the Case functions of Appendix A, the P + Instrumental of (11.11) expresses [Locus[X-essive]], while the P + Accusative of (11.11') expresses [Goal[X-essive]]. The cleanest account of these P + Case relations, then, is that the primary spatial functions, Locus and Goal, select the Locative and Accusative Case, respectively, while the secondary functions, Subessive, Superessive, Posterior, and Anterior, select the preposition. In other words, function determines Case endings and prepositions alike but independently.

Notice that the marking in (11.11) structurally parallels that of the spatial adjectival Cases in Lezghian illustrated in (11.7) above. Consider the spatial II and III Cases in that listing for a moment:

(11.12) a. Locative II   sevre-x^h "behind the bear"
       b. Ablative II   sevre-x^h-aj "(out) from behind the bear"

c. Goal II   sevre-x^h-di "to the bear"
d. Locative III   sevre-k "under the bear"
e. Ablative III   sevre-k-aj "(out) from under the bear"
f. Goal III   sevre-k-di "(to) under the bear"

Ignoring the Ergative stem (*-re*), which is used vacuously throughout the spatial Case system, the final suffix, *-di*, *-aj*, or *-∅*, changes with the primary function, Locus, Origin, Goal, just as does Case in (11.11). The initial marker, *-x^h* or *-k*, however, changes with the secondary function, Subessive, Posterior, and so on, like the prepositions in (11.11). In neither case does one set of markers govern the other.

11.4.3 Scope Reversal among Adpositions

In organizing adpositional semantics so that syntactic structures such as that of (11.9) reflect semantic scope, inexplicable morphosemantic mismatches arise. Since *from* and *to*, and *on* and *under* express antonymous functions, each of these pairs will have to be assigned to the same superordinate category; the former with primary, the latter, with secondary functions. Their markers generally reflect their semantic counterparts isomorphically when they are combined. Thus, the relation of the motion FROM or TO in reference to a position UNDER or ON usually stands in isomorphic relation to the physical markers, the Ps, as (11.13) illustrates.

(11.13)   a. [from [under the desk]]   structurally
           b. [FROM [UNDER THE DESK]   semantically

The syntactic and semantic structural relations of (11.14) and (11.15) present quite a different picture, however.

(11.14)   a. [in [to the desk]]   structurally
           b. [TO [IN THE DESK]]   semantically

(11.15)   a. [on [to the desk]]   structurally
           b. [TO [ON THE DESK]]   semantically

Jackendoff (1990: 53), for instance, expresses the R-representation of *into*, the antonym of *from under*, as [$_{Path}$TO($_{Place}$IN([ ]))], with TO dominating IN to express the scope it exercises over IN. The R-representation of *onto* is formulated similarly. If these prepositions are true lexical items, then by Principle I their argument structure would have to directly and isomorphically parallel their phonological form. Yet (11.14) and (11.15) demonstrate that the forms of these expressions are reversed in comparison to the scope relations of their meanings.

The problem could be reduced to idiosyncrasy by claiming that, since *into* and *onto* are written together, they are in fact lexical compounds which lexically block **to in* and **to on*. This tack will not work, however, since we do not find such scope violations even among the most idiosyncratic analytic compounds of the uncontroversial lexical classes. Not even the most idiomatic analytic compounds, for example, *pinhead,* can have a reverse-scope meaning, "head pin." This includes the classical morphosemantic mismatches such as *moral philosopher, criminal lawyer.* Moreover, the productive forms predicted by LMH here, **to-in* and **to-on*, are clearly unacceptable. Even if *pinhead* is not perfectly symmetric with its idiomatic extension, its productive meaning "the head of a pin" is not blocked.[4]

The only workable account of reversed Ps departs on the assumption that *into* and *onto* are the idiomatic output of an MS-operation which inserts them under the condition [Goal[Inessive]] and [Goal[Adessive]], respectively. Their idiomaticity is explained by the arbitrariness of morphological spelling. The analogy then is not to be found among lexical compounds like *pickpocket* but among agglutinative suffixes whose order often reverses the scope of the correlate semantic categories, as in the Turkish examples mentioned in chapter 3:

(11.16)   a. gelir-ler-se "if they come"
          b. gelir-se-ler "if they come"

The English Ps *into* and *onto* have simply crystallized in reverse order due to the phonological infelicity of the combinations **to-in* and **to-on*. The morphological account is strengthened by the fact that part of these Ps are omissible so that *in* and *on* are synonymous with *into* and *onto*. Scope reversals, then, are rare in the lexicon but at home in morphology.

11.4.4 The Distribution of Adpositions and Case Endings

If Ps are morphological spellings on phrases in a class with desinences, the two should share limits on (i) the number of them allowed in a PP, (ii) the kind and number of specifiers they permit, and (iii) other morphological attributes not dependent on their specific phrasal and lexical status, that is, the possibility of zero and empty variants. This section argues that Case functions cannot be concatenated as can lexical classes and that the number of functions per PP is limited to two, one of which must be a primary one. Thus, triple Case-marked nouns must contain a compound marker with a single function, an empty morpheme, or a locational Delimiter homophonous with a function marker. The second point of this subsection is that neither adpositions nor Case endings may be modified by more than one Delimiter, as in *far/just/right under the house.*

Limitations on the Distribution of Case Endings

Let us assume that something like the Theta Criterion holds for the nominal grammatical functions. Given the discernability of at least two functions in the secondary relations illustrated in (11.8–11.10), a single primary and a single secondary function, the Theta Criterion will have to be modified, say, in the following way, call it now the GRAMMATICAL FUNCTION CRITERION:

(11.17)   a. *All NPs must bear one primary nominal grammatical function.*
          b. *NPs with a primary function may bear one additional secondary function.*

This formulation obviates the undergeneration caused by Chomsky's Case Filter and Theta Criterion by allowing a maximum of two functions to be assigned Case-marked NPs and PPs under restricted conditions. Notice also the simplification offered at this point by LMBM: while an equivalent of the Theta Criterion is maintained, Case Theory is eliminated altogether. Nonetheless, the overall theory works better both morphologically and syntactically.

The autonomous MS-component of chapter 3 can account for the possible range of function markers. It predicts possible disjunctions between the number of functions and the number of markers. If only one function is present, it may condition one or more markers. However, while additional markers may be present, conditions other than the primary function must account for them. Specifically, such markers must constitute extended exponence (see section 6.3.1) with another affix, that is, serve purely morphological or phonological purposes. In (11.7), for example, the Genitive and Dative forms of *sev* "bear", *sev-re-n* and *sev-re-z* exhibit two recognizable markers. However, *-re* is found on all oblique Cases, where it serves merely as a stem classifier in the sense of Aronoff (1993), associated with the Ergative functions only if no other ending follows it. (11.17) therefore does not prevent two or more recognizable affixes or Ps from realizing a single function; the number of affixes is limited by the MS-module.

If PPs may bear a maximum of two functions and these functions may be realized by compound markers, we might expect to find some PPs with four ostensible Ps, and Case-marked nouns with four ostensible desinences. Primary functions, however, are in some sense more "basic" than secondary ones. For this reason they tend to be marked by the simplest means available, such as phrase position or unaccented ending alone. In languages where neither of these options are available, the simplest clitics or asyllabic adpositions will mark them. No evidence of single functions realized by three desinences or Ps emerged in the research upon which this book is based.

Secondary functions may be expressed by two markers if they constitute extended exponence. Extended exponence may comprise a set of endings such as those in the Lezghian data of (11.7), for example, *sev-re-k-aj,* which bears three Case endings but only two functions, [Origin[Subessive]]. If Ps are Case markers in a class with nominal desinences, a complex marker might be a preposition plus ending. The [Origin [Inessive]] (= Ablative) function in Russian is marked by the Genitive Case ending plus the preposition *iz: ja vyšel* **iz** komnat-y "I came **out-of** the-room". It is traditional to simply specify the preposition as *iz* + Gen, since the P and Case do not distinguish discrete functions but combine to mark one set. However, within the current working hypothesis, P + Case amounts to complex Case marking equivalent to the P + P construction of English *out of.* Case markers therefore may comprise as many as three distinguishable morphemes in the marking of secondary functions and (11.20) prevents more than two functions being assigned to any NP, so that however complex the marker, it may be conditioned by no more than two functions.[5]

Further examples of complex markers of single functions are not difficult to find. The Mongolian languages often combine two Case endings to realize a single function. The Mongolian Ablative ending may be combined with the Locative ending to the same effect as Ablative alone. In fact, the contemporary *-Ača* is a combination of an earlier Ablative marker *-ča* with the Locative marker *-A.* However, one also finds in the classical language combinations of the regular Ablative with the Locative *-DA* (Poppe 1954: 78):

(11.18)   a. ger-eče "from the house"   a′. ger-te-če "from the house"
           b. morin-ača "from the   b′. morin-da-ča "from the horse"
              horse"

The Locative markers in (11.18) seem to be used emptily in marking the Origin function. Locus does not appear involved in any way with the Ablative NPs, since semantically distinct forms with the Ablative but without the Locative do occur.

More problematic for all theories are the combinations of Genitive *-yIn* + Locative *-dUr* seen in (11.19) and Comitative (*-tEi*) + all other Cases as illustrated in (11.20). In both instances the double marking reflects double primary functions.

(11.19)   a. baʁši-yin-dur "to the teacher's, at the teacher's"
           b. eke-yin-dür "to mother's, at mother's"
           c. noyan-ai-dur "to the prince's, at the prince's"

(11.20)   a. Genitive: eke-tei-yin "[mother and someone else]'s"
           b. Dative/Locative: eke-tei-dür "to/at [mother and someone
              else]'s"
           c. Accusative: eke-tei-yi "[mother and someone else]"
           d. Ablative: eke-tei-eče "from [mother and someone else]('s)"
           e. Instrumental: eke-tei-ber "by [mother and someone else]"

Mongolian languages allow the combination of what seem to be two primary functions. The spatial functions Locus, Goal, and Origin generally
combine only with secondary spatial functions. In Mongolian, however,
Locus combines with another primary function, Possession.[6]

The Sociative is a borderline primary-secondary function in IE languages. Although it originally did not require an adverb augment in Vedic,
in Classical Sanskrit the inclusion of *saha* became common, suggesting a
shift to secondary status. If Sociative is a secondary function, (11.20) presents less of a problem, although it still combines with all other primary
Case functions rather than just with the spatial ones. However, the fact that
Mongolian languages generally mark Sociative with a single Case ending
and no adposition militates strongly against this speculation. Mongolian
languages, therefore, may require a special theory of function combination; however, they do not violate the limitation of two inflectional functions expressed in (11.17).

In general, then, (11.17) holds cross-linguistically: an NP may possess
either one primary or a primary plus a secondary function for a total of
two functions. The primary function may be marked by one or two morphemes but tends to be expressed by only one; a secondary function may
be expressed by two markers. However, the number of recognizable morphemes marking functions is a matter of morphological spelling as defined
in chapter three. No limit on the number of Case function markers is set
by the theory of grammatical functions. Finally, (11.17) seems to hold for
both affixal and adpositional function markers.

Limitations on the Distribution of Adpositions

Structural relations in much of the current GB research are derived from
semantic relations under the assumption of a syntax-semantics homomorphism (Napoli 1989 makes the same point). That is, semantic relations
are widely assumed to be isomorphic with syntactic structures except for
disjunctures between Negation, Quantifier, and adverbial structures, and
their corresponding semantic scope for which Logical Form accounts. The

syntactic relation of *out, from,* and *under* in *out from under the rock* is presumed to be that of (11.21):

(11.21)   [out[from[under[the rock]]]]

Here the syntactic bracketing reflects the semantic scope of each of the prepositional concepts. *From under the rock* denotes where the mouse ran out in the sentence *the mouse ran out from under the rock. Under the rock* is where the mouse ran out from. To the extent that PP may serve as a PP complement, the number of such embeddings should be infinite, given recent X-bar theory. If (11.21) is correct, the answer to the question "out from where did the mouse run" should be "under the rock". This seems to be the case. However, if *out,* too, is a P, "from under the rock" should be the answer to the question "*out where did the mouse run from under". *Out where,* however, does not reflect Origin as it should under the assumption that *out* is a transitive P, whose complement is *from under the rock.*

A disparity therefore arises between the scope relations in *out from under* and the structural representation [*out*[*from*[*under*]]] similar to that of *into* and *onto.* While FROM does have scope over UNDER in phrases like *from under the rock,* the position of OUT is not so clear. Historically, *out* is an adverb. As a preposition, however, it has a peculiarly specific meaning; one may say *he came out the door* but not **he came out the house.* It is by no means the antonym of *in* despite the anonymy of their adverbial variants, *in(side)* and *out(side).* The preposition *out* means "outwardly through". This is not the meaning it reflects in *out from under N* or *out from N.* There are three possible explanations of its appearance in *out from under.*

Out-from might be a compound P like *into, onto* but simply not written so, a common failing of the English spelling system. This hypothesis is undermined by its independent accent (*oút from únder*) and the referential difference between (11.22a) and (11.22b):

(11.22)   a. she came out from under the house
          b. she came from under the house

(11.22b) is indifferent between an interpretation *she came out from under the house* and *she came in/up/*and so on *from under the house. Out* here would seem to be an independent modifier.

The second possible explanation of *out* is that it is simply a specifier of *from.* This hypothesis is supported by the accentuation and also the fact that *out* may be attached initially to any spatial PP: *out to the car, out from the living room, out on the roof, out over the street, out through the window (we saw his face). Out, up,* and *down,* by this interpretation, are homophonous spellings of two kinds of morphological categories, P and De-limiter, not an uncommon phenomenon in morphology, as we already have seen on many occasions.[7]

A second plausible hypothesis is that *out* is an adverb which may gov-ern a wide variety of NP or PP complements. An Origin-Subessive comple-ment takes the compound P *from-under,* explaining [*out* [*from-under* [*the house*]]]$_{AdvP}$. This hypothesis is supported by the fact that *out* in (11.22a) has its adverbial meaning rather than its prepositional meaning, that is, it does not imply THROUGH([ ]). The third hypothesis is also supported by the fact that this phrase fits uncomfortably as an NP adjunct where PPs are otherwise comfortable:

(11.23)   a.   the man from under the house
           a'.   *the man out from under the house
           b.   the man in the door
           b'.   *the man out the door

The antonym of *in(to)* in English is not *out from* but *out-of.* This suggests that the adverb *out* governs the prepositions *of* and *from,* as well as the simple Accusative Case, under different semantic interpretations. Notice that not only must the Origin-Subessive marker be specified in the ques-tion, *out from-under where did the mouse run,* it must be repeated in the answer: *from-under the rock; under the rock* will not do.

We are now in a position to provide three accounts for PPs which seem to contain three Ps. This allows us to constrain PPs with multiple Ps to adjectival relations comprising two grammatical functions. Triple Ps con-tain a compound P marking a single function, two Ps plus a Delimiter homophonous with some other P, or a homophonous adverb which sub-categorizes a spatial relation and hence can have a PP complement. Some-times it is not perfectly clear which of these three options is involved; however, one always provides a better account of the relation of the Ps in a PP with three or more Ps than the simple leftward or rightward scope bracketing of the P&P story.

The conclusion, then, is that however many markers are present in a PP, they can mark a maximum of two functions. The maximum number of Case endings and/or Ps in a PP is the maximum number allowed by the MS-component to mark two functions; this seems to be about four. We should take this as a sign that a unified, universal theory of Case markings with adpositions in a class with Case endings might be possible if the range of specifiers on Case-marked NPs and PPs is the same. We examine this issue next.

Limitations on the Distribution of Specifiers of P and Case

Having established limits on the possible number of Ps in PP and determined that the initial P of a PP with two Ps may exercise semantic scope over the second, let us now see if the distribution of Spec$_P$ also supports the hypothesis that Ps are Case markers. In fact, another embarrassment to the Lexical P Hypothesis is that the number of adpositional specifiers is restricted to one Delimiter. The [Origin[Locus]] PPs like *from-under* seem to indicate several Quantifier (11.24) and Delimiter (11.25) positions which control scope relations.

(11.24)   a.   ?The mouse ran [five inches] from under the rock
          b.   The mouse ran from [five inches] under the rock
          c.   *The mouse ran from under [five inches] the rock

(11.25)   a.   ?The mouse ran [right] from under the rock
          b.   The mouse ran from [right] under the rock
          c.   *The mouse ran under from [right] the rock

But the movement of Delimiters and QPs through these positions results in unforeseen oddities. The first is that placement of the specifiers before the first P creates a vague semantic reading. It is not clear that it is five inches from under the rock that the mouse is located after running, as opposed to, say, five inches that the mouse ran. In the latter case the QP modifies the VP, not the PP.

To control whether the Quantifier modifies the PP or the VP, we need to test the modification by eliminating the VP. Since PPs may also adjoin NPs, we may try the same PPs in (11.25) and (11.26) as an NP adjunct, for example:

(11.26)   a.   *the mouse [five inches] from under the rock
          b.   the mouse from [five inches] under the rock
          c.   *the mouse from under [five inches] the rock

(11.27)   a.   *the mouse [right] from under the rock
          b.   the mouse from [right] under the rock
          c.   *the mouse under from [right] the rock

As a nominal adjunct, the same PP allows specifiers only between the first and second P. Hence we may be sure that (i) only two Ps are allowed in PPs and (ii) only one specifier is allowed per PP, and (iii) it is positioned before a single P (*the mouse five inches from the rock*) or between double Ps (11.26b, 11.27b).

The same principle applies to van Riemsdijk's examples of P-PP constructions (van Riemsdijk 1982: 58–60).

(11.28)   a. De cognac is [voor [bij de koffie]]
               The cognac is for with the coffee
               "The cognac is to go with the coffee"

           b. Deze cognac is [van [voor de oorlog]]
               "This cognac is from before the war"

Riemsdijk points out only that the inner P may be specified (e-mail, 1991).[8]

(11.29)   Deze cognac is [van [meerdere jaren voor de oorlog]]
           "This cognac is from several years before the war"

The issue, however, is whether the outer P may also be specified at all. Indeed, specification before the first preposition is blocked as it is in (11.26) and (11.27):

(11.30)   *cognac is [meerdere jaren van [voor de oorlog]]
           "This cognac is several years from before the war"

Notice, in conclusion, that both Ps cannot be specified or quantified simultaneously.

(11.31)   a. *The mouse just from five inches under the rock
           b. *The mouse right from just under the rock
           c. *The mouse five inches from right under the rock

If the two Ps were heads of their own PP, functional or lexical, each should accept its own spatial specification independent of each other, but that is not possible. Rather, specification of PPs, no matter how complex, is restricted to one position: before a single P or between two Ps.

It also seems possible to restrict modification of the Delimiter in an extreme way, by one category, Intensification. Notice that non-intensificational modification of Delimiters is impermissible (11.32), and that the Delimiters and Intensifiers in (11.33) may not be switched.

(11.32)   a. *the mouse immediately just under the house
           b. *the mouse hardly barely under the house
           c. *the mouse directly right under the house

(11.33)   a. the mouse very far under the house
           b. the mouse just barely under the house

    c. *the mouse very barely under the house
    d. *the mouse just far under the house

The number of Ps in PPs seems to be restricted to three with a maximum of two functions, modified by one Spec$_P$ in a fixed position. The specifier in English is positioned before a single P, as in *right/far/way under the rock* but between any two Ps, as in *(the mouse) from right/far/way under the rock*. Contrast these examples with *(the mouse)* *right/far/way from under the rock*. Given the ungrammaticality of the latter construction and the (a) variants of (11.24–11.27), it would seem that the scope of a PP specifier is limited to the second function of secondary Case-marked NPs. I will not speculate at this point why this should be the case, but only note that it is a factor in PP modification in English. It now seems quite possible that PPs and Case-marked NPs in languages with Case morphology are compatible, since we would expect a maximum of one specifier of any given Case on an NP.

Case Specifiers in Klamath

Klamath also has Intensifiers which reflect some of the same functions as the adpositional Intensifers, but which are affixal and appear with Case endings rather than Ps. The marker for the spatial Intensifier, meaning "right" or "just", is a partially reduplicative infix positioned between the stem and the Case ending, yet it exercises semantic scope over the Case ending to its right and the stem to its left, as the English gloss indicates (Barker 1964).

(11.34)   a. sdo-tga "by the road"   sdo-tda-tga "right by the road"

        b. habaa-ksi "at the treetop"   haaba-ksa-ksi "right at the treetop"

        c. čii-s-ksi "at the house"   čii-s-ksa-ksi "just at the house"

The ordering of Klamath morphology would seem to be linear, in that it lacks word-internal structure. (11.34a) can neither be bracketed [*sdo* [*tda*[*tga*]]] nor [[[*sdo*]*tda*]*tga*]. The scope relations of these forms, as we have seen time and again, must also be purely semantic.

    We have now established a distinction between adverbs and adpositions so that the latter may be constrained to two functional occurrences per PP with a single specifier, itself possibly intensified once. The same numbers apply to the maximum number of Case endings and affixal Delimiters. These discoveries contradict both the Case Filter and the Theta Criterion of current P&P theory, which limit NPs to one Case and one theta role each. The interpretation offered here obviates the need of a Case filter or a syntactic Case theory in general. All that is required under the present hypothesis is the Grammatical Function Criterion (11.17), which was suggested as a replacement for the Theta criterion.

11.5 CONCLUSION

The purpose of this chapter was to take the conclusion of chapter 10, that adpositions are not a governing lexical class, a step further toward an integrated theory of grammatical functions and function marking by demonstrating the adposition's compatibility with affixal Case markers. The central point throughout this chapter is that the extended set of Case functions, disambiguated from semantic theta roles by chapter 9, are central to the system of syntactic relations, as abstract Case is not. The Case paradigm is a purely morphological phenomenon required only by fusional synthetic languages; Case in this (traditional) sense is not involved in syntax in any way whatever. However, while Case is an optional morphological system, the grammatical functions which underlie Case paradigms are a critical universal component of the syntactic system. Some functions are marked by Case endings, others, by adpositions, and yet others by a combination of the two. The marking system, adpositions and desinences, however, constitute an integrated set of operations of the MS-component. Chapter 12 will demonstrate how that set of operations works.

NOTES

1. Lexically determined Case assignment amounts to the MS-component recognizing a lexical condition on the assignment of Case endings. Since Case endings are assigned by the MS-component in a LMBM model, lexically conditioned Case assignment does not necessarily involve syntax, either. The assignment of, say, the Dative endings to mark the DO of German *helfen* "help", for example, is a matter of the MS-component, not syntax, recognizing the special lexical subcategorization of that verb under LMBM.

2. The variation of /n/, the basic consonant of the Accusative desinence in the Academy Grammar's representation indicates that the /n/ is retained only before vowels. Before voiceless consonants it is replaced by /t/ and before voiced consonants it is replaced by /d/ or /ð/. The high mid-vowel /y/ participates in harmony. "IntrVOM" in the "Function Context" column stands for "Intransitive verb of motion".

3. In fact, Material may not be a grammatical function at all but rather a semantic operator MADE-OF($[_{Artifact}$], $[_{Material}$]) interpreted as the Origin function at the grammatical level. The assumption that it is a grammati-

cal function simply follows traditional grammars. Evidence against its being a grammatical function comes from the lack of any language with a specific Material Case or adposition, and the fact that it universally receives the Case indicating Origin or Comitation, as in *made (out) of/from steel* or *made with steel*.

4. The same is true of idiomatic V + N compounds like *scofflaw* and *pickpocket*: they do not block the regular interpretation, for example, "a pocket for picks".

5. The constraint on the number of desinences marking a given Case no doubt derives from either the Paradigm Economy Principle (Carstairs, 1987) or the Principle of Contrast (Carstairs-McCarthy 1992b; 1993). These principles limit the number of affixes marking a given Case and the extent of synonymy with a paradigm.

6. The combinations in (11.19) are not without parallel; English combines the same two functions in its own way, expressing them with two logically appropriate markers, as in *to mother's, at mother's, from mother's*. It is more common, however, for two primary functions in one PP to be interpreted as a conflict subjected to resolution rules in the sense of Corbett (1983). In Russian, for example, the same function as those in (11.19b) surface in a Dative Case construction, for example, *k mater-i* "to mother's", with no marking of Possession. Presumably, resolution rules assign precedence to Dative over Genitive, since the same two senses are present in the Russian locution as they are in the Mongolian one.

7. This account would extend to the German examples discussed by van Riemsdijk (1990): *der Blick [vom Fenster aus]* = the view from.the window out "the view out of the window". The positioning of the P and its specifier here may be morphologically defined in terms of the PP brackets and discrete lexical precedence rules (see sections 12.4.1 for Anderson's General Theory of Affixation and 15.2.2 for a morphological theory of bracket erasure).

8. According to van Riemsdijk, the initial P in a double-P PP may occasionally be specified, as in *recht van voren* "directly from before (in-front-of)". But as noted throughout this chapter, the specifiers are limited to those Intensifiers meaning "right, just" and are restricted to Ps marking spatial functions. Otherwise, Ps marking nonspatial primary functions in Dutch, as in English, resist specification:

*pal tot overmorgen "right until day after tomorrow"
*3 dagen sinds de vrede "3 days since the peace"

Chapter Twelve

The Defective Adjective Hypothesis

12.1 CASE FUNCTIONS IN THE BASE

Chapter 11 established several facts for which a theory of Case must account. First, unlike the theta roles controlled by the Theta Criterion, PPs must be able to bear more than one Case function in certain positions, but also unlike Jackendoff's conceptual theta roles, PPs may bear no more than two functions and those only under highly constrained circumstances: one from a closed set of primary functions plus one secondary function. Chapter 11 also established parallels between Case and adpositional marking systems, showing that in Case systems, up to three Case endings may mark an adjectival PP with maximally two functions, just as in adpositional languages up to three adpositions or adpositions + Case endings may mark PPs with maximally two functions. These chapters for the first time account for PPs of up to four adpositions. Finally, both Case endings and adpositions, multiple or single, allow a maximum of one specifier, restricted to a QP or a Delimiter (which itself may be specified by a single Intensifier). Specifiers of nonspatial primary functions like Manner, Means, Purpose, Possession, Possessivity, Partitivity, Cause do not permit QPs and are further restricted to the occasional Intensifier.

All the parallels between Case endings and adpositions have set the stage for demonstrating how Case systems may be conflated universally with adposition marking systems. This process will require a definition of Case and adpositions and a category for these markers, since chapter 10 argued that adpositions do not constitute an independent lexical class. The first step is to provide syntax with a means of operating over the Case functions of Appendix A so as to distinguish the argument functions, Subject and Objects, from oblique adjectival functions such as Manner, Locus, and Subessive. The logical way to do this is to introduce the direct Case functions as features on structural NP positions. Chomsky's Minimalist Program, with its AgrS and AgrO functions, suffices for this: Infl assigns these functions to the appropriate structural positions and the functions

follow the Subject and Object to their surface positions, [Spec, IP] and
[NP, VP]. The curious may turn to Chomsky (1992) for details of his analy-
sis of Subject and Object positions; other interpretations, with and without
VP-internal subjects, are possible.

Let us hypothesize that all DPs not contained in PPs expand into NP
+ [Subject], [Object1], or [Object2]. The placement of the phrasal markers for these functions, as in Japanese, for example, or Case endings, as in
Latin, will follow from the General Theory of Affixation to be presented
in section 12.4.1. Hence neither adpositions, particles, nor Case endings
marking structural Case positions require a structural position of the base.
This approach predicts that all adpositional Subject and Object markers are
affixes attached to N or clitics attached to the peripheral element of the NP
by the General Theory.

Adverbal Cases and Ps, on the other hand, because they may attain the
power to move in syntax or remain stranded to mark an empty NP position
after NP movement, require a rather different account. Adverbal PPs and
adverbal Case-marked NPs are in fact APs when adjoined to VPs, IPs, or
NPs. This interpretation is an entailment of the treatment of BARE NP AD-
VERBS in Bresnan and Grimshaw (1978: 347) and ADVERBAL CASE NPs in
Emonds (1985: 223–37). Emonds' approach is designed to accomplish the
same goal as chapters 11 and 12 here: to provide a consistent treatment of
adjectival PPs or Case-marked NPs across languages. Emonds wishes to
be able to treat the English Dative phrase *to the man* and its German and
Russian counterparts, *d-em Mann* and *mužčin-e*, identically at D-structure.
English "bare" NP adverbs like *(she did it) this way, Friday night, some
place,* would then become the normal phenomenon theoretically that they
seem to be empirically, not requiring the special lexical treatment Larson
(1985) proposes. Emonds suggests that a structure like (12.1) underlies
these surface adjectival types. Notice that Emonds postulates grammatical
functions as heads of PPs without overt Ps so that P becomes phrasal function markings in a class with Case markers. This leaves the question of the
relation of PPs to APs, to which we now turn.

(12.1)

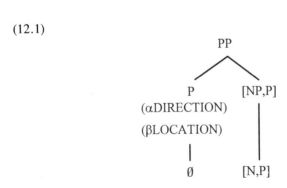

12.2 ADPOSITIONS, THE RESIDUE OF ADVERBS, AND ADJECTIVES

Section 8.3 concluded that Manner adverbs do not represent a discrete lexical class but are merely the form that qualitative adjectives (QAdjs) assume when they modify verbs and adjectives. The vast majority if not all Manner adverbs are derived from QAdjs.[1] If we exclude Delimiters from the class of adverbs as Jackendoff (1977) has proposed, only a relatively small residue of adverbs remain. If this residue could be explained without reference to a special class, adverbs and AdvPs could be obviated altogether from the theory of grammar.

12.2.1 Defective QAdjs (DAdjs)

The residue class of adverbs contains items of three types: (i) some of Jackendoff's "intransitive prepositions," for example, *back, home, here, there,* to which we might add *uptown, upright, downwind, downstate, downriver, beforehand,* (ii) a substantial and marginally productive class prefixed with *a-,* (see 12.2) and (iii) a smaller set suffixed with *-s, -ward, -wise* and *-side* (12.3):[2]

(12.2) abloom, ablaze, aboard, abroad, adrift, afar, afield, afire, afloat, afoot, afraid, afresh, agleam, aglitter, aglow, aground, ajar, alike, alive, aloft, alone, aloud, amuck, anew, apace, apart, apiece, aplomb, aright, around, ashore, aside, askance, askew, asleep, aslant, aslope, astride, astray, atop, atwitter, awake, away, awash

(12.3) a. indoors, outdoors, downstairs, upstairs
       b. homeward(s), outward(s), northward(s), afterward(s),
            backward(s), upward(s), downward(s), earthward(s)
       c. clockwise, slantwise, lengthwise
       d. topside, outside, inside, broadside, stateside

Most of the items in (12.2) and (12.3) are denominal and deverbal forms which are as much adjectival as they are adverbal. In addition to occurring in predicate adjectival position, they also appear comfortably in postnominal AP position (12.4); those ending on *-ward* and *-way(s)* even appear sporadically in attributive position (12.5), less the suffix *-s*.

(12.4) a. motion backwards
       b. a pool indoors
       c. the people aboard
       d. a park abloom with roses

(12.5)   a. backward motion
         b. an indoor pool
         c. *the aboard people
         d. *the abloom park

A few of those on -*ward* even nominalize, however idiomatically: *backwardness, forwardness*. Those prefixed with schwa usually appear with a complement inside an NP, as in *those aboard the ship, a park abloom with roses, eyes ablaze with passion*. With or without complements, they are restricted to predicate and postnominal positions, like all APs with complements. However, both sets serve both predicate and attributive adjunct functions.

We may justifiably set aside these forms as a class of QAdjs called "defective qualitative adjectives" (DAdjs), because they occur as a class only in predicate and postnominal positions and do not undergo the range of lexical and syntactic derivations that proper QAdjs are subject to. The result of this step is the final obviation of the class "Adverb" from the lexicon and of "AdvP" from syntax. Adjectives now come in three varieties distinguished by distribution, inflectional properties, and the range of L-derivation each is subject to. RAdjs, which appear only in attributive position, DAdjs, which appear in predicate and postnominal attributive positions, and QAdjs, which appear in all A positions. QAdjs undergo all adjectival derivations; RAdjs and DAdjs are subject to no derivation, including Gradation. RAdjs and QAdjs agree with their head nouns in attributive position, while DAdjs do not. Finally, QAdjs and DAdjs serve as both nominal and nonnominal adjuncts; RAdjs modify only nouns.

12.2.2 The Distribution of APs and PPs

An interesting semantic attribute of DAdjs is that the majority describe Manner, Direction, Place, and State—the major functions of oblique Ps. This overlap places us in a position to eliminate PPs altogether by collapsing them with APs. Geis (1985) adopts this position explicitly in order to achieve a uniform nontransformational treatment of adverbs, AdvPs, PPs, and adverbal subordinate clauses with preposition-like conjunctions, for example, *before I go, since I came, after I left*. He attributes the notion to Jespersen (1949–1958: II.1.15), but it has been discussed periodically in Europe for at least a century. Here the hypothesis has been adjusted to include PPs specifically in a subclass of APs, call it the DEFECTIVE ADJECTIVE HYPOTHESIS. Let us begin our examination of the distributional evidence for this hypothesis with a review of the distribution of AP.

In comparing the syntactic distribution of APs and PPs, we should keep in mind that the claim here places PPs in a class with a subclass of adjectives which exhibit special behavior vis-à-vis the class A as a whole, those in (12.2) and (12.3). DAdjs occur in predicate and postnominal positions, do not compare or nominalize, but may be used adverbally without any manner adverb morphology. In fact, the distribution of PPs is identical with that of DAdjs with one exception: adjectives are not encountered in NP complement position. Because they are phrases, they are not expected to appear in prenominal or preverbal positions, which preclude heavy APs. In the examples to follow, a and b are QAdjs, and c is always a DAdj. To their right, a′, b′, c′ will be typical PPs for comparison.

(12.6) **in NP complement position**
    a. *   a′. a student of physics
    b. *   b′. his reply to my insult
    c. *   c′. his encounter with art

(12.7) **in postnominal adjunct position**
    a. a book yellow with age   a′. a book on the shelf
    b. a book full of pictures   b′. a book about flowers
    c. a man asleep   c′. a man with a good life

(12.8) **in prenominal adjunct position**
    a. *a yellow with age book a′. *an on the shelf book
    b. *a full of pictures book b′. *an about flowers book
    c. *an asleep man   c′. *a with a good life man

PPs, QAdjs, and DAdjs also occur in various predicate positions: predicate adjective (12.9), VP complement position (12.10), in "state" adjunct positions (12.11), and in postverbal (12.12) but not preverbal adjunct position (12.13).

(12.9) **in predicate position**
    a. the house is red   a′. the house is in Smoketown
    b. John is happy   b′. John is in ecstasy
    c. John is aboard   c′. John is on board/on the ship

(12.10) **in VP complement position**
    a. look good   a′. remain in flames
    b. feel happy   b′. feel on top of the world
    c. remain ablaze   c′. look like a million bucks

(12.11) **in "state" adjunct positions**
    a. John arrived sick   a′. John arrived in a tuxedo
    b. John found the goat dead b′. John found the goat on a spit
    c. John set the skiff adrift   c′. John set the skiff in the water

(12.12) **in postverbal adjunct position**
    a. John ate fish preparatory to   a'. John ate fish before dinner
       departure
    b. John ate fish subsequent to   b'. John ate fish in the diner
       leaving
    c. John thought aloud   c'. John thought about home

(12.13) **in preverbal adjunct position**
    a. *John preparatory to lunch   a'. *John before dinner ate fish
       ate fish
    b. *John subsequent to leaving   b'. *John in the diner ate fish
       ate fish
    c. *John aloud thought   c'. *John about home thought

This interpretation of P accounts for both the usage of some P isolates in adjectival positions such as predicate position (12.14) and the idiosyncrasy of their adjectival distribution in (12.15).

(12.14) a. The cat came in
       b. The dog rolled over
       c. The needle came through

(12.15) a. The cat is in   *the in cat
       b. The play is over   *an over play
       c. The actor is through   *a through actor

The restricted range and idiosyncrasy of Ps in the predicate adjective position is consistent with their serving as grammatical function markers, PRO-NOMINAL DAdjs, whose primary job is to mark the different types of adjunct and complement relations available in language. Since adjectives constitute a lexical class primarily associated with adjunction, these *pro*-markers tend to be associated with adjectivity. The fact that they are not lexical QAdjs leads to cranky constraints and idiosyncratic distribution vis-à-vis QAdjs.

    If Ps are pronominal DAdjs, we can account for their being functional, as Emonds most recently noted, and thus for their forming a closed class. This would also explain the prominence of prepositionless, Case-marked NP adverbials in all languages, since null realization of pronouns is usual. It further accounts for another curious fact about languages: while languages with pure adpositional systems and Case + adpositional systems exist, there is no language with a pure Case system, that is, without any adpositions at all. Archi has 40 Cases and Tabassaran, 52; still, both use adpositions for marking some nominal adverb functions. If Ps were pronominals of some type and Case-marked adverbal nouns simply exhibited the null pronoun, we would not expect pure Case languages without adpositions since purely zero grammatical systems do not exist in general.

APs and PPs in NP Complement Position

The prominence of PP nominal and verbal complements and the AP's evasion of that service represents the only serious misalignment of the distribution of PPs and APs. PPs occur much more freely as complements of NPs and VPs than do APs in general. The reason for this might be that the PPs in complements are not PPs at all but $X + NP$ constructions whose NP complement relation is coincidentally marked by the same system of Ps. Chomsky (1981) noted that PPs in NPs marked by *of* in English and elsewhere by the Genitive are NPs. The preposition in these instances is an empty Case marker. Thus in (12.6a'), *student of physics,* the relation of *student* to *physics* is the same as that of *study* and *physics* in the VP *study physics.* The preposition *of* marks the Genitive of Object1. For this reason, most such constructions are deverbal nominalizations; however, underived such constructions also occur: *letter of condolence, woman of distinction, book of witchcraft.* That these complements do not accept the classic [Spec, PP] Delimiters or nonnominal adjuncts, as (12.16) illustrates, strengthens the argument that such complements are NPs rather than PPs.

(12.16)   a. a student *right/*almost/*barely of physics
          b. a student *certainly/*specifically/*eternally of physics

Other PP nominal complements seem to be restricted to those Ps like *to, for, with, as, from, at,* which mark primary functions. This also suggests that these PP complements are lexically Case-marked NPs rather than APs. Most are, again, nominalizations derived from verbs which subcategorize the Case function marked by the oblique P, or subcategorize the P as a grammatically and semantically empty Object marker, such as *reply to my insult, longing for home, interest in Baghdad.* However, underived nouns with oblique Ps and derived nouns whose complement is marked differently from the underlying verb also occur. These nouns must subcategorize those functions themselves lexically, as in *letter to my brother, sympathy for students, pain from the injection.* (12.17) and (12.18) illustrate typical cases.[3]

(12.17)   a. the letter *right/*almost/*barely/*way to my brother
          b. the letter *directly/*completely/*physically to my brother

(12.18)   a. the letter right/almost/barely/way under the table
          b. the letter directly/completely/physically under the table

PPs which serve as NP complements do not behave adjectivally; they do not allow [Spec, AP] or the nonnominal adjuncts associated with PPs. PPs which serve as adjuncts behave like normal PPs. The most promising interpretation of all these facts, then, is that PPs in NP complement position are in fact regularly or lexically Case-marked NPs and not APs, while adjunct PPs are APs.[4]

The Defective Adjective Hypothesis and Marked Cases

A secure hypothesis predicts not only the unmarked case, but the most likely marked cases and speech errors. If adjunct PPs are DAdj APs with a pronominal DAdj, we would expect them to occur marginally in some prohibited AP position in the marked case rather than in any NP or VP position. If adjunct PPs are APs, the most likely marked position in which they might occur is the prenominal, attributive A position. Moreover, since that is an A^0 position which precludes complements in English, they would be most likely to move to that position if they were somehow reanalyzed as a simple lexical adjective rather than as an AP. Such reanalysis occurs most commonly when phrases are idiomatized; thus, we find derivational violations like *oneupsmanship, sticktoitiveness, do-gooder*, where phrases lose their compositionality and begin behaving like a single lexical item. Although we do not expect to find PPs in A^0 prenominal positions in languages where this position requires morphological agreement, this would be the most likely marked position in which they would emerge in marked instances in languages which do not require NP internal agreement.

English is one such language and it does allow a wide variety of PPs in attribute position in instances where the PPs are fixed phrases; that is, where the semantics of the PP has become noncompositional and the phrase is treated more like an X^0-level item than a phrase.

(12.19)   a. sales over the counter   a'. over-the-counter sales
          b. activity behind the scenes   b'. behind-the-scenes activity
          c. reductions across the board c'. across-the-board reductions
          d. a dress off the shoulder   d'. an off-the-shoulder dress

When PPs behave like X^0-level objects, they behave like As. That PPs behave like As when they lose their compositionality is strong evidence indeed that PPs in general are some sort of AP.

The factor obstructing the full grammaticality of the examples in (12.19) is their phrasality, the presence of inflectional markers like *a, the, -s,* and the Ps themselves. If the idiomatized phrases in (12.19) are in fact adjectives, it should be possible to prenominalize simple Case-marked nouns if they first undergo lexical adjectivization. Since the position in question is attribute position, we would expect the output of such rules to be RAdjs. English also has a series of adjectives which fit this description under the assumption that they receive null suffixation: *in-house, off-color, for-profit, on-target*. These constructs do not seem to be much more productive than those based on lexicalized phrases in (12.19).

Many languages do, however, possess a derivation called RELATIVIZATION which productively converts Case-marked NP adverbs and PPs into RAdjs. Turkish, for example, uses the suffix *-ki* to convert a predicate adverbal noun into a RAdj (Underhill 1976: 210):

(12.20) a. kitap masa-da   a'. masa-da-ki kitap
            book the.table-Loc   the.table-Loc-Rel book
            "the book on the table"   "the on-table book"
         b. binalar Ankara-da   b'. Ankara-da-ki binalar
            buildings Ankara-Loc   Ankara-Loc-Rel buildings
            "the buildings in Ankara"   "the in-Ankara buildings"

Basque exhibits similar rules of relativization which convert adjuncts into RAdjs and suffixes them with *-ko*. Saltarelli (1988: 73–80, 163–164) sometimes refers to the underlying structures as adjuncts and, other times, as complements. All seem to be adjuncts, however.

(12.21) a. ama-rentzat   erosi   ditut   lore-ak
            mother-Ben   bought   I.have   flower-AbsPl
            "I bought flowers for mother"
         a'. ama-rentza-ko   lore-ak   larrosa-k   dira
            mother-Ben-Rel   flower-AbsPl   rose-AbsPl   are
            "the for-mother flowers are roses"
         b. etxe hau ladrilu-z   egina   da
            house this brick-InsSg   made   it.is
            "this house is made of brick"
         b'. ladrilu-z-ko   etxe-a
            brick-InsSg-Rel   house
            "a brick house"
         c. etxe hau ladrilu(-rik)   gabe   egin   zuten
            house this brick(-Prt)   without   made   they-have
            "they made this house without bricks"
         c'. ladrilu-rik gabe-ko   etxe-ak   triste-ak   iruditzen
            brick-Prt without-Rel   house-AbsPl   sad-AbsPl   seem
            "without-brick houses seem sad"

Saltarelli gives more examples involving other Cases. The important point is that the evidence suggests that *-ko* is a suffix which distinguishes RAdjs, for it also attaches to nouns alone, generating RAdjs: *eskola-ko neska* "school girl". Its attaching to PPs, as in (12.21), legitimizes prenominal PPs as RAdjs. The absence of such derivational legitimation no doubt prevents phrases like those in (12.19′) from becoming a productive English derivation.

Schachter and Otanes (1972: 195) go so far as to call secondary function PPs "locative adjective phrases", pointing out parallels in Tagalog similar to those found in Turkish and Basque. Most attributive adjectives may be placed on either side of their head noun in Tagalog (12.22a) so long as they are accompanied by a LINKER; so can Locative PPs (12.22b):

(12.22)   a. Binili niya ang [bahay na mahal/mahal na bahay]
              buy.PST he the [house LNKR expensive/expensive LNKR
              house]
              "he bought the expensive house"
          b. Binili niya ang [bahay na nasa probinsya/nasa probinsya-ng
              bahay]
              buy.PST the [house LNKR in provinces/in provinces-LNKR
              house]
              "he bought the house in the provinces"

All of the possible Locative phrases listed by Schachter and Otanes (1972: 254–59) express secondary functions except for the primary locational function. The primary functions on case-marked NPs are conspicuously absent.

There is further support for the interpretation of adjunct PPs as APs and complement PPs as Case-marked NPs here. If PP complements are in fact Case-marked NPs, they would be precluded from the sort of PP prenominalization just witnessed. We would predict that (12.19) would exemplify a class of adjuncts and would exclude NP complements like those (12.23).

(12.23)   a. *an of-physics student
          b. *a to-the-insult reply
          c. *a with-art encounter

The English evidence supports this prediction; further research in other languages is required to firmly establish the point, however.

In conclusion then, the distribution of PPs correlate to that of DAdj APs in all positions except NP and most VP complement positions. In these positions, PPs are restricted to those with Ps marking primary Case functions which characterize NPs rather than APs. This suggests that PPs in complement positions are not APs but are, in fact, Case-marked NPs, where the P is the Case marker. There is no doubt of this in the case of the preposition *of* in NPs and *to* marking Object2, points made by Chomsky and Emonds. The syntactic position of Ps marking the other primary functions is only slightly less clear; however, the evidence in this section supports their inclusion in this same treatment.

12.2.3 The Specifiers of APs and PPs

The distributional evidence suggests that PPs are either NPs or APs, the P representing a simple Case marker in the former instance and a pronominal DAdj, in the latter. This section will examine the specifiers of PPs and APs to see if their distribution also supports this account. If so, we may develop a theory of grammar eliminating PPs by more clearly defining Case and the lexical class "Adjective". An added advantage of including PPs under the rubric of AP is that we conflate all adjectival and adverbal adjuncts (A, Adv, P) into one lexical class. PPs like *at that place, at that time, at this time* share the same meanings and distribution with traditional adjective-adverbs as *there, then, now*. The same applies to other such PPs as *in a soft way, with vigor, from fear*, and the adjectives *soft(ly), vigorous(ly), fearful(ly)*. Functionally and distributionally these simple and complex forms behave almost identically in syntax.

The specifiers of both classes also form a closed set; adjective specifiers and PP specifiers are restricted to Delimiters, QPs, and lexicalized adverbs. However, those Delimiters which are "degree words", that is, which apply only to gradable concepts, sometimes apply differently to PPs. First, let us consider the Delimiters which specify DAdjs and Ps indifferently. Attenuative Delimiters only marginally discriminate the various subtypes of adjectives, specifying QAdj, DAdj, and P (DAdj pronoun) alike. When they do, DAdjs and PPs behave identically.

(12.24) **Attenuative Delimiters**
    a. QAdj: the mouse is sorta/barely/rather happy/sad/brown
    b. DAdj: the mouse is sorta/barely/*rather alive/adrift/asleep
    c. PP: the mouse is sorta/barely/*rather under the porch

(12.25–12.27) show that the same pattern holds with other Delimiters. (The asterisk outside the parenthesis indicates that the construction is ungrammatical WITHOUT the parenthesized material; an asterisk inside the parentheses indicates that the construction is ungrammatical WITH the parenthesized material.)

(12.25) **Intensive Delimiter**
    a. QAdj: the mouse is very (*much) happy/revolting/brown
    b. DAdj: the mouse is very *(much/far) alive/asleep/adrift/
        outside

    c. PP: the mouse is very *(much/far) under the porch/in love/
       out of sorts

(12.26) **Excessive Delimiter**
    a. QAdj: the mouse is too (*much) happy/revolting/brown
    b. DAdj: the mouse is too *(much/far) alive/asleep/adrift/aglow
    c. PP: the mouse is too *(much/far) under the porch/in love/out
       of sorts

(12.27) **Comparative Delimiter**
    a. QAdj: the mouse is as (*much) happy as he is brown
    b. DAdj: the mouse is as *(much) alive/asleep/adrift as not
    c. PP: the mouse is as *(much) under the porch/in love/out of
       sorts as not

The distribution of PPs seems to parallel that of DAdj APs and they serve
the same syntactic function, adjunction. A logical a priori hypothesis is
that APs, like NPs and VPs, are also introduced by a functional category
such as Abney's DegP (Abney 1987), and that PP is a functional category
derived in the same base structure. The implication is that P is to A as
auxiliaries are to verbs. Van Riemsdijk's CATEGORY IDENTITY THESIS (van
Riemsdijk 1990) provides support for this view. Van Riemsdijk reminds
us that the functional categories for nouns and verbs seem to belong to the
same category as their complements. Determiners are often used as Ns (as
is English *that*) and auxiliaries possess all the attributes of verbs. There are
always limitations on the categorial identity, however. Auxiliaries cannot
be used alone as verbs, and determiners, too, must be adjoined to, or co-
referenced with, a lexical noun. The relation of P to A conforms to both
these criteria: while P behaves much like an A, it follows the pattern of
defective adjectives, and that imperfectly. However, there is enough evidence to hypothesize that at least secondary Ps represent a functional category of AP. The remainder of the chapter explores this hypothesis.

12.3 THE DELP RULES

The functional categories of the current P&P theory represent the means
of introducing grammatical functions into syntax. Since the argument here
is that structural Ps are expressions of a universal set of adjectival (adjunct)
functions, a functional syntactic category is the logical means of introducing them. A functional category, DELIMITER, which dominates AP, is a
logical point to set out from, so let us couch APs in DelP projections in
the spirit of Abney's DegPs (Abney 1987). Consider (12.28) as a first
approximation.

(12.28)   a. DelP → Intensifier Del'
          b. Del' → [Primary, Spatial] AP
          c. AP → Spec$_A$ A'
          d. A' → A (DP, IP, CP)
          e. [Spatial] → [Locus[ ]], [Goal[ ]], [Origin[ ]],
             ([Perlation[ ]], . . .)
          f. [ ] → [Subessive], [Superessive], [Anterior],
             [Posterior], . . .)

The rules in (12.28) are approximate universal parameters of adjunct phrases (DelP). Marked instances emerge which ostensibly will require language-specific parameter settings. Mongol, for example, will require a [Sociative] rule which expands this feature by each of the remaining primary functions. [Sociative] → [Sociative [Possessive]], and [Sociative [Purpose]] (11.20). Dutch will require a rule expanding [Purpose] to account for the constructions meaning "for with cognac", "for after the war" (11.28). The rules above which specify dependency relations among Case functions, along with the Grammatical Functional Criterion (11.17), form the universal parameters of grammatical functions. The Functional Criterion sets the limit on the number of functions that an adverbal NP may bear at two: a primary plus a secondary one. (12.28) stipulates the relation of any two functions and their place in syntax.

The rules in (12.28) take advantage of the distinction between the functional and lexical categories of P&P, but their specificity violates the spirit of the Minimalist Program advanced within the P&P framework (Chomsky 1992). Chomsky would now rid grammar altogether of D-structure in favor of minimal principles of X-bar theory and lexical and functional categories selected from the lexicon. However, there is no general principle beyond (11.17) which can specify the diverse relations among adjunct functions, and preceding chapters pointed out the difficulties in maintaining Ps in the lexicon. Indeed, the parallels we have seen between adpositional and Case functions are lost under Chomsky's assumption. At this writing, the Minimalist Program remains vaguely defined so that its impact on linguistic theory in general and LMBM in particular cannot be fully appraised. To the extent it is obliged to define Ps as lexical items and most grammatical functions as semantic theta roles, it cannot cope with the tightly closed, definable universal system of grammatical categories at the base of this book.

According to (12.28) then, DelP initially develops specifier, head, and complement nodes like other functional projections (12.28abc). The specifier may be only a single Intensifier chosen from among the Delimiter functions. The DelP complement is an AP. Only DP, IP, and CP are permitted as complements of DelPs (12.28d). This may require adjustment to include

pronominal DelPs; however, it seems plausible that the ostensible PP complements of adjectives are, like those of NPs, simply Case-marked NPs.
Generally, APs with PP complements allow only one P. In English this P
is always selected from those which mark primary functions, those closely
associated with NP and VP complements, and never from among those
marking secondary ones, as (12.29) illustrates:

(12.29)   a. ready for danger with my new computer
          b. full of warmth from the reverend's words
          c. mad at John for his crude remark

The first PP in each example of (12.29) is a complement; it neither conjoins
nor permutes felicitously with the second PP. The second PP, presumably
an adjunct, may be replaced by a simple A (12.30), while the initial one
may not (12.31):

(12.30)   a. ready for danger computationally
          b. ready for danger computer-wise

(12.31)   a. *ready dangerously with my new computer
          b. *ready danger-wise with my new computer

Assuming that *ready* subcategorizes an Object2 $NP_{Purpose}$, we predict that
any NP immediately following it will be assigned *for* and cannot be per-
muted with an adjunct nor replaced by a simple A. There is no need to
refer to this NP as a DelP if we extend NP grammatical functions to include
all the primary functions.

The evidence seems to indicate that PPs in complement positions are
Case-marked NPs, while in adjunct positions they are APs. The difference
between complements and adjuncts derives from whether the head controls
the selection of the grammatical function or whether selection is free in
syntax. A Case-marked NP does not need a syntactic position for the P,
since the P is a Case-ending or clitic directly attached to some constituent
of the NP by the MS-component. Because complements necessarily have
primary functions, and since primary functions are marked by endings or
clitic Ps, this account adds to the explanation of why complements are
more tightly bound to the head of XP than adjuncts and why they are
always marked by Case-endings or cliticizable Ps.

(12.28f–12.28h) next specify the superordinate nominal function categories as discussed in previous chapters according to primary, spatial, and
secondary types. It first replaces the spatial function with one of the three
primary spatial functions, Locus, Goal, or Origin (12.28f). The rules may
stop applying at this point and the MS-component will assign *in, on,* or *at*

to [Locus], *to* or *for* to [Goal], or *from* to [Origin]. However, the three spatial functions may also be optionally combined with one of the secondary functions (12.28f–12.28h) as described in chapters 10 and 11.[5] If neither [Primary] nor [Spatial] are expanded, the lexicon is free to insert lexical adjectives. If either [Primary] or [Spatial] is deployed, presumably the lexicon is blocked from operating unless it possesses a DAdj semantically compatible with the specified function. This selection parameter thus distinguishes DAdjs from other QAdjs.

(12.28) preserves the possibility of a head which is not overtly expressed, as suggested by Bresnan and Grimshaw and elaborated by Emonds. The head is required to contain either a lexical item (all of which are phonologically overt) or a phonologically covert adjectival *pro* to be defined in chapter 15; either suffices as a head. The analogy is with ''headless'' NPs like *der Rote* ''the red one'' in German, where the head is an array of lexically determined features which effect agreement but is not overtly expressed itself. Chapter 15 will contend, however, that heads which are not overtly expressed must contain lexically controlled features. Presumably PPs are determined by the features for DAdjs, say [±Defective], for the time being.

We are now in a position to derive the English PP *just under the bear* in the same manner in which the Lezghian *sevrekaj* is generated and in a way compatible with the derivation of APs. (12.32) illustrates the base structure of an AP (adjunct phrase) realized as a PP as projected by (12.28).

The positioning of Delimiters is an issue discrete from the question of their immediate dominance. It has become clear recently that models of

(12.32)

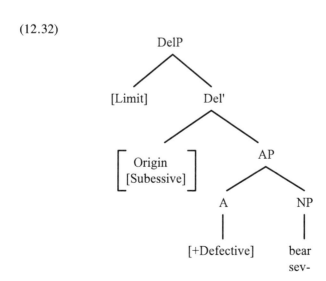

grammar need to distinguish what advocates of GPSG call "immediate dominance" and "linear precedence". GPSG models such as that of Gazdar et al. (1985) comprise a pair consisting of a set of ID and LP rules. Constructions are grammatical only if they conform to both sets of rules. There is no need to provide a position for Delimiters before and between the prepositions under the assumption of the separation of structure and precedence rules. Since the Delimiters constitute a closed category of grammatical functions marked by affixation in some languages, they must be handled entirely by the MS-component. It is therefore entirely appropriate that they are introduced in a functional rather than lexical projection. The MS-component, however, may attach the marker in accord with its own principles. Chapter 10 suggested that Delimiters are generally attached to the P closest to the NP because their scope only extends over the second function of complex secondary functions or the only function of primary ones.

Short head raising brings A to the Del node as in (12.33), where it may receive allomorphy from the MS-component. When A is raised, the DelP functions amalgamate with it and the phrase is ready for MS-interpretation. The assumption is that nominal PP adjuncts also receive Agreement in appropriate positions; however, only in languages like Basque and Turkish (see 12.20–12.21), which provide RAdj morphology to PPs, will Agreement be realized phonologically. Whether a language uses free morphemes or bound Case endings to mark the functions of a DelP is a matter of morphological spelling irrelevant to syntax. The analogy here is the

(12.33)

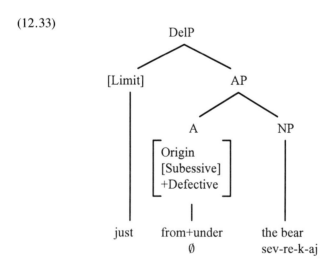

Semantic interpretation: [FROM([LIMIT([UNDER([BEAR])])])]

variation in marking person with free personal pronouns, conjugational endings, or both. However, if the function markers are attached to the complement, we must assume that the head A position is phonologically but not functionally empty.

12.4 TWO PROBLEMS: COMPLEMENT MARKING AND
PREPOSITION STRANDING

This section will briefly examine a complex area of current syntactic theory directly relevant to adjectival adpositions: preposition stranding. It will demonstrate that this is a marked phenomenon in Dutch, English, and the Scandinavian languages which represents no greater problem for LMBM than for other theories. In fact, the morphological framework of LMBM makes more accurate predictions about stranding than LMH. Before examining this area, however, we must address a question raised by the Defective Adjective Hypothesis: if complement PPs are NPs whose P is a Case marker, how do we account for the position of the P in those NPs? DelPs provide a head position which is the logical position for P if Ps are proadjectives (12.32), but NPs do not. How then do we account for the syntactic relation of the P in complement NPs marked by Ps?

12.4.1 A General Theory of Affixation

The answer to the question of what syntactic position Ps occupy in complement PPs occupy, is none. Since the Ps in these P-marked NPs do not allow specifiers or adjuncts, they always occur in phrase-initial or phrase-final position. We have already noted that these NPs are either marked by Case ending alone or by a primary function P—all of which are clitics or have an optional clitic form. The PP *about people* in *a story about people* cannot, therefore, be a complement because the P is neither a primary function marker nor a potential clitic. Thus *a story in the book about good people* is as grammatical as *a story about good people in the book* and both phrases may be coreferential. However, **a story in the book of good people* is not a coreferential, grammatically acceptable alternate of *a story of good people in the book*. It follows that no syntactic position is required for Ps marking complements in a LMBM model, so long as that model provides a morphological account of P positioning, an integrated theory of lexical and phrasal affixation.

The title of Anderson (1986; also 1992, chapter 8), "Clitics are Phrasal Affixes", probably expresses the current consensus among morphologists (see also Zwicky 1977, 1985; Carstairs 1981; Klavans 1985). Anderson folds in the theory of clitics with that of affixation, predicting the placement of both on the basis of a consistent set of parameters, those of (12.34):

(12.34) a. *Affixes and clitics are located within the scope of some constituent which constitutes its domain. The domain of an affix is the word; the domain of the clitic is the phrase.*

b. *Affixes and clitics are located by reference to the periphery (beginning vs. end) or the head of the constituent in which they appear. The head of a phrase is the element occupying position X^0; the head of the word is the syllable receiving stress.*

c. *Affixes and clitics either immediately precede or immediately follow their point of reference.*

This set of parameters, call it the GENERAL THEORY OF AFFIXATION, limits the distribution of lexical and phrasal affixes to positions on either side of the initial or final element in words or phrases, or on either side of the head of words or phrases. Lexical affixation is restricted to (i) prefixation and suffixation, (ii) infixation to positions located immediately inside the initial or final phoneme or syllable, and (iii) infixation to positions immediately preceding or following the accented syllable. Clitics are restricted to positions either immediately preceding or following the head, the initial or final word or constituent of the matrix phrase. Hence, the distribution of the two are identical once their hosts are defined in terms of "heads" and "peripheral elements".

(12.34) makes the positioning of affixes and clitics morphologically predictable, thus obviating any need for assigning positions for clitic adpositions in syntactic structure. To predict any clitic positioning, the MS-component must simply have enough memory to read an entire phrase, then mark the grammatical functions of the head on lexical elements at the periphery of its domain. (Chapter 15 discusses this capacity in more detail.) All asyllabic and monosyllabic Ps behave like clitics syntactically, and hence follow (12.34); they syntactically affix (cliticize) to some host and hence cannot accept any freestanding specifiers. (12.34) then provides the parameters for assigning all grammatical morphemes not occupying a syntactic position.

The General Theory of Affixation accounts for the positioning of adpositions and Case endings marking direct and oblique NP complements as a single, unified allomorphic category, BOUND GRAMMATICAL MORPHEMES, of the MS-component. Ps which mark primary functions must, then, have two forms: a free and a bound form. The free form is necessary in cases of P-stranding (see the next section) while the bound form is used when a suitable host is available, as in *who did John give it tó* [tu] versus *I gave it to* [tə] *John*. Important to us, the clitic form is used to mark NP complements with oblique Case functions as phrasal affixes.

12.4.2 Preposition Stranding[6]

LMH enjoys an ostensible advantage over LMBM and the Defective Adjective Hypothesis in its account of PREPOSITION STRANDING. Since LMBM postulates prepositions as Case markers inserted over abstract grammatical functions late in the derivation process, the very concept of "stranding prepositions" is alien to it. At the time of the movement which strands prepositions, prepositions are not even present in the syntactic derivation of an LMBM model. LMH, however, provides prepositions during lexical selection, so Ps are available for stranding. LMBM does, however, offer an account of P-stranding at least as compelling as that of LMH.

English, Dutch, and the Scandinavian languages are the only languages thus far discovered which allow preposition stranding. In all these languages stranding is restricted to one movement rule: *wh*-to-Comp raising, where stranding is optional, as (12.35) demonstrates. English additionally permits stranding during NP raising, the result of which are PSEUDOPASSIVES like those in (12.36). (12.35) and (12.36) are taken from Chomsky (1981: 292).

(12.35) a. Who did John speak to (To whom did John speak)
        b. Who did John give the book to (To whom did John give the book)
        c. *Which meal did John speak to Bill after (After which meal . . . .)

(12.36) a. Tom was spoken to
        b. *Tom was given the book to
        c. *The meal was spoken to Bill after

Van Riemsdijk (1982) noted that the two types of preposition stranding are asymmetrical; that is, the conditions on them are not the same. Notice that the NPs cannot be moved from PPs outside the VP in the pseudopassives of (12.37), while *wh* may be moved out of any PP (12.38).

(12.37) a. *his mother is traveled with (by John)
        b. *the third round/May was lost in (by Rocky)
        c. *Switzerland is bought many houses in (by Germans)

(12.38) a. Who did John's mother travel with?
        b. Which round/month did Rocky lose in?
        c. (Switzerland is the country) which Germans buy many houses in

The constraint on PPs c-commanded by V therefore applies constantly only to pseudopassives, which is to say, only in English.

Finally, as Hornstein and Weinberg (1981: 60, fn.) point out, P-PP constructions cannot be broken up if their PPs may be extracted at all.

(12.39)   a.   *Under what did John jump out from?
        a′. What did John jump out from under?
        b.   *Behind what did John jump from?
        b′. What did John jump from behind?

Hornstein and Weinberg mark all the constructions in (12.39) as ungrammatical. If constructions which extract NP from double Ps (12.39a′–12.39b′) are ungrammatical, as Hornstein and Weinberg suggest, they are markedly less so than examples which extract PP (12.39a–12.39b).

Bresnan's and Hornstein and Weinberg's Solution

Hornstein and Weinberg, like Bresnan (1982b), account for both types of stranding in terms of PREDICATE REANALYSIS based on principles of Case assignment. Hornstein and Weinberg's version rests on the three assumptions listed in (12.40).

(12.40)   a.   There is a universal filter of the form *$[_{NP}\, e_{oblique}]$
        b.   There is a general syntactic rule of Reanalysis which says that in the domain of VP, a V and any set of contiguous elements to its right can form a complex V, i.e. V → V* (where V c-commands all elements of V*)
        c.   There are Case-marking rules which occur after all transformation rules have applied and before filters apply

Under the assumption that adpositions normally assign oblique Case, the filter (12.40a) prevents any movement from an NP position c-commanded by P. This filter prevents NPs from being extracted from the domain PP, the norm in all languages save the Germanic. The reanalysis rule allows, among other things, a VP in an active sentence, $[_{VP}V\, +\, [_{PP}P[NP]]]$, to be reanalyzed as $[_{VP}[_{V}V\, +\, P]NP]$. Case-marking in English crucially follows reanalysis and applies after all transformations, assigning Nominative to any NP governed by Tense, Accusative to any NP governed by V, and Oblique to any NP governed by P. *Wh*-forms are assigned the Case of the closest trace which bears its index. (12.40) rules out *what time did John arrive at t* because the trace receives oblique marking, violating (12.40a) and *arrive at* cannot be reanalyzed because *at what time* falls outside the VP. Sentences like *who did John talk to Harry about* are permitted because *about who* is a daughter of the VP.

While predicate reanalysis accounts for the markedness of the phenomenon of stranding by positing a marked operation, it does not explain why English but not other languages with free adpositions developed such an ad hoc operation. Also, (12.40) predicts that the Ps in P-PP constructions are subject to reanalysis as are the Ps in P-NP constructions; however, as we see in (12.39), they are not. The examples in (12.39) are taken from a footnote in Hornstein and Weinberg which intimates that they are the result of "dialect-specific variation" to be expected in a marked phenomenon. Finally, van Riemsdijk and others distinguish stranding by *wh*-movement from that found in pseudopassives, noting that predicate reanalysis applies to the latter but not the former. It seems that Dutch (van Riemsdijk), Icelandic (Maling and Zaenen 1985), and Norwegian (Christensen 1986, Lødrup 1991) do not allow genuine pseudopassives, thus exhibit only *wh*-movement stranding. This type of stranding is also less constrained in English than pseudopassive stranding, as (12.37–12.38) show. The job facing LMBM, therefore, is to account for the optional stranding accompanying *wh*-movement in the Germanic languages which exhibit it and the obligatory stranding in pseudopassives for English only.

The LMBM Solution

LMBM eliminates Case as a syntactic factor, replacing it with a system of adjectival grammatical functions uniting the grammatical effects of Case and theta roles in grammar. The morphological account requires no reanalysis for stranding in *wh*-movement and only slight reworking of reanalysis to account for English pseudopassives. At the point in derivation where NP- and *wh*-movement occurs, lexical items and grammatical functions are present without morphological form. *Who did John speak to* will have the base constituent structure illustrated in (12.41).

$$\begin{bmatrix} +\text{wh} \\ \text{Goal} \end{bmatrix} \quad \text{Syntactic (Inflectional)}\ \text{functions}$$

(12.41)   John [Past speak [NP]]

$$\begin{bmatrix} 3\text{rdP} \\ +\text{An} \end{bmatrix} \quad \text{Lexical (pronominal) func-}\ \text{tions}$$

(12.41) assumes that Object2 in English may be a preposition-marked NP, as already discussed.[7] Movement then rewrites (12.41) as (12.42):

$$\begin{bmatrix} +\text{wh} \\ \text{Goal} \end{bmatrix} \qquad \begin{bmatrix} +\text{wh} \\ \text{Goal} \end{bmatrix}$$

(12.42) $[NP_i]_{\text{COMP}}$ John [Past speak t_i]

$$\begin{bmatrix} 3\text{rdP} \\ +\text{An} \end{bmatrix} \qquad \begin{bmatrix} 3\text{rdP} \\ +\text{An} \end{bmatrix}$$

The grammatical and syntactic functions of the interrogative pronoun now are associated with the proper node; however, it is coindexed with its trace, giving the trace position access to the same functional information available to the AP. Coindexation is tantamount to simply copying this information to Comp, leaving the original behind rather than literally moving it (copying it to Comp and erasing it from VP). When (12.42) arrives at the MS-component, the spelling mechanism has four logical options, three of which are realized in English:

(12.43)   a.   John spoke to whom
        b.   To whom$_i$ did John speak e$_i$
        c.   Who$_i$ did John speak to e$_i$
        d.   *To did John speak who(m)

(12.43d) is ruled out under the assumption that movement is restricted to lexical XPs; functions move only if they are realized on a lexical item. (12.43d) is thus ruled out by independent constraints on movement. All other options occur in English. The reason adpositions generally follow their NP (PIED-PIPING) is that adpositions are Case function markers of NP under LMBM. They should therefore behave like Case endings and follow any NP which they mark for grammatical function. Case markers follow any NP which they mark because movement presumably copies all the morphological information in a node, leaving the MS-component with the decision as to where to phonologically realize features, individually or as a group.

P&P and other theories with LMH assume lexical adpositions in a class with verbs. Now, since V certainly may be "stranded" by NP movement, these theories predict P-stranding under normal conditions, hence require a special filter (12.40a) to prevent the unmarked case. Not only may V be stranded, V itself may move and strand its object in many languages, such as in German questions like *bringt Mark das Buch* = brings Mark the book, "is Mark bringing the book". If P is a lexical class whose transitivity is similar to that of verbs, as has been assumed at least since Jackendoff (1973), LMH theories must also explain why P does not similarly move and strand its object, as in **for the book was brought whom*. Since Ps and Case endings are both Case markers under LMBM, it predicts the unmarked phenomenon of adpositional pied-piping without special principles.

LMBM with the theory of primary and secondary grammatical functions outlined in the previous chapter also explains why PPs cannot be extracted from P-PP constructions. Under LMBM these constructions are actually P + P-NP constructions, with the dual Ps sometimes marking single functions, sometimes marking nested double functions. However either

P behaves in such a construction, the other P should behave the same—and so it does. NP may be extraposed from these constructions, but not the ostensible PP. The question facing LMBM is why some types of Case markers, that is, freestanding adpositions, are stranded in a few Germanic languages, when we would expect them to be morphologically fixed to their NPs like clitic adpositions and Case endings.

In order for a language to be a candidate for P-stranding, all its Ps must be potentially free morphemes, like those of English, rather than lexical or phrasal affixes. It follows that syntax must be capable of providing Ps with structural positions in AP. In nonstranding languages, Ps are clitics or endings which demand a phonological host; they therefore cannot occur in isolation. Russian, for example, has asyllabic Ps like *v, k, s* which are inarticulable without a syllabic host. Even accented Ps are associated indissolubly with some Case and must remain in the domain of the host of that Case's marker, the PP complement. Take the Russian preposition *ókolo* + Gen "around," as in *ókolo dóm-a* "around the house," for example. P is an overt extension of the Genitive Case marker, specifying one of that Case's functions and distinguishing it from others. Since the Genitive Case ending presupposes the P-representation of some noun, and since *okolo* is bound to its host expressing the Genitive, it must remain in the domain of that NP which bears the Genitive ending. To the extent that English Ps are not indissolubly conjoined with a phonologically marked Case, it conforms with the first constraint on stranding.

Evidence also indicates that the prevalence of absolutely free particles functionally and phonologically identical with free prepositions is related to the unusual freedom of English prepositions (Maling 1977). However, this part of the story remains far from complete. German has separable preverbs but no stranding; Norwegian has separable preverbs and exhibits stranding. No final answers to this question of Germanic grammar will be presented here. The important point is that not only does LMBM concede nothing vis-à-vis stranding to LMH, it structurally predicts pied-piping and rules out the extraction of PPs from complex PPs. When a complete account of stranding is finally achieved, it is much more likely that the framework of that account will be LMBM than LMH.

12.5 CONCLUSION

This chapter has raised persuasive evidence that PPs represent two distinct phenomena. Adjunct PPs are a functional category of APs whose head is a pronominal DAdj, a subset of A restricted to predicate and postnominal positions. Complement PPs, on the other hand, are Case-marked NPs. The Case-marked NPs are distinguished from adpositional APs in that they have no syntactic position for their Case-marking; rather, the MS-component inserts that marking in the form of a simple Case ending or a P + Case ending complex following the General Theory of Affixation (12.34). This means that the position of these Ps is predictable on a morphological basis alone by (12.34) and does not require a syntactic projection.

Perhaps the major attraction of this direction in the resolution of the adposition question is that it identifies the adjunct function with a single lexical class: adjectives. It is true that many languages, like English, allow NP attributive adjuncts such as *downtown renovation campaign committee*. In most inflectional languages, however, these nouns must be converted into RAdjs so that they may agree with their head noun. Since such agreement is not required of English, noun attributes may well be zero-marked RAdjs, all of which are derived from nouns. Whether the attributive nouns are in fact nouns or null-marked RAdjs is a question for future research, but even if we must concede them NPs, the range of possible lexical classes serving as adjuncts is significantly reduced by conflating AP, AdvP, and PP and identifying them principally with one functional category, DelP, and one lexical class, A.

Functional categories like DelP, DP, and IP are nothing but a syntactic means of introducing morphosyntactic category functions (features) into syntax. All GB theories now concede the necessity of these categories in addition to lexical classes. Aronoff (1993) and Halle and Marantz (1993) must be correct in claiming that syntax contains an independent morphosyntactic module which assigns these categories to functional projections. Functional projections conveniently provide positions for free morphemes, as chapter 15 will discuss in more detail.

Having established that Ps are Case markers in a class with declensional desinences, marking the same set of Case functions, we are now in a position to establish the ultimate conditions on functional L-derivation: the same set of Case functions marked by Case endings and Ps.

NOTES

1. Zwicky (1989: 87) points out that there is at least one "single-purpose, Adv-only lexeme", namely *soon*. He notes that *often* also appears to have the properties of an adverb. To the extent that predicate position is an indication of adjectivity, however, *soon* represents no radical departure from the norm; *my birthday is soon* is grammatical in many dialects, as is *my dental appointments are too often*.

2. See Kuiper (1987) for a more in-depth analysis of the entire class of *a*-adjectives. (12.2) is a sampling of about one third of this subclass of adjective currently in use.

3. Occasionally, ostensible Delimiters seem to occur in [Spec, PP]

position of these complement PPs: *a letter only to John.* However, these turn out to be instances of variable ordering. Notice that this phrase is synonymous with *a letter to only John.* The difference between the [Spec, PP] (Limitative) Delimiter and the [Spec, NP] Delimiter is semantically detectible in adverbal PPs *she went only up to the house* and *she went up to only the house.*

4. The fact that these Ps may be stranded as in *who is the picture of* and *who was the letter to* does not speak to the issue of their role in complements and adjuncts. The interpretation of Ps as clitics on complements and adjectival pronouns in adjunct phrases allows them to serve as surface markers of empty categories in whichever categorial role they serve. The crucial factor here is that in either service they are grammatical morphemes rather than lexemes and hence may be used as free or bound function markers.

5. Some of the secondary funcitons, for example, Prolative (*along, by*), Perlative (*through*), and Privative (*without*) do not obviously follow this pattern. Hence these rules of (12.28) reflect some parametrical flexibility. Archi and other Caucasian languages subordinate all the secondary functions available to the three primary spatial functions to Perlation, as well.

6. This section especially has benefitted from the comments of Joan Maling. The author is deeply grateful for the time and effort which she invested in reading several chapters of this book.

7. This book does not address the question of the distinction between the Indirect Object and Goal, instead combining the two functions to maintain clarity in discussions of other matters. Eventually this question will have to be sorted out, since the Indirect Object represents a type of Addressee function which is distinct in many parts of syntax from the directional Goal function.

Chapter Thirteen

The Unitary Grammatical Function Hypothesis

13.1 Constraints on Functional L-derivations: Background

Word Syntax constrains the semantic range of functional derivations to argument relations, the theta roles of subcategorization frames. The implication of section 7.5, however, was that noun incorporation is a variety of functional L-derivation determined by a much broader range of functions than is found in subcategorization frames. This chapter will argue that functional L-derivation is constrained by the same set of nominal functions that determine Case.

Appendix A represents a relatively complete list of the nominal grammatical functions correlated with their syntactic markings in English, Sanskrit, and Serbo-Croatian, illustrated with an example of each function determining a Serbo-Croatian functional L-derivation. The list itself is derived from a study of languages across all language stocks. Appendix A contains 44 relations, 22 primary functions and three primary spatial functions. The three primary spatial functions commonly combine with secondary spatial functions in accord with (11.17), producing complex functions such as [Origin [Subessive]] = *from + under,* [Locus [Subessive]] = *under,* [Goal[Subessive]] = *under.* The majority of languages with word formation derive words from only the most pragmatically useful of these functions. More are found in compounds than in simple L-derivations. Individual languages, therefore, do maintain further restrictions on this overall set of possibilities; further universal restrictions, however, are unlikely.

This chapter will assume that the functions catalogued in Appendix A determine the nominal inflection systems of all languages, as argued in chapters 10 and 11. This chapter and the next, then, will demonstrate that the same set of functions determines functional L-derivation in the following sense:

(13.1) *The number and nature of Case property functions and the functions of the functional L-derivation rules are both determined by the universal set of primitive grammatical relations listed in Appendix A.*

In other words, the system of functions listed in Appendix A operate at both the lexical and inflectional levels of grammar. This position will be called the UNITARY GRAMMATICAL FUNCTION HYPOTHESIS or simply UGF. UGF is the ultimate constraint on the functional L-derivations examined by Roeper and Siegel, Selkirk, Lieber, and Baker, and discussed in section 7.5. Examination of their work revealed that a looser set of constraints is required for functional L-derivations. UGF seems appropriate to the task.

Several problems previously obstructing the association of Case functions with L-derivations have now been obviated. The first problem was the assumption that thematic relations are semantic. Jackendoff (1990) removes theta roles altogether from grammar, accounting for them in the lexical entries of Vs and Ps (see also Dowty 1991). Chapter 9 argued that this approach to theta roles does not eliminate the need for a set of grammatical functions, since theta roles do not map isomorphically onto Case or Case functions, a point also made by Bresnan and Kanerva (1989). Chapters 10 and 11 showed that neither grammatical functions nor theta roles may be derived from lexical adpositions. Adpositions are a morphological phenomenon in a class with Case endings, in that they are pronominal function markers, not function bearers. Indeed, Case proper is a purely morphological phenomenon, present only in fusional synthetic languages; the universal aspect of Case systems is the system of nominal category functions.

13.2 THE HYPOTHESIS AND ITS PREDICTIONS

The type of L-derivation referred to as "functional" in chapter 7 differs from transposition and value switches in that it adds a meaningful element to the bases on which it operates. Functional derivation differs from the affective derivations in that it is capable of adding a wide range of meaning to the base lexeme. The meaningful elements added by functional derivation are grammatical relations: Subject, Object, Means, Locus, and so on, which are also the fundamental functions of the Case categories Nominative, Accusative, Instrumental, and Locative. A logical suspicion, then, is that functional L-derivation operates on whatever class these functions belong to.

The obvious point of departure for proving UGF is the wide range of correlations among the Case functions and word formation rules of IE languages. The IE correlations are set forth in Appendix A for Serbo-Cro-

atian, the contemporary IE language with arguably the richest word formation output. Once we examine the functions of L-derivation independent of
the more complex system of morphological marking, it becomes clear that
the range of correlation is too substantial to be considered coincidental.
However, this simple correlation alone does not prove that the relation is
causal. The next question is then, what sort of predictions emerge from
UGF beyond the correlations of Appendix A.

If L- and I-derivation were determined by the same system of grammatical functions, we would expect that (i) *if either has a subclassification
system, the system would be the same for both*. Since Case functions under
the present interpretation are subdivided into primary, primary spatial, and
secondary functions, the former two most often marked by endings alone
and the last usually marked by adpositions and endings or complex endings, we would expect to find a parallel subdivision among L-derivation
rules if the two are causally related. We would also expect, given integrated
morphology, instances where (ii) *the same morpheme marks L-derivations
and inflectional categories sharing an identical function*. The MS-component in this case would overlook the distinct lexical and syntactic derivational origins and mark the common function. Given the integrated morphological spelling component described in chapter 3, in languages with a
mixed inflection-adposition marking system, we would predict the possibility of a morpheme surfacing as both an affix and adposition in different
contexts, lexical and syntactic, respectively, marking the same functions.

Since morphemes frequently mark more than one function, as the Instrumental morpheme marks Means, Manner, and Subject, even if the
L- and I-derivations were distinguished by morphological marking, we
might reasonably expect instances of (iii) PARALLEL POLYSEMY, *where one
affix marks the same set L-derivation functions that are marked by some
single Case marker even though the affixes differ*, as in Means and Manner,
two common functions of the Instrumental, or the Dative functions, Goal
and Purpose. Finally, we would expect to find (iv) *typologically* and (v)
historically parallel development in lexical and inflectional derivation.
That is, typological differences in inflection should be reflected in L-derivation across languages, and historical similarities and differences in the
inflectional systems of language families should emerge analogically in L-
derivational development. Historically, Case functions which merge or
split over time should cause similar mergers or splits of derivational categories. (See Carstairs-McCarthy 1992a, chapter 5 for a discussion of the importance of diachronic proof.)

13.3 THE EVIDENCE

We find in the morphological data of synthetic languages widespread corroboration of all the predictions of UGF reviewed in section 13.2. The

remainder of this chapter will review a sampling of that corroboration (see Beard 1990 for details of one aspect of it, parallel polysemy).

13.3.1 Primary and Secondary Lexical Derivation Rules

The first prediction of UGF is that if inflectional functions are systematic, the same system should be evident among L-derivation functions. Indeed, Chapter 10 discovered that not all inflectional functions enjoy the same status in morphology. The NP complement functions tend to be marked by Case ending alone in Case languages and word order or a single P in isolating languages. Other functions tend to be marked by Case ending plus adpositions, or double adpositions in isolating languages. Chapter 10 referred to this distinction as the primary and secondary functions, respectively. If this functional dichotomy underlies the I-derivation system, we predict evidence of a similar phonological distinctions among L-derivations.

Indeed, in IE languages some lexically derived words are marked by suffix alone while others are marked by a suffix plus a prefix. Moreover, where the derived word is marked with a prefix, the prefix is often the same morpheme as the preposition marking the corresponding secondary inflectional function. At least 13 Serbo-Croatian morphemes mark the same function in both lexical and inflectional derivations, strong formal evidence that the paired functions are identical. Five are illustrated in (13.2).

(13.2)   a. nad-zem-ni kamen   nad zemlj-om
             'aboveground stone [tombstone]''   ''above the ground''
         b. među-grad-ski saobraćaj   među grad-ov-ima
             ''intercity traffic''   ''between cities''
         c. posle-diplom-ske studije   posle diplom-e
             ''postdiploma [graduate] studies''   ''after the diploma''
         d. bez-briž-an momak   bez brige
             ''carefree boy''   ''without (a) care''
         e. pod-ljud-sko biće   pod ljud-ima
             ''subhuman being''   ''below/beneath people''

The productivity of omissive morphology among L-derivation suffixes complicates the English data. The data is further beclouded by the habit of substituting prefixes borrowed from Latin or Greek for their Germanic correlates in derived words based on Latinate stems. However, the underlying pattern remains quite distinct. The selection in Table 13.1 is taken from Table 10.1.

The distinction between primary and secondary functions at both levels seems to hinge on the compositional complexity of the functions dis-

Table 13.1   The English Preposition-Prefixes

Preposition	Prefix	Function
a. with	co-worker, co-author	Sociative
b. before	fore-tell, pre-dispose	Anterior
d. behind	hind-sight, after-burner	Posterior
e. above/over	over-fly, super-class	Superessive
f. below/under	under-pay, sub-category	Subessive
g. across/over	cross-walk, over-pass	Transessive
h. between	between-class, inter-national	Intermediate
i. near/by	by-law, by-stander, ...?	Proximate
j. in	in-house, in-state, input	Inessive
k. on	on-line, on-shore, ...?	Adessive

cussed in chapter ten. Most of the secondary functions are based on the primary spatial functions, Locus, Origin, Goal, plus some more specified sublocative function. Anteriority thus implies Locus plus some function Ante "before, in front of". A few nonspatial secondary functions also are found; Privative (*without*), for example, implies Negated Possession. The motional semantics, omitted from Appendix A but distinctly marked in many Uralic and Caucasian languages such as Lezghian, involve similar combinations, for example Allative = [Goal[Addessive]] (*onto*). This interpretation accounts for the tendency to single-mark the primary functions and double-mark the secondary ones, whether by double suffixes (Lezghian, Archi, Basque) or adposition + suffix (German, Latin, Russian).

LMH is stressed to explain the absence of primary function prepositions like *of, at, for, with, to, from, by,* in its P + X "compounds." Serbo-Croatian *za,* for example, is productively used to mark the secondary function of Posteriority (13.3), but we never find it in L-derivations marking the primary Purposive function (13.4), even though it marks both functions in syntax.[1]

(13.3)   a. za gor-ama   za-gor-j-e
             "beyond the mountains" "transmontane region"
         b. za rek-om   za-reč-j-e
             "beyond the river"   "region beyond the river"

(13.4)   a. karte za igra-nj-e   (*za)igra-ć-e karte
             "cards for playing"   "(*for)playing cards"

b. hartija za pisa-nj-e   (*za)pisa-ć-a hartija
    "paper for writing"   "(*for)writing paper"
c. za pošt-u   (*za)pošt-ar-in-a
    "(in exchange) for the-mail" "(*for)postage"

While English L-derivations like *oversized* and *underprivileged* require the prepositions *over* and *under*, others, such as *blue-eyed* "with blue eyes" and *friendly* "like a friend," neither require nor allow the prepositions *with* and *like*, even though precisely these prepositional meanings are present in the L-derivates. Given *oversized* and *underprivileged*, why are *withblueeyed* and *likeboyish* impossible, and potential adjectives like *privileged* or *privilegy*, in the sense of "under-" or "overprivileged," all ungrammatical? Precisely those prepositions that mark the primary functions—*of, at, for, with, to, from*, and *by*—never appear in theoretically projected compounds, even though their functions do occur productively in L-derivates. No theory depending on prepositions and affixes defined as lexical items can capture either the unity of the functional system or the systematic gaps in the prepositional system used in L-derivation and compounding.

The argument for a causal relation between the systems of inflectional and L-derivation functions is weakened by an imperfect correlation between those inflections requiring a preposition and those derived words requiring a prefix. In the Slavic languages, some of the primary functions of L-derivation are now expressed by P + Case in the inflectional system. The *IE Purpose function (*IE Dative) is marked in contemporary Slavic languages with a combination P + Case: Serbo-Croatian *za njega*, Russian *dlja nego* "for him."[2] (13.4), however, shows that the corresponding L-derivation is unprefixed. The Locus function also requires prepositions: Serbo-Croatian *u grad-u* "in the city", but not the L-derivation: (∅)*pekarnja* "bakery." The Origin relation is now commonly marked by clitic prepositions, as in Serbo-Croatian *iz* + Genitive "out of, from," without any concomitant use of prefixes to mark the Originative lexical derivation rule.

(13.5) a. iz Beograd-a   beograd-ski   Beograd-an-in
            from Beograd   Beograd (A)   Belgradian (N)
        b. iz Amerik-e   američ-ki   amerik-an-ac
            from America   American (A)   American (N)

The primary Case functions do not automatically and directly determine the formal primary-secondary split among derived words in Slavic. But this difficulty is obliquely predicted by the Separation Hypothesis: if conditions on marking are generally independent of conditions on assigning functions, we would expect to find the inexact correlations between the two systems.

The key to this problem is related to another major argument for autonomous morphology: diachronic change of grammatical functions proceeds at a much slower rate than diachronic change of affixation. Table 13.2 illustrates this.

Table 13.2 Six Lexical Derivations in IE Languages

FUNCTION	English	French	Russian	Pashto
Subjective noun	writ-**er**	écriv-**ain**	pisa-**tel'**	lik-**unk-ay**
Locative noun	(ant-hill)	fourmi-li-**ere**	muravej-**nik**	meža-**tun**
Originative Adj	Chin-**ese**	Chin-**ois**	kitaj-**sk-ij**	čin-**āy-i**
Adverbalization	quick-**ly**	prompte-**ment**	bystr-**o**	žər-**∅**
Similitudinal Adj	child-**ish**	enfant-**in**	det-**sk-ij**	tifl-**āna**
Possessional Adj	sorrow-**ful**	doulour-**eux**	pečal'-**n-yj**	ɣam-**jən**

Table 13.2 represents five of the IE lexical derivation categories of Appendix A, plus the adverbal adjective, across four IE language families. Grammatical functions slowly realign under different Cases as the paradigm swells and contracts, but the affixes that realize these functions develop dramatically. While the core of underlying derivational functions has remained remarkably intact in the 4,000 years since *IE, only closely related languages share even partially similar markers. If the phonology of the affixation system changes more rapidly than the system of inflectional and lexical derivation functions, we would expect a closer correlation between the present-day division of primary and secondary functions than between the primary-secondary phonological markings.

The data of Table 13.2 do not reflect circumstances idiosyncratic to IE languages. The same effect may be found in relatively closely related non-IE dialects which have existed for a substantial period. Menovshchikov (1967: 53–54) notes that the markers of the Delimiter functions of the Yupik verb system differ radically from dialect to dialect, even though the functions themselves remain constant. Table 13.3 confirms the IE picture in Table 13.2: category functions exhibit much greater diachronic stability than the phonological material expressing them.[3]

Returning now to the IE languages, if we compare the *IE Case functions with the meanings of the lexical derivation rules in any contemporary IE language, we find a remarkable correlation (see Appendix A, the data in parenthesis). That is, the prefixless derived words in all contemporary IE

Table 13.3   Verbal Delimiter Functions in Three Yupik Dialects

Grammatical Function	Semantic Reading	Chaplin dialect	Naukan dialect	Imaklik dialect
Iterative	"again"	-lata	-vre	-igu
Microdeetic	"barely"	-vzi	-ləqja	-naʁlu
Conclusive	"finally"	-msax	-toχ	-toq
Tardive	"slowly"	-kəsta	-kəsita	-mawpa
Celerative	"fast"	-raxki	-ʁaχqu	-lutuq
Durative	"long time"	-ɬqiina	-kəŋa	. . .

languages correspond perfectly with the Sanskrit primary Case functions without any Case-sensitive adpositional. In *IE the conceptually simple primary functions were marked by the morphologically simplest means, while conceptually complex functions were marked by more complex morphology. The tendency continues today; however, in languages like English, where prepositions have taken over the marking of most of the primary functions as well as the secondary ones, this fact has been obscured.

13.3.2 Markers of Lexical and Syntactic Duplicates

We suspect that the same set of the functions operates at the L- and I-level and that both are marked by a single, integrated MS-component. Under these conditions, even languages which distinguish L-derivation from inflection should have contexts where the distinction breaks down and the marker normally used to express an I-function is used to express the same function at the L-derivation level. In these instances, the MS-component would ignore the distinction between L- and I-derivation and mark only the function in question.

Inflectional Markers Inside Lexical Markers

Obvious cases of inflectional endings in L-derivational service are found in Turkic, Mongol, and other languages (recall the Turkish and Basque examples of (12.20) and (12.21)). Buryat, a Mongol language spoken in Central Asia, exhibits inflectional affixes inside a denominal RAdj suffix, *-xi*. (13.6) illustrates nouns marked with the Locative *-DA* and the Instrumental ending *-gAAr*, preserving the grammatical function, Locus, at the L-derivation level (Sanzheev 1962, 115–16).

(13.6)   a. ara-da ''in/on the back''   ara-da-xi ''hind, rear''
         b. zaxa-da ''at the extremity''   zaxa-da-xi ''extreme''

    c. urd-uur "in the front"   urd-uur-xi "frontal"

    d. üglöö-güür "in the morning"   üglöö-güür-xi "morning's"

    RAdjs, then, are not derived from inflected forms, since L-derivation cannot apply after inflection in any current model of morphology. However, if Levi and Warren are correct (section 8.2.2), they are derived from a set of functions shared commonly by RAdjs and Case. Thus, while we certainly would expect the MS-component to distinguish RAdjs from Case, we might expect some languages to identify the common functions with identical affixes. Basque, Buryat, and Turkish seem to identify the common Locus function with a Locus marker common to both I- and L-derivation. The MS-modules of these languages identify the RAdjs as lexical rather than inflectional derivations by positioning the RAdj suffix (Buryat *-xi*, Turkish *-ki*, Basque *-ko*) outside the ostensibly inflectional markers. Since the Locus markers are invisible to syntax, they cannot in fact be inflectional and hence must be markers of Locus at both levels, marking L-derivation in these examples.

    Archi is a Caucasian isolate spoken in and around one village of the same name in Dagestan, USSR, by roughly 1,000 people. It possesses a nominal word formation suffix, *-an*, which attaches to nouns, converting them to other nouns denoting an indiscriminate class of objects (Kibrik et al. 1977: 90–91).

(13.7)   a. aq-li-ti-k "onto the foot" : aqǝltǝk-an "footwear"
             foot-ERG-ADES-GOAL
        b. lagi-l-a-k "into the stomach" : lagilak-an "snack"
             stomach-ERG-INES-GOAL
        c. qaq-a-∅ "on the back" : qaq-an "backpack"
             back-INES-LOC

    As in all the languages of Dagestan, Archi has a complex Case system with an especially elaborate set of 30 spatial Cases based on the Ergative stem (marked by *-li*). Locative functions like Adessive ("on"), Inessive ("in"), Subessive ("under"), Intermediative ("between"), may be combined with the directional functions Origin ("from"), Goal ("to"), Perlative ("through"), and Terminative ("up-to, as far as") in a manner similar to the Lezghian combinations of some of the same functions. In (13.7) we see these heavily inflected forms reflecting precisely the meanings associated with the Case markers, but in lexically derived nouns. Although the output in Archi is a noun rather than an adjective, the situation is the same that we find in Buryat. The nouns in (13.7) represent a kind of "relational noun" based on the grammatical functions, distinguished by the "inflectional" markers functioning here to mark L-derivations.

Dual Level Affixes

If L- and I-derivation operate on the same set of functions, and if the allomorphy of both is integrated and autonomous, we would expect instances where one affix alone marks the same function at both levels. In the IE languages it is common for the Present Active participle to serve as a marker of Subjective nominalization. The Active participle differs from the Passive in that it binds the Subject function of the underlying verb syntactically to the head N it modifies. Thus the Subject of *drench* in *drenching rain* is *rain*. The Subjective nominalization, as in English *drench-er*, also binds the Subject of its base. However, since participles come in Past, Present, and Future varieties, and since chapter 6 concluded that Tense is purely inflectional, participles must be I-derivations. The Subjective nominalization, however, is lexical because it does not preserve any verbal inflectional functions and its product possesses all the properties and attributes inherent to a noun: Number, Animacy, Gender, and Noun class.

Despite the crucial differences between participles and the Subjective nominalization, the Present Active participle ending is a common marker of Subjective nominalizations and the Past Passive participle doubles as an Objective nominalization. In French, for example, we find forms like those in (13.8):

(13.8) a. resist-er   resist-ant(e) "resisting; resistance fighter"
        b. resid-er   resid-ent(e) "residing; resident"
        c. émigr-er   émigr-ant(e) "emigrating; emigrant"

(13.9) a. émigr-er   émigr-é(e) "emigrated; emigre"
        b. employ-er   emploi-é(e) "employed; employee"
        c. évacu-er   évacu-é(e) "evacuated; evacuee"

(See also the Chukchee examples in 13.18.)

A common explanation of this phenomenon is that the nominalizations originate in a headless NP; that is, phrases parallel to *homme resist-ant* "resisting man". In contemporary terms we might refer to a null head adjunct, where the head contains all the requisite nominal features but no allomorphy. The problem is that null head adjuncts exist in addition to the nominalizations in (13.8–13.9). All adjectives in inflectional languages may be used alone as nominals but in a way which is purely syntactic, as the Russian and German examples in (13.10) illustrate:

(13.10) a. krasnyj   der Rote   "the red one (Mas)"
        b. krasnoe   das Rote   "the red one (Neu)"
        c. krasnaja   die Rote   "the red one (Fem)"
        d. krasnye   die Roten   "the red ones (Pl)"

These constructions, however, refer syntactically; they describe specific situations and do not name lexical categories. *Der Rote* does not refer to all red objects, only to a specific one recently mentioned. Like its English correlate, *the red one,* this form is nonreferential out of deictic context. *Resident* (13.8b), on the other hand, refers to the class of all objects who reside, just as the uncontroversial Subjective nominalization *lis-eur* "reader" refers to the class of all objects which read. (13.8–13.9), therefore, are not "adjectives used as nouns"; they are lexical nouns.[4]

13.3.3 Parallel Polyfunctionality

The literature has frequently noted the formal parallels between the Subjective and Instrumental lexical derivations in IE languages (Panagl 1975). Russian, for example, marks Subjective and Modalic nominalizations with the suffix *-tel'*, as Table 13.4 demonstrates.

Table 13.4   Russian Subjective and Modalic Nominalizations

Subjective	*Means*
čita-tel' "reader"	podogreva-tel' "heater"
uči-tel' "teacher"	krasi-tel' "colorant, dye"
stroi-tel' "builder"	uskori-tel' "accelerator"

Russian also marks both Passive Subject (13.11a) and Active Modalic functions (13.11b) with simple Instrumental endings as they were marked in *IE:

(13.11)   a. Ivan porazil   Boris-a   svo-im   um-om
             Ivan stunned Boris-Acc   REFLEX-INST wit-INST
             "Ivan stunned Boris with his wit"
          b. Boris byl poražën Ivan-om
             Boris was stunned Ivan-INST
             "Boris was stunned by Ivan"

Thus, the same affixes, those of the Instrumental, mark both Subjects and Means in the inflectional system and the same affix *-tel'* marks Subjective and Modalic derivates in the lexical derivation system, even though the sets of suffixes are different for L- and I-derivation. Beard (1990) provides many more examples and demonstrates how affixal polyfunctionality may even be predicted, given UGF.

13.3.4 Typologically Parallel Development: Ergative and Accusative

We have until now concluded that animate nominalizations like *bak-er* and *employ-ee* are Subjective and Objective. UGF predicts that these nominalizations derive from underlying grammatical categories, those of Subject and Object in Accusative languages. We have also assumed that the grammatical functions in Appendix A are universal; however, while Accusative systems mark Subject-Object, Ergative systems mark something more nearly like the semantic Agent-Patient. To the extent that Ergative languages mark Subject-Object relations distinctively, deverbal nominalizations should be similarly distinctive. The UGF hypothesis predicts that Ergative languages should exhibit Agent and Patient nominalizations, corresponding to the basic functions of the Ergative and Absolutive Cases, where the Agentive is crucially distinguished by its animacy.[5] Since the claim that the derivations in Accusative languages are in fact Subjective and Objective rather than Agentive and Patientive is itself controversial, evidence of this prediction might be taken as an effect of definition. There is, however, an uncontroversial test of the Accusative-Ergative distinction.

The reason that the Subjective nominalization is more productive than the Objective in Accusative languages is that the former logically has more potential referents. According to Plank (1979: 15), the Transitive Agent (= Subject) is the grammaticalized topic in Accusative languages. The referents of the Subject function comprise first arguments of Transitive and Intransitive verbs. Subjective nominalizations like *employer* (Transitive base), *sitter* (Intransitive base), and *loner* (QAdj or qualitative verb base) are more common in Accusative languages than objective nominalizations like *employee*, because the Subject function is possible with a larger number of verbal subclasses than the Object relation. In addition, the Subject is not restricted to animate terms, as is the Agent.

In Ergative languages the argument of Intransitive verbs is interpreted as the category which also includes the second arguments of transitives and the argument of QAdjs. In Plank's terms, the transitive Patient becomes the grammaticalized topic in Ergative languages. Here UGF predicts a predominance of L-derivations like *employee* (Transitive base), *escapee* (Intransitive base), and *absentee* (QAdj or qualitative verb base) for the same reasons. In Ergative languages we would expect (a) no Subjective nominalizations and (b) that Patientive nominalizations would outproduce Agentives, given the greater range of potential referents and the absence of the animacy constraint.

In Tongan, Lezghian, Gilyak, and Chukchee, the UGF prediction is precisely what we find. According to Churchward (1953: 240ff), Tongan, a split Ergative Polynesian language, has highly productive Locative, Possessional, and Patientive L-derivations, the latter marked most widely with the suffix *-(V)nga*.

(13.12) a. toe "to remain"   toe-nga   "a remainder"
         b. fotu "to appear"   fotu-nga   "appearance, countenance"
         c. taka "to go about   taka-nga   "a companion"
            together"
         d. takai "to roll,   takai-nga   "a roll, coil"
            coil"

Churchward lists no animate or inanimate L-derivations at all in his grammar or dictionary with this or any other suffix referring to the class of possible first arguments of an underlying Transitive verb. The closest approximation to Agentive L-derivates is a group of denominal animate nominalizations illustrated in (13.13). However, it is not clear that they are not compounds, since the ostensible prefix Churchward mentions, *fai,* is also a verb meaning "do."

(13.13) a. mākoni "radio"   fai-mākoni "radio operator"
         b. lēsista "register"   fai-lēsista "registrar"
         c. kalama "grammar"   fai-kalama "grammarian"
         d. fakatau "buy(ing)/sell(ing)"   fai-fakatau "merchant"

According to Gaidarov (1966) and Talibov (1966), Lezghian also contains no productive Subjective or Agentive deverbal L-derivations, though many Patientives and denominal Agentives emerge in their grammars. The productive suffixes *-Ac, -či, -Ak, -kar, -ban,* and *-q-an* attach to adjectives and nouns but apparently not to transitive verbs.[6]

(13.14) a. lap-u "lazy"   lap-uc "lazy bones"
         b. alḳ-un "be stuck to"   alḳ-ac "bed-ridden person"
         c. kukum-un "fester"   ḳm-ac "person with sickly face"
         d. qel "insult, spite"   qil-ec "obnoxious person"

(13.15) a. ɣu'rč "hunt (N)"   ɣu'rč-q-an "hunter"
         b. χpe (χeb) "sheep"   χpe-q-an "shepherd"
         c. čapla "left (A)"   čapla-q-an "left-hander"
         d. jaç "obesity"   jaç-q-an "fat person"

The evidence here parallels that of Tongan. Subjective deverbal nominalizations do not seem to exist, while Agentives are at best as marginal as Objectives in English. Rather, derivations referring to professions derive from forms which are by their nature generally Intransitive and nonagentive: adjectives or nouns.

Panfilov (1962: 43) claims that in Nivkh (Gilyak) "the possibility of deriving nouns of this semantic group [*nomina agentis*] with the suffix *-s* is

very limited; the instances of such derivations exhibit a unique character''
[author's translation]. But virtually all of his examples are in fact Patientives, that is, animate Subjects of Intransitive verbals or Objects of Transitive ones. Moreover, his characterization of -*s* fits the productive suffix -*k*
equally well.

(13.16) a. xrəɣrə-d′ ''serve''   xrəɣrə-s ''servant'' (who serves)
         b. jətŋu-d′ ''guard''   jətŋu-s ''a guard'' (who guards)
         c. xov-d′ ''wrap up''   xov-s ''package'' (which is wrapped)
         d. emq-t′ ''cut''   moq-s ''piece'' (which is cut off)
         e. pulkul-d′ ''be round''   pulku-s ''circle'' (which is round)
         f. per-d′ ''be heavy''   per-s ''weight'' (which is heavy)

(13.17) a. ŋarla-d′ ''be fat''   ŋarla-k ''fat person'' (who is fat)
         b. polm-d′ ''be blind''   polm-k ''blind person''(who is blind)

Skorik lists no Agentive nominalizations for Chukchee; however, he
devotes a separate chapter to NOMINAL PARTICIPLES (Skorik 1961: 345–
387) which productively fill that function. These ''participles'' derive from
nouns, adjectives, and verbs and may be used as Active participles or nominals (see 13.8 above).

(13.18) a. rəjuk ''to herd deer''   rəju-lʔ(ən) ''herding, herder''
         b. əʔtt-ən ''a dog''   əʔtt-lʔ(ən) ''having dogs, dog owner''
         c. gəteŋ ''be beautiful''   gətiŋ-lʔ(ən) ''beautiful, a beauty''

Skorik is struck by the fact that ''in the substantive meaning nominal participles emerge only independently—as names of persons'' (Skorik 1961:
346; author's translation). Thus, the attributives are not restricted to persons but the free Agentives are. The construction meaning ''herding dog''
may refer to a dog but the bare participle, which refers to a herder, does
not. I take ''personhood'' to be simply a stricter specification of the Agentivity which characterizes all these nominalizations. It certainly precludes
inanimate Subjective L-derivates like *sparkler, sizzler, sinker* based on this
derivation in Chukchee. The distinction between Ergative and Accusative
nominalizations predicted by UGF again appears in the data.

13.3.5 Historically Parallel Development: The Slavic Locative

The *IE Locative apparently marked Locus without any distinction between the specific functions Inessive ''in'' and Adessive ''on''. The Slavic
Locative, however, distinguishes the two Locus functions with two prepositions, the Inessive *u* + Loc ''in'' and the Adessive *na* + Loc ''on''. The
original Locus lost its unique marker and became a metaphoric function of

both Locative prepositions, as in Serbo-Croatian *u park-u* "in/at the park", *na polj-u* "on/at the field". When the Locative split, apparently, the secondary Inessive and Addessive functions were promoted to primary status, since they then bore the primary function metaphorically. In striking accord with the predictions of the UGF Hypothesis, the derivational system shifted in tandem with the inflectional, splitting the Locative nominalization in two only in the Slavic languages[7]. In no other non-Slavic language do we find the derivational distinction.

(13.19) a. raditi u "work in" rad-io-nica "workshop"
  a'. raditi na "work on" rad-il-išt-e "work site"

  b. kupati se u "bathe in" kup-ao-na "bathroom"
  b'. kupati se na "bathe on" kup-al-išt-e "bathing beach"

  c. vežbati se u "do gymnastics in" vežb-ao-nica "gymnasium"
  c'. vežbati se na "drill, practice on" vežb-al-išt-e "drill field"

The distinction is still productive not only in Serbo-Croatian, as demonstrated in (13.19), but also in Polish and Ukrainian; it is not productive in Russian today.

The correlate Origin functions did not split lexically, even though we find a parallel split of the Origin I-derivation *iz* + Gen "out of, from" and *sa* + Gen "off of, from", corresponding to the respective Locative functions represented by *u* and *na*.

(13.20) a. ići u škol-u biti u škol-i ići iz škol-e
  go in school + Acc be in school + Loc come out-of school + Gen
  "go to school" "be in school" "come from school"
  b. ići na pijac-u biti na pijac-i ići sa pijac-e
  go on market + Acc be on market + Loc come off-of market + Gen
  "go to the market" "be at the market" "come from the market"

Serbo-Croatian has not developed similar distinct Ablative L-derivations but retains one Originative L-derivation, as in *amerik-an-ac* "American, someone from America", *gor-ac* "mountaineer, someone from the mountains."

Two reasons for this asymmetry present themselves. The grammatical reason is that the Inessive and Adessive functions have been promoted to primary status within the Locative, while the Illative and Allative functions remain secondary. This is reinforced by the fact that the Locative Case has been retained in all Slavic languages while the Ablative, whose central function is Origin, has disappeared. The pragmatic reason is that the Ablative distinction has much less referential value for the language. While there may be a logical distinction between something which comes from inside America and something which comes down from a mountain, this amounts to little practically. We do not find instances where the distinction is as crucial as that between a place in which one works and a place on which one works.

13.3.6 The Last Transposition

UGF is intended to apply to verbal as well as nominal functions. The PARTICIPIAL ADJECTIVES, described in terms of transposition in chapter 8, may also be explained in terms of grammatical functions operating at both lexical and syntactic levels. Section 8.2.5 did not close the question of deverbal adjectival transposition but promised to return to it in this chapter. Now is the time to reconsider the whole issue of the so-called participial adjectives. Recall that it is quite common for languages to have what seem to be lexical versions of the Active and Passive participles. They are commonly called the ''Agentive'' and ''Patientive'' adjectives but will be called ''Subjective'' and ''Objective'' adjectives here since, like the Subjective and Objective nominalizations, their reference need not be animate, as the referent of Agents usually is. Now consider the examples of the Active participle and Subjective QAdj presented in Table 8.3, reiterated here as Table 13.5. In Table 13.5 the difference between the lexically derived adjective and the syntactic participle is marked by a different series of affixes added to most Latinate stems, while -*ing* marks all participles. Participles, recall, are distinguished by their incompatibility with the ad-

Table 13.5 (8.3)   Subjective Qualitative Adjectives and Active Participles

Affixes	Subjective Adjective	Active Participle
Distinct	is (very/un)product-ive is (very/un)repent-ent is (very/un)complement-ary	(not) produc-ing (very much) (not) repent-ing (very much) (not) complement-ing (very much)
Same	is (very/un)surpris-ing is (very/un)excit-ing is (very/un)mov-ing	(not) surpris-ing (very many) (not) exciting-ing (very much) (not) mov-ing (very much)

jectival prefix *un-* and adjectival intensifiers like *very*; they require *not* and *very much/a lot* (Borer 1990). Since it is a QAdj, the adjective but not the participle also compares and nominalizes (*more productive, productivity* versus **more producing (it), *producingness*).

Table 13.6 demonstrates that the evidence for a similar division is found among Passive participles and Objective QAdjs, except that the Objective QAdj does not differ at all allomorphically from the corresponding Passive participle in English. Even the most idiosyncratic affixes are used without exception to mark L- and I-derivations based on the same function. All other syntactic and semantic differences are present, however.[8]

Table 13.6 (8.4)   Objective Qualitative Adjectives and Passive Participles

Adjectives	*Participles*
is (very/un) surpris-ed	(*very/not) surpris-ed (very much)
is (very/un) mov-ed	(*very/not) mov-ed (very much)
is (very/un) bent	(*very/not) bent (very much)
is (very/un) swoll-en	(*very/not) swoll-en (very much)

Again, the adjectives in Table 13.6 reflect lexical properties, while the participles all possess the properties of syntactic descriptions.

Since all their properties are syntactic, the participles must be generated by syntactic rules, whether "move α" (Babby 1973, 1975) or the simple insertion of Vs in A nodes (Beard 1981), a form of syntactic transposition. The lexical treatments of Past participles by Bresnan (1982b), Lieber (1981), Sproat (1985: 306–312), Levin and Rappaport (1986) do not account for the semantic differences between participles and adjectives. Levin and Rappaport, for example, explain the difference between the participles and adjectives in Table 13.6 as differences between verbs and adjectives. However, while participles do have verbal functions in such constructions as the English Progressive and Perfective, they also serve adjectivally, and it is the adjectival functions of participles which parallel those of the Subjective and Objective QAdjs.

Since the evidence for functional L-derivations is overwhelming, and since Subject and Object are grammatical functions, it is impossible to exclude the possibility of functional derivations operating over Subject and Object features. Chomsky (1992) has joined the advocates of Relational Grammar, LFG, and HPSG in introducing Subject and Object projections in deep structure. Chapter 14 will demonstrate how L-derivation rules may operate over deep structure to generate precisely the range of L-derivation meanings found in the data. Thus, a plausible account of participles and participial adjectives is that both are generated from Subject and Object functions, the former by syntax, the latter by the lexicon.

The final question, of course, is this: if the participial adjectives may be explained as either transpositions or functional L-derivations, how do we decide which account is preferable? The answer to that question is that we do not have to decide. Recall the discussion in section 9.4.2, where it was noted that the Possessional and Similitudinal adjectives could be explained both as a single t⟋osition and as two functional derivations based on the Possession ⟋ ⟋anner functions. Beard (1993) speculates that the most highly prod ⟋e L-derivations, as well as those most likely to remain when morphol ⟋al systems deteriorate, will be those which are both semantically and g ⟋matically generable in this way. In other words, while the set of categ ⟋s in Appendix A is the ultimate constraint on L-derivation, and the ⟋e lexical classes, N, V, and A, represent the ultimate constraint on tr ⟋position, derived lexemes which may be generated both by transpositio⟋ ⟋nd L-derivation are materially more productive than those which may b⟋ ⟋enerated by only one means.

This is the sit ⟋ion which we again see in the participial adjectives, the Subjective an⟋ ⟋bjective QAdjs; they are predicted both by transposition and by the f⟋ ⟋tions Subject and Object in Appendix A under UGF. It follows that the⟋ ⟋djectives are much more likely to be found in languages than are Purpo⟋ ⟋, Comitative, or Modalic QAdjs; moreover, they should be much more⟋ ⟋oductive. This conclusion supports the Word Syntax position that nom⟋ ⟋lizations with functions corresponding to subcategorized arguments or⟋ ⟋ntrolled by ECP are far more likely to occur than adverbial L-derivation⟋ ⟋For this reason, Beard (1993) concludes that both Word Syntax and LM⟋ ⟋ are correct on this point.

13.4 SUFFICIENT CONDITIONS

We have now established that the functions of Appendix A do determine both inflectional and some L-derivational functions. An equally important question, however, is whether all the functions of all L-derivations not determined by lexical categories, like Number and Gender, fall within the range of grammatical functions. In other words, are these conditions sufficient as well as necessary to define the range of functional L-derivations? If we extend the term to include all grammatical functions, verbal as well as nominal, they do seem to be.

13.4.1 Potential Objective Adjectives like **Breakable**

IE languages generally exhibit a Potential Objective adjective like English *breakable* ''can be broken''. Potentiality is a fundamental Modal function expressed in English by the auxiliaries *can* and *may*. Indeed, examples like (6.14b), *John plays the piano,* suggest that Potentiality is a modality implicit in all verbal meanings. If auxiliaries were lexemes rather than grammatical morphemes, this adjective might represent an exception to UGF. The strong version of LMBM, however, with its clear distinction of closed- and open-class items, treats auxiliary verbs as grammatical morphemes, differing only in the predictable ways in which a free form differs from a bound one. Their functions are thus fair game for UGF.

Puzzles do remain, however. It is not clear why we find Potential involved in L-derivation but apparently not Obligative, Optative, Subjunctive. Why we find a Potential Objective adjective in IE languages but no distinctively marked Potential Subjective is not totally clear; however, a reasonable estimation is that this L-derivation represents another instance of derivational overlap. This time the Subjective QAdj overlaps the Potential Subjective function, so that, for instance, *deceptive* means "(tends to) deceive" and includes "may/can deceive" in a way that *deceived* does not include *deceivable*, rendering it redundant. Another explanation virtually indistinguishable from the first is that both derivations do exist; however, because of the functional and semantic similarity, the MS-component does not formally distinguish them. Little more on the subject can be said without further investigation. UGF only predicts the range of potential derivational functions from among which actual L-derivations of language L may be chosen; it does not predict exactly which will be chosen and used in specific languages.

13.4.2 Nouns like Marxism

Other ostensible exceptions generally turn out to be misinterpreted L-derivations or compounds. Derivates on *-logy*, *-graphy*, and the like, behave more like NEOCLASSICAL COMPOUNDS (Bauer 1983: 213–16) than N + Suf derivates. Beard (1981: 225–26) suggests that derivates on *-ism*, for example, *Marxism*, might in fact be compounds rather than L-derivates meaning "philosophy or belief in N" in English, since *ism* is now listed as an independent noun in all dictionaries. UGF does predict that a nonexpressive derivation not controlled by some grammatical function must be eliminated. Reanalysis into a compound is a highly probable method of elimination in such Cases.

Another tack is also available to UGF. Beard (1984) assumes that proper nouns like *Marx* are subject to a performance process known widely as COMMONIZATION, which applies to proper names referring to people distinguished by a special attribute such as the special property distinguishing Napoleon discussed in chapter 9. This feature defines the semantic domain along which a person is evaluated for appropriateness of a commonization, for example, *he is a (young) Marx* is true if the referent reflects the property of Karl Marx which distinguishes Marx from other people, that is, his interpretation of capitalism.

Such commonizations and other common nouns are then subject to the Similitudinal adjectivization also discussed in chapter nine. Parallel to *friend* : *friendly, boor* : *boorish* we derive the adjectives of (13.21):

(13.21) a. (a) Marx   Marxist (A)   *Marxistry
         b. (a) Darwin   Darwinist (A)   *Darwinistness
         c. (a) Nixon   Nixonian (A)   *Nixonianity

Notice that the resultant adjectives here are not subject to the highly productive deadjectival nominalization productively marked by *-ness* in English: *Marx-ist (A)* : **Marx-ist-ness*, even though they fit the description of true adjectives. However, this presents no problem to theories based on autonomous morphology, so long as we can find some affix marking the predicted nominalizations of these adjectives.

An interesting peculiarity of the nominalization of Similitudinal adjectives based on [+Human] nouns discussed in section 9.4.2 is that their meaning names the special characteristic which distinguishes the [+Human] noun in their base. Just as *friendliness* is that property distinguishing friends, and *boorishness* is that property distinguishing boors, the special characteristic of Marx which distinguished him is his interpretation of capitalism, i.e. his *Marxism*. *Darwinism* is that special attribute which distinguishes Darwin and *malapropisms* constitute the attribute which distinguishes Mrs. Malaprop. It is therefore a straightforward matter to derive the nouns on *-ism* from the QAdjs on *-ist* so long as the affixation is separate from the L-derivation. Separation in this case allows the MS-component to insert either *-ist,* if only adjectival features are present, or *-ism,* if adjectival and nominal features are present in the L-derivation.

This section does not cover all the possible L-derivations which ostensibly fall outside the UGF Hypothesis. Instead, it has examined two typical types of apparent exceptions to the hypothesis and has demonstrated how they are explained within the LMBM framework. By and large, if the correlate inflectional function is properly interpreted and compared with the potential meaning of the appropriate L-derivation, UGF works. L-derivations with meanings which lie outside the range of grammatical functions pass rather quickly from the use. This was the case with the so-called ''*-in*'' derivations of the '60's: *sit-in, love-in, be-in.* Otherwise, they are reanalyzed as compounds, the suffix entering regular usage as a fully fledged lexeme.

13.5 CONCLUSION

This chapter has attempted to establish the ultimate constraint on perhaps the largest class of L-derivations, the functional L-derivations, those associated with the basic grammatical functions of nouns and verbs. UGF claims that both L- and I-derivation are restricted to these functions, that these functions are available to both the lexicon and syntax (inflection). The few derivational functions which do not ultimately conform to the predictions of UGF are explained in the main by transposition, expressive derivation, or the value switches described in previous chapters.

Recent research on these derivational types in the P&P framework assumes that the deverbal derivations are constrained by the subcategorization frames of the base or the ECP applied to those functions which lexical items subcategorize. These are generally taken to include at most Subject, Object, and Goal. The research upon which this book is based found a much larger range of functions represented in L-derivation; these functions are listed in Appendix A. It is true that Subjective and Objective nominalizations occur more frequently than L-derivations based on other functions. Under LMBM these salient derivations may be generated both by transposition, assuming featural composition, and by L-derivation operating on the grammatical functions Subject and Object. If such simultaneous dual derivation accounts for the particularly high productivity of these forms, then both the advocates of Word Syntax and LMBM are correct on this point.

NOTES

1. Recall also from section 10.3.2 that prepositions in these derivations cannot be considered constituents of compounds because they lack interfixes in languages which maintain interfixes.

2. "*IE" will be used here to refer to the protolanguage of all IE languages. "IE" is used to refer to the contemporary members of the family.

3. Yupik is spoken in several dialects on the Chukotka Peninsula. The largest enclave, comprising about 550 speakers residing to the south of the peninsula, speaks the Chaplin dialect. Two smaller groups in the north speak the Naukan and Imaklik dialects. The former group comprised about 350 and the latter, about 100 speakers in the 1960s.

4. This is why they are listed in the dictionary, the official list of names, but those like (13.10) never are.

5. This chapter has nothing to say about the actual nature of the direct functions in Ergative languages; the terms "Agent" and "Patient" are used here heuristically because they are familiar terms which approach in meaning the major functions of "Ergative" and "Absolutive" Cases. The assumption here is simply that there exist two functions similar to traditional concepts of "Agent" and "Patient" in Ergative languages at the

same level as "Subject" and "Object" in Accusative languages. Whether they are semantically reducible to Subject and Object is also irrelevant to the arguments of this chapter. A possible third type of Case system, which Mithun (1991) calls ACTIVE/AGENTIVE, could not be incorporated in this study.

6. The initial suffix in the last complex of (13.21), *-q*, serves also as a Locative Case suffix meaning "at, by," leading Gaidarov to believe that these derivations are based on inflected stems. Within the framework advocated here, however, and in the absence of any syntactic motivation for Locative in this L-derivation, it may be interpreted as just another multifunctional, multilevel affix, whose presence in this instance, given its ostensible semantic vacuity, is arbitrary.

7. The morphological complex between the root and the affixes in (13.20) is the verb theme, /i/ or /a/, plus the morpheme *-l*, which is replaced by *-o* except before vowels. Recent neologisms like *general* : **generao* (N) "general"; *generalni* : **generaoni* (A) "general" suggest that this replacement is a phonological rule recently become morphological.

8. They do, however, in other languages such as Bashkir, for example. See n. 10, p. 203 for an example.

Chapter Fourteen

The Base Rule Theory

14.1 INTRODUCTION

Having examined evidence that a fixed set of grammatical functions determine both L- and I-derivation, we need next to ask: how do the specific operations of L- and I-derivation feed on the same set of functions, yet maintain independent inflectional and lexical attributes? The answer to this question relies on a framework in which the Case functions are simultaneously accessible to both lexical and inflectional operations and which at the same time preserves the distinctive outputs of the lexical and syntactic modules. The strong LMBM position developed here has maintained the strictest boundaries between the lexicon and syntax, and between these and the semantic module. Mapping between all modules is regulated by algorithmic correspondence rules, allowing for the consistent though asymmetric relations between the categories and functions of distinct modules that we have seen time and again. The ideal would be to maintain this distinction in the strictest sense. But then how do both the lexicon and syntax bleed the same set of functions? The answer proposed here is that the functions themselves are the output of a third module which feeds both the lexicon and syntax: the base.

14.2 THE HISTORY OF BASE RULES

The only viable means for expressing the identity of L- and I-derivational functions is what Botha calls THE BASE RULE THEORY (Botha 1980; 1981). According to Botha, the base generates syntactic structures whose nodes bear the morphosyntactic categories demanded by the work of Aronoff (1993), Don (1993), Halle and Marantz (1993), Szymanek (1985), and others, but these are subject to lexical as well as inflectional rules. L-rules transform certain types of underspecified phrases into simple and compound derived words, while movement rules transform them into S-structures. In my own variant (Beard 1981, 1988), the base is a general grammatical component, a categorial component which accounts for all the grammatical relations of language common to syntax, inflection, and the lexicon. Only after lexical selection are lexical and syntactic structures distinguished.

The purpose of the Base Rule Theory is to account for simple and compound derivations with a single set of principles. The next section explores approaches toward achieving this end.

14.2.1 Simple and Compound Derivation

The detail of Botha's theory was aimed at the question of the relation of simple and compound derivations. Roeper and Siegel (1978) had claimed that deverbal synthetic compounds are derived by suffixation rules distinct from those rules which produce simple derivations with the same suffixes. They supported their claim by citing compounds for which no simple correlate is attested, as in *church-goer*, for which, according to Roeper and Siegel, no simple correlate, *goer*, "exists".[1] The compounding rules, with an empty frame for an attribute noun, must be distinguished from the simple derivation rules which do not bear such a frame. This conclusion is forced by Roeper and Siegel's First Sister Principle, which holds that the first sister of a subcategorization frame must be satisfied within a synthetic compound (see section 7.5.1 for details). If a verb like *carry* subcategorizes for an obligatory Object NP, that argument must be satisfied in any lexical derivation. Thus *rug-carrier* is legitimate but *carrier* alone should not be. In order to avert contradictory evidence such as the common use of nouns like *carrier,* Roeper and Siegel claimed that simple lexical derivations are generated by rules with conditions independent of those determining synthetic compounds.

Botha (1984: 17–19) began his case against this COMPLEXITY BASED lexical rule typology proposed by Roeper and Siegel by pointing out that whether a form "exists" is untestable; whether it is attested, or FAMILIAR in Meijs' terminology (Meijs 1975), is grammatically irrelevant, of no more importance to morphology than to syntax. Morphology, like syntax, describes the range of grammatically potential forms; it does not presuppose knowledge of attested derived forms (Corbin 1987 makes the point most elegantly). If we postulate pairs of affixes, one for simple, the other for compound derivations, the affixes in such pairs would not differ from each other in any respect: not phonologically, allomorphically, or semantically. No basis exists, therefore, for serious consideration of synthetic compounds and simple derivations as anything other than a single set of L-derivations which permit an optional modifier.

The result of Botha's critique of Roeper and Siegel is that simple derivations and synthetic compounds bearing identical affixes now may be assumed to be the output of single operations, allowing optional modifiers, on base lexemes. Botha's simplification implies that functional relations like Subject, Object, Means, in synthetic compounds are the same as those in simple derivations. However, their origin cannot be the subcategorization frames proposed by Roeper and Siegel, since most of the functions found in functional L-derivations are not subcategorized (section 7.5.1). The alternate source is the base component.

14.2.2 Botha's Version of the Base Rule Theory

Despite the criticism by Hoeksema and others, the most promising approach to a solution of the problem of this chapter remains the Base Rule Theory. Botha's theory, which he restricts to Afrikaans, comprises two basic hypotheses: the Deep Structure Hypothesis and the Affixation Hypothesis, quoted from Botha (1981: 5) in (14.1) and (14.2), respectively.

(14.1) THE DEEP STRUCTURE HYPOTHESIS:
Afrikaans synthetic compounds have as their bases syntactic deep structures which are generated by independently motivated rules.

(14.2) THE AFFIXATION HYPOTHESIS:
The rules by means of which Afrikaans synthetic compounds are formed on the basis of deep structure phrases are affixation rules which (i) are also used for the formation of simple derived words, and which (ii) apply in accordance with proper constraints.

The Affixation Hypothesis makes it clear that Botha is adapting his assumption to the Lexicalist Hypothesis, so that compounds are derived by the same rules which derive simple forms. However, the Affixation Hypothesis also establishes Botha's adherence to LMH, since his derivation rules are themselves affixation rules. Obviously, this aspect of his theory must be materially readjusted in light of the evidence against LMH raised in the preceding chapters of this book. Before adjusting the Base Rule Theory to LMBM, however, let us examine Hoeksema's criticisms of it to see whether they may be set aside.

14.2.3 Hoeksema's Criticism of the Base Rule Theory

Hoeksema (1985) presents two fundamental criticisms of the Base Rule Theory: (i) the Base Rule Theory introduces so much abstraction as to render the theory unfalsifiable and (ii) in order to work outside Afrikaans, the theory requires T-rules hence does not achieve one of its primary goals, a theory simpler than that afforded by Word Syntax.[2] Let us examine these criticisms individually to estimate their real impact on the Base Rule Theory.

Abstractness

Hoeksema claims that the most convincing argument for phrasal origins of derived words are "compounds" which preserve their grammatical morphemes:

(14.3)   a. agter-die-muur rook-er "behind-the-wall smoker"
          b. laag-bij-de-grond-s "low-at-the-ground-AFF, vulgar"
          c. laat-in-die-bed-kom-ery "late-to-the-bed-com-ing"

Yet Botha's theory excludes these forms as ungrammatical because they contain grammatical morphemes which are not available to the base module at the moment lexical affixation takes place. If grammatical morphemes are not present in the base module, how are these constructions explained?

English, like Afrikaans, allows PPs to serve marginally as attributive adjectives, as (12.19), reintroduced here as (14.4) for convenience, demonstrates.

(14.4)   a. sales over the counter   a′. over-the-counter sales
          b. activity behind the scenes   b′. behind-the-scenes activity
          c. reductions across the board   c′. across-the-board reductions
          d. a dress off the shoulder   d′. an off-the-shoulder dress

However, we never find fully productive paradigms like (14.5) and (14.6) among these forms, as (14.7) and (14.8) illustrate.

(14.5)   a. lion-hunter
          b. tiger-hunter
          c. elephant-hunter

(14.6)   a. lion-hunter
          b. lion-trainer
          c. lion-tamer

(14.7)   a. #over-the-counter
          b. *at-the-counter
          c. *behind-the-counter

(14.8)   a. #over-the-counter
          b. *over-the-table
          c. *over-the-garage

The acceptable forms in (14.7) and (14.8) are marked with a pound sign to indicate that it is not clear that these constructions are grammatical. The crucial fact about (14.4) is that they are idioms; *over-the-counter sales* is based on an idiom since **over-the-counter handshake, *over-the-counter picture* are all unacceptable in formal or colloquial English, even though *they shook hands over the counter* and *they hung the picture over the counter* are perfectly acceptable.

We concluded in section 12.2.2 that idiomatization stimulates the conversion of PPs into simple As. PPs which idiomatize reduce semantically to simple adjectives and tend to behave more like simple adjectives syntactically than productively generated PPs. This allows them to be moved to attributive position, a position from which PPs and other DAdjs are usually proscribed. This hypothesis is supported by marginal appearances of idiomatized PPs in other adjectival positions, such as in the predicate (14.9a), with adjectival Delimiters (14.9a), and in Comparative structures (14.9b). Productive PPs are unacceptable in any of these positions (14.9c):

(14.9)   a. ?Her dress was very "off-the-shoulder"
         b. ?He was so "off-the-wall"/"off his rocker", I couldn't believe it
         c. *He was so off-the-road/off-the-chair, I couldn't believe it

That these collocations might be acceptable but not grammatical is reflected in their spelling: either the constituents of the phrase are connected by hyphens, the phrase is set in quotation marks, or both. The adjectivized PPs are thus explained by the general AP structure of PPs and the nature of lexical idiomatization in performance.

Lexical Movement

Hoeksema next raises a point about the order of the lexemes in synthetic compounds. Botha derived deverbal compounds like Afrikaans *leeu-byter* "lion-biter" from the Afrikaans base structure [leeu$_{NP}$[byt]$_V$]$_{VP}$. Afrikaans being an SOV language, the order of the Object noun and verb remains the same in deep and surface structure and is the same in compounds and in phrases. Hoeksema notes that in the corresponding English compound the order of the verb and its Object is reversed from that of the phrase: *lion-biter* : [[bite]$_V$lion$_{NP}$]$_{VP}$. To Hoeksema's mind, a transformational account like that of Roeper and Siegel is still required if Botha's approach is to be universal.[3]

In fact, a modifier may occupy only two positions in relation to its head: it may precede or succeed it. Either position causes problems for the affixation of synthetic compounds, assuming that spelling must apply to the head of a compound. This assumption has been suggested recently by Hoeksema himself and Stump. Hoeksema (1985) proposed that at least some morphological rules are HEAD OPERATIONS. Head operations represent a constraint on the morphology of compounds such that rules of inflectional spelling apply to the head of the compound even though the semantic scope of inflectional categories is the compound as a whole. The morphological spelling of the Past Tense, then, applies only to the head of *understand*, producing *understood*. The semantic scope of Past, however, is the entire word. It follows that in a morphosemantic mismatch like *unhappier*, the comparative suffix attaches to the head, *happy*, even though its semantic scope includes the entire adjective *unhappy*.

Stump (1991) extends Hoeksema's insight with his H(EAD)-APPLICATION DEFAULT. Stump argues that the appearance of inflectional markers inside L-derivational markers supports Hoeksema's principle; moreover, as the name of Stump's variant implies, head application is the default. The ordering of inflectional markers inside L-derivational markers, such as the Preterite affix in Sanskrit which occurs inside the preverbs (for example, *pari-ṇayati* "he marries" : *pary-a-ṇayat* "he married"), reflects the operation of inflectional morphology on the head even when the morpheme's logical scope encompasses parts of the derivation on either side of it. Indeed, there is evidence of conflicts between restrictions on affixation and this constraint that accounts for null morphology on compounds and for the distribution of compound constituents including some affixes.

To get at these principles of distribution, let us begin with a strong version of Hoeksema's principle friendly to the General Theory of Affixation, say, (14.10).

(14.10)   THE HEAD SPELLING DEFAULT

All morphological spelling applies to the phrasal or morphological head of an L-derivation.

That is, in the unmarked case, morphological spelling applies to the lexical peripheries of phrasal heads. The morphological head of a simple L-derivation is always the lexeme or, more precisely, the P-representation of the lexeme. Compounds are either coordinative or subordinative, and the latter comprise minimally two constituents whose relation is that of a phrasal head and modifier. A modifier is the correlate of a base structure complement or adjunct. In the unmarked case, if the compound is synthetic, the morphology is attached to the phrasal head, as in *light-headed, truck-driver, fast-baking*.

Syntactically and semantically, the relation of *lion* to *bite* is that of a complement to its head. Lexically, the relation of *lion* to *biter* is that of a modifier to its head. In both instances *lion* is subordinate to *bite*. Let us suppose that rather than a syntactic projection, some independent principle positions all English, Afrikaans, and Dutch lexical and syntactic modifiers before their heads, if they consist of a single lexical item. This rule would be of the sort of late ordering rule Chomsky (1981) refers to, or a linear precedence rule in HPSG terms.

If modifier position were determined by independent principles, we would have an explanation of why languages generally position nominal and verbal modifiers both before and after their heads, though usually in a principled way. Two positions are logically possible and both are used; however, those languages which restrict single-item syntactic modifiers to pre-head position will limit lexical modifiers to the same position if the rule is general within any specific language. Those which order single attributes after their head would be expected to restrict lexical modifiers to that position. Let us next examine the question of how such a principle would interact with the Head Spelling Default (14.10).

If a language positions lexical modifiers in NPs and noun compounds before the head, no conflict with (14.10) arises if the language also suffixes. Since the compound head lies to the right of the modifier, and since suffixes attach to the right, the head may be suffixed. If, however, such a language prefixes its synthetic compounds, a conflict will arise if it positions its modifiers before the head, since prefixes would have to attach to the modifier. If a language generally situates modifiers after the head, no conflict arises with prefixing; the modifier will not be situated to the left of the head where prefixes attach. However, if the language supports post-head modifiers and suffixes, a conflict will arise, since any suffix would have to be added to the modifier.

Where conflicts arise between head-spelling and lexical modifier positioning, the alternatives are to (i) affix the head internally, (ii) affix the modifier, (iii) forego compound L-derivation, or (iv) forego affixation. Since the first alternative violates lexicalism, the second violates the Head Spelling Default, and the third would seriously curtail lexical productivity, we would predict that the fourth alternative would be prominent across languages: modifier-affixation conflict will be resolved most often by omissive marking on synthetic compounds.

We have already examined some suffixing Indo-European languages which place their nominal modifiers before the head and follow the same pattern in their synthetic compounds. Regardless of whether the languages are SOV (German, Afrikaans) or SVO (English, Russian), the order of the constituents in compound nouns is modifier + head if that is the order of constituents in NPs with a single, unmodified attributive adjunct. French, however, is a predominantly suffixing language which places its lexical nominal modifiers in postnominal position, as in *une femme formidable* "a formidable woman". French, for example, suffixes its Subjective and Instrumental nominalization, as (14.11) indicates.

(14.11) a. essuy-eur "wiper"
         b. attrap-eur "cheat, trickster"
         c. coup-eur "cutter, cutting machine"

These two tendencies present a conflict to the Head Spelling Default in the case of synthetic compounds. The prediction then is that French Subjective and Instrumental compounds like *lion-biter* and *wire-cutter* will not be affixed.

French resolves the conflict exactly as predicted; that is, it omits suffixation on such compounds rather than affixing the modifier. Not only does it do this for V + N compounds such as those in (14.12), it responds in the same way for V + A compounds (14.13). Compare (14.11) with (14.12) and (14.13).

(14.12) a. essui-glace = wipe-glass "glass wiper"
　　　　　b. attrape-nigaud = trap booby "booby trap"
　　　　　c. coupe-fil = cut wire "wire-cutters"

(14.13) a. gagne-petit = earn-little "low wage earner"
　　　　　b. couche-tard = go-to-bed late "late bed-goer"
　　　　　c. lève-tôt = rise-early "early riser"

The French data is not coincidental. Yoruba, which uses the same head + modifier order as French, incurs no conflict since it is a primarily prefixing language. Notice first that lexical noun modifiers without complements follow their head in Yoruba. (The reduplicative prefix marks the adjective's transposition from its original status as a qualitative verb to that of an attributive QAdj.)

(14.14) a. ọtí lí-le = liquor strong "strong liquor"
　　　　　b. ipò gí-ga = position lofty "lofty position"
　　　　　c. omi kí-korò = water bitter "bitter water"

Subjective compounds exhibit the same order of head and modifier, sustaining the prefix on the head (Rowlands 1969: 121, 182).

(14.15) a. pa "kill"　　ẹja "fish"　　　a-p-ẹja "fisherman"
　　　　　b. kọ "write"　ìwé "paper"　　a-kọ-wé "clerk"
　　　　　c. kọ́ "learn"　èkọ́ "learning"　a-k-ẹ́kọ̌ "student"

Compound ordering, therefore, is probably unrelated to the Base Rule Theory but rather is determined by the interaction of the Head Spelling Default and Lexicalism. That N + V is the normal order of Afrikaans VPs and synthetic compounds thus represents two unrelated facts, which neither motivate movement rules in L-derivation nor undermine the Base Rule Theory.[4]

14.3 THE BASE AS A GENERAL GRAMMATICAL COMPONENT

Chapters 9 through 12 established that Case and adposition functions are universal grammatical (not semantic) functions while Case itself is not; Case may be demonstrated only for fusional synthetic languages where it is a purely morphological phenomenon with no ties to syntax at all. It follows that the base must account for grammatical functions though not for Case. Chapter 13 next showed that the same Case functions which determine the syntactic relations of nouns also determine the functions for functional L-derivation. We now need to describe the mechanism by which the same set of base-generated grammatical functions emerge in both lexical and syntactic derivations. The common source in the base provided by the Base Rule Theory is precisely the framework that LMBM/UGF requires. Having cleared the path of known impediments, this section sets about the task of resetting this theory in a LMBM framework.[5]

To provide a common source of grammatical functions for the lexical and syntactic rule components while maintaining the distinguishing properties of these two components, the base must serve as a common but independent input for both components. If the base does this, it becomes not a strictly syntactic component, but a general grammatical one. The specific lexical or syntactic nature of its output is determined by post-base operations. If the base is so conceived, the Base Rule Theory accounts for the fact that the same set of functions underly both the Case-adposition system and L-derivation. However, if the functions marked by adpositions are not introduced lexically, we need to understand how the whole set of Case functions described in (12.28) is manipulated in the base.

If the input of L-derivation operations is base structures and the output, lexical items, the general structure of a functional L-derivation will be XP → X, where X is a lexical category. We will naturally assume that the lexicon can operate only on the categories available in the lexicon so that functional categories (including adpositions) will not undergo L-derivation. That functional categories are unavailable for any sort of derivation is a fundamental empirical fact of L-derivation which LMH is at pains to explain. Let us begin with the null hypothesis, namely, that no further constraints hold on this operation. In other words, we expect to find the following realizations of L-derivation:

(14.16)   a. VP → V
          b. NP → N
          c. AP → A

Having already noted that most specialists consider noun incorporation a form of verbal L-derivation, let us begin our investigation of the data with an examination of noun incorporation, to see if it fits the description of (14.16a).

14.3.1 Verbalization and the Base: Noun Incorporation

An interesting aspect of languages with noun incorporation is that they always have exactly two structural means of expressing the complex concept underlying an incorporative verb: the incorporation and a correlate syntactic phrase. According to most specialists, the former bears the properties of a lexical item such as the Chukchee example in (14.17a), while the latter bears those of a syntactic phrase, as in the Chukchee sentence of (14.17b).

(14.17) a. mən -nəki - ure -qepl-uvičven-mək
             IMP-night-long.time-ball - play - IPL
             "Let's-night-long-ball-play"
         b. nəki-te   n-ur-gev   mən-uvičven-mək qepl-e
             night-LOC ADV-long-ADV IMP-play-IPL   ball-INST
             "Let us play ball all night long"

Sapir, Bloomfield, and others have interpreted formal differences in pairs such as that of (14.17) as the difference between lexical and syntactic derivation. Mithun (1984) and Grimshaw and Mester (1985) pointedly argue that incorporation is a purely lexical process distinguished from syntactic processes in all the ways described here. Skorik (1977) finds essentially the same quality in Chukchee incorporation. Sapir (1922: 68) and Skorik (1977: 241) point out that in both Takelma and Chukchee, phrases may be both lexically and syntactically derived so long as the input to the lexical rule(s) contains no subordinate phrases.

Grammatical theory must account for the fact that two and only two means of expressing a sentiment exist universally and relate that fact to the central roles of lexical and syntactic components in all languages. It must explain why the morphology of (14.17a) is that of a single word while that of (14.17b) is that of a sentence.[6] The Base Rule Theory accounts for this parallel duality by denying that base structure is specifically syntactic and claiming instead that it is a general grammatical component which feeds both the lexicon and syntax. The lexicon operates on certain types of base structures, reducing them to words, just as movement and agreement rules convert them to PF- and, perhaps, LF-representations. The underlying structure of both (14.17a) and (14.17b), then, is (14.18).

LMBM facilitates the Base Rule Theory by delaying morphological spelling, derivational and inflectional, until after all lexical and syntactic rules have been executed. The decision to spell out lexical or inflectional allomorphy does not have to be made at the point of L-derivation as Botha

(14.18)

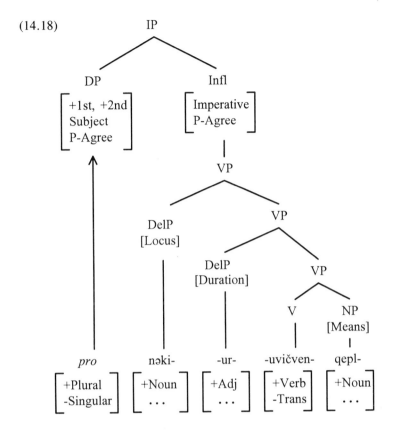

and Hoeksema assumed. If L-derivation does not take place, each NP will be assigned the appropriate Case marker by morphological spelling rules, conditioned by the functional projections. If L-derivation does take place, inflectional information should not be recognized, hence should be ignored by the lexical rules. However, chapters 12 and 13 taught us that at least the Case functions are recognized and preserved by the functional L-derivation rules. What, then, is the L-derivation process which unites the four lexemes of (14.18) into the single lexeme *-nəki-ur-qepl-uvičven-*, incorporating the function markers [Means], [Locus], and [Duration]?

Two lexical operations are required to account for the verbal compounding of the sort illustrated in (14.18). Both are required for syntax as well. First, the head (V) must be raised to Infl, AMALGAMATING the object and the adverbs along its way, in much the same sense as Chomsky (1989) uses the term in referring to verbal inflectional affixes. The difference is that, while syntactic amalgamation applies only to functional categories, the lexicon amalgamates lexical items as well, a difference which goes a long way toward accounting for the semantic difference between lexical and syntactic derivations. (14.19) illustrates the outcome of lexical Raising to Infl.

(14.19)

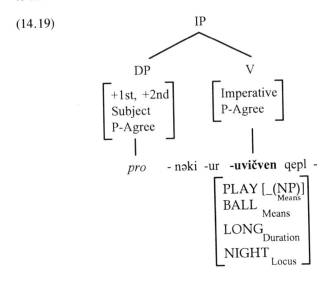

The second operation required of a theory of functional L-derivation is the repositioning of the underlying complement, the Means, *qepl-* "ball", which derivation converts to an attributive modifier, to prehead position. Since the normal position for both single and multiple noun adjuncts in Chukchee is before the head, and since Chukchee is a primarily suffixing language, linear precedence conditions force the correct *nəki-ur-qepl-uvič-ven-*.[7] The new lexical item then passes on to the MS-component for appropriate affixation. Again, following the most productive case of verbal derivation in English, Chukchee zero-marks the L-derivation and adds only inflectional markers in exterior prefix and suffix positions.

We have already seen that the same morphemes which realize inflectional adverbal functions sometimes emerge inside L-derivations, usually marking the same function. The Nahuatl verbal compound in (7.32), therefore, raises no new issues: the same morpheme marks Locus functions lexically and inflectionally.[8]

(14.20)   te - tla -ix -co -maca
           Sub-Obj - face-Loc - give
           "someone-something-in(to)-face-give"
           "to tell someone his faults to his face"

Since the LMBM MS-component accounts for adpositions (= DAdj pronouns), they are available for L- as well as I-derivation. In (14.20) an adposition functions as an affix to mark an incorporated Locative function (see section 13.3.1 for parallels), as predicted, on the head of the verbal compound. Under LMBM, ''inflectional'' affixes may occur inside derivational ones, but only if serving a derivational function. They are only prevented from serving an inflectional function derivation-internally (recall the discussion of 12.20–12.21).

If L-derivation does not occur, syntax will recognize the syntactic and inflectional categories and operate on them, moving categories subject to movement and allowing the remaining features to migrate wherever appropriate. The MS-component will then operate on each of the base lexemes independently, providing those of (14.18) with the more diversified inflectional morphology seen in (14.17b). The differences between syntactic and lexical operations on the same underlying structure explain the distinctions between lexical and syntactic operations. Their operation over a common base accounts for the close correspondence between inflectional and L-derivational relations long noted by linguists.

Hoeksema claims that additional powers must be accorded the lexicon if we are to account for the complexity of examples like (14.17a) and the parallels with syntactic structures which they exhibit. Botha's constraints rule out synthetic compounds based on phrases with internal constituent structure. His Complexity Constraint, which rules out Roeper and Siegel's example *good-dark-coffee-maker*, will also prohibit *truck-man-bought-last-week-driver*. Exceptions like English *over-the-counter* and Afrikaans *agter-de-muur rooker* ''behind-the-wall smoker'', have been explained above, as have the derived words with internal inflectional markers. The assumption now is that compounds are simply complex L-derivations and that the same set of rules derives both. Certainly synthetic compounds are derived by lexical operations which allow one or more optional modifiers.

14.3.2 Nominalizations

Deverbal nominals may be derived from base NPs just as compound verbs are derived from VPs. Infl provides the Case function for Subject (if it is not the default function); other functions are provided by the V or DelPs. The base structure underlying *driver, driver of the truck,* and *truck-driver* is illustrated in (14.21).

(14.21) may be called a LEXICALLY MINIMAL phrase structure in that it contains only two lexemes for a considerable amount of structure. When this construction leaves the lexicon, all lexical nodes must be filled. However, recall that the lexicon has two options for achieving this goal: it may erase the empty nodes and raise the VP to N, generating an L-derivate, or

(14.21)

```
                        DP
                    [Function F]
                     /      \
                  Det        NP
              [±Definite]    /  \
                           N     CP
                      [Function F]  |
                                    IP
                                  /    \
                                DP      VP
                             [Subject]  /  \
                                      V     DP
                                      |   [Object]
                                      |      |
                                    drive   truck
                                   [+Trans]
```

it may fill the nodes with categories under its control. If it follows the latter tack, its output will resemble (14.22). In (14.22), the matrices in the empty nodes are featural descriptions of *pro*. They will have to be marked appropriately by the MS-component, which spells all closed-class markers, bound and free alike. Further on we will examine the results of syntactic processing of L-derivation bases in more detail and provide a surface interpretation for (14.22).

Returning now to (14.21): four operations are required to convert this construction into a single lexical item, *truck-driver*. First, it requires the functional L-derivation, which raises the VP to N because of the lack of any intervening lexical material. Since the lexicon cannot ''see'' Case functions, [Subject] is blindly incorporated into the stem of the verb. The result, however, is a conflict: a VP heading an NP. While this situation is syntactically inadmissible, the lexicon has a natural process which can resolve the conflict: transposition. Transposition, as we saw in chapter 8, is capable of changing the lexical class of any lexical item to any other. Here it adjusts the lexical representation of the verb to its phrasal context by providing it with the nominal features, [± Plural, ± Singular, ± Animate].

The raising operation presumably follows the principles of bracket erasure outlined in section 6.4.2. Lexical raising essentially removes the

(14.22)

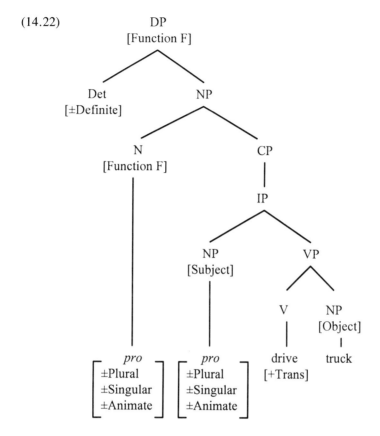

brackets between lower XPs so that they merge head-head, specifier-specifier, complement-complement with the higher ones until the newly derived lexical category features (those of N in this case) match the syntactic category features. In other words, obeying the constraints of subjacency and bounding theory, the operation rewrites the lower VP over the higher NP before the pronominal features of (14.22) are inserted. Since the LMBM lexicon contains only three classes, N, V, and A, and since these are the only classes or categories involved in L-derivation, the operation of functional L-derivation rules are naturally constrained to the appropriate lexical classes by the theoretical architecture of LMBM.

(14.23) represents the results of the first two operations on (14.22). This is the correct configuration for phrases like *the driver of the truck*. [Subject] now marks, not the relation of the [Spec, IP] to the verb, but the relation of the L-derivate to its base. The MS-component will read the incorporated [Subject] feature under the V stem *drive* and extend the stem

(14.23)

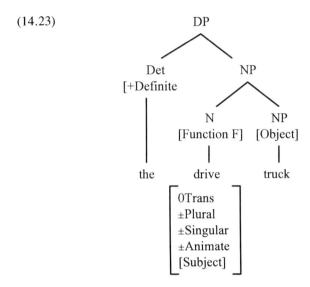

by suffixing /r/. Assuming with Chomsky (1981) that *of* is an empty nominal Case marker, the MS-component will assign it, too, after the now internal feature, [Subject], generating *the driver of the truck*. Since of (/əv/) is a clitic, its position may be determined by the General Theory of Affixation and thus requires no structural position.

Now let us assume that the L-derivation process goes a step further toward the kind of effect we see in (14.19) and (14.21), and incorporates the Object into the head noun. The results of this action is illustrated in (14.24).[9]

(14.24)

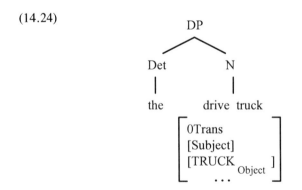

The fourth operation required for the correct derivation of *truck-driver*, illustrated in (14.25), is modifier ordering, discussed in the preceding section. The parameter for the English modifier position is set for head antecedence and hence *truck* is forced to that position. At which point this principle applies to (14.24) is of no direct relevance to L-derivation; however, the principle does provide the final derived form of the L-derivation, illustrated in (14.25).

(14.25)

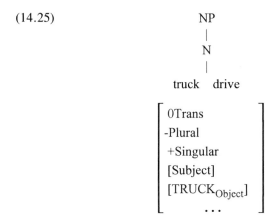

$$
\begin{array}{c}
NP \\
| \\
N \\
| \\
\text{truck} \quad \text{drive}
\end{array}
$$

$$
\begin{bmatrix}
\text{0Trans} \\
\text{-Plural} \\
\text{+Singular} \\
\text{[Subject]} \\
\text{[TRUCK}_{\text{Object}}] \\
\cdots
\end{bmatrix}
$$

Nothing more is required of derivation. All of the four operations required, (i) function incorporation, (ii) bracket erasure, (iii) transposition, and (iv) modifier ordering, are independently motivated. All in all then, the operations required by LMBM/UGF are independently motivated operations of the modified GB theory assumed here.

Since functional L-derivation is optional, it is natural to ask what happens to (14.21) if L-derivation does not operate. Remember first that in an LMBM model, free grammatical morphemes as well as bound morphemes are handled by the MS-component. The MS-component must be capable of spelling freestanding grammatical markers in syntactically supplied positions or spelling clitics on the P-representations of head and phrase-peripheral lexemes. The MS-component requires only that appropriate conditions for its operations reach it. This is guaranteed by the general rule that all minimal projections must be appropriately filled when a base generated construction exits the lexicon. (14.22) illustrates how the lexicon accomplishes this should the lexicon choose not to lexically derive the phrase of (14.21): it simply fills each X^0 with the appropriate features under its control. For the class N, those features for English are [± Plural, ± Singular, ± Animate], what Lieber (1992: 88–91) calls the nominal CATEGORIAL SIGNATURE. This is the LMBM definition of "*pro*" and the relative pronoun "*wh*".

Notice first that in this instance the CP and IP nodes have been projected, for while they are irrelevant to L-derivation, they are relevant for

(14.26)

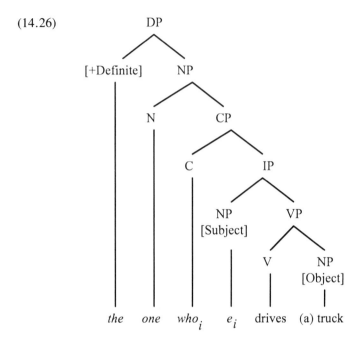

syntax. Also, LMBM does not require any special *wh*-form for relative pronouns, in keeping with the fact that relative pronouns are definable in terms of grammatical functions. The relative pronoun is simply the nominal categorial signature in the complementizer position. This interpretation of *pro* automatically sets limitations on its content, namely, *pro* can contain only grammatical features controlled by the lexicon and the features of functional categories. The latter may include Case and Person features from syntax in the case of nominal pronouns. This seems to be exactly the constraint required, for *pro* is semantically empty and can only reflect Case and Person plus whatever other categories are expressed by nouns in language L.

14.3.3 Adjectivization and Bahuvrihis

It is possible to include at least some analytic compounds under the same rubric as synthetic compounds but only in an LMBM framework, which invests no importance in the distinction between overtly and nonovertly marked derivations. Indeed, if L-derivations operate independent of affix spelling operations, analytic compounds immediately fall under suspicion of being simply zero-marked compounds of the same sort as are synthetic. Possessional or BAHUVRIHI COMPOUNDS certainly are. All IE languages, as mentioned before, exhibit a Possessional adjective (OPAdj), which is sometimes affixed and sometimes not, and a Bahuvrihi compound with the same meaning, which also may or may not be affixed. In English, OPAdjs are productively marked with the suffix *-ed*, while the nouns are zero-marked. However, there is no doubt that both derivates undergo the same L-derivation, for both the noun and the adjective are idiomatized in exactly the same way(s).

(14.27) a. a hardhead a′. hardhead-ed
         b. a blueblood b′. blueblood-ed
         c. a peabrain   c′. peabrain-ed
         d. a hardnose   d′. hardnos-ed

The forms of (14.27) share the same basic derivational relation, Possessional, that is, they map onto the predicate POSSESS([ ] [ ]). OPAdjs are used literally, metaphorically, and idiomatically, but the English Possessional nouns are for some mysterious reason seldom used literally. *Hardheaded* may refer to something with a literally or figuratively hard head, but the noun *hardhead* is used only to refer to someone who is obstinate or stubborn. The interesting point, however, is that the adjectives and nouns share precisely the same idiomatic and metaphoric interpretations. It follows that the meaning of the bahuvrihis must originate somewhere other than in the suffix. The nouns and adjectives share the same functional derivation, Possessional, but while the MS-component marks the adjective, it omits marking on the noun for its own reasons.[10]

(14.28)

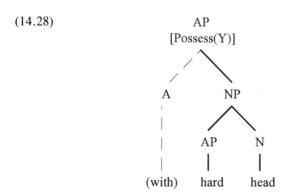

(14.28) illustrates the input of the L-derivation of the OPAdj. The feature [Possess(Y)] will distinguish it from the Possessive (SPAdj), which might have the feature [Possess(X)]. In the former case the underlying noun is linked as the Subject of Possession; in the latter case, it is linked as the Object. The difference in meaning reduces to a difference in which the argument of the function is incorporated into the compound. (14.28) represents a raised AP (DelP) as described in chapter 12. Bracket erasure generates *hard* + *head* and MS-rules spell -*ed* on the head of this stem to produce *hard-headed*. Since functional L-derivation also operates on APs, the prediction that this derivation is of the form XP → X (14.16) is verified. Recall that chapter 12 defined Ps as pronominal As and PPs as APs. This interpretation of PPs explained many adpositional phenomena; here it also accounts for the semantic and distributional similarities of Possessional adjectives like *hard-headed* and syntactic PPs like *with a hard head*.

(14.29)

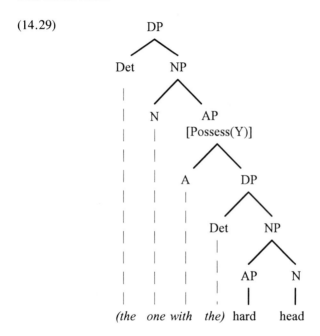

The same structure serving as an adjunct to a headless NP accounts for bahuvrihi nouns, as (14.29) illustrates. The inflectional morphology which provides the syntactic realization of (14.29) is represented by broken descenders. Notice that all the content of those X^{Min} with broken descenders derives from closed grammatical categories; none has lexical content. If the lower NP is not raised, the result will be that represented in (14.29). If it is raised, the result will be *hard-headed*.

The previous section mentioned the Head Spelling Default but no other restrictions on the operations of L-derivation have been discussed. Obviously, other constraints apply to functional L-derivations. While virtually all functions are available for RAdjs, only Possessional, Manner, and perhaps one or two more are available to QAdjs. The number of items allowed in compounds seems to be restricted to two in IE languages, although the Chukchee example in (14.17) demonstrates that this is not a universal constraint. The next section will examine two possibly universal constraints which account for these limitations.

14.4 CONSTRAINTS ON FUNCTIONAL L-DERIVATION

Botha (1981) posits two constraints on Afrikaans synthetic compounds which in fact seem to approach universal constraints on functional L-derivation: the CONTIGUITY CONSTRAINT and the COMPLEXITY CONSTRAINT. Both will require some adjustment for LMBM and the data examined in the research underlying this work. A third issue, that of derivational recursivity, also needs to be examined; however, final disposition of this question must await further research.[11]

14.4.1 The Contiguity Constraint

The first of Botha's constraints is the Contiguity Constraint, a Base Rule Theory version of Roeper and Siegel's First Sister Principle (Botha 1981: 28).

(14.30)   The Contiguity Constraint
   The affixation rules involved in the formation of Afrikaans synthetic compounds can take as their bases only those deep structure phrases of which the head and peripheral constituent are both linearly and structurally contiguous.

This constraint is of no service to the present model as stated since it relies on affixation. If we assume that linearity is the result of independent linear precedence rules, linearity must also be removed as a criterion of this constraint. Let us rewrite (14.30) as a general constraint based purely on structural relations.

(14.31)   The Lexical Head Constraint
   L-derivation rules can take as their base only a single, base-generated phrase headed by a single lexeme with optional lexical complements or adjuncts.

(14.31) is a complex constraint which replaces (14.30). (14.30) has been relaxed to allow any subcategorized item which falls within the maximal projection of the head in an analytic or synthetic compound. However, any subordinate modifier must be a lexical complement or adjunct; specifiers are excluded, because they constitute a functional category, as are sentential adjuncts and all (other) functional categories. *Late-blooming* and *pale-skinned* reflect universally well-formed compounds but **perhaps-blooming* and **that-skinned* are universally ill-formed. (14.31) guarantees that every L-derivation will have a lexical base and that if it contains more than one lexeme, one will be a head. It therefore excludes DVANDVA COMPOUNDS as it stands and will have to be modified at some point.

The LMBM lexicon, which includes only N, V, and A lexemes, excludes pronominal heads and modifiers so that compounds like English *she-goat* and *she-wolf* cannot be derived by L-derivation. As footnote 2 on pages 40–41 indicate, the meanings of these compounds are not "3rdSg-Fem goat" and "3rdSgFem wolf" but "female goat" and "female wolf", respectively. If these forms are not extra-grammatically derived (Beard 1987b), the pronoun here functions as a prefixal Femininizer rather than a compound modifier. The same interpretation applies to Turkish *ben-lik* = I-ism "self, selfishness, egotism" and English *selfish*. In both cases the pronominal morphological marker has been lexicalized, as in English *the self*. *Selfish* does not even mean "like the self" or "having a self," but rather, "greedy," and hence is idiomatic. Turkish, moreover, does not allow forms corresponding to "you-ism", "(s)he-ism", undermining any claim that *ben-lik* is rule-generated.

14.4.2 The Complexity Constraint

The second of Botha's constraints on Afrikaans synthetic compounds is called "the Complexity Constraint". Its function is to restrict compounds to those whose subordinate constituent contains no specifiers or complements. Botha's version reads as follows:

(14.32)   The Complexity Constraint (Botha 1981: 41)
   The peripheral constituent of an Afrikaans synthetic compound cannot be syntactically complex, that is, it cannot have internal constituent structure.

The complements and adjuncts permitted by the Lexical Head Constraint (14.31) must be simple unmodified heads themselves. It is clear that most IE languages and many others further constrain all synthetic compounds to a maximum of one modifier of any sort. However, the Eskimo, Chukchee, and Amerindian evidence makes it evident that such restrictions are language-specific and do not hold universally. Indeed, considerable data becloud the universality of (14.32), suggesting that it is too restrictive. Complex nominal compounds like the classic German *Donaudampfschif-fahrtsgesellschaft* "Danube steamship travel company" and the Turkish example in (8.35) suggest that modifiers with subordinate clauses are possible in analytic compounds for some languages.

14.5 Conclusion: Base Categories Cannot Be Derived from the Lexicon

This chapter has reopened the discussion of the Base Rule Theory by showing that its viability is enhanced by recent advances in LMBM and GB. The LMBM lexicon is strictly constrained to the storage of open-class items, while GB theories now distinguish functional from lexical categories. The LMBM distinction accounts for the fact that lexical derivation, simple and compound alike, operates only on open-class items. We avoid mixing modules by simply recognizing that if the base generates structures accessible to both the lexicon and syntax, it must be part of neither, but rather a third independent module whose output is available to both components. Given all these assumptions, the operation of functional L-derivation reduces to a lexical variety of raising with the amalgamation (incorporation) of complements and adjuncts. These two processes are followed by a narrow range of linear precedence rules whose parameters are determined by the Head Spelling Default and the language-specific ordering of head modifiers.

The Base Rule Hypothesis also explains an ostensible contradiction in LMBM: If lexical and inflectional functional operations are distinct, how can L-derivation operate on the functions of an inflectional category? The answer, of course, is that Case functions are not syntactic for the base must serve both the lexicon and syntax. Chapter 5 distinguished Case and Agreement as the nominal inflectional categories. Chapter 11, however, removed Case from syntax to the MS-component. The Case functions must be part of the base since they determine both lexical and syntactic relations. This fact complicates the P&P Minimalist program to eliminate D-structure in favor of a set of broad principles, for it would seem that Case functions and other morphological categories for which the lexicon cannot account must be introduced there.

The Base Rule Theory accommodates UGF, a major linguistic generalization which contemporary syntactic theory has heretofore failed to discover, let alone explain. The range of potential relations between a functional L-derivate and its underlying base, and between the modifier and head of compounds, is far greater than subcategorization can account for. However, the range of L-derivation functions is identical with that of I-derivation. The best approach to a universal constraint on functional L-derivation, therefore, is a base component sharing a common set of primitive grammatical relations with both L- and I-derivation.

NOTES

1. In fact, *goer* is used widely in Australia and New Zealand, for example, *he is a real goer,* in the sense of a lively or persevering person (or race horse as Elizabeth Gordon and Andrew Carstairs-McCarthy have confirmed by e-mail, 1994). Since the derivation and its meaning are available to all speakers of English, it is not clear what the ''existence'' of this form refers to.

2. Hoeksema's third argument against the Base Rule Theory is that it violates Partee's Well-Formedness Constraint. Partee maintained that the input and output of transformation rules must be structurally acceptable forms in language. Since Hoeksema subscribes to LMH, he assumes that in order for an affix to be present in the surface, it must be present in the base. This book provides ample rationalization for the distinction of lexemes and affixation and the late application of affixation rules. Moreover, the version of Botha's theory adopted here reduces movement to head-head raising and modifier ordering. Hoeksema's third argument against the Base Rule Theory, therefore, has no thrust against a LMBM model.

3. See also Roeper (1988: 215–220), who reminds us that the word–order consistency in compounds must be accounted for. He remains convinced that transformations are the only solution in English.

4. An initial study of some 50 languages sustains this interpretation generally. However, languages which place nominal modifiers on either side of the noun do not seem to conform to the hypothesis. Work is currently underway to clarify the complete range of this parameter.

5. Chomsky (1992) proposes the elimination of D-structure in favor of a generalized transformation (GT) which projects lexical items onto X-bar structures, $X \rightarrow [X' \, X] \rightarrow [X'' \, [X' \, X]]$. This proposal goes through only if the lexicon projects functional categories, such as CP, IP, DP, as well as lexical ones, or if GT is expanded to account for functional categories. Since functional categories are excluded from the lexicon by all the arguments raised at the beginning of this book, I am assuming either that GT will provide these categories external to the lexicon or that D-structure is generated by a general categorial component.

6. Chukchee exhibits front-back vowel harmony whose domain is the lexical word. Although (14.17a) is not a good example of this, the phonological evidence elsewhere that constructs like (14.17a) are single lexical items is conclusive.

7. (14.19) shamelessly combines grammatical and semantic categories and relations for the sake of expediency. This chapter, of course, ultimately assumes the sort of mapping from grammatical to semantic levels outlined in chapters 8–9 and the semantic composition in verbal R-representations described in Jackendoff 1990.

8. It is also possible that (14.20) represents an instance where Nahuatl incorporates an idiom whole, as in the case of English forms like *over-the-counter* discussed above. This would imply however, that such incorporations containing Ps are unproductive, based on lexicalized phrases. The references to Nahuatl and its contemporary dialects make no mention of such a constraint.

9. It is not clear at this point whether the third step is a different type of operation or simply a second cycle of raising. This ultimately depends on the final theories of XP raising and bracket erasure. Since it is not a critical question for the theory of functional L-derivation, the issue will not be pursued here.

10. In Serbo-Croatian the situation is the reverse of that in English; the noun is suffixed and OPAdj is not: *tvrd-o-glav* "hard-headed" *tvrd-o-glav-ac* "a hardhead." Affixation is clearly arbitrary here.

11. Recall the mystery surrounding expressive derivations (chapter 5), which are most prone to recursivity.

Chapter Fifteen

Free Grammatical Morphemes

15.1 INTRODUCTION

The relation of bound and free grammatical morphemes has been accorded no place in current theories of grammar because these theories rely on the simplified lexicon described in chapter 2. This chapter establishes the relation of free to bound morphemes under LMBM, showing that the theory of bound morphology outlined in chapter 3 accommodates an equally restrictive account of free grammatical morphemes. It then examines the problems of morpheme ordering facing a theory of morphological spelling. It shows how LMBM, with the General Theory of Affixation introduced in section 12.4.1, provides a consistent and broadly comprehensive theory of spelling. These two theories reduce if not obviate the problems of pronoun and verb movement and promise a unified, universal theory of auxiliaries and pronominals.

15.1.1 The Similarities of Bound and Free Grammatical Morphemes

Because free grammatical morphemes share much in common with lexemes, it is not clear that the same component accounts for bound and free morphemes. Free morphemes such as determiners, pronouns, and auxiliaries are often movable and themselves may be affixed with bound morphemes. However, the similarities they share with bound morphemes are much more striking. First, free morphemes belong to closed classes like bound morphemes, and some even form paradigms. Second, because they belong to closed paradigmatic classes, they are subject to omissive (zero) morphology and cumulative exponence. Third, they reflect the same morphological categories as do affixes in other languages. The interaction of the English Definite and Indefinite articles with Number exemplifies all three of these attributes. The article *the* marks Definite in both Singular and Plural. Indefinite, however, is marked by *a(n)* in the Singular and by the omission of any article at all in the Plural, as illustrated in Table 15.1.

Section 2.3.1 established the high improbability of zero lexemes. As-

Table 15.1   The English Articles

	Singular	*Plural*
Definite	the buffalo	the buffalo
Indefinite	a buffalo	Ø buffalo

suming then that free morphemes must be either lexemes or grammatical morphemes, their ability to vary with omissive morphology forces them into the MS-component under strict LMBM. Moreover, their interaction with affixally marked categories such as Number in (15.1) confirms this account.

Another compelling piece of evidence that free morphemes are in a class with bound morphemes and not lexemes is the fact that they often alternate with bound variants themselves. Table 10.2, for example, displays a substantial catalogue of prepositions which must be free because they may be stranded; however, they also serve, with the same form and function, as prefixes: *by-pass, after-taste, over-pay, under-pay, input, off-shore*. Other free morphemes alternate with clitics or contractionally bound variants, as in (15.1).

(15.1)   a. I háve : Í've
         b. I wóuld háve : I wóuld've: Í'd've
         c. he ís nót : he's nót : he ísn't

Lexemes, by contrast, never contract or serve as affixes or clitics except historically via grammaticalization.

It is true that some free morphemes seem to alternate as lexemes. The Ps in sentences like *the cat is in, the oven is on, our team is behind, the play is over,* behave more like lexical DAdjs than like grammatical morphemes. However, the high level of idiomaticity involved in this usage suggests that these instances are diachronic lexicalizations. The predicates *in, behind, on,* and *over* in these examples are used in much more restricted senses than the corresponding P; for instance, *in* in phrases like *the cat is in* cannot have the functions it expresses in *in five minutes, in love, in opening the letter.* Moreover, while the common interpretation of *the cat is in* is that the cat is located inside some unspecified physical object, under no circumstances may *our team is behind* mean that our team is located behind any physical object.

The final property which free morphemes share with bound ones is that they are not subject to L-derivation, simple or compound. The rare exceptions like *she-goat, she-wolf,* and *selfish* (discussed in section 14.4.1) which do occur are always idiomatic, suggesting that such forms enter the language diachronically via stock expansion rules rather than by regular derivation (Beard 1987b). We have also seen that case markers find their way into compounds and derivations in German, Slavic, and other languages but as affixes, never as lexical constituents. Free grammatical morphemes participate only exceptionally and always idiomatically in L-derivations.

Some pronouns do take affixes which are elsewhere used derivationally. For example, the Serbo-Croatian Demonstrative bases may be converted into a proadjective system with the suffixes *-ak* and *-av:*

(15.2) a. t(o)   t-ak-o   t-ak-av($\emptyset$)
              "that"   "that way"   "that kind of"

         b. ov(o)   ov-ak-o   ov-ak-av($\emptyset$)
              "this"   "this way"   "this kind of"

The affixes in (15.2), however, simply mark systematic positions in a paradigm. A suffix *-ak* may be posited only in those Serbo-Croatian dialects which have lost distinctions of vowel length. In those dialects it might merge with the marginal deadjectival Subjective marker *-āk* that we see in *levi* "left(hand)": *lev-āk* "left-hander." The suffix *-av* productively marks Possessional adjectives (*bubljic(a)* "pimple" : *bubljič-av* "pimply") and, marginally, Subjective adjectives (*vriska-* "shriek" : *vrisk-av* "shrill"). However, neither *-ak* nor *-av* express any such grammatical functions when attached to the pronominal stems of (15.2). Rather, they simply distinguish the classes N, adverbal A, and adnominal A for which these forms serve as pronouns.

That auxiliaries do not undergo L-derivation or participate in compounding also complicates the claim that they are regular verbs. Auxiliaries are in fact inaccessible to any type of L-derivation, including deverbal verbalizations such as transitivization, causativization, reflexivization. We simply do not find derivations like **unmust, *overmust, *dewill, *oughter, *willer.* The auxiliary's lack of access to verbal L-derivation is explained by the fact that auxiliaries are grammatical morphemes which are not in the lexicon and hence are unavailable for lexical derivation.[1]

15.1.2 The Differences between Bound and Free Grammatical Morphemes

The overwhelming similarities uniting bound and free morphemes forces the inclusion of both in the MS-component of an LMBM model. This in no way handicaps the model in predicting the grammatical functions they express, as chapters 5 and 6 demonstrated. There are, however, three distinguishing attributes of free morphemes which must be accounted for, all involving syntax. Auxiliaries may be moved and prepositions may be stranded in the sense in which "stranding" was defined in section 12.4.2. Both these properties suggest that free morphemes, unlike bound ones, must be assigned syntactic positions. Third, free morphemes may themselves be affixed with bound morphemes, as (15.2) shows. Assigning free but not bound morphemes to syntactic positions and inserting them before bound MS-operations apply accounts for all three of these capacities.

15.2 Spelling Auxiliary Categories

Abney (1987), Chomsky (1989, 1992), Pollock (1989), Halle and Marantz (1993) and others assume that in addition to the major lexical categories of X-bar theory, that is, NP, VP, AP, there are nonlexical, functional categories, namely CP, IP, DP, plus an adjunct category, DegP. The category IP has momentous implications for a theory of morphology since it accounts not only for modal auxiliaries, but for Tense and Agreement functions (features) as well. The Tense and Agreement affixes introduced under IP amalgamate with the verb stem in the correct order during verb-to-Infl raising, redefined in chapter six as simple bracket erasure. Those affixes which fail to amalgamate in the correct order "move" from their base position under Infl to their appropriate morphological positions at the end of the auxiliary or main verb, during what Chomsky calls SPELL-OUT. The reasons for rejecting any type of affix movement were sorted out in section 6.3.2. The program here is to demonstrate how LMBM achieves better results without affix movement.

15.2.1 Analytic Versus Synthetic Auxiliary Categories

A theory of grammar must account for the fact that grammatical functions are marked by free morphemes in some languages and by affixes in others. Free auxiliaries, as mentioned, require a syntactic position to the extent that they are subject to movement and stranding. Lexical and phrasal affixes, however, cannot be assigned a syntactic position because their position is always morphologically determined by the General Theory of Affixation. One way to handle this distinction is to divide languages into those which require free morpheme positions (analytic) and those which do not (synthetic). This tack is discouraged by two aspects of verbal morphology.

First, languages are not so neatly divided; most languages mark some grammatical functions with free morphemes and others with affixes, and the mix of free and bound morphemes marking the same categories varies widely across languages. Turkish marks Potential and Dubitative with verbal affixes but all other modal functions with free morphemes. Basque marks the Potential and Conditional with affixes and all other modal functions with conjugable auxiliaries. English marks all modal functions with free morphemes. Each language would have to be specified for the modal functions which it marks with free morphemes, making it difficult if not impossible to maintain a universal theory. The second problem is that all morphological systems seem to mark the same catalogue of functions described throughout this book. Although it is possible, it seems unlikely that two different marking systems express the same catalogue of functions. The most promising hypothesis, therefore, is that the base generates one set of universal grammatical functions, while syntax and morphology account for the differences between free and bound morphological spelling.

The problem facing LMBM is that since affixation is postsyntactic, affixes are not available in syntax for amalgamation during raising. Only grammatical features may be amalgamated as the verb is raised to Infl. These features are marked by affixation only when the amalgamation is complete. The question for LMBM, then, is, how does syntax anticipate the needs of morphology, amalgamating just those projections which will be marked affixally and preserving those which are to be filled with free auxiliaries? Will there have to be some form of communication between the operations of syntax and MS that weakens strict modularity?

15.2.2 Raising and Bracket Erasure

The crucial issue, then, is accounting for where raising occurs and where it does not. GB assumes that raising is a syntactic operation; however, there is no convincing syntactic motivation for such an operation as supporters of LFG, HPSG, and RG have long noted. The effect of raising, however, is to erase brackets and bracket erasure is an operation required for phonological interpretation. Since the MS-component under LMBM is more closely associated with phonology than syntax, chapter 6 hypothesized that one of its tasks is to erase all brackets as it inserts morphemes. The General Theory of Affixation provides prima facie evidence for this hypothesis, for it limits phrasal affixation to peripheral constituents and the head of XPs, precisely the points where the brackets most relevant for recognizing XP would be erased. Inflectional spelling thus becomes syntactic bracket marking under LMBM.[2]

If the MS-component erases syntactic brackets, it will be a natural matter for it to choose which nodes are incorporated under lexemes and which are assigned free morphemes. Indeed, a morphological principle of head-head raising may be combined with the General Affixation Theory and stated roughly as (15.3):

(15.3) *As syntactic brackets are erased, the features not marked by free morphemes are phonologically spelled out on the realization of the free item (morpheme or lexeme) nearest one of the brackets enclosing the head or maximal projection of the phrase.*

Notice that (15.3) specifies only the positioning of bound morphemes; it is ambiguous as to the stem on which a morpheme will be spelled. The nearest lexical stem may lie outside the maximal bracket and hence outside the scope of the feature which the morpheme marks, or inside the bracket and thus inside the scope of that feature. Which stem the phrasal affix selects is determined by the definition of the affix, whether it is a proclitic or enclitic, prefix, suffix, or infix.

When the brackets around Mod', [Mod VP], are erased in analytic languages, the MS-component will insert a free morpheme which spells [+Potential]. In Polish, a highly inflectional language, that morpheme is the auxiliary *mog-*. (15.3) will not apply since free morphemes are exempt from that principle. The output of the free morpheme MS-operations on the structure introduced in (6.28) in Polish is illustrated in (15.4).

(15.4)

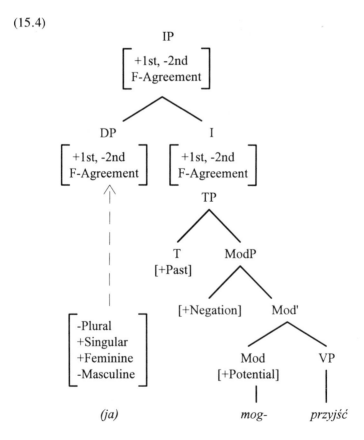

The first brackets requiring erasure are those of ModP, [+Negation Mod']. [+Negation] is expressed by the Polish proclitic, *nie*. The stem to the right of that feature is now *mog-*, so *nie* must be spelled out on it, providing *nie* + *mog-* as its brackets are erased. Next, the IP bracketing [+Past ModP] will be erased. The MS-marker for [+Past] in Polish is the suffix *-ł*, so it is attached to the nearest appropriate stem, now the Mod *nie* + *mog-* at this stage of spelling. The result is *nie* + *mog-ł-*. Gender and Person features are added next and are realized by *-a* and *-m*, respectively. The results of all feature accumulation are illustrated in (15.5).

(15.5)

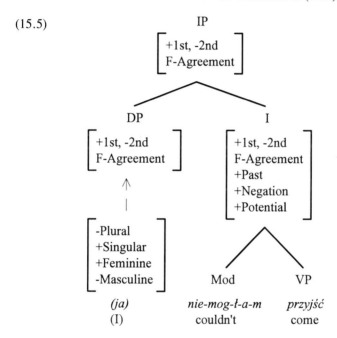

If the MS-component erases the syntactic brackets, therefore, it will be a natural matter for it to choose which functional features are incorporated under lexemes and free morphemes and which are assigned free morphemes. The underlying base of Turkish *gelemedim* "I could not come", described in chapter 6, would be the same as (15.4), but the output would be (15.6).

The base structure for this construction in Polish, English, and Turkish would be identical except for the Agreement categories and the presence of ModP after raising. ModP on this interpretation becomes an AuxP projection which controls the number of free auxiliaries in a given language by establishing the number of expansions within its domain. ModP will now be raised if it is filled; otherwise, VP will be raised. Infl may be

(15.6)

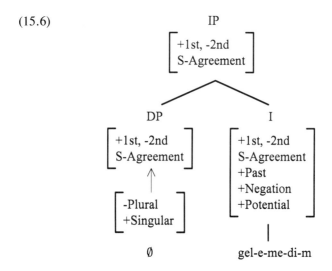

moved to Comp in IE questions, where the first Mod feature or V will have to follow in order to receive conjugational features. In English V does not follow; rather, the conjugational features are realized on the morphologically empty verbal pronominal *do* in Comp. The MS-module spells all the ModP head features, as free or bound morphemes, wherever they appear in syntax, including the full P-representation of *do*.

The bracket erasure hypothesis does not obviate the problem of verb-Comp movement in questions:

(15.7)   a. Have you *e* not been coming?
          b. Haven't you *e* been coming?
          c. Did you come?
          d. Kommst du *e* denn? "Are you coming" (German)

In IE languages, the inflected form of a verbal complex, auxiliary or main verb, is moved to Comp in questions. In most Germanic and Slavic languages the main verb is moved in the absence of an auxiliary (15.7d); in English, however, the main verb is exempt from this movement. If no auxiliary is present in an English phrase bearing the conditions for verb movement, a default auxiliary *do* is inflected and inserted by MS (15.7c). Finally, particles cliticized to this form may follow it to Comp (15.7b); free morphemes marking the same functions do not (15.7a).

We could account for the fact that the inflected form of the verbal complex is always moved to sentence-initial position either by moving Infl to Comp or by assigning the Infl features to Comp in the base structure of phrases bearing a [+ wh] feature. This would force whichever verb form that must bear inflectional Agreement features to that position. However, auxiliary complexes like *wouldn't* require information from several different nodes and hence would have to be moved to Comp only after some raising has taken place. Beard (ms.) points out that if raising were an MS-operation under LMBM, another alternative is available which obviates movement while explaining it in these cases. Since this alternative is a type of long-distance spelling related to cliticization, discussion of it will be delayed until that subject is covered in the next section.

To conclude this section, then, a modest adjustment already suggested in the syntactic literature renders current GB theories of IP compatible with the strong version of the LMBM hypothesis. In the strong version of LMBM, all and only closed-class items, including free grammatical morphemes, are controlled by the MS-component, while the content of the lexicon is restricted to all and only open class items. Free morphemes, like lexemes, must be assigned their own position. However, languages vary as to how many verbal functions are realized phonologically by free morphemes and how many by bound morphemes.

15.3 PRONOUNS

Languages also vary as to whether the Subject (and Object) pronominals must be expressed by an overt morpheme or simply by the Agreement affixation of the verb. All languages maintain a Subject NP projection for full noun Subjects. However, in *pro*-drop languages like Bashkir and Serbo-Croatian, the Subject NP position goes unfilled unless intensified; in non-*pro*-drop languages like English and Russian it will be filled by a closed-class morpheme such as English *I, you, she,* and the Russian correlates, *ja, ty, ona.* These morphemes are semantically empty, which is to say that they express nothing more than the grammatical functions represented in the features of the structural positions which they fill. They then serve a purpose identical with that of verbal suffixes such as *-u, -š, -t* in the Russian conjugation, for example, *ja slyš-u* "I hear", *ty slyši-š* "you hear", *ona slyši-t* "she hears", even though the pronouns differ allomorphically from the suffixes in that they are free and hence require a syntactic (NP) position. Not only does nothing else distinguish the two sets of paradigmatic forms, but they interact with each other in perfect sequence at all times: *ja . . . -u, ty . . . -š, on(a) . . . -t.*

The structure of the MS-component can easily account for the superficial differences between *pro*-drop and non-*pro*-drop languages if we maintain the assumption that the MS-component contains a list of free morpheme spelling rules as well as stem-bound spelling operations. Pronoun spelling, like auxiliary spelling, may be counted among the spelling rules of the MS-component. The selection and copying of free morphemes must precede stem modifications since free morphemes may themselves be modified by bound morphemes. In Russian, for example, the 3rd Person pronouns receive regular predicate Agreement markings, that is, M-Agreement, F-Agreement, N-Agreement, and P-Agreement, as (15.8) demonstrates:

(15.8)　a. on-∅ "he, it" ("Masculine," or M-Agreement)
　　　　b. on-**a** "she, it" ("Feminine", or F-Agreement)
　　　　c. on-**o** "it" ("Neuter", or N-Agreement)
　　　　d. on-**i** "they" ("Plural", or P-Agreement)

While the "Masculine" and "Feminine" forms may indirectly reflect natural Gender, the presence of "Neuter", along with the fact that these forms may coindex any noun of the appropriate Agreement class, make it clear that these suffixes express Agreement classes rather than Gender as defined in chapter 5.

According to chapter 5, Agreement functions are derived by algorithm from the inherent features of a lexical noun. The Russian algorithm, Table 5.3, assigns F-Agreement to a node containing a noun with natural Feminine Gender or, in the absence of natural Gender, to the same node if the noun belongs to either Class 2 or Class 3. The point is that lexical features are not allowed to enter syntactic structures; rather, syntax interprets the features of lexical output and translates them into its own terms.

However, this interpretation of the lexicon-syntax interface causes a conflict with the present account of pronouns in Subject NP position. If pronouns are empty morphological markers introduced postsyntactically by the MS-component, they may contain no lexical features to be interpreted syntactically.[3] Apparently, the LMH approach, which posits pronouns as lexical items containing appropriate lexical features, would be more adequate. LMBM could match this advantage by allowing the lexicon complete and unrestrained control over its own categories; that is, the lexical selection rule may copy, in addition to fully specified lexemes, pure lexical categories without P- or R-representations. This amounts to a universal constraint on all pronominals, to the effect that:

(15.9) *a pronominal (pronoun, proadjective, proverb) is a bare G-representation (Lieber's categorial signature) of a lexical class mapped to X^0.*

(15.9) defines pronominals as pure lexical functions such as [± Feminine, ± Masculine], [± Plural, ± Singular], and [Noun Class X]. The operation involved in their derivation to X^0 is essentially that of transposition; however, instead of inserting category features into lexical items, this variant of transposition copies them via a lexico-syntactic conversion algorithm like Table 5.3 directly into a syntactic position. Semantically, this option describes reference to an object by its sex and quantity without attributing to it any specific semantic properties. (15.9) does not restrict pronominals to nouns; it also predicts verbal and adjectival pronouns with features like [±Transitive] and [±Gradable] with the all the capacities of regular verbs and adjectives. All languages seem to possess such forms.

This definition applies the appropriate constraint on pronouns. In an LMBM model so configured, the underlying form of the Russian 3rd Person Singular "Feminine" pronoun would be that of (15.10):

(15.10)

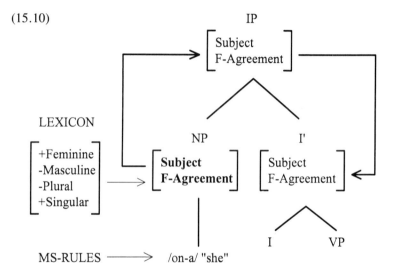

(15.10) indicates that the Subject is the list of all nominal lexical categories with their values set arbitrarily to Feminine Singular. These features have been translated into [F-Agreement] by the lexical-syntactic translation algorithm shown in Table 5.3. That feature has combined with the Case function [Subject] to form a bundle which migrates freely throughout IP, blocked only by preexisting features of the same category; that is, DP² will not accumulate the features of DP¹ but all non-DP categories will.

This accounts for the realization of NP features on verbs regardless of whether they derive from a specifier (as in the case of Subject Agreement) or a complement (as in the case of Object Agreement).[4] When V merges with Infl through bracket erasure, Subject agreement features become available, as in other versions of GB. They will be joined by a similar bundle also containing Object inherited from DP². We may assume that features like these migrate freely throughout IP, since the MS mechanism described in chapter three responds only to those features which condition its operations. If a language has verbal affixes conditioned by Object Noun Class and Person features, as do Swahili, Chukchee, and Potawatomi, they will be attached to the verb or auxiliary stem in accord with their description as prefixes, suffixes, and so on. If a language lacks such affixation, as do the IE languages, obviously no such affixation can be carried out.[5]

To conclude this section, the problems of IP in the preceding section are special problems which do not extend to DP. This is because morphological categories do not move from inside DP as the auxiliary moves out of IP to Comp. Since all NP morphological functions remain in DP once they are assigned, it is irrelevant whether their position is assigned a free morpheme by morphological spelling or whether a bound morpheme is attached to some specified lexeme in the NP domain. The assumption is that the General Theory of Affixation will determine the distribution of such affixes if syntax does not. Assuming that phonologically null syntactic positions are permissible so long as their categorial content is realized by some means somewhere in the appropriate domain, the categories of articles and pronouns may be assigned to N^0 positions and realized there morphologically by free or bound morphemes. If not, however, they must be realized elsewhere, that is, on the auxiliary or the verb.

15.4 LONG-DISTANCE SPELLING: THE QUESTION OF CLITICS

One of the problems facing contemporary theories of syntax is the fact that lexical items and clitic pronouns of the same class and with the same grammatical function often appear in different phrasal positions. In French the Object NP generally appears after the V; if it is a pronoun, however, it is placed before the verb.

(15.11) a. Je vois Jean "I see Jean"
         b. Je le vois "I see him"

The usual solution to this problem is Move α (Pollock 1989). LMBM, however, proposes to replace Move α with Affix α, the General Theory of Affixation.

15.4.1 Cliticization and Contraction

The separation of morphological spelling from functional assignment and the realization of grammatical morphemes like pronouns in the MS-component account for French pronoun positioning with considerable explanatory power. It ensures that clitic pronouns will be positioned according to the General Theory of Affixation, which constrains morphologically the latitude of pronoun distribution. This latitude accounts for the variation of clitic pronoun distribution from that which syntax predicts via a preestablished morphological principle. We may assume that the French base assigns all Objects, nominal or pronominal, a postverbal position, as in the diagram of *je le vois* or *je l'ai vu* in (15.12):[6]

Syntactically, then, all pronominal positions, null or expressed, are nodes filled exclusively with lexical and inflectional G-representations, as in (15.12).

(15.12)

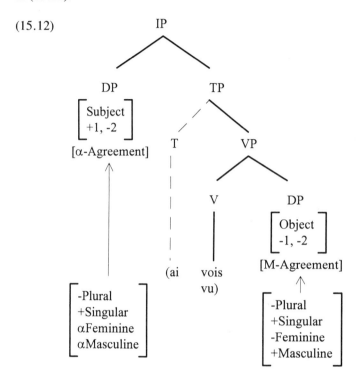

In keeping with the Separation Hypothesis, pronominal functions are proper to syntax, but their phonological realization is the responsibility of the MS-module. How is this accomplished? Since all NPs reflect 1st, 2nd, or 3rd Person, let us imagine that rather than assigned by Agr, these features are specified by the functional category DP, as suggested in chapter 6. These features then percolate to IP along with Case function and Agreement features. That is, every DP is minimally $[\pm 1, \pm 2]_{NP}$, where any value setting other than [-1, -2] precludes the selection of a noun and forces the copying of the pure category signature (G-representation) which defines pronouns, as in (15.12). If the Person setting is [-1, -2], selection of a noun is permissible.

When the spelling mechanism of the French MS-component looks up the conditioning features of the 3rd Person Object pronoun required by (15.12), it finds in its catalogue of operations a procedure which provides a proclitic defined as prefixation to the initial periphery of TP, excluding phrase-initial position (see footnote 6). The Object proclitic thus marks both the pronominal Object and the boundary between the Subject and predicate, cf. *je l'[ai vue]* "I have seen him". The MS-component is both empowered and constrained by the General Theory of Affixation. It reads the Object NP position in constructions like (15.12), but is licensed to affix the entire phrase TP in which the Object NP is an internal argument. This capacity leaves the impression of movement in theories based on LMH, when in fact movement need not be invoked at all. Indeed, the positioning of clitic pronouns cannot be universally predicted by movement rules, since the positions of all clitics and affixes are determined by their unique definition which, in turn, is constrained broadly by the principles of the General Affixation Theory.[7]

A final advantage of the morphological solution to the problem of Object NP distribution is that it simplifies semantics, since the base structure of (15.12) does not change: it may be interpreted identically at all syntactic levels. This, in fact, explains why the "movement" of clitics does not affect scope relations. The positioning of clitics and affixes is relevant only to phonology and thus does not require any restructuring of syntax by correspondence rules at semantic level.

Cliticization under LMBM is a problem of ordering affixational application: phrasal affixes are added after all lexical affixes have been attached. Clitic rules must also preserve Zwicky's distinction between special clitics (CLITICS) and regular clitics (CONTRACTIONS). The position of the latter is determined partially by syntax, while the General Theory determines the former. None of these variations present any problem for LMBM so further detail is unnecessary at this point. A more interesting question is this: if long-distant clitic spelling obviates pronominal movement, can it explain other types of movement? Perhaps so.

15.4.2 Long-Distance Spelling and Move α

Recall from section 15.2.2 that no decision was made as to how raising to Comp should be treated in an LMBM model. Auxiliaries are grammatical morphemes like pronouns under LMBM. Could they be simply spelled out in Comp for questions in IE languages? If inflectional derivation is separate from spelling, and if the spelling of a specific set of inflectional conditions need not occur on the specific position containing those conditions (cliticization), LMBM could spell auxiliaries out on Comp without any movement of the conditioning features. All that is required is a language-specific condition at MS-level similar to (15.13):

(15.13)   iff [+wh]: spell [+Tense] over the left-most IP bracket

(15.13) is the interrogative "morpheme" for English. Under LMBM, such a long-distance MS-rule could spell any English auxiliary phrase-initially after bracket erasure has amalgamated all the Infl features, including Tense. The claim here is that Infl-Comp movement in English is a matter of marking the IP-initial bracket with the spelling of [+Tense], forcing the spelling of the auxiliary and its dependencies there, while their amalgamated G-representation remains under Infl. As (15.14) illustrates, not even metaphorical movement is involved:

(15.14)

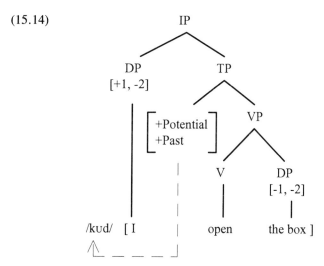

Movement in (15.14) is reduced to a disjunction of grammatical and spellout markers. MS reads the featural conditions for *could* under Infl but writes their phonological realization on the leftmost constituent of IP, just as it reads the conditions for the French pronouns in NP$_{Obj}$ position but writes them out on the leftmost constituent of TP. Constraints on this type of movement are those provided by the General Theory Affixation: movement should be restricted from the head X to the either side of a peripheral constituent of XP, where that constituent may be Y or YP but nothing else.[8]

The immediate problem with this explanation of Infl-Comp movement is that in other Germanic languages, when no auxiliary is present, rather than invoking Do-Support, the lexical verb moves to Comp, as (15.15) demonstrates.

(15.15)   a. Der junge Mann **kommt** heute abend
              "The young man is coming this evening"

b. **Kommt** der junge Mann heute abend?
   "Is the young man coming this evening?"

Under LMBM auxiliaries are not lexical items, hence are not phonologically present in D-Structure phrase markers. Lexical verbs, however, possess obligatory P-representations which are inserted at D-structure with the lexical item. Surely the only way for them to reach Comp is via Move α.

LMBM currently has had nothing to say about the spellout of lexical items, even though the assumption that syntax at any point contains phonological material represents an unpleasant violation of modularity. Beard (1981: 166–69, 311–12) argues that the P-representation of lexemes must be pure abstraction. That is, the P-representation of a lexical item cannot be any form of its surface phonological realization; Chomsky's claim that the phonological module is an interpretive device must be taken literally (Chomsky 1957). It is difficult to conclude otherwise since allomorphy, certainly an MS enterprise, applies to stem as well as affix phonology. This means either that MS may be the interpretive device which gives lexical P-representations phonological substance or is part of the phonological component which does.[9]

The positioning of clitics demonstrates that MS can spell a morpheme far from the functional features which condition the spelling. MS also has the authority to reduplicate a lexical P-representation. These two capacities of MS allow us to hypothesize that in those Germanic languages which seem to raise verbs to Comp in questions, no raising takes place at all. Rather, MS spells the P-representation (only) of the lexical verb on Comp.

(15.16)

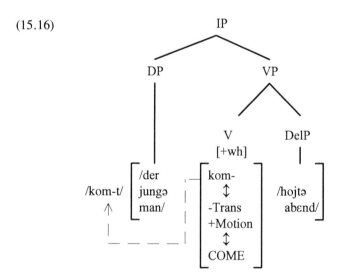

(15.16) illustrates this process for a structure essentially identical to (15.14) in German. (15.16) predicts that Interrogatives will normally be marked on the verb (as in Japanese and Yupik) but that the only alternatives are before or after the initial constituent of IP (English and other IE languages) or before or after the final constituent of IP (English tag questions, Quechua question markers).

Further, this account adds empirical substance to two previously mysterious syntactic notions. TRACES, for example, become the entire abstract lexical representation of the verb. Rather than actual movement, the distinction between V_i and $[e_i]_V$ is that between the position where the lexical information is stored and where the surface phonological representation is realized. If the G-representation of lexemes and pronominals were moved with the P-representation, nothing would be left to motivate resumptive pronouns. If the G-representation is left in its underlying position, it provides powerful motivation for resumption. Finally, coindexation, under this interpretation, is simply the morphological rule which realizes a grammatical morpheme in a position other than that occupied by its grammatical or lexical features. No further definition is required.

This section certainly has not done justice to a theory of movement as long-distance spelling; rather, it has attempted simply to demonstrate that a complete LMBM model of morphology offers promising new ways to deal with old, intractable problems. Only grammars with morphological components capable of long-distance spelling separate from derivation can account for cliticization under the General Theory of Affixation. However, if the MS-component can perform long-distant spelling and has the power to copy lexemes (reduplication), it is capable of copying to positions other than the one for which lexemes are selected. The result is an account which explains why movement does not effect grammatical or semantic relations: grammatical and semantic features never move.

15.5 THE ORDER OF AFFIXES

The MS-model outlined in chapter 3 assumes that the order of morphological operations on lexical stems follows the order of features in the lexical G-representation of the lexeme and that of the inflectional G-features in the node above it. The order of the features is presumed to be language-specific, although nothing of substance for LMBM hangs on this presumption.[10] The fact that inflectional features always occur in a syntactic position, while L-derivation features are part of the G-representation internal to the lexeme occupying that position, explains why inflectional affixes occur outside those of L-derivation when their function is syntactic. Given the Separation Hypothesis of LMBM and the Integrated Spelling Hypothesis, it does not follow that all inflectional markers will always appear only outside all L-derivation markers; indeed, it is meaningless to even speak of dedicated "inflectional markers" and "L-derivation markers" except in terms of a specific language. The advantage of LMBM in this regard is its account of cumulative and extended exponence. This section examines these two phenomena of fusional languages.

15.5.1 Cumulative Exponence

An MS-rule cannot ignore features in the G-representation of an L-derivate which satisfy its conditions; however, since MS conditions are independent of those on the L-rules which insert features, the possibility arises under LMBM of a wider range of function-spelling relations than are available to LMH. In other words, a condition on an MS-rule may include features from more than one L-operation, part of the features inserted by one L-operation, or a combination of inherent lexical features and derivation features. For example, the conditions on some MS-rule might be [+ Negation, − Singular, − Plural] or [+ Gradable, + Potential, + Negation], even though the L-rules operating over Negation, Number, Gradation, and Potentiality are all independent.

A good example of cumulative exponence based on L-derivation is found in Serbo-Croatian. Serbo-Croatian derived and underived adjectives widely undergo Subject nominalization. (15.17) illustrates how the suffix *-ac* most commonly marks these derivations when they are based on Possessional adjectives.

(15.17)   a. dronj-av "ragged"   dronj-av-ac "a ragged person"
          b. čađ-av "soot-y"   čađ-av-ac "sooty person"
          c. vaš-ljiv "lous-y"   vaš-ljiv-ac "lousy person" (literally)

If, however, the noun stem underlying a Possessional adjective belongs to a lexical class of about 50 commonly used nouns referring to salient body parts, the adjective and noun affixes are not concatenated, as (15.18) shows.

(15.18)   a. rog   rog-at   *rog-at-ac/rog-onj(a)
             "horn"   "horned"   "horned male"
          b. glav-a   glav-at   (*)glav-at-ac[11]/glav-onj(a)
             "head"   "(big) headed" "big-headed male"
          c. brad-a   brad-at   *brad-at-ac/brad-onj(a)
             "beard"   "bearded"   "bearded male"

We cannot claim that (15.17) and (15.18) are identical except for the truncation of *-at* before *-onj(a),* since truncation is unfalsifiable; in this case such an account would require a rule to remove an affix inserted by a previous rule. To avoid such unruly rules, we must conclude that in the case of (15.18) a single MS-rule marks features inserted by two different L-rules, the same two L-rules marked by two MS-operations in (15.17). The suffix *-onj(a)* responds to both the adjectival feature, say, [+ Gradation], and the nominal features, circumventing *-at,* which normally responds to the adjectival feature alone in a purely QAdj context.

The Subject nominals are formally unrelated to the adjectives but their functional behavior proves them derivationally identical. Even idiomatic meanings which hold for the adjective emerge in the noun. For example, *rep-at* "tailed" and *rep-onj-a* "tailed one" are derived from the noun *rep* "tail". Most often both QAdj and noun refer, as might be expected, to animals. *Repat,* however, has two rather unusual referents: people with tail-like vertebral extensions and the Devil. The adjective *rep-at* may be used nominally in its Definite form, which is *rep-at-i,* to refer to "the tailed one" or "the Tailed One = Devil". Both these idiomatic interpretations turn up in the noun, *reponja.* In fact, all idiosyncratic senses which appear in the adjectives of this class also occur in the corresponding nouns on *-onj(a),* a situation which would not be expected were the two L-derivations as unrelated as the MS-derivations.

We must conclude that the derivation of the class of nouns represented in (15.18) is based on that of the corresponding adjectives and that only affixation differs. The N $\rightarrow$ QAdj transposition adds the QAdj grammatical feature, [+ Gradation] and converts the underlying N to a property, [HORN{[ ]}], at conceptual level (see section 9.4.2). Gender and Number are then added by the nominal transposition as indicated by the left side of Figure 15.1. The MS-rule inserting the single suffix *-onj(a)* is thus conditioned by features located at all three levels of the G-representation: an inherent feature <(Salient) Body-Part>, the Possessional adjectival feature, and the nominal features added by transposition and adjusted by feature switches.

The MS-component of chapter 3 derives a capacity to "look ahead" at subsequent conditions from its short-term memory. It can hold condition C_1 in memory if it does not match any of its operations, and then move on to conditions C_2, C_3, and so on until it finds a combination of conditions which corresponds to some operation. The operation "suffix *at*" relies on this capacity. Since it, too, is conditioned not only by [<(Salient) Body-Part>] but by [+ Gradation] as well, *-at* cannot be copied if the derived G-representation contains [0Gradation]. If it does, the operation "suffix *onj(a)*" is executed.

15.5.2 Extended Exponence

Cumulative exponence is the result of a single MS-operation expressing several L-derivation operations; extended exponence results from a single

Figure 15.1

The Derivation and Affixation of rogonja *"horned male"*

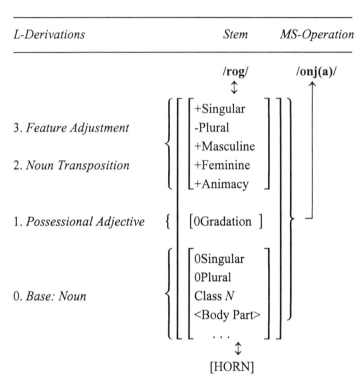

L-derivation conditioning several MS-operations. The Russian femininization of Subjective nominals ending on *-tel'*, such as *uči-tel'*, represents a
typical example. This derivation is marked by the suffix complex *-n-ic(a)*,
as in *uči-tel'-n-ic(a)* "teacher". Figure 15.2 represents *uči-tel'-n-ic(a)*,
which has undergone three L-derivations. The first is responsible for [Sub-
ject] and its coindexation with the argument structure of its verbal base.
The second is a transposition which changes the lexical class of the derivate
from verb to noun by copying the nominal features of Number and Natural
Gender which determine its Agentivity. Finally, femininization adjusts the
values of the Natural Gender features inserted by transposition to [− Masculine, + Feminine]. While one suffix, *-tel'*, marks both subjectification
and nominalization, two mark femininization: *-n* and *-ic(a)*. Hence Figure
15.2 in fact contains an instance each of cumulative and extended exponence.

The rules required to mark *uči-tel'nica* are summarized in (15.19). The

Figure 15.2

Derivation and Affixation of Russian učitel'nica *"teacher"*

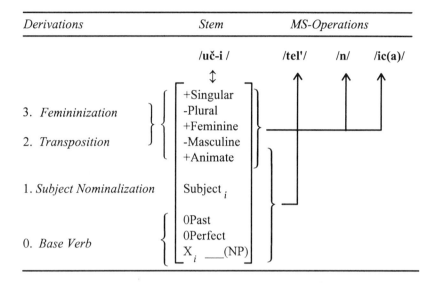

Derivations	Stem	MS-Operations

suffix *-tel'* marks the first two derivations, subjectivization and nominal transposition, and is selected from among other Subjective markers on the basis of stem type. The two suffixes *-n* + *ic(a)* together mark the feature adjustment to Femininity.

(15.19) a. $\emptyset \rightarrow$ -tel'   / $\left[\begin{array}{l} +\text{Animate} \\ \text{Subject} \end{array} \right]$

b. $\emptyset \rightarrow$ -n   / -tel'___
       [− Masculine, + Feminine, . . .]

c. $\emptyset \rightarrow$ -ic(a) / -n___
       [− Masculine, + Feminine, . . .]

Cumulative and extended exponence provide vivid evidence of the Separation Hypothesis that is as compelling as omissive and empty morphology. They graphically reflect the fact that conditions on affixation are only obliquely related to those on derivation. Lexical material provided by several rules may be interpreted by a single MS-rule, or several MS-rules may combine to interpret the material inserted by a single L-rule. Moreover, inherent lexical material often forms a part of conditions on L-derivation and MS-rules.

15.6 CONCLUSION

This chapter completes the description of universal morphological spelling begun in chapter 3. Much detail still begs clarification, but the general nature of the module is certainly discernible. The MS-component controls free morphemes just as it controls bound ones. Like bound morphemes, free morphemes are semantically empty markers of inflectional (never lexical) functions. Most interesting is the fact that the long-distant spelling described here may be extended in a minor way to obviate various types of movement, not only French clitic movement, but Infl-Comp movement as well. Under LMBM, movement is a matter of spelling to positions other than that occupied by conditioning grammatical functions or lexical items. The restrictions on such spelling are provided by Anderson's General Theory of Affixation. While all the details of long-distance spelling were not pursued here, the promise of obviating movement from syntax, while explaining trace, coindexation, and resumption, reflects the type of exciting new avenues opened by LMBM.

NOTES

1. Auxiliaries are available to L-derivation precisely to the extent lexical meaning may be attributed to them, that is, to the extent they may be copied into the lexicon. Thus *being* is a word to the extent the meaning EXIST can be inferred from it. A *doer* is someone who acts, not someone who is emphatic, the meaning derivable from the auxiliary's Emphatic grammatical function.

2. The interpretation of movement as bracket erasure and long-distance spelling in this chapter is equally available to the Distributed Morphology of Halle and Marantz (1993), who depend heavily on LMBM.

3. Chomsky's reference to these pronouns as empty categories is misleading. The categories (that is, nodes) are not empty but are in fact positions filled with grammatical functions which are not phonologically realized. A more descriptive term would be "zero category".

4. Why A ([±Gradable]) and V features do not similarly migrate to DP remains as much a mystery in LMBM as in other theories.

5. I am assuming that these features are bundled so that Subject and Object feature bundles are distinct and neither blocks the amalgamation of the other. This suggests structural factors at work similar to those proposed by Halle and Marantz (1993); however, details are currently unavailable.

6. The complete algorithm controlling the placement of the French pronouns, of course, is more complex than represented here. Another con-

straint prevents assignment to initial position. This inhibits preverbal positioning in positive but not Negative Imperatives:

Donnez le moi!	*Le me donnez! "Give it to me!"
*Ne donnez le moi pas!	Ne me le donnez pas "Don't give it to me!"

These additional complexities have no bearing on the issue at hand.

7. If we expand the General Theory of Affixation to include all grammatical morphemes, free and bound, we predict that some auxiliaries may also occur before the Subject NP, since the domain of Infl, IP, includes Subject NP. This is, of course, where the conjugated auxiliary occurs in questions for most IE languages: *Would your friend from Canada do it.* The General Theory of Affixation may well be a General Theory of Grammatical Morphemes with very important implications for linguistic theory that deserve serious thought and intensive study.

8. If the details of this approach can be worked out, it will offer an interesting account of Wackernagel's Law, too. Second position is simply the "enclitic" variant of movement to Comp, that being simply spelling in the "proclitic" position (Anderson 1993).

9. Because Distributed Morphology (Halle and Marantz 1993) includes both grammatical morphemes and lexemes in their lexicon but supports late lexical insertion, it is in a better position to predict that grammatical morphemes and lexemes will behave similarly here. However, the problems in maintaining a single morpheme discussed in earlier chapters are simply too great in number to justify this position in an overall theory of morphology.

10. Halle and Marantz (1993), for example, assume that affixes are structured like phrases, although the structure is morphological rather than syntactic. LMBM is comfortable with this proposal; indeed, this proposal assumes deep structural relations of those category features which may be represented in some language by free morphemes. However, given the fact that affixes end up sequentially ordered, it would seem that their structure must be erased at some point. The question then is whether erasure occurs before or after affixation.

11. Forms like *glav-at-ac* do occur but with a highly idiomatized reference, for example, *zub-at* "toothy": *zub-at-ac* = a species of fish; *ok-at* "(big-)eyed": *ok-at-ac* = a species of grape; *glav-at* "(big-)headed": *glav-at-ac* = a species of plant. Because these derivates are nondescriptive (do not refer to the entire class of objects with teeth, eyes, heads, and so on) and are unproductive, they are better explained in terms of stock expansion, which uses morphological "junk" in the sense of Lass (1990).

Chapter Sixteen

LMBM and the Agenda of Morphology

16.1 THE AGENDA OF MORPHOLOGY REVISITED

Chapter 1 concluded with an agenda for morphology, a catalogue of six fundamental goals for a theory of morphology derived from an examination of the ancient and modern literature. The succeeding chapters designed a morphological theory to achieve those goals, a framework referred to throughout the book as Lexeme-Morpheme Base Morphology (LMBM). This book, however, is organized as an argument against the only other complete modern theory of morphology, the Lexical Morpheme Hypothesis (LMH), and not around the six goals discovered in chapter 1. This final chapter will address this shortcoming by comparing the conclusions of intervening chapters with the goals of chapter 1 in an attempt to assess the success of LMBM in achieving them. The structure of this chapter is quite simple: each of the six goals of the agenda of morphology will be reexamined against the conclusions of this book, each in its own section and in the order in which they were presented in chapter 1.

16.1.1 What are the Grammatical Atoms, the Basic Elements of Language?

Time and again throughout this book we have seen evidence indicating that theories of grammar based on only one basic element, the morpheme, cannot account for the rich array of facts generally associated with morphology. Rather, any successful theory of grammar must provide for two means of meaning: the lexeme, with its necessary isomorphism of sound and cognitive meaning, and the grammatical morpheme, with its indirectly mapped association of sound and grammatical function. Grammatical morphemes, in fact, are semantically empty spelling operations, which range from the insertion of lexeme-like free morphemes requiring syntactic positions to modifications of the phonological representation of a lexeme. Grammatical morphemes may even be omitted altogether in transparent

377

contexts where other means of deducing the grammatical function(s) they express are available.

Chapter 2 demonstrated that, unlike uncontroversial lexemes, affixes serve without semantic content and often without grammatical function (empty morphemes), yet the meanings otherwise associated with them may be present in their absence (omissive or zero morphology). Affixes belong to rigorously closed classes which cannot be expanded by derivation rules. Chapter 9 demonstrated that the reason for this is that phrasal and lexical affixes express only the purely grammatical categories which define grammar. Unlike the lexeme, which may belong to one and only one lexical class, the same affix may mark derivates belonging to all three major lexical classes; thus, the categorization of affixes cannot be determined by the lexicon.

Finally, bound derivational morphemes must be described as processes distinct from the selection-copy process that accounts for the presence of lexical items in phrases. Affix-spelling and the spelling of free morphemes may be described as operations; however, stem mutations, revowelling, prosodic morphemes, and reduplication cannot be described as lexical selection-copying without ad hoc enrichment of both the lexicon and the phonological realization rules. It follows that the simplest and most consistent universal theory of morphology will represent grammatical morphemes as purely phonological operations on lexemes or phrasal positions, not as listable objects. The underlying principle uniting all methods of L- and I-derivation spelling is that these methods presuppose lexemes. Lexemes, on the other hand, presuppose nothing and, in fact, have an existence independent of grammar as identifying labels on objects in the real world.

The chapters following chapter 2 demonstrated a host of areas where the maintenance of a sharp distinction between lexemes and grammatical morphemes facilitates progress in developing a workable grammatical theory. Chapter 4 discovered a new generalization about L-derivational morphology: consistent, predictable Gender across several phonologically different affixes marking the same derivation. Chapter 5 determined how Natural Gender and Lexical Class are interpreted by a distinct I-category of Agreement. Because the same affixes often mark both L- and I-functions, just as *-ing* marks Progressive Aspect, Action and Resultative Nominalizations, and Present participles in English, LMH models without the Separation Hypothesis are ill-equipped for discovering these generalities. Under LMH, when two morphological variants are phonologically similar and share similar functions, the inevitable conclusion is that the two are variants of the same morpheme unless evidence of homonymy presents itself. In an LMBM model, variants of grammatical functions must be proved identical independent of any proofs that their markers are identical, since several markers may express a single function and several functions may be spelled out by a single marker.

Free grammatical morphemes behave like lexemes not only in their requirement of syntactic positions, but they also accept inflectional morphology like lexemes, as in the Russian Potential auxiliary *mog-* : *mog-u* "I can," *mož-eš'* "you can," *mož-et* "he/she can," and so on. The line between lexemes and free grammatical morphemes, is therefore not as sharp as that between lexemes and bound morphemes but it is nonetheless there. Inflectible free morphemes such as pronouns and auxiliaries share all four of the defining properties of bound morphemes discussed in chapter 2: they allow omissive and empty morphology, morphological asymmetry, and paradigmaticity, as do bound morphemes. Free grammatical morphemes also express only the closed classes of grammatical categories and never those of general cognition, and are not susceptible to L-derivation. Inflectibility, therefore, must be an entailment of phonological freedom rather than lexicality.

Free morphemes presuppose lexemes just as do bound morphemes. Only personal pronouns may occur in sentences as NPs independent of any other lexical element in the sentence; demonstratives, articles, auxiliaries, conjunctions, and prepositions appear only in the presence of some specific lexical class or syntactic category elsewhere in the sentence. However, free pronouns presuppose nominal lexical categories, since they are wholly determined by them (section 15.3). Unlike lexical nouns, pronouns cannot function extragrammatically as labels, as do terms like *men, exit, restaurant,* except as idiosyncratic surrogates for true lexemes as in "hers" and "his" towels, where they facetiously supplant "wife's" and "husband's".

Natural languages, then, are based on a single lexical element, the lexeme, a linguistic sign; however, grammatical processes are marked by output from an array of operations on phrases and the P-representation of lexemes limited only by the nature of that representation itself. The grammatical morpheme therefore represents a much wider selection of processes than lexical selection, although free morpheme insertion is one option. The basic elements of language, then, must be lexemes, narrowly defined, and bound grammatical morphemes, including clitics, must be operations on lexemes and free morphemes. Free grammatical morphemes have some of the phonological properties of lexemes, but all of the defining properties of grammatical morphemes.

16.1.2 How are Phonological, Grammatical, and Semantic Representations of the Basic Grammatical Elements Related to Each Other at their Respective Levels?

The answer to this question is the definition of "morphology" and the description of its role in language. In fact, morphology is the glue which holds the various levels of language together. Grammatical functions map lexical classes and syntactic categories (L- and I-derivation, respectively) onto semantics. The MS-module maps grammatical functions to phonology. Neither in the lexicon nor in syntax do we find the sound-meaning isomorphism widely assumed.

Sound-meaning isomorphism characterizes only the lexicon: the direct association of P-, G-, and R-representations of Figure 3.2, in fact, defines the lexeme. However, chapters 2 and 3 demonstrated that the relation between the G- and P-representations of the grammatical morphemes, which constitute the operation of the lexicon, word formation, is mediated by independent sets of conditions on either. On the phonological side, the L-derivational categories added to the G-representations of derived words stimulate the MS-operations to modify the P-representations of derived lexemes. These MS modifications intervene between the derivational categories and phonology, for they and the effects which they have on the stem must be interpreted allomorphically before they are interpreted by postcyclic phonological operations. MS-operations, it follows, map lexical G-representations onto phonology and vice versa.

On the semantic side, the same morpholexical categories are interpreted by semantics, as we saw in chapter 9 and elsewhere. Again, the mapping is not isomorphic: semantic TIME and PLACE are mapped onto a single set of Locative constructions while the single [POSSESS([ ], [ ])] feature is mapped onto two grammatical functions, Possessive and Possessional. Again, the function of morphology is to map from grammar to semantics and vice versa.

The same picture holds for syntax. On the one hand, inflectional categories like Subject and Object are crucial in identifying arguments and mapping them onto syntax. The Locative and Accusative Case endings or adpositions identify TIME and PLACE expressions but only via Locus, Goal, Origin, Duration category functions. On the other hand, the MS-component maps inflectional functions like these onto phonology, just as it maps lexical functions onto phonology. Again, the mapping is not one-one; the Progressive function of the VP, for instance, may be phonologically mapped onto the Subject NP, as in *John's coming*, or the Possessive function of the head of an NP may be mapped to the periphery of the NP, as in *the king of England's hat*. Morphology, therefore, comprises sets of mapping rules which glue syntax to semantics, on the one hand, and to phonology, on the other.

This description of morphology as a class of mapping systems from syntax and the lexicon to semantics and phonology depicts it as the all-pervasive linguistic system. However, it serves yet another mapping function in inflectional languages; it maps syntax to the lexicon via the Base Rule Theory, and lexicon to syntax via such Agreement algorithms as Table 5.4. Thus, it seems that morphology is the product of modularity. If grammar comprises various independent modules, it requires a system of transducers to translate the language of one module into that of any module it feeds. Morphology is that system.

If morphology is the set of intermodular translation mechanisms of language, it would seem to follow that isolating languages lack modularity since they ostensibly lack morphology. However, isolating languages only lack one side of morphology: allomorphy. Allomorphy is required only if a language relies on bound MS-operations. Isolating languages like Vietnamese and Chinese use lexical items to mark inflectional categories; for example, productive verbs and nouns serve double function as prepositions, as illustrated in (16.1), where the verb for "follow" functions at the inflectional level to mark the Accordant Case function:

(16.1)   a. Có   ba   đúǎ   **theo**   chúng ta
            there-be three   rascal follow   group 1stPER
            "There are three rascals following us"

         b. Anh   làm   **theo**   mẫu   này
            (brother) make   follow   model   this
            "Make it according to this model"

The allomorphy of MS is not required, since nothing is phonologically attached to the lexical stems which would require MS allomorphic operations. However, isolating languages do possess lexical and syntactic grammatical categories such as Noun Classes, Subject and Object positions, and other inflectional functions marked by adpositions. Evidence indicates that these categories serve the same function of mapping lexical and syntactic derivations onto semantics.

The only place in language, then, where semantic, grammatical, and phonological representations are directly related to each other, is the lexicon. The direct relation of these representations defines the lexeme. Elsewhere, at the syntactic, semantic, and phonological levels, information from one domain must be translated into the representations of any other domain which employs that information. Morphology does all the translating.

16.1.3 How Many Morphologies are There?

Matthews (1972, 1992) concluded that there must be two morphological components: one which accounts for lexical, the other, for inflectional morphology. The basis of this conclusion is the assumption that inflectional morphology is productive and consistently predictable while word formation is not. At the time Matthews was working on his classic WP model, linguistics was laboring under perceptions of morphology introduced by Chomsky (1970). Chomsky's version of Lexicalism assumed Bloomfield's position that the lexicon was essentially a depository of idiomatic information, a "collection of the lawless", as Di Sciullo and Williams have recently expressed it. Chomsky examined a few problems in English word formation such as the spelling variation in examples like *recite : recital : recitation* and concluded that word formation in toto is unpredictable. He strengthened his case with examples containing the effects of semantic intensification (*read : readable*) and Reflexive L-derivations like *self-addressed*, which he failed to recognize as regularities. Matthews accepted this interpretation of word formation even while rejecting other aspects of EST. He concluded on the basis of this assumption that inflection is a matter of syntax, which Chomsky assumed to comprise fully productive, exceptionless rules, while word formation comprises a set of less predictable if not unpredictable lexical operations.

Not only is the underlying assumptions here unreliable, evidence of the opposite conclusion far outweighs that supporting Matthews. Halle (1973) first demonstrated that inflection is not exceptionless. Meijs (1975) and Beard (1976b, 1977, 1981) demonstrated that most of Chomsky's other examples follow rules under adequate analysis. By the middle of the 70's, therefore, the original case for separating word formation from inflection had fallen. In fact, those who argue for Split Morphology and those who argue for Integrated Morphology are both partially correct: L- and I-derivation are discrete, but only one set of MS-operations serves to mark both. The crucial evidence for this conclusion comes from the fact that in many languages the most productive morphological markers express both lexical and inflectional grammatical functions.

Recall (2.17–2.20), reorganized below as (16.2–16.4), which demonstrates the range of functions marked by the most productive suffix in English, *-ing*.

(16.2)   The boy is **cutting** flowers   (Progressive Aspect)

(16.3)   a. The boy **cutting** the flowers   (Present participle)
          b. His **cutting** the flowers   (Gerundive)
             dismayed us

(16.4)   a. **Cutting** is for the birds   (Imperfective nominalization)
          b. He brought his **cuttings** in   (Objective nominalization)
          c. a very **cutting** remark   (Subjective adjective)

At the inflectional level this suffix marks the Progressive Aspect (16.2), the Present participle, and gerundive (16.3). However, it also expresses the

Imperfective and Resultative nominalizations and the Subjective adjective (16.4), which are unquestionably L-derivations. The exposition following (2.17–2.20) mentions several other suffixes in English and German which pose the same problem for the Split Morphology Hypothesis.

In order for the Split Morphology hypothesis to account for these facts, it will have to posit two sets of -*ing* suffixes and introduce one set in the lexicon and the other in syntax. The lexical set will be directly associated with a grammatical function or semantic reference. The inflectional set must consist of purely phonological operations in the sense developed in this book. The only motivation for such a division, however, is purely theoretical; there is no phonological, historical, or other empirical evidence that English has more than one suffix, -*ing*. The set of lexical affixes is hence a result of the assumption that L-derivation cannot be defined in terms of regularities while I-derivation may be so defined. However, we have seen throughout this book that idiomaticity is not the prerogative of any one grammatical module. Memorized linguistic material includes output of the base, the lexicon, the syntactic and phonological components. The proportion of memorized versus productively generated material is an issue of quantity, not quality, and of performance, not competence. The correct conclusion would seem to be that L- and I-derivation are discrete; however, only one set of MS-operations serves to mark the output of both.

16.1.4 What are the Categories of Morphology?

Chapter 9 reviewed substantive evidence indicating that the outer limit on the number of morphological categories is arbitrary and grammatically controlled. The many asymmetries between the grammatical and semantic categories are particularly persuasive evidence. Speakers may generate semantic categories at will (Jackendoff 1983) but they cannot generate grammatical categories at all. There is evidence of grammatical categories falling into desuetude, as Gender has dropped from the English language; however, no compelling evidence was found to indicate that any language contains grammatical categories which are in principle impossible in other languages. Specifically, the evidence upon which this study was based suggests a universal set of grammatical categories from which specific languages select. A core of these categories appears in all languages.

Even more interesting is the evidence of chapter 13 that the same set of grammatical categories determines each level of grammar which operates on categories. That chapter introduced the Unitary Grammatical Function Hypothesis, which postulates one set of grammatical functions for both L- and I-derivations, that is, which is available to both the lexicon and syntax. Chapter 14 accounted for this with a refinement of the Base Rule Theory, which assumes the base to be a general categorial component whose output is accessible to both the rules of the lexicon and those of syntax. This interpretation of the base predicts that languages will have two and only two types of categorially defined derivations, those of the lexicon (lexical) and those of syntax (inflectional). These two types of derivations should not differ in terms of base structure but only in terms of surface realization. L-derivations should name cognitive categories and functions while I-derivations should define relations in specific events. The complex nominal compounds of Germanic languages and the complex verbal compounds of Chukchee and Yupik exhibit all the properties of L-derivation, yet also reflect phrasal relations. Cognitive categories, on the other hand, should not be named by sentences. This, too, seems to be a universally excluded possibility.

16.1.5 What Are Morphological Rules?

The theory of morphology which has dominated linguistic research for the past century, referred to as LMH here, has assumed that morphological rules comprise lexical selection and allomorphy. Chapter 2 and subsequent chapters demonstrated faults in this assumption which account for the failure to predict some of the most common morphological phenomena, such as omissive and empty morphology, morphological asymmetry, and morphological operations like revoweling and reduplication. Morphological rules do not coincide with the principles and operations of syntax as proponents of Word Syntax maintain, although they do operate on the same set of grammatical functions. The roles of lexical and syntactic derivation, as just mentioned, are radically different.

Lexical derivation internalizes the functions of these categories in a way that I-derivation does not. While the Subject function of *bake* is present both lexically and inflectionally in *the baker bakes,* in the L-derivation that function relates the output of the L-derivation to its input, the base *bake*. The result is a lexeme, the name of a cognitive cateogory. The syntactic Subject reflects the same relation to a distinct word in the phrase, the verb *bakes*. The Subject function here participates in a description of a momentary event. The function is the same but it is precisely the nature of the lexical and syntactic operations which differentiates the Subject function in the derived noun from the same function in the phrase.

The rules of L- and I-derivation must execute at least four different tasks. First, both must be able to switch the values of binary grammatical features between " + " and " − ." Nonbinary features have other values. Agreement and Noun Class, for example, seem to be categories containing distinguishable properties: F-, M-, N-, and P-Agreement, Noun Class 1, 2, 3, and so forth. Binary features are special and the nature of that specialness is defined by the interplay between their values discussed in chapter

7. An important point to keep in mind is that this process is not a typical syntactic process and hence relies on an autonomous morphological component comprising discrete derivation and spelling operations.

Second, L-derivation must be capable of incorporating grammatical function features from base structure into a word. Syntactic rules are capable of amalgamating Infl features in the auxiliary or main verb nodes as they are raised (chapters 6 and 15). Chapter 14 demonstrated that L-rules incorporate such features into the lexical description of the word itself, as the example *the baker bakes* just mentioned indicates. However, the output of the functional L-derivation rule is both formally and semantically distinct from the output of syntactic rules operating on the same category functions. We therefore cannot sympathize with the position of Word Syntax, that morphology may be reduced to the principles of syntax.

Third, L-rules must possess the capacity to insert L-features not only into L-derivations, as in the case of transposition (chapter 8), but also into X^0 nodes. The latter capacity is required to account for pronouns, which are a set of often phonologically null L-features, such as [± Plural, ± Singular], [± Feminine, ± Masculine]. These features are recognized by syntax as lexical, not syntactic, since they are interpreted in terms of F-, M-, or P-Agreement for purposes of Agreement, just as they are when they appear in fully specified lexemes. Finally, the L-rule component must account for the mysterious expressive derivations. Nothing in LMBM or LMH predicts the semantics of Diminutive, Augmentative, Pejorative, or Affectionate forms. Honorific morphemes may belong to the same category.

Scalise (1984: 131–33), claims that the morphological component requires an independent module for expressive morphology. He reaches his conclusion on the basis of the fact that unlike either L- or I-derivation, expressive derivations are recursive, as in Italian *fuoco* ''fire'' → *fuocherello* ''little fire'' → *fuoch-erell-ino* ''nice little fire''. But Scalise's radical solution, and Stump's (1993) alternative, beg the question of why languages contain these functions at all. Are they grammatical, semantic — or pragmatic, as Dressler and Kiefer maintain? The traditional grammars of Slavic languages generally maintain that these derivations are asemantic and simply reflect an attitude of the speaker. A diminutive may certainly refer to an object small for its category, but it may also reflect either an affectionate or pejorative attitude on the part of the speaker toward the referent. It is not the referent which limits the semantic interpretation of a diminutive. Using a diminutive in referring to a large, burly man results in a pejorative connotation, but in reference to one's wife, regardless of her size, the effect is affectionate. This weak referentiality suggests semantic, perhaps pragmatic, rather than grammatical categories. Before we can decide which module accounts for these derivations, we must clarify the nature of the categories involved.

16.1.6 What Adjustments to Syntactic Theory Are Required to Accommodate a Theory of Morphology?

The inclusion of a clearly articulated MS-module in grammatical theory can no longer be avoided. The principles of syntax deal with structure, yet the categories discussed in this book cannot be reduced to structure. Anderson, Aronoff, Bazell, Carstairs-McCarthy, Halle, Kiefer, Leitner, Marantz, Stump, and Zwicky have compiled an enormous stock of evidence for autonomous morphology. However, the operations of lexical and inflectional morphological spelling are identical, excepting only the exclusive use of free morphemes to mark I-derivation. Affixes and other types of stem modifications are used for both types of derivation. However one accounts for inflectional marking, therefore, the same component must account for the marking of L-derivation.

Some of the L-derivation rules will operate over the same categories as syntax, even though the results of the two types of operations on these categories differ. Any account of the identity of derivational and inflectional categories expressed by the Unitary Grammatical Function Hypothesis will require a categorial module in the base that introduces grammatical functions, in such a way as to allow lexical and inflectional rules equal access to them.

As has already been proposed in HPSG, linear precedence rules must be stated independent of rules of hierarchic dominance. Proper analysis of linear sequencing led to the important discovery of the General Theory of Affixation by Anderson mentioned above, which establishes limits on the phonological distribution of all bound morphemes, affixes and clitics alike. This constraint will have to be adopted by any serious theory of grammar and possibly extended to free morphemes. Incorporating the General Theory into grammatical theory will not only provide better predictability for morphological spelling, but also will significantly reduce the number of movement types, since it predicts the distribution of clitics much better than do clitic movement rules.

Recall the differences between the Possessive and Plural NP constructions:

(16.5)   a. the kings of England
          b. the king of England's hat

The "long-distance" spelling of the Possessivity of *king* in (16.5a) suggests that grammatical features located in one position of a phrase may be expressed on a lexeme in a different position so long as it remains in the domain of the projection to which it is relevant and complies with the General Theory of Affixation.

The common way to explain such long-distance marking is via clitic movement at some level. The General Affixation Theory, however, obviates clitic and affix movement in favor of general principles, which account for all morpheme positioning. MS-operations, however, must be capable of reading features of a head and then spelling them out either on the head or on the periphery of its maximal projection. The interpretation of clitics in chapter 15 also requires no syntactic position for morphological clitics (as opposed to contractions); clitics are phrasal affixes, attached to lexemes just as lexical affixes are. The burden of proof now falls on those who claim that clitics enjoy structural relations with their host.

The scope of Plurality in (16.7) is the same as that of Possessivity in (16.6). However, the Plurality marker is attached to the head of the NP rather than to its peripheral lexical element.

(16.6)

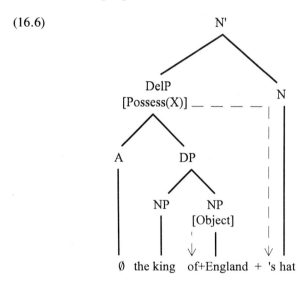

The point is that clitics are attached to the heads of phrases or to the periphery of the head's maximal projection. The range of clitic positions is therefore predictable, although the specific position is not. The specific position of an affix, phrasal or lexical, is determined by the definition of the affix itself. This means that no affix or clitic movement rules of any generality can be devised, yet the definitions of specific affixes are tightly constrained by such morphological concepts as ''head'' and ''governing domain'' and ''periphery''.

The morphological theory of Case presented in chapter 11 also has

(16.7)

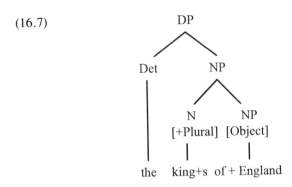

serious repercussions for syntactic theory. The catalogue of syntactic principles dependent upon Case Theory is indeed large. The evidence examined here indicates that up to two Case markers may appear on NPs, assuming that P is a Case marker, not a governor. So, Case theory and the Theta Criterion need revision. Chapter 11 concludes that Case is a purely morphological phenomenon restricted to fusional languages.

Finally, the morphological account of movement in chapter 15 may mitigate the problems associated with movement. Anderson (1993) has proposed extending the General Theory of Affixation to verb movement to second IP position; chapter 15 suggests defining some movement to Comp in terms of first IP position. Rethinking syntax in light of the foregoing will no doubt reduce its role in grammar considerably—the right direction, according to Minimalism.

16.2 THE FINAL WORD

All in all, LMBM provides a much more tightly constrained model of grammar. First, it defines in new and intriguing ways a range of terms which have long defied definition; "empty category," "pronoun," "lexicon," "lexical item," "morpheme," "functional category," "lexical category," "grammatical category," "grammatical function," "Case," "inflection," "trace," "coindexation," and "movement" are some of the fundamental theoretical terms which have been defined morphologically in this book. The central and perhaps most important of these terms is "lexicon," which LMBM totally disambiguates from grammar. LMBM defines the lexicon as an open class of cognitive category and function names comprising three and only three open classes, N, V, and A. Grammar comprises, in addition to the structural relations of syntax, a set of morphological categories, each of which contains a set of properties (functions). Finally, the MS-component deals exclusively with the phonological expression of grammatical categories.

LMBM not only preserves strict modularity, it further defines it. All the borders between all linguistic modules have now been defined as morphological interfaces comprising algorithms which convert the representations of one module to those of the other. These conversions are generally signalled by phonological modifications of the lexemes involved; thus, an intermediary between grammar and phonology is required.

We saw this in the algorithm required to convert lexical features into Agreement features across the lexicon/syntax boundary and the algorithms required of the MS-component to translate inflectional syntactic information into phonological. Beard (1991, 1993) and the preceding chapters also provide evidence of algorithms required by a semantic theory to translate lexical and syntactic information into conceptual structure.

There is one last significant ramification of LMBM, this one important for research into cognitive processing: indirect articulation is not the logically simplest means of signalling meaning. As the Natural Morphologists have correctly emphasized, the simplest means of expressing meaning verbally is the direct articulation of the linguistic sign, assumed to be the only primitive element of grammar from Aristotle to Chomsky. The lexicon takes advantage of this simplicity; grammar does not. The rise of conditioned indirect articulation reveals an extremely interesting property of the human brain: it can process conditional relations as efficiently as it can direct, isomorphic ones. The reason seems to be that the speaking organism is capable of extremely rapid deductive logic. Perhaps this logic is built into individual processing circuits or perhaps it is an independent parallel faculty. Either way, theories of language processing must be reinforced by a morphological component, which maps sound to meaning in a way radically different from the way lexemes do, a way which distinguishes the human communication system from those of other species.

Appendix A

Appendix A lists all the grammatical (category) functions of the *IE and contemporary IE Case system(s) alongside examples of L-derivations with the same functions. Examples are given for Serbo-Croatian; however, the corresponding Case for Sanskrit and preposition for English are given in parenthesis. Possessivity (Genitive : of) indicates that the possessor was marked by the Genitive in Sanskrit (thus probably in *IE), and in English, it is indicated by the preposition *of*. The Serbo-Croatian grammatical marking for the given function is provided in brackets. Since Sanskrit did not have a Possessional (Qualitative) Genitive, the Greek (Gk) is given; presumably it was an *IE function. The table does not imply a perfect correlation between the functions of Serbo-Croatian, Sanskrit Case, and English adpositions, only an overlap in the relevant one. All of the locational secondary functions imply the primary function Location (*at*) and may also be combined with Goal and Origin as discussed in chapters 9 and 10, for example, *go under, come from under*. These combinations have been omitted here.

Finally, *up* and *down* are not included because they function primarily as adverbs in most languages and, even in English, they appear sometimes as adverbs, sometimes as prepositions, and sometimes seem to be prepositional modifiers, as in *up under, up over, up into, up out of*. It is clear that these functions, along with their subfunctions such as *upstream* and *downstream*, beg further study.

I. Primary Declensional Functions

GRAMMATICAL FUNCTIONS (SKT : ENG)	LEXICAL DERIVATIONS
1. **Agent** (Ergative: Not in IE Languages)	
2. **Patient** (Absolutive: Not in IE Languages)	
3. **Subject** (Nominative: Word Order)	**Subjective Nominals**
čovek radi [Nom]	*rad-nik*
"the-man works"	"worker"

4. **Object** (Accusative: Word Order)
   zatvorili su čovek-a [Acc]
   "they-imprisoned the-man"

   Objective Nominals
   zatvor-en(-nik)
   "imprisoned (one)"

5. **Possessivity** (Genitive: of)
   plave oči čovek-a [Gen]
   "the-blue eyes of-the-man"

   Possessive Adjective
   čovek-ov-e plave oči
   "the-man's blue eyes"

6. **Possession** ((Gk) Genitive: with/of)
   čovek plav-ih oč-iju [Gen]
   "a-man with-blue eyes"

   Possessional Adjective
   plav-o-ok čovek
   "blue-eyed man"

7. **Measure** (Accusative: Word Order)
   idemo pet kilometara [Acc]
   "we-are-going five kilometers"

   Mensurative Nominals
   kilometr-až-a
   "(mileage)"

8. **Material** (Genitive: (out) of)
   sto od hrast-a [od + Gen]
   "a-table from oak"

   Material Nominals
   hrast-ov sto
   "oak(en) table"

9. **Partitivity** (Genitive: of)
   drvo od hrast-a [od + Gen]
   "wood from an-oak"
   meso od jagnj-et-a [od + Gen]
   "meat from a-lamb"

   Partitive Nominals
   hrast-ov-ina
   "oak (wood)"
   jagnj-et-ina
   "lamb (meat)"

10. **Distinction** (Ablative: than)
    brž-e od konj-a [od + Gen]
    "faster than a-horse"

    [Specialized usage:
    determined by
    comparative adjectives]

11. **Absolute** (Ablative: Word Order)
    . . .

    [Sentence Adverbs]

12. **Means** (Instrumental: by/with)
    žanje kos-om [Instr]
    "he-reaps with-a-scythe"

    Modalic Nominals
    kos-ac
    "reap-er" (machine)

13. **Route** (Instrumental: by/via)
    ploviti mor-em [Instr]
    "travel by-sea"

    Vialic Adjective
    mor-sk-a (plovidba)
    "sea (voyage)"

14. **Manner** (Acc/Instr: like)
    živeti rob-om [Instr; kao + Nom]
    "to-live like a-slave"

    Similitudinal Adjective
    rop-sk-i
    "slav-ish"

15. **Ession** (Acc/Instr: as)
    raditi kao lekar [kao + Nom]
    "to-work as a-doctor"

    Essive Adjective
    lekar-sk-i
    "doctor-ly, medical"

16. **Duration** (Instrumental: (for))
    čitav-o let-o smo radili [Acc]
    "the-whole summer we worked"

    Durative Adjective
    let-nj-i raspust
    "summer holidays"

17. **Iteration** (. . . ?: (on) . . . s)
    nedelj-om idemo (u crkvu) [Instr]
    "(on) Sunday(s) we go (to church)"

    Iterative Adjective
    nedelj-n-a (misa)
    "Sunday (mass)"

18. **Accordance** (Ablative: by)
    po zakon-u [*po* + Loc]
    "according to the law"

    Accordant Nominals
    zakon-it
    "lawful"

19. **Purpose** (Dative: to/for)
    karte za igr-anj-e [*za* + Acc]
    "cards for playing"
    (platiti) za pošt-u [*za* + Acc]
    "(pay) for the mail"

    Purposive Nominals
    igr-ać-e kart-e
    "playing cards"
    pošt-ar-in-a
    "post-age"

20. **Exchange** (? : for)
    za pet dinara [*za* + Acc]
    "(buy the book) for 5 dinars"

    Permutative
    . ? .
    . ? .

21. **Cause** (Ablative: from/out of)
    pocrvenio je od stid-a [Various Ps]
    "he blushed from shame"

    . ? .
    . ? .
    . ? .

22. **Sociation** (*saha* + Instrumental: with)
    raditi sa čovek-om [*sa* + Instr]
    "to-work with a-person"

    Sociative Noun
    sa-rad-nik
    "co-work-er"

SPATIAL

*23a. **Location** (Locative: at/in/on)
    raditi u pekarnic-i [*u* + Loc]
    "to-work at a-bakery"

    Locative Nouns
    rad-io-nic-a
    "work-shop"

*23b. (Temporal = Punctuality: at/in/on)
    u noć, u veče(r) [*u* + Acc]
    "at night", "in the evening"

    Relational Adjective
    večer-nje izdanje
    "evening edition"

*24. **Goal** (Accusative/Locative: to)
    voz za Beograd [*u/na/za* + Acc]
    "train for Beograde"

    Goal Nominals
    beograd-sk-i voz
    "Belgrade train"

*25. **Origin** (Ablative: from/of)
    čovek iz Amerik-e [*iz* + Gen]
    "a-person from America"
    voz iz Beograd-a [*iz* + Gen]
    "train from Belgrade"

    Originative Nominals
    Amerik-an-ac
    "(an) American"
    beograd-sk-i voz
    "Belgrade train"

II. Secondary Declensional Categories

SPATIAL

26. **Inession**(Locative: in)
    raditi u pekarnic-i [*u* + Loc]
    "to-work at a-bakery"

    Locative Nouns
    rad-io-nic-a
    "work-shop"

27. **Adession**(Locative: on)
    raditi na ulic-i [*na* + Loc]
    "to-work on the-street"

    Locative Nouns
    rad-il-išt-e
    "work site"

28a. **Anteriority** (*agre* + Gen: in front of)
pred sob-om [*pred* + Instr]
"in-front-of the-room"

Anterior Nominals
pred-sob-lj-e
"anteroom"

28b. (Temporal: *pūrva* + Abl: before)
pred rat [*pred* + Acc]
"before the-war"

Antecedent Nominals
pred-rat-n-i
"prewar"

29a. **Posteriority** (*paścāt* + Abl: behind)
za gor-ama [*za* + Instr]
"behind the-mountains"

Posterior Nominals
za-gor-sk-i/za-gor-j-e
"transmontane (region)"

29b. (Temporal: *parena* + Abl: after)
posle rat-a [*posle* + Gen]
"after the-war"

Subsequential Nominals
po(sle)-rat-n-i
"postwar"

30. **Superession** (*upari* + Gen: over)
nad zem-lj-om [*nad* + Instr]
"above the-ground"

Superessive Nominals
nad-zem-n-i
"overground"

31. **Subession** (*adhas* + Acc: under)
pod vod-om [*pod* + Instr]
"under the-water"

Subessive Nominals
pod-vod-n-i
"underwater"

32. **Transession** (*adhi* + Acc: across)
preko mor-a [*preko* + Gen]
"*across the-ocean*"

Transessive Nominals
*preko-mor-sk-i/preko-
mor-j-e*"overseas"

33. **Intermediacy** (*antar* + Acc: between)
medu narod-ima [*medu* + Instr]
"bet ween nations"

Intermediative Nominals
medu-narod-n-i
"international"

34. **Prolation** (*anu* + Acc: along)
duž Dunav-a [*duž* + Gen]
"along the-Danube"

Prolative Nominals
*po-dunav-sk-i/po-dunav-
lj-e* "Danubian (basin)"

35. **Proximity** (*abhyāśe* + Gen: by/near/at)
pri mor-u [*pri* + Dat]
"by the-sea"

Proximate Nominals
pri-mor-sk-i/pri-mor-j-e
"coastal (region)"

36. **Opposition** (*prati* + Acc: against)
protiv avion-a [*protiv* + Gen]
"against aircraft"

Oppositive Adjective
protiv-avion-sk-i
"anti-aircraft"

37. **Perlation** (*tiras* + Acc: through)
kroz šum-u [*kroz* + Acc]*pro-laz*
"through the-woods"

Perlative Nominals?
(deverbal nominalization)
"throughway"

38. **Circumession** (*pari* + Acc: around)
oko kuć-e [*oko* + Gen]
"around the house"

Circumessive
oko-vrat-nik
"collar" (*vrat* "neck")

39. **Termination** (? + ?: up to)
do kuć-e [*do* + Gen]
"as far as the house"

Terminative
. ? .
. ? .

NONSPATIAL

40. **Concession** (. ? .)   **Concessive**
    uprkos čovek-u [uprkos + Dat]   . ? .
    "despite the man"   . ? .

41. **Distribution** (. ? .)   **Distributive?**
    po deset dinara [po + Loc]   . ? .
    "ten dinars apiece"   . ? .

42. **Exception** (. ? .)   **Exceptive?**
    [Negative [Sociation]]   . ? .
    osim čovek-a [osim/izuzev + Gen]   . ? .
    "except the man"   . ? .

43. **Privation** (*ré, vinā* + Inst: without)   **Privative Adjective**
    [Negative [Possession]]
    bez vod-e [bez + Gen]   *bez-vod-an*
    "without water"   "waterless, arid"

44. **Thematicity** (*pari* + Acc: about)   . ? .
    (misliti) o kuć-i [o + Loc]   . ? .
    "(think) about the house"   . ? .

III. Tertiary (Recent) Declensional Functions

SERBO-CROATIAN

kod "at someone's (chez)" *mesto* "instead of"
sred "amid"   *radi* "for the sake of"
zbog "thanks to"   *prema* "toward, opposite"

ENGLISH

atop	amid	alongside	but	since	until
astride	among	save	opposite	including	during
aboard	beside	except	near	toward	besides

Appendix B

Productive Yupik Denominal Verbalizations

1. **-(s)ja**   Purpose

     "go to V"
     "go for N"

qəpχaʁ- "work": *qəpχaʁ-ja-* "go (in order) to work"
uŋuna- "tell": *uŋuna-sja-* "go to tell"
nəχsaq "seal": *nəχsaʁ-ja-* "go after seals"

2. **-ni(ʁ)**   Purpose (food)

     "go for N"

ajvə-q "walrus": *ajvəʁ-niʁ-* "hunt for walrus"
əɬqwa-q "water lilies": *əɬqwaʁ-niʁ* "pick water lilies"

3. **-qu**   Purpose (non-food)

     "go for N"

iljaŋqu-q "ice": *iljaŋqu-qu-* "go for ice"
aŋwaʁun "oar": *aŋwaʁut-qu-* "go for an oar"

4. **-ta**   Goal

     "go to N"

Uŋaziq "Ungazik": *Uŋaziχ-ta-* "go to Ungazik"
porta "port": *porta-ta-* "head for port"

5. **-tu**   Patient

     "eat N"

iqaɬjuk "fish": *iqaɬjux-tu* "eat fish"
əɬqwaq "sea cabbage": *əɬqwaχ-tu* "eat sea cabbage"

6. **-sjugni**   Manner

     "be like N"

juk "person": *jux-sugni-* "be like a person"
aŋjaq "canoe": *aŋjaχ-sugni-* "be like a canoe"

7. **-pagni**   Manner

     "be like N"

əɬqwaq "sea cabbage": *əɬqwaχ-pagni-* "smell like s. c."
ujgaq "stone": *ujgaχ-pagni* "be hard, tough"

8. **-(ŋ)iraʁ**   Manner?

     "play at N"
     "act like N"

ama "wolf": *ama-ŋiraʁ* "play wolf' "
ama-ŋiraq "a game of 'wolf' "

9. **-lgu**   Possessive

     "have N"

kamə-k "shoes": *kamə-lgu-q* "he has shoes"
savi-k "knife": *savi-lgu-ŋa* "I have a knife"

     Part. *-lək + u*   "having N"

juk kamə-lgu-q "the man having shoes . . ."

10. **-tu**   Poss + Intens

     "have many N"

kaməx-tu-ŋa "I have many shoes"

11. **-ŋ**   Inchoative

     "get N"

iga-q "book": *iqa-ŋ-a-qu-q* "he gets a book"

     Possessive   (Intrans)

pana "spear": *pana-ŋ-a-qu-ŋa* "I get a spear"

12. *-li*   Caus + Poss   "provide
           Transitive: "with N"   *javuqun* "oar": *javuqut-əli-* "provide X
                                                with oars"

           Intransitive: "prepare N"   *ajvə-q* "walrus": *ajvə-li-* "prepare
                                                walrus"

13. *-ŋļja*   Causative   "cause N"   *pana* "spear": *pana-ŋļja-* "make a
                                                spear"

           Trans/Intrans   *məŋtəʁa-q* "house": *məŋtəʁa-ŋļja-*
                                                "build a house"

Appendix C

Chukchee Denominal Verbalizations

1. **-tku** — Instrumental (Intransitive)
   rəpe-ŋə "hammer" rəpe-tku-k "to hammer"
   walə "knife" walə-tku-k "to cut"
   wəlpə "shovel" wəlpə-tku-k "to shovel"

2. **-lʔAt** — Instrumental (Intransitive)
   əʔtw-ʔet "boat" əʔtw-əlʔet-ə k "to boat"
   əʔtt-ʔən "dog" əʔtt-əlʔet-ək "go by dogs"
   (Restricted to means of Transportation)
   n-ejməsq-əqin "sticky" ejməsq-et-ək "to stick"

3. **-twE** — Inchoative Adjectives
   nə-čiwm-əqin "short" čiwm-ətvi-k "to get short"
   nə-wəlg-əqen "thin" wəlg-ətve-k "to thin down"

4. **-rʔO** — Inchoative Intransitive
   piŋepiŋ "snowfall" piŋe-rʔu-k "snowfall set in"
   (Restricted to natural phenomena)

5. **-twa** — Intransitive
   nəm-nəm "settlement" nəm-ətwa-k "live, get along"
   — from Ns & As
   n-untəm-qin "quiet" ontəm-ətwa-k "be peaceful"

6. **-jp/ep** — Possessive?
   pamʔja-lgən "fur socks" pamʔja-jp-ək "put on fur socks"
   — Intransitive
   ewirʔ-ən "clothes" awerʔ-ep-ək "dress"
   kʔeli "cap" kʔale-jp-ək "put on a cap"
   BUT: anŋen "anger" anŋena-jp-ək "get mad"

7. **-tw** — Reversive
   plek-ət "shoes" plek-ətw-ək "take off shoes"
   ričit "belt" ričit-ətw-ək "unbelt"

8. **-O** — Intransitive
   a. Hunt N
   rʔew-ət "whales" rʔew-u-k "to whale"
   meməl-te "seals" meməl-o-l "to seal"
   b. Consume N
   tekičg-ən "meat" tekičg-u-k "eat meat"
   kəmček-ət "potatoes" kəmček-o-k "eat potatoes"
   c. Take
   kimitʔ-ət "goods" kimitʔ-u-k "take goods"
   əʔtw-ət "boats" əʔtw-u-k "take boats"

9. **-ŋEt** — Durational
   lʔele-ŋ "winter" lʔele-ŋit-ək "to winter"
   ele-n "summer" ele-ŋit-ək "to summer"

10. **t(A)- . . . -ŋ** — Make Intransitive
    lili-t "sleeves" te-lili-ŋ-ək "make sleeves"
    pamʔja-t "fur socks" ta-pamʔja-ŋ-ək "make fur socks"

11. **-At** — Intransitive from Ns & As
    wenn-əwen "envy" wenn-et-ək "to envy"
    alpəŋŋ-lgən "payment" alpəŋŋ-at-ək "make a payment"

12. **-Aw** — Intransitive from Ns & As
    tumgətum "friend" tumg-ew-ək "become friends"
    nə-korg-əqen "happy" korg-aw-ək "rejoice"

399

TRANSITIVIZING CIRCUMFIXES

13. **rə- . . . -Aw**	Transitive	*ačəŋ* "loan" *r-ačəŋ-aw-ək* "borrow"
rə- . . . -At	from Ns & As	*kim-ə-kim* "mixture" *rə-kim-ew-ək* "mix"
		ačgət "row" *r-ačgət-aw-ək* "put in a row"
		mumkəl "coat loop" *rə-mumkəl-ew-ək* "fasten"
		qergəqer "light" *rə-qerg-aw-ək* "illuminate"
		wətgər "crack" *rə-wətgər-ew-ək* "put in crack"
	Also used	*anŋenajn-ək* "get mad" *r-anŋenajn-aw-ək* "anger"
	to Transi-	*piŋku-k* "go out" *rə-piŋku-w-ək* "put out, exting."
	tivize Vs	*təŋe-k* "grow" *rə-təŋe-w-ək* "grow N, raise N"
		gagčaw-ək "hurry" *rə-gagčaw-at-ək* "hurry N"
		nəwil-ək "stop" *rə-nwil-et-ək* "stop N"

Bibliography

Abney, Steven 1987. *The English Noun Phrase in its Sentential Aspect.* Ph.D. dissertation, MIT.

Adelaar, Willem 1977. *Tarma Quechua: Grammar, Texts, Dictionary.* Lisse: Peter de Ridder.

Allen, Margaret 1978. *Morphological Investigations.* PhD Dissertation, University of Connecticut.

Anceaux, J. C. 1965. *The Nimboran Language: Phonology and Morphology.* The Hague: Martinus Nijhoff.

Anderson, John 1971. *The Grammar of Case: Towards a Localistic Theory.* Cambridge: Cambridge University Press.

———— 1977. *On Case Grammar: Prolegomena to a Theory of Grammatical Relations.* London-Cambridge: Croom Helm.

Anderson, Stephen R. 1982. Where's Morphology? *Linguistic Inquiry* 13.571–612.

———— 1984. On Representations in Morphology: Case Marking, Agreement and Inversion in Georgian. *Natural Language & Linguistic Theory* 2.157–218.

———— 1986. Clitics are Phrasal Affixes. II. International Morphology Meeting, "Theoretical Approaches to Morphology," Veszprém.

———— 1992. *A-Morphous Morphology.* Cambridge: Cambridge University Press.

———— 1993. Wackernagel's Revenge: Clitics, Morphology, and the Syntax of Verb-Second Position. *Language* 69.68–98.

Archangeli, Diana 1983. The Root CV-Template as a Property of the Affix: Evidence from Yawelmani. *Natural Language & Linguistic Theory* 1.347–84.

Aronoff, Mark 1976. *Word Formation in Generative Grammar.* Linguistic Inquiry Monograph 1. Cambridge, MA: MIT Press.

———— 1980. Contextuals. *Language* 56.744–58.

———— 1992. Stems in Latin Verbal Morphology. *Morphology Now,* ed. Mark Aronoff. Albany: SUNY Press.

———— 1993. *Morphology by Itself; Stems and Inflectional Classes.* Cambridge, MA: MIT Press.

Babby, Leonard 1973. The Deep Structure of Adjectives and Participles in Russian. *Language* 49.349–60.

—— 1975. *A Transformational Grammar of Russian Adjectives.* The Hague: Mouton.

—— 1980a. *Existential Sentences and Negation in Russian.* Linguistica Extranea, Studia 8. Ann Arbor, MI: Karoma.

—— 1980b. The Syntax of Surface Case Marking. *Cornell Working Papers in Linguistics.* Ithaca, NY: Department of Languages and Linguistics, Cornell University, 1.1–32.

Baker, Mark 1985. The Mirror Principle and Morphosyntactic Explanation. *Linguistic Inquiry* 16.373–415.

—— 1988a. *Incorporation: A Theory of Grammatical Function Changing.* Chicago: University of Chicago Press.

—— 1988b. Morphology and Syntax: An Interlocking Independence. *Morphology and Modularity. In Honour of Henk Schultink,* Publications in Language Sciences 29, ed. Martin Everaert, Arnold Evers, Riny Huybregts, and Mieke Trommelen. Foris: Dordrecht, 9–32.

——, Kyle Johnson, and Ian Roberts 1989. Passive Arguments Raised. *Linguistic Inquiry* 20.219–51.

Barker, M. A. R. 1964. *Klamath Grammar.* University of California Publications in Linguistics, 32. Berkeley, CA: University of California Press.

Battistella, Edwin 1990. *Markedness: The Evaluative Structure of Language.* Albany: State University of New York Press.

Baudouin de Courtenay, Jan 1889. O zadaniach językoznawstwa. *Prace filologiczne* 3.92–115. [Translation in Stankiewicz 1972, 125–143.]

—— 1895. *Versuch einer Theorie phonetischer Alternationen: Ein Kapitel aus der Psychophonetik.* Strassburg/Crakow. [Translation in Stankiewicz 1972, 144–212.]

Bauer, Laurie 1983. *English Word-Formation.* Cambridge Textbooks in Linguistics. Cambridge: Cambridge University Press.

Bazell, C. E. 1949. On the Problem of the Morpheme. *Archivum Linguisticum* 1.1–15. [Reprinted in Hamp, Householder, and Austerlitz, eds., 216–26].

—— 1952. The Correspondence Fallacy in Structural Linguistics. *Studies by Members of the English Department, Istanbul University* 3.1–41.

Beard, Robert 1976a. A Semantically Based Model of a Generative Lexical Word Formation Rule for Russian. *Language* 52.108–20.

—— 1976b. Derivational Intensification in IE Languages. *Chicago Linguistic Society* 12.49–58.

—— 1977. On the Extent and Nature of Irregularity in the Lexicon. *Lingua* 42.305–42.

——— 1981. *The Indo-European Lexicon: A Full Synchronic Theory.* North-Holland Linguistic Series, 44. Amsterdam: North-Holland.

——— 1982. Plural as a Lexical Derivation (Word Formation). *Glossa* 16.133–48.

——— 1984. Optimism, Pessimism and Finer Distinctions. *Quaderni di semantica* 5.277–87.

——— 1985. Is Separation Natural? *Studia grammatyczne* 7.119–34.

——— 1986. The Gender-Animacy Hypothesis. Paper presented at the American Association of Teachers of Slavic and East European Languages, New York (to appear in *Journal of Slavic Linguistics*).

——— 1987a. Morpheme Order in a Lexeme/Morpheme Based morphology. *Lingua* 72.73–116.

——— 1987b. Lexical Stock Expansion. *Rules and the Lexicon: Studies in Word Formation,* ed. Edmund Gussmann. Lublin: Catholic University Press, 24–41.

——— 1988. On the Separation of Derivation from Morphology: Toward a Lexeme/Morpheme Based Morphology. *Quaderni di semantica* 9.3–59.

——— 1990. The Nature and Origins of Derivational Polysemy. *Lingua* 81.101–40.

——— 1991. Decompositional Composition: The Semantics of Scope Ambiguities and 'Bracketing Paradoxes'. *Natural Language & Linguistic Theory* 9.195–229.

——— 1993. Simultaneous Dual Derivational Origin. *Language* 69.716–41.

——— ms. Movement as Morphology. Lewisburg, PA: Bucknell University.

Beller, Richard and Patricia Beller 1979. Huasteca. Modern Aztec Grammatical Sketches, Vol. 2, ed. Ronald Langacker. Dallas: SIL 199–306.

Belousov, Viacheslav, Irina Kovtunova and Irina Kruchinina 1989. *Kratkaia russkaia grammatika.* Moscow: Russkii iazyk.

Bennett, Charles 1914. *Syntax in Early Latin.* Vol. 2: *The Cases.* Boston: Allyn and Bacon.

Berwick, Robert and Amy Weinberg 1984. *The Grammatical Basis of Linguistic Performance: Language Use and Acquisition.* Cambridge, MA: MIT Press.

Bierwisch, Manfred 1988. On the Grammar of Local Prepositions. *Syntax, Semantik und Lexikon,* Studia Grammatica, 29, ed. Manfred Bierwisch, Wolfgang Motsch, and Ilse Zimmerman. Akademie-Verlag: Berlin, 1–65.

Bloomfield, Leonard 1933. *Language.* New York: Henry Holt.

—— 1939. Menomini Morphophonemics. *Travaux du Cercle Linguistique de Prague* 8.105–15.

—— 1962. *The Menomini Language.* New Haven, Yale University Press.

Booij, Geert 1988. The Relation between Inheritance and Argument Linking: Deverbal Nouns in Dutch. *Morphology and Modularity. In Honor of Henk Schultink,* ed. Martin Everaert, Arnold Evers, Riny Huybregts and Mieke Tommelen. Dordrecht: Foris, 57–73.

—— 1993. Against Split Morphology. *Yearbook of Morphology 1993,* ed. Geert Booij and Jaap van Marle. Dordrecht: Kluwer, 27–49.

Booij, Geert and Jerzy Rubach 1987. Postcyclic versus Postlexical Rules in Lexical Phonology. *Linguistic Inquiry* 18.1–44.

Borer, Hagit 1990. V + ing: It Walks Like an Adjective, It Talks Like an Adjective. *Linguistic Inquiry* 21.95–103.

Botha, Rudolf 1980. *Word-Based Morphology and Synthetic Compounding.* Stellenbosch Papers in Linguistics, 5. Stellenbosch: University of Stellenbosch.

—— 1981. A Base Rule Theory of Afrikaans Synthetic Compounding. In Moortgat, van der Hulst, and Hoekstra, 1–77.

—— 1984. *Morphological Mechanisms: Lexicalist Analysis of Synthetic Compounds.* Language & Communication Series, 7. Oxford: Pergamon Press.

Brauner, Siegmund and Irmtraud Herms 1986. *Lehrbuch des modernen Swahili.* Leipzig: VEB Verlag Enzyklopädie.

Brekke, M. 1988. The Experiencer Constraint. *Linguistic Inquiry* 19.169–80.

Bresnan, Joan 1978. A Realistic Transformational Grammar. *Linguistic Theory and Psychological Reality,* MIT Bicentennial Studies, ed. Morris Halle, Joan Bresnan, and George Miller. Cambridge, MA: MIT Press, 1–59.

—— ed. 1982a. *The Mental Representation of Grammatical Relations.* Cambridge, MA: MIT Press.

—— 1982b. The Passive in Lexical Theory. In Bresnan, 1982a, 3–86.

—— and Jane Grimshaw 1978. The Syntax of Free Relatives in English. *Linguistic Inquiry* 9.331–91.

—— and Jonni Kanerva 1989. Locative Inversion in Chichewa: A Case Study of Factorization in Grammar. *Linguistic Inquiry* 20.1–50.

Brown, Cecil 1985. Polysemy, Overt Marking, and Function Words. *Language Science* 7.283–332.

Bybee, Joan 1985. *Morphology: A Study of the Relation between Meaning and Form.* Amsterdam: John Benjamins.

Carrier-Duncan, Jill 1985. Linking of Thematic Roles in Derivational Word Formation. *Linguistic Inquiry* 16.1–34.

Carstairs, Andrew 1981. *Notes on Affixes, Clitics and Paradigms.* Bloomington, IN: Indiana University Linguistics Club.

———— 1987. *Allomorphy in Inflexion.* Croom Helm Linguistics Series, London: Croom Helm.

———— 1990. Phonologically Conditioned Suppletion. In Dressler et al., 17–24.

Carstairs-McCarthy, Andrew 1989. Review of Szymanek, Categories and Categorization in Morphology. *Journal of Linguistics* 25.506–509.

———— 1992a. *Current Morphology.* London: Routledge.

———— 1992b. Uses for Junk: A New Look at Inflection Classes. International Morphology Meeting, Krems, August 8–11.

———— 1993. Gender and Inflection Class: Syntagmatic and Paradigmatic Synonymy-Avoidance. Paper read at the Typology and Parameters Workshop, 11th ICHL, UCLA, August, 1993.

Chomsky, Noam 1957. *Syntactic Structures.* The Hague: Mouton.

———— 1965. *Aspects of the Theory of Syntax.* Cambridge, MA: MIT Press.

———— 1970. Remarks on Nominalization. *Readings in English Transformational Grammar,* ed. Roderick Jacobs and Peter Rosenbaum. Waltham, MA: Ginn & Company, 184–221.

———— 1981. *Lectures on Government and Binding.* Dordrecht: Foris.

———— 1989. Some Notes on Economy of Derivation and Representation. Functional Heads and Clause Structure, *MIT Working Papers in Linguistics,* 10.43–74.

———— 1992. *A Minimalist Program for Linguistic Theory.* MIT Occasional Papers in Linguistics, 1. Cambridge, MA: Department of Linguistics and Philosophy, MIT.

———— and Morris Halle 1968. *The Sound Pattern of English.* Studies in Language. New York: Harper & Row.

Christensen, Kirsti 1986. Complex Passives, Reanalysis, and Word Formation. *Nordic Journal of Linguistics* 9.135–62.

Churchward, C. Maxwell. 1953. *Tongan Grammar.* London: Oxford University Press.

Chvany, Catherine 1975. *On the Syntax of BE-Sentences in Russian.* Columbus, OH: Slavica.

Clark, Eve and Herbert Clark 1979. When Nouns Surface as Verbs. *Language* 55.767–811.

Cole, Peter 1985. *Imbabura Quechua.* Croom Helm Descriptive Grammars. London: Croom Helm.

Cook, Walter 1989. *Case Grammar Theory.* Washington: Georgetown University Press.

Corbett, Greville 1983. *Heirarchies, Targets and Controllers: Agreement*

Patterns in Slavic. University Park, PA: Pennsylvania State University Press.

———— 1987. The Morphology/Syntax Interface. *Language* 63.299–345.

———— 1991. *Gender*. Cambridge Textbooks in Linguistics. Cambridge: Cambridge University Press.

Corbin, Danielle 1987. *Morphologie dérivationelle et structuration du lexique*, Vol. 1. Linguistische Arbeiten 193. Tübingen: Max Niemeyer.

Coulson, Michael 1976. *Sanskrit: An Introduction to the Classical Language*. Teach Yourself Books. London: Hodder and Stoughton.

De Saussure, Ferdinand 1916. *Cours de linguistique générale*. Lausanne/Paris.

Dik, Simon 1981. *Functional Grammar*. Dordrecht: Foris.

DiSciullo, Anna M. and Edwin Williams 1987. *On the Definition of Word*. Linguistic Inquiry Monograph 14. Cambridge, MA: MIT Press.

Dixon, R. M. W. 1988. *A Grammar of Boumaa Fijian*. Chicago: University of Chicago Press.

Don, Jan 1993. *Morphological Conversion*. OTS Dissertation Series. Utrecht: Research Institute for Language and Speech.

Dowty, David 1991. Thematic Proto-Roles and Argument Selection. *Language* 67.547–619.

Dressler, Wolfgang 1980. Universalien von Agens-Wortbildung. *Wege zur Universalienforschung; Festschrift für Hansjakob Seiler*, ed. G. Bretschneider and C. Lehmann.

———— and Ursula Doleschal 1990–91. Gender Agreement via Derivational Morphology. *Acta Linguistica Hungarica* 40.115–37.

———— and Ferenc Kiefer 1990. Austro-Hungarian Morphopragmatics. In Dressler et al., 69–77.

————, Hans Luschützky, Oskar Pfeiffer, and John Rennison (eds.) 1990. *Contemporary Morphology*. Berlin: Mouton de Gruyter.

Dryer, Matthew 1989. Plural words. *Linguistics* 27.865–95.

Ellis, Annette 1987. The Status of Prepositions in Syntax and the Lexicon. Unpublished manuscript. Lewisburg, PA: Linguistics Program, Bucknell University.

Emonds, Joseph 1972. Evidence that Indirect Object Movement is a Structure-preserving Rule. *Foundations of Language* 8.546–61.

———— 1985. *A Unified Theory of Syntactic Categories*. Dordrecht: Foris.

Fabb, Nigel 1988. English Suffixation is Constrained only by Selectional Restrictions. *Natural Language & Linguistic Theory* 6.527–39.

Falk, Jehuda 1991. Case: Abstract and Morphological. *Linguistics* 29.197–230.

Fillmore, Charles 1968. The Case for Case. *Universals of Linguistic Theory*, ed. Emond Bach and Robert Harms. New York: Holt, Rinehart and Winston: 1–88.

Fleischer, Wolfgang 1975. *Wortbildung der deutschen Gegenwartssprache*. 4th edition. Tübingen: Max Niemeyer.

Fodor, Jerry 1983. *The Modularity of Mind: An Essay on Faculty Psychology*. Cambridge, MA: MIT Press.

Gaidarov, R. I. 1966. *Leksika lezginskogo iazyka*. Makhachkala, USSR: Daguchpedgiz.

Gazdar, Gerald, Ewan Klein, Geoffrey Pullum, and Ivan Sag 1985. *Generalized Phrase Structure Grammar*. Cambridge, MA: Harvard University Press.

Geis, Michael 1985. The Syntax of Conditional Sentences. *Working Papers in Linguistics*. Columbus, OH: Deparment of Linguistics, Ohio State University, 31.130–59.

Givón, Talmy 1970. Notes on the Semantic Structure of English Adjectives. *Language* 46.816–37.

Glinert, Lewis 1989. *The Grammar of Modern Hebrew*. Cambridge: Cambridge University Press.

Greenberg, Gerald, and Steven Franks 1991. A Parametric Approach to Dative Subjects and the Second Dative in Slavic. *Slavic and East European Journal* 35.71–97.

Grimshaw, Jane and Ralf-Armin Mester 1985. Complex Verb Formations in Eskimo. *Natural Language & Linguistic Theory* 3.1–20.

Guilbert, Louis 1975. *La créativité lexicale*. Langue et Langage. Paris: Librarie Larousse.

Hale, William and Carl Buck 1966. *A Latin Grammar*. Alabama Linguistic and Philological Series 8. University, AL: Alabama University Press.

Halle, Morris 1973. Prolegomena to a Theory of Word Formation. *Linguistic Inquiry* 4.3–16.

———— 1990. An Approach to Morphology. *North East Linguistics Society* Amherst, MA: Linguistics Department, University of Massachusetts. 20.150–84.

———— and K. P. Mohanan 1985. Segmental Phonology of Modern English. *Linguistic Inquiry* 16.57–116.

———— and Alec Marantz 1993. Distributed Morphology and the Pieces of Inflection. *The View from Building 20: Essays in Linguistics in Honor of Sylvain Bromberger*, ed. Kenneth Hale and S. Jay Keyser. Cambridge, MA: MIT Press, 111–76.

Hammond, Michael and Michael Noonan, eds. 1988. *Theoretical Morphology: Approaches in Modern Linguistics*. San Diego, CA: Academic Press.

Hamp, Eric, Fred Householder, and Robert Austerlitz, eds. 1966. *Readings in Linguistics*, Vol. 2. Chicago: University of Chicago Press.

Hjelmslev Louis 1972. *La catégorie des cas, étude de grammaire génér-*

ale. Internationale Bibliothek fur allgemeine Linguistik, 25. Munich: Wilhelm Fink.

Hoeksema, Jack 1985. *Categorial Morphology*. Outstanding Dissertations in Linguistics. New York: Garland Press.

———— 1987. Relating Word Structure and Logical Form. *Linguistic Inquiry* 18.119–26.

Hooper, Joan 1976. *An Introduction to Natural Generative Phonology*. New York: Academic Press.

Hornstein, Norbert and Amy Weinberg 1981. Case Theory and Preposition Stranding. *Linguistic Inquiry* 12.55–91.

Iatridou, Sabine 1990. About Agr(P). *Linguistic Inquiry* 21.551–77.

Inkelas, Sharon 1993. Nimboran Position Class Morphology. *Natural Language & Linguistic Theory* 11.559–624.

Iuldashev, A. A., ed. 1981. *Grammatika sovremennogo bashkirskogo iazyka*. Moscow: Nauka.

Jackendoff, Ray 1973. The Base Rules for Prepositional Phrases. *A Festschrift for Morris Halle*, ed. Stephen Anderson and Paul Kiparsky. New York: Holt, Rinehart and Winston, 345–56.

———— 1977. *X-Syntax: A Study of Phrase Structure*. Linguistic Inquiry Monograph 2. Cambridge, MA: MIT Press.

———— 1983. *Semantics and Cognition*. Current Studies in Linguistics 8. Cambridge, MA: MIT Press.

———— 1987. The Status of Thematic Relations in Linguistic Theory. *Linguistic Inquiry* 18.369–411.

———— 1990. *Semantic Structures*. Current Studies in Linguistics 18. Cambridge, MA: MIT Press.

Jaeggli, Osvaldo 1986. Passive. *Linguistic Inquiry* 17. 587–622.

Jakobson, Roman 1932. Zur Struktur des russischen Verbums. *Charisteria V. Mathesio oblata*. Geneva: Georg, 74–83. [Reprinted in Hamp, Householder, and Austerlitz, 22–30].

———— 1939. Le signe zéro. *Mélanges de linguistique offert à Charles Bally*, 143–52. [Reprinted in Hamp, Householder, and Austerlitz, 109–115].

———— 1957. ''Shifters, Verbal Categories, and the Russian Verb.'' Descriptive Analysis of Contemporary Standard Russian. Department of Slavic Languages, Columbia University, New York. [Reprinted in *Selected Writings*, II, *Word and Language*. Mouton: The Hague, 1971, 130–47].

Janda, Richard 1982. ''Morphemes Aren't Something that Grows on Trees: Morphology as More the Phonology than the Syntax of Words''. *Papers from the Parasession on the Interplay of Phonology, Morphology, and Syntax*, ed. John Richardson, Mitchell Marks, and Amy Chukerman. Chicago: Chicago Linguistics Society, 79–95.

Jensen, John 1990. *Morphology: Word Structure in Generative Grammar*. Current Issues in Linguistic Theory 70. Amsterdam: John Benjamins.

Jespersen, Otto 1949–1958. *A Modern English Grammar on Historical Principles*. London: George Allen & Unwin.

Karcevskij, Sergei 1929. Du dualisme asymmetrique du signe linguistique. *Travaux du cercle linguistique de Prague* 1.88–93.

Kibrik, A. E., S. V. Kodzasov, I. P. Oloviannikova, and D. S. Samedov 1977. *Opyt strukturnogo opisaniia archinskogo iazyka*. Publikacii otdeleniia strukturnoi i prikladnoi lingvistiki. Moscow: University of Moscow Press, 11–14.

Kiel, Heinrich, ed. 1857–1880. *Grammatici Latini*. 8 volumes. Leipzig: B. G. Teubner.

Kiparsky, Paul 1982. Lexical Morphology and Phonology. *Linguistics in the Morning Calm*, ed. I. S. Yang. Seoul: Hanshin, 3–91.

———— 1983. Word-Formation and the Lexicon. *1982 Mid-America Linguistics Conference Papers*, ed. F. Ingemann. Lawrence, KA: Department of Linguistics, University of Kansas, 3–29.

Klavans, Judith 1980. *Some Problems in a Theory of Clitics*. Ph.D. dissertation, University College of London. Published by Indiana University Linguistics Club, Bloomington, IN, 1982.

———— 1985. The Independence of Syntax and Phonology in Cliticization. *Language* 61.95–120.

Klima, Edward 1965. *Studies in Diachronic Syntax*. Ph.D. dissertation, Harvard University.

Korigodskii, Robert, Oleg Kondrashkin, and Boris Zinov'ev 1961. *Indoneziisko-russkii slovar'*. Moscow: Gosudarstvennoe izdatel'stvo inostrannykh i nacional'nykh slovarei.

Korkina, E. I., E. I. Ubriatova, L. N. Kharitonov, and N. E. Petrov 1982. *Grammatika sovremennogo iakutskogo literaturnogo iazyka*. Moscow: Nauka.

Köpcke, Klaus-Michael 1982. *Untersuchungen zum Genussystem der deutschen Gegenwartssprache*. Tübingen: Max Niemeyer.

Kühner, Raphael and Bernhard Gerth 1963. *Ausführliche Grammatik der griechischen Sprache*. Vol. 2: *Satzlehre*. 4th edition. Munich: M. Hueber Verlag.

Kuiper, Koenraad 1987. Feature Percolation and the Prefix *a-*. *De Reo* 30.55–78.

Kuryłowicz, Jerzy 1936. Dérivation lexicale et dérivation syntaxique; contribution à la théorie des parties du discours. *Bulletin de la Société de Linguistique de Paris* 37: 79–92. [Reprinted in Hamp, Householder, and Austerlitz, 42–50].

———— 1949. Le probléme du classement des cas. *Towarzystwa Językoznawczego* 9.20–43.

Larson, Richard 1985. Bare NP Adverbs. *Linguistic Inquiry* 16.595–621.

Lass, Roger 1990. How to Do Things with Junk: Exaptation in Language Evolution. *Journal of Linguistics* 26.79–102.

Lefebvre, Claire and Pieter Muysken 1988. *Mixed Categories: Nominalizations in Quechua*. Studies in Natural Language & Linguistic Theory. Dordrecht: Kluwer.

Levi, Judith, 1978. *The Syntax and Semantics of Complex Nominals*. New York: Academic Press.

Levin, Beth and Malka Rappaport 1986. The Formation of Adjectival Passives. *Linguistic Inquiry* 17.623–62.

Lewis, Geoffrey 1974. *Turkish grammar*. Oxford: Clarendon Press, 1967.

Lieber, Rochelle 1981a. *On the Organization of the Lexicon*. Bloomington, IN: Indiana University Linguistics Club.

———— 1981b. Morphological Conversion within a Restricted Theory of the Lexicon. In Moortgat, van der Hulst, and Hoekstra, 161–200.

———— 1983. Argument Linking and Compounds in English. *Linguistic Inquiry* 14.251–85.

———— 1987. *An Integrated Theory of Autosegmental Processes*. Albany NY: State University of New York Press.

———— 1992. *Deconstructing Morphology: Word Formation in Syntactic Theory*. Chicago: University of Chicago Press.

Lødrup, Helge 1991. The Norwegian Pseudopassive in Lexical Theory. *Working Papers in Scandinavian Syntax* 47.118–29

Maling, Joan 1977. A Typology of Preposition Stranding. Unpublished paper, GLOW Conference, Amsterdam.

———— and Annie Zaenen 1985. Preposition-Stranding and Passive. *Nordic Journal of Linguistics* 8.197–209.

Marantz, Alec 1982. Re Reduplication. *Linguistic Inquiry* 13.435–82.

———— 1984. *On the Nature of Grammatical Relations*. Linguistic Inquiry Monographs 10. Cambridge, MA: MIT Press.

Marchand, Hans 1967. Expansion, Transposition, and Derivation. *La Linguistique* 1.13–26. [Reprinted in *Studies in Syntax and Word-Formation: Selected Articles by Hans Marchand*, ed. Dieter Kastovsky. Munich: Wilhelm Fink (1974), 322–36.]

Matthews, P. H. 1972. *Inflectional Morphology: A Theoretical Study Based on Aspects of Latin Verb Conjugation*. Cambridge Studies in Linguistics 6. Cambridge: Cambridge University Press.

———— 1991. *Morphology. An Introduction to the Theory of Word-Structure*. 2nd. ed. Cambridge Textbooks in Linguistics. Cambridge: Cambridge University Press.

Mayerthaler, Willi 1981. *Morphologische Natürlichkeit*. Wiesbaden: Athenäum.

McCarthy, John 1981. A Prosodic Theory of Nonconcatenative Morphology. *Linguistic Inquiry* 12.373–418.

——— 1982. Prosodic Templates, Morphemic Templates, and Morphemic Tiers. *The Structure of Phonological Representations*, Vol. 2, ed. Harry van der Hulst and Norval Smith. Dordrecht: Foris, 191–223.

——— 1984. Prosodic Organization in Morphology. *Language, Sound, Structure*, ed. Mark Aronoff and Richard Oehrle. Cambridge, MA: MIT Press, 299–317.

Meier, Barbara 1988. *The Role of Females and the Rule of Femininization in Russian*. Honors thesis, Bucknell University, Lewisburg, PA.

Meijs (Meys), Willem 1975. *Compound Adjectives in English and the Ideal Speaker-Listener: A Study of Compounding in a Transformational-Generative Framework*. North-Holland Linguistic Series 18. Amsterdam: North-Holland.

Mel'čuk, Igor 1979. Syntactic, or Lexical Zero in Natural Language. *Berkeley Linguistics Society* 5.224–60.

Menovshchikov, Georgii 1967. *Grammatika iazyka aziatskikh èskimosov*, Vol. 2: *Glagol, prichastie, narechie, sluzhebnie slova*. Leningrad: Nauka.

——— 1980. *Iazyk èskimosov Beringova proliva*. Leningrad: Nauka.

——— and Nikolai Vakhtin 1983. *Eskimosskii iazyk*. Leningrad: Prosveshchenie.

Milojević, Miloš 1934. Jedan prilog za nekoliko naziva. *Naš jezik* 2.209–10.

Milsark, Gary 1988. Singl-ing. *Linguistic Inquiry* 19.611–34.

Mithun, Marianne 1984. The Evolution of Noun Incorporation. *Language* 60.847–94.

——— 1991. Active/Agentive Case Marking and its Motivation. *Language* 67.510–46.

Moortgat, Michael, Harry van der Hulst, and Teun Hoekstra, eds. 1981. *The Scope of Lexical Rules*. Dordrecht: Foris.

Motsch, Wolfgang 1987. On Inactivity, Productivity and Analogy in Derivational Processes. XIV International Congress of Linguists, Berlin, August 10–15, 1987.

Muysken, Pieter and Claire Lefebvre 1988. *Mixed Categories: Nominalizations in Quechua*. Studies in Natural Language & Linguistic Theory. Dordrecht: Kluwer.

Napoli, Donna Jo 1989. *Predication Theory: A Case Study for Indexing Theory*. Cambridge: Cambridge University Press.

Nida, Eugene 1946. *Morphology*. Ann Arbor, MI: University of Michigan Press.

Osborne, C. R. 1974. *The Tiwi Language, Grammar, Myths and a Dic-*

tionary of the Tiwi Language. Australian Aboriginal Studies, Linguistic Series 21. Canberra: Austrailian Institute of Aboriginal Studies.

Ouhalla, Jamal 1990. Sentential Negation, Relativised Minimality and the Aspectual Status of Auxiliaries. *Linguistic Review* 7.183–231.

Panagl, Oswald 1975. Kasustheorie und Nomina agentis. *Flexion und Wortbildung, Akten der V. Fachtagung der Indogermanischen Gesellschaft, Regensburg, 9.-14. September, 1973,* ed. H. Rix Wiesbaden: L. Reichert Verlag, 232–46.

Panfilov, Vladimir 1962. *Grammatika nivkhskoyo iazyka*. Moscow: USSR Academy of Sciences.

Perlmutter, David 1988. The Split Morphology Hypothesis: Evidence from Yiddish. In Hammond and Noonan, 79–100.

Pesetsky, David 1985. Morphology and Logical Form. *Linguistic Inquiry* 16.193–248.

Plank, Frans 1979. *Ergativity: Toward a Theory of Grammatical Relations*. London: Academic Press.

Pollock, Yves 1989. Verb Movement, Universal Grammar, and the Structure of IP. *Linguistic Inquiry* 20.365–424.

Poppe, Nicholas 1954. *Grammar of Written Mongolian*. Porta Linguarum Orientalium, Wiesbaden: Otto Harrassowitz.

Pustejowski, James 1991. The Generative Lexicon. *Computational Linguistics* 17.409–41.

Reuchlin, Johannes 1506. *De Rudimentis hebraicis*. Pforzheim: Thomas Anshelm.

Roeper, Thomas. 1987. Implicit Arguments and the Head-Complement Relation. *Linguistic Inquiry* 18.267–310.

———— 1988. Compound Syntax and Head Movement. *Yearbook of Morphology,* 1.187–228.

———— and Muffy Siegel 1978. A Lexical Transformation for Verbal Compounds. *Linguistic Inquiry* 9.199–260.

Rosch, Eleanor 1977. Human Categorization. *Studies in Cross-Cultural Psychology* 1.1–49.

————, C. Mervis, W. Gray, D. Johnson, and P. Boyes-Braem 1976. Basic Objects in Natural Categories. *Cognitive Psychology* 8.382–439.

Ross, John 1972. Double -ing. *Linguistic Inquiry* 3.61–86.

Rowlands, E. C. 1969. *Teach Yourself Yoruba*. Teach Yourself Books. London: Hodder and Stoughton.

Rumelhart, David and James McClelland 1987. *Parallel Distributed Processing: Explorations in the Microstructure of Cognition*. Cambridge, MA: MIT Press.

Saltarelli, Mario 1988. *Basque*. Croom Helm Descriptive Grammar Series. London: Croom Helm.

Sanzheev, Garma 1962. *Grammatika buriatskogo iazyka: fonetika i morfologiia.* Moscow: USSR Academy of Sciences, Izdatel'stvo vostochnoi literatury.

Sapir, Edward 1911. The Problem of Noun Incorporation in American Languages. *American Anthropologist,* n. s. 13.250–82.

———— 1922. Takelma. *Handbook of American Indian Languages,* Part 2, ed. Franz Boas. Bureau of American Ethnology, Bulletin 40. Washington: Government Printing Office, 1–296.

Scalise, Sergio 1984. *Generative Morphology.* Studies in Generative Grammar 18. Dordrecht: Foris.

———— 1988. Inflection and Derivation. *Linguistics* 26.561–81.

Schachter, Paul and Fe Otanes 1972. *Tagalog Reference Grammar.* Berkeley, CA: University of California Press.

Schleicher, August. 1859. Zur Morphologie der Sprache. *Mémoires de l'Académie imperiale des sciences de St. Pétersbourg* 7. St. Petersburg: Imperial Academy of Sciences, 1–38.

Schottelius, Justus. 1663. *Ausführliche arbeit von der teutschen haubt sprache.* Braunschweig: C. F. Zilligern.

Selkirk, Elizabeth 1982. *The Syntax of Words.* Cambridge, MA: MIT Press.

Shepardson, Kenneth 1983. An Integrated Analysis of Swahili Augmentative-Diminutives. *Studies in African Linguistics* 13.53–92.

Siegel, Dorothy 1974. *Topics in English Morphology.* PhD Dissertation, MIT. Published by Garland Press, New York, Outstanding Dissertations in Linguistics, 1979.

Skorik, Petr 1961. *Grammatika chukotskogo iazyka.* Vol. 1: *Fonetika i morfologiia imennykh chastei rechi.* Moscow-Leningrad: Academy of Sciences, USSR.

———— 1977. *Grammatika chukotskogo iazyka.* Vol. 2: *Glagol, narechie, sluzhebnye slova.* Leningrad: Academy of Sciences, USSR.

Slobin, Dan, ed. 1985. *The Crosslinguistic Study of Language Acquisition,* Vol. 2: *Theoretical Issues.* Hillsdale, NJ: Lawrence Erlbaum.

Smyth, Herbert 1920. *A Greek Grammar for Colleges.* New York: American Book Company.

Speijer, J. S. 1886. *Sanskrit Syntax.* Leiden: E. J. Brill.

Sproat, Richard 1985. *On Deriving the Lexicon.* Ph.D. Dissertation, Cambridge, MA: MIT.

Stankiewicz, Edward 1972. *A Baudouin de Courtenay Anthology.* Bloomington, IN: University of Indiana Press.

Starosta, Stanley 1978. The One Per Sent Solution. *Valence, Semantic Case and Grammatical Relations,* Studies in Language Companion Series 1, ed. Werner Abraham. John Benjamins: Amsterdam, 459–571.

Stump, Gregory 1991. A Paradigm-Based Theory of Morphosemantic Mismatches. *Language* 67.675–725.

―――― 1993. How Peculiar is Evaluative Morphology? *Journal of Linguistics* 29.1–36.

Sullivan, Thelma 1988. *Thelma D. Sullivan's Compendium of Nahuatl Grammar*. Salt Lake City, UT: University of Utah Press.

Szymanek, Bogdan 1985. *English and Polish Adjectives: A Study in Lexicalist Word-Formation*. Lublin: Catholic University Press.

―――― 1988. *Categories and Categorization in Morphology*. Lublin: Catholic University Press.

Talibov, B. 1966. *Grammaticheskii ocherk lezghinskogo iazyka. Lezginsko-russkii slovar'*, ed. B. Talibov and M. Gadzhiev. Sovetskaia entsiklopediia: Moscow.

Talmy, Leonard 1978. The Relation of Grammar to Cognition. *Theoretical Issues in Natural Language Processing*, Vol. 2, ed. D. Waltz, Champaign, IL: Coordinated Science Laboratory, University of Illinois.

―――― 1983. How Language Structures Space. *Spatial Orientation: Theory, Research, and Application*, ed. Herbert Pick and Linda Acredolo. New York: Plenum Press, 225–82.

―――― 1985. Lexicalization Patterns: Semantic Structures in Lexical Forms. *Language Typology and Syntactic Description*, Vol. III: *Grammatical Categories and the Lexicon*, ed. Tim Shopen. Cambridge: Cambridge University Press, 57–149.

Thomason, Sarah 1988. *Language, Contact, Creolization, and Genetic Linguistics*. Berkeley: University of California Press.

Underhill, Robert 1976. *Turkish Grammar*. Cambridge, MA: MIT Press.

van Riemsdijk, Henk 1982. *A Case Study in Syntactic Markedness: The Binding Nature of Prepositional Phrases*. 2nd edition. Dordrecht: Foris.

―――― 1990. Functional Prepositions. *Unity in Diversity*, ed. Harm Pinkster and Inge Genee. Dordrecht: Foris, 229–41.

―――― and Edwin Williams 1986. *Introduction to the Theory of Grammar*. Current Studies in Linguistics, 12. Cambridge, MA: MIT Press.

von Humboldt, Wilhelm. 1836. *Über die Verschiedenheit des menschlichen Sprachbaues und ihren Einfluss auf die geistige Entwickelung des Menschengeschlects*. Berlin: Royal Academy of Sciences.

Warren, Beatrice 1984. *Classifying Adjectives*. Göteborg: Acta Universitatis Gothoburgensis.

Wasow, Thomas 1977. Transformations and the Lexicon. *Formal Syntax*, ed. Peter Culicover, Thomas Wasow, and Adrian Akmajian. New York: Academic Press, 327–60.

Whitney, William 1967. *Sanskrit Grammar*. 2nd edition. Cambridge, MA: Harvard University Press.

Williams, Edwin 1981. On the Notions 'Lexically Related', and 'Head of a Word'. *Linguistic Inquiry* 12.245–74.

Woodcock, Eric 1959. *A New Latin Syntax*. Cambridge, MA: Harvard University Press.

Wurzel, Wolfgang 1984. *Flexionsmorphologie und Natürlichkeit: ein Beitrag zur morphologischen Theoriebildung*. Studia Grammatica 21. Berlin: Academy of Sciences, GDR.

Yip, Moira 1982. Reduplication and the C-V Skeleta in Chinese Secret Languages. *Linguistic Inquiry* 13.637–61.

Zaitseva, Marija 1978. *Suffiksal'noe glagol'noe slovoobrazovanie v vepsskom jazyke*. Leningrad: Nauka.

Zalizniak, A. 1964. K voprosu o grammaticheskikh kategoriiakh v sovremennom russkom iazyke. *Voprosy iazykoznaniia* 4.25–40.

Žepic, Stanko 1970. Izvedenice sa sufiksima za tvorbu mjesnih imenica (nomina loci). *Jezik* 18.83–90, 195–209.

Zubin, David and Klaus-Michael Köpcke 1984a. Affect Classification in the German Gender System. *Lingua* 63.41–96.

———— 1984b. Gender: A Less than Arbitrary Grammatical Category. *Chicago Linguistics Society,* 17.439–49.

———— 1986. Gender and Folk Taxonomy: The Indexical Relation between Grammatical and Lexical Categorization. *Noun Classes and Categorization,* Typological Studies in Language 7, ed. Collette Craig. Amsterdam: John Benjamins, 139–180.

Zubizarreta, Maria-Luisa 1985. The Relation between Morphophonology and Morphosyntax: the Case of Romance Causatives. *Linguistic Inquiry* 16: 247–90.

Zwicky, Arnold 1977. *On Clitics*. Bloomington, IN: Indiana University Linguistics Club.

———— 1985. Clitics and Particles. *Language* 61.283–305.

———— 1989. Quicker, More Quickly, *Quicklier. *Ohio State Working Papers in Linguistics* 37.84–99.

Author Index

Language Index

Subject Index